Customer Relationship Management

VSF

Customer Relationship Management

Concepts and Tools

Francis Buttle

ELSEVIER
BUTTERWORTH
HEINEMANN

AMSTERDAM BOSTON HEIDELBERG LONDON NEW YORK OXFORD PARIS
SAN DIEGO SAN FRANCISCO SINGAPORE SYDNEY TOKYO

Elsevier Butterworth-Heinemann
Linacre House, Jordan Hill, Oxford OX2 8DP
200 Wheeler Road, Burlington, MA 01803

First published 2004

British Library Cataloguing in Publication Data
A catalogue record for this book is available from the British Library

Library of Congress Cataloguing in Publication Data
A catalogue record for this book is available from the Library of Congress

ISBN 0 7506 5502 X

For information on all Elsevier Butterworth-Heinemann publications
visit our website at: www.bh.com

Composition by Genesis Typesetting Limited, Rochester, Kent
Printed and bound in Italy

Contents

Foreword

Customer relationship management (CRM) is no longer something that only leading-edge enterprises use to gain competitive advantage. It is now a necessity for survival.

Customer relationship management is a complex and difficult way of doing business. Much as some would like us to believe, CRM is not just about installing software or automating customer touchpoints. It is about the reinvention of our enterprises around the customer. It is about becoming and remaining customer-centric.

As such, it can be fraught with perils. So what is an enterprise to do? Should we say that CRM is too difficult and turn back to our old, product-centric way of doing things? The reality is that we cannot. Customer relationship management is here to stay because customers, both consumers and business entities, now expect suppliers to be customer-centric. Customers expect to be able to deal with enterprises when they want, where they want and how they want. Enterprises are expected to remember past interactions and to build on those interactions in the future.

Customers know that they hold the ultimate trump card, their loyalty. Enterprises that do not re-engineer their business processes to become more customer-centric risk the mass defection of their customers and, with them, their associated revenues. Therefore, CRM is no longer a competitive differentiator; rather, it is a business necessity of the twenty-first century.

Customer relationship management has had some bad publicity of late. High levels of CRM failure have been reported. Does this mean that CRM is a business necessity with a high risk of failure? That would be an alarming combination. Today, we are finding that companies are increasingly asking tough, but correct, questions and looking for the associated answers before they embark on CRM. Gartner's clients work on issues such as business justification, customer acceptance, process redesign, and training and compensation issues. All reflect a greater maturity about CRM as enterprises try to avoid the mistakes of their predecessors.

Gartner predicts that in the next few years, enterprises will consider CRM critical to corporate strategy, but will be considerably more

...

pragmatic. The days when CRM fever started to break out in boardrooms across the world seem a 'technology lifetime' ago.

The *new* new economy is a lot like the old economy before the *old* new economy distorted all of the expectations. The good news about a slower economy is that we have breathing room to absorb the technologies and applications that have poured out of high-technology enterprises during the past several years. We also have a mandate to do more with less, which has introduced a healthy pragmatism.

Regardless of who you ask in management about the role of data for marketing, sales and service, there is a consensus that data are highly valued. However, identifying, extracting and transforming data into actionable information is an ongoing challenge. Enterprises need to go beyond basic measurement and reporting to enhance their ability to leverage more valuable insights. Analytical CRM is an enabler of such customer insight.

Companies are demanding more return from their investments in operational CRM applications such as sales-force automation, marketing automation and service automation. Enterprises need to be careful about their choice of software vendors. Many companies have bought over-specified CRM suites, rather than the applications that are best suited to their particular needs. This is changing. Enterprises are beginning to seek support for specific functions such as incentive compensation, partner relationship management and e-commerce-related applications. Customer relationship management software vendors are responding by unbundling total solution packages to gain entry to new accounts.

A continued determination to lower service costs while delivering higher levels of customer care continues to drive investments and interest in e-service and self-service. Recent studies show that although 70 per cent of enterprises believe they have a well-run contact centre that provides their customers with good customer service, less than half of their clients report being satisfied with the service. World-class e-service requires enterprises to adapt to users' needs and requirements. Customers are demanding more information, easier and expanded access, and support through newer channels.

Customer relationship management has had a tough run in the recent past, but we believe that it is here to stay. There is no substitute for customer-centricity. Many believe that the basic task of a business is to create and keep customers. The task of CRM is to enable companies to do just that. A more professional approach to CRM is emerging and we welcome the contribution that this book makes towards that goal.

Kristian Steenstrup
Research Director, Gartner Inc.

Preface

This book has been written to meet a perceived need in the CRM literature. Most CRM books are either produced by, or represent the interests of, software vendors or CRM consultants. This book is different. It is an impartial, academically independent review of CRM that is written to be a learning resource. It is designed to enable any interested party – student, practitioner, critic or professor – to study the subject and develop a better understanding and appreciation of CRM.

The book views CRM as the core business strategy that integrates internal processes and functions, and external networks, to create and deliver value to targeted customers at a profit. Customer relationship management is grounded on high-quality customer data and enabled by information technology.

The idea for the book emerged after a frustrating and ultimately fruitless search for a core CRM text to use on a course I was due to teach. I couldn't find one, so I wrote this book.

Audience for the book

The book is written for a number of audiences, all of whom share an interest in improving their understanding of CRM:

- MBA and Masters students, and upper level undergraduates studying CRM or related advanced marketing courses, including courses in database marketing, relationship marketing, strategic management and customer value management
- students on diploma courses of professional organizations such as the Chartered Institute of Marketing
- practitioners of CRM who want to make sense of this complex area. Practitioners often work on small areas of CRM such as data quality projects, campaign management and website development, and can benefit from an overview of the field of CRM, to see where their work fits.

Key features of the book

- The book has been widely researched to ensure that it is theoretically sound and managerially relevant: it is intended to be a useful CRM textbook from both the student's and the practitioner's point of view. The book draws on content from a wide range of disciplines, including strategic management, marketing, sales, human resources, information technology, operations, leadership and change management.
- Academically independent, the book is free of CRM software vendor and CRM consultancy bias.
- The book views CRM as a core business strategy that organizes the business and its network to create value for customers at a profit. It is not a book about IT. It is a book that shows how IT can be used to support customer acquisition, retention and development processes across marketing, sales and service functions.
- The book is organized around the CRM value chain model. The model provides a helicopter overview of CRM. The value chain model identifies five primary stages through which organizations pass in creating profitable customer relationships. These are customer portfolio analysis, customer intimacy, network development, value proposition development and managing the customer lifecycle. These primary stages are enabled by a number of supporting conditions: culture and leadership, data and IT, people, and processes. The model has been tested and developed over about 6 years in a large number of organizations and classrooms. I believe that it provides a simple overview of this complex field.
- To help you to learn, the book's chapters are standardized in format and content: learning outcomes, text, case illustrations and references.

Chapter titles

The book is organized into 10 chapters:

1 Making sense of customer relationship management
2 The customer relationship management value chain
3 Information technology for customer relationship management
4 Customer portfolio analysis
5 Customer intimacy
6 Creating and managing networks
7 Creating value for customers
8 Managing the customer lifecycle: customer acquisition
9 Managing the customer lifecycle: customer retention and development
10 Organizing for customer relationship management

I hope that you find the book is a comprehensive and fully developed text on CRM. If you've ever tried writing a book, painting a picture or composing a song, you will know that you never reach a point when you can say you've completed the task. There's always more you can do. When you've read the book you may well think that it has missed some important issue or simply got something wrong. If you do, I invite you to write to me at francis.buttle@mq.edu.au

Enjoy the book!

Francis Buttle
Sydney

Acknowledgements

Many people have contributed to this book, both directly and indirectly. I appreciate their assistance in helping to bring the book to completion.

Extra special thanks go to John Turnbull, who wrote Chapter 3 – Information technology for customer relationship management. John's experience in the IT domain provides balance and is a great and necessary value-add to the managerial bias of the rest of the book. He also helped with the IT elements of my chapters across the rest of the book. John has worked on the vendor side for CRM giants Siebel and PeopleSoft. He now runs the CRM consultancy Customer Connect (www. customerconnect.com.au), helping companies to get more from their CRM investments.

Another notable contributor was Paul Benning. Paul was a doctoral student at Macquarie Graduate School of Management when the book was written. He searched out and drafted many of the case illustrations that are a feature of the book.

Thank are due to Kristian Steenstrup of Gartner Inc., who kindly wrote the Foreword. Gartner provides a calm and independent voice in the maelstrom of CRM hype and publicity.

Among others who deserve special mention are the many MBA-level students who have taken my CRM courses at Manchester Business School (UK) and Macquarie Graduate School of Management (Sydney, Australia). Their perceptive minds and sometimes sharp criticism have given pause for thought. Among them are Jon Baker, Mark Ferguson, Gillie Kirk, Jan Kitshoff, Megan Maack, Samantha Parkhurst and Lee Williams, all of whom commented on early drafts of the chapters.

Thanks also to the executives who have attended my CRM management development courses in Sydney and Manchester. You were exposed to many ideas that were at times 'work-in-progress'. Not one of you asked for your money back . . . thanks for the generosity!

A number of consulting clients have been test beds for some of the ideas in the book. I particularly appreciate the opportunities to work with Frost Rowley, Hewlett Packard, IBM, KPMG, Littlewoods, Medica and Microsoft.

Colleagues and friends at Manchester, Macquarie and elsewhere have been generous with their support. Among them are Rizal Ahmad,

Lawrence Ang, Professor Gayle Avery, Sergio Biggemann, Nick Buttle, Sue Creswick, Professor Robert East, Guy Ford, Max Frost, Professor James Guthrie, Charles Hobson, Professor John A. Murphy, Professor Sharon Murray, Professor Peter Naudé, Professor Alan Thomas, Martin Williams and Professor Steve Worthington.

Many other clients, colleagues, friends and students have contributed to the development of this book. Mostly, I have sought their input but on occasion they have been unaware that they have contributed. They have simply said something that has triggered the spark of an idea. Thanks to them.

I would like to thank the many authors and publishers who have granted permission for their copyright materials to be included in this book. Full references to these materials appear in the text or in reference materials at the end of the chapters. While every effort has been made to trace copyright owners, I may not have always been successful. I apologize if there has been any infringement of copyright or failure to acknowledge original sources. Any corrections advised to the publishers will be included in future printings.

Finally, I would like to thank everyone who has contributed in any way to the creation of this book, whether mentioned here or not.

About the authors

Francis Buttle

Francis Buttle is Professor of Marketing and Customer Relationship Management at Macquarie Graduate School of Management (MGSM) in Sydney, Australia, Principal of Francis Buttle & Associates and a Director of Listening Post Pty Ltd. In 2002 the Economist Intelligence Unit ranked MGSM the number one MBA programme in Asia–Pacific and among the top forty worldwide.

Before joining MGSM, Francis held the world's first sponsored Professorship of CRM at Manchester Business School in the UK. He has also worked at Cranfield School of Management (UK) and the University of Massachusetts (USA). He has degrees in management science, marketing, and communication. His PhD is from the University of Massachusetts.

In addition to three books Francis has written nearly 250 papers in practitioner and academic journals.

Francis works with a number of associates on research into CRM effectiveness, CRM competencies, word-of-mouth customer referrals and relationship quality. He teaches MBA-level courses on CRM, services marketing and marketing management, and runs customized executive-level short courses on CRM and marketing. He is an elected Fellow of the Chartered Institute of Marketing in recognition of his service to the field.

Francis has consulted and advised on customer relationship management and marketing issues for many businesses and other organizations in recent years. These cover many sectors and sizes of client, including, for example, KPMG, Microsoft, Littlewoods, Medica, the European Patent Office and Frost Rowley.

Francis is a qualified Rugby Union referee and enjoys golf, skiing and cricket.

Francis can be contacted at:

Macquarie Graduate School of Management
Sydney
NSW 2109
Australia

E-mail: francis.buttle@mq.edu.au

John Turnbull

John Turnbull is the author of Chapter 3, Information technology for customer relationship management.

John Turnbull is the founder and Managing Director of Customer Connect Australia Pty Ltd, a specialist CRM consulting and education organization. The mission of Customer Connect Australia is to work with clients to help them realize the business benefits of customer relationship management.

John is an experienced practitioner of CRM, with over twenty years' experience in industry and technology. His industry experience includes hands-on roles in field service, engineering, sales and marketing support. Since joining the enterprise application software (EAS) sector thirteen years ago, John has worked in education, consulting, implementation, sales consulting and management roles. During this time, John spent a number of years managing the sales consulting organizations in Australia and New Zealand for two of the major CRM vendors.

Recent CRM engagements have focused on CRM strategy development, CRM implementation, effectiveness reviews, CRM concepts and business practice education. John has also presented on CRM at a number of public conferences.

John is currently involved in ongoing CRM consulting and education activities at Customer Connect Australia, and supporting lecturing activities in CRM at Macquarie Graduate School of Management. His qualifications include an honours degree at the University of Technology, Sydney, and an MBA majoring in marketing at the University of New England.

John enjoys a number of outdoor pursuits including cycling, bushwalking, canyoning and canoeing, and spending time with his wife, Jane, and three children, Adele, Olivia and Emilia.

John can be contacted at Customer Connect Australia Pty Ltd:

Website: www.customerconnect.com.au
E-mail: jturnbull@customerconnect.com.au

Chapter 1

Making sense of customer relationship management

By the end of the chapter, you will understand:

1 three major and different perspectives on CRM
2 several general misunderstandings about CRM
3 why companies and customers are motivated to establish and maintain relationships with each other, or not
4 the importance of trust and commitment within a relationship
5 how customer satisfaction, customer loyalty and business performance are connected
6 the five constituencies having an interest in CRM
7 how to define CRM.

Introduction

Customer relationship management, or CRM, means different things to different people. Even the meaning of the three-letter abbreviation CRM is contested. Most people use CRM to refer to customer relationship management. Others use CRM to mean customer relationship marketing.[1] Another group, in the belief that not all customers want a relationship with a supplier, omit the word relationship, preferring the term customer management.[2] Still others opt for the expression relationship marketing.[3,4] Whatever it is called, CRM is clearly a business practice focused on customers.

The term CRM has only been in use for a few years. One view, held by some of the information technology (IT) companies, is that the term CRM

Level of CRM	Dominant characteristic
Strategic	A top–down perspective on CRM which views CRM as a core customer-centric business strategy that aims at winning and keeping profitable customers
Operational	A perspective on CRM which focuses on major automation projects such as service automation, sales force automation or marketing automation
Analytical	A bottom–up perspective on CRM which focuses on the intelligent mining of customer data for strategic or tactical purposes

Figure 1.1
Levels of CRM

is used to describe software applications that automate the marketing, selling and service functions of businesses. Although the market for CRM software is now populated with many players it began back in 1993, when Tom Siebel founded Siebel Systems Inc. Use of the term CRM can be traced back to that period.

Because of its relatively short history there is still debate about the meaning of CRM. Some of the confusion arises because the term is used in a number of different ways.

We can think about CRM at three levels: strategic, operational and analytical, as summarized in Fig. 1.1 and described below.

Strategic CRM

Strategic CRM is focused on the development of a customer-centric business culture. This culture is dedicated to winning and keeping customers by creating and delivering value better than competitors. The culture is reflected in leadership behaviours, the design of formal systems of the company, and the myths and stories that are created within the firm. In a customer-centric culture you would expect resources to be allocated where they would best enhance customer value, reward systems to promote employee behaviours that enhance customer satisfaction, and customer information to be collected, shared and applied across the business. You would also expect to find the heroes of the business to be those who deliver outstanding value or service to customers. Many businesses claim to be customer-centric, customer-led, customer-focused or customer-oriented, but few are. Indeed, there can be very few companies of any size that do not claim to be on a mission to satisfy customer requirements profitably.

Customer-centricity competes with other business logics. Kotler identifies three other major business orientations: product, production and selling.[5]

Product-oriented businesses believe that customers choose products with the best quality, performance, design or features. These are often highly innovative and entrepreneurial firms. Many new business start-ups are product-oriented. In these firms it is common for the customer's voice to be missing when important marketing decisions are made. Little or no customer research is conducted. Management makes assumptions about what customers want. The outcome is that products are overspecified or overengineered for the requirements of the market, and therefore too costly for the majority of customers. That said, marketers have identified a subset of relatively price-insensitive customers whom they dub 'innovators', who are likely to respond positively to company claims about product excellence. Unfortunately, this is a relatively small segment, no more than 2.5 per cent of the potential market.[6]

Production-oriented businesses believe that customers choose low-price products. Consequently, they strive to keep operating costs low, and develop low-cost routes to market. This may well be appropriate in developing economies or in subsistence segments of developed economies, but the majority of customers have other requirements. Drivers of BMWs would not be attracted to the brand if they knew that the company only sourced inputs such as braking systems from the lowest cost supplier. Henry Ford did not face this problem in the early stages of development of the automobile market. It was enough to tell customers they could have any car they wanted as long as it was black. But then came competition, and customer expectations changed.

Sales-oriented businesses make the assumption that if they invest enough in advertising, selling, public relations (PR) and sales promotion, customers will be persuaded to buy. Very often, a sales orientation follows a production orientation. The company produces low-cost products and then has to promote them heavily to shift inventory.

A **customer or market-oriented** company shares a set of beliefs about putting the customer first. It collects, disseminates and uses customer and competitive information to develop better value propositions for customers. A customer-centric firm is a learning firm that constantly adapts to customer requirements and competitive conditions. There is evidence that customer-centricity correlates strongly with business performance.[7]

Many managers would argue that customer-centricity must be right for all companies. However, at different stages of market or economic development, other orientations may have stronger appeal.

Operational CRM

Operational CRM is focused on the automation of the customer-facing parts of businesses. Various CRM software applications enable the marketing, selling and service functions to be automated. The major applications within operational CRM appear in Fig. 1.2.

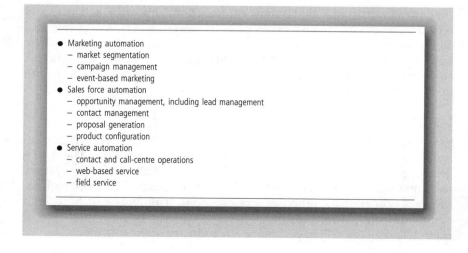

- Marketing automation
  - market segmentation
  - campaign management
  - event-based marketing
- Sales force automation
  - opportunity management, including lead management
  - contact management
  - proposal generation
  - product configuration
- Service automation
  - contact and call-centre operations
  - web-based service
  - field service

Figure 1.2
Forms of
operational CRM

Marketing automation

Marketing automation (MA) applies technology to marketing processes. Several capabilities are offered by MA software: customer segmentation, campaign management and event-based marketing. Software enables users to explore their customer data in order to develop targeted communications and offers. Segmentation, in some cases, is possible at the level of the individual customer. Unique offers may be made to a single customer at an appropriate point in time.

Marketing automation enables companies to develop, budget and execute communication campaigns. It automates the multiperson work-flow that delivers the communication output. Typically, a print-based communication campaign will involve a number of people such as marketing manager, market analyst, copywriters, artists, printers, sales-people and media buyers. Their contributions to the campaign can be co-ordinated with the help of the software. MA can also audit and analyse campaign performance, and direct leads from advertising campaigns to the most appropriate sales channel.

In multichannel environments, campaign management is particularly challenging. Some fashion retailers, for example, have city stores, an e-tail website, home shopping, catalogue stores and perhaps even a TV shopping channel. Some customers may be unique to a single channel, but most will be multichannel prospects, if not already customers of several channels. Integration of communication strategies and evaluation of performance require a substantial amount of information collection and distribution, and of people management across these channels.

Event-based marketing is also known as trigger-based marketing. Typically, sales or service actions are initiated by a company in response to some action by the customer. The customer action triggers the company response. If a business customer emails in a request for information, this might initiate a sales process that commences with a courtesy call to thank the customer for the request. When a credit-card user calls a contact centre to enquire about the current rate of interest, this might be taken as an indication that the customer is comparing alternatives, and might switch to a different provider. This event may trigger an offer designed to retain the customer. Companies can trawl their transactional histories, and sales and service records, to identify exploitable connections between events and outcomes. For example, it might be discovered that many customers who buy flights to exotic destinations also buy high value health insurance. A company that has learned about this connection can target health insurance products to the traveller.

Sales-force automation

Sales-force automation (SFA) was the original form of CRM. It applies technology to the management of a company's selling activities. The selling process can be decomposed into a number of stages such as lead generation, lead qualification, needs identification, development of specifications, proposal generation, proposal presentation, handling objections and closing the sale. Sales-force automation software can be configured so that is modelled on the selling process of any industry or organization.

Sales-force automation software enables companies automatically to record leads and track opportunities as they progress through the sales pipeline towards closure. Intelligent applications of SFA are based on comprehensive customer data made available in a timely fashion to salespeople through various media such as desktops, laptop and handheld computers, personal digital assistants (PDAs) and cell-phones. Sales-force automation software has several capabilities, including opportunity management, contact management, proposal generation and product configuration.

Opportunity management lets users identify and progress opportunities to sell from lead status through to closure and beyond, into after-sales support. Opportunity management software usually contains lead management and sales forecasting applications. Lead management applications enable users to qualify leads and direct them, perhaps automatically, to the appropriate salesperson. Sales forecasting applications generally use transactional histories and salesperson estimates to produce estimates of future sales.

Contact management lets users manage their communications programme with customers. Customer databases are developed in which contact histories are recorded. Contact management applications often have features such as automatic customer dialling, the salesperson's personal calendar and e-mail functionality. For example, it is usually possible to build e-mail templates in Microsoft Outlook that can be customized with individual customers' details before delivery. Templates can be built that thank a client for an order, or to present a quotation. Sales-force automation is grounded on the right customer information being made available to the right sales team members and/or customers at the right point of time. In multiperson decision-making units, it is important to identify which people need what information. Companies should try to get the right information to the right person (see Case 1.1).

Case 1.1

Sales-force automation at Roche

Roche is one of the world's leading research-based healthcare organizations, active in the discovery, development and manufacture of pharmaceuticals and diagnostic systems. The organization has traditionally been product-centric and quite poor in the area of customer management. Roche's customers are medical practitioners prescribing products to patients. Customer information was previously collected through several mutually exclusive sources, ranging from personal visits to handwritten correspondence, and not integrated into a database or central filing system, giving incomplete views of the customer. Roche identified the need to adopt a more customer-centric approach to understand their customers better, to improve services offered to them and to increase sales effectiveness.

Roche implemented a sales-force automation system where all data and interactions with customers are stored in a central database which can be accessed throughout the organization. This has resulted in Roche being able to create customer profiles, segment customers, and communicate with existing and potential customers. Since its implementation Roche has been more successful in identifying, winning and retaining customers.

Proposal generation applications allow the salesperson to automate the production of proposals for customers. The salesperson enters details such as product codes, volumes, customer name and delivery requirements, and the software automatically generates a priced quotation that takes into account the customer's relational status. Casual customers can generally expect to pay more than strategically significant customers.

Product configuration software allows salespeople automatically to design and price customized solutions to customer problems. Configurators are useful when the product is particularly complex, such as IT solutions. Configurators are based on an 'if . . . then' rules structure. The general case of this rule is 'If X is chosen, then Y is required or prohibited or legitimated or unaffected.' For example, if the customer chooses a particular feature (say, a particular hard drive for a computer), then this rules out certain other choices or related features that are technologically incompatible or too costly or complex to manufacture.

The technology side of SFA is normally accompanied by an effort to improve and standardize the selling process. This involves the implementation of a sales methodology. Sales methodologies allow sales team members and management to adopt a standardized view of the sales cycle, and a common language for discussion of sales issues. Many methodologies have been developed over the years, including SPIN (Fig. 1.3),[8] Target Account Selling (TAS),[9] RADAR[10] and Strategic Selling.[11]

Some companies face particularly complex selling tasks. This is especially true of mission-critical multimillion dollar sales such as the sales of defence systems to national governments. Here, a team of people from the supply side will sell to a team from the government/customer side over a long period, possibly several years. There will be a large number of contact episodes to understand, develop and deliver to very demanding customer specifications. It is clearly essential to track carefully the status of the opportunity and manage contacts in the most effective and efficient way. Even where the selling context is significantly less complex, SFA still holds out the promise of better contact and opportunity management.

Figure 1.3
SPIN selling methodology (Source: Neil Rackham, Huthwaite Corporation)

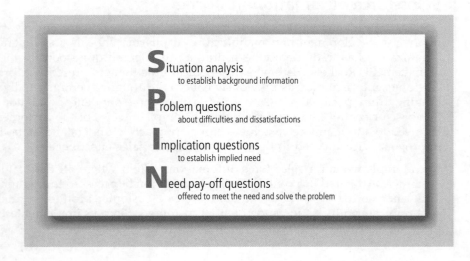

Situation analysis
to establish background information

Problem questions
about difficulties and dissatisfactions

Implication questions
to establish implied need

Need pay-off questions
offered to meet the need and solve the problem

Service automation

Service automation allows companies to automate their service operations, whether delivered through a call centre, a contact centre, the web or face-to-face in the field.[i] Software enables companies to manage and co-ordinate their service-related in-bound and out-bound communications across all channels. Software vendors claim that this enables companies to become more efficient and effective, by reducing service costs, improving service quality, lifting productivity and increasing customer satisfaction.

Service automation differs significantly depending on the product being serviced. Consumer products are normally serviced through retail outlets, the web or a call centre as the point of first contact. These contact channels are often supported by online scripting tools to help to diagnose a problem on first contact. Several technologies are common in service automation. Call-routing software can be used to direct inbound calls to the most appropriate handler. Technologies such as interactive voice response (IVR) enable customers to interact with company computers. Customers can input to an IVR system after listening to menu instructions either by telephone keypad (key 1 for option A, key 2 for option B) or by voice. If first contact problem resolution is not possible, the service process may then involve authorizing a return of goods, and a repair cycle involving a third party service provider. Examples of such a process include mobile phones and cameras.

Service automation for large capital equipment is quite different. This normally involves diagnostic and corrective action to be taken in the field, at the location of the equipment. Examples of this type of service include industrial air-conditioning and refrigeration. In these cases, service automation may involve providing the service technician with diagnostics, repair manuals, inventory management and job information on a laptop. This information is then synchronized at regular intervals to update the central CRM system.

Many companies use a combination of direct and indirect channels especially for sales and service functions. When indirect channels are employed, operational CRM supports this function through partner relationship management (PRM). This technology allows partners to communicate with the supplier through a portal, to manage leads, sales orders, product information and incentives.

Analytical CRM

Analytical CRM is concerned with exploiting customer data to enhance both customer and company value.

Analytical CRM builds on the foundation of customer information. Customer data may be found in enterprise-wide repositories: sales data

---

[i] Contact centres differ from call centres in that they handle not only phone calls, but also communications in other media such as mail, fax, e-mail and SMS.

(purchase history), financial data (payment history, credit score), marketing data (campaign response, loyalty scheme data), service data. To these internal data can be added data from external sources: geodemographic and lifestyle data from business intelligence organizations, for example. With the application of data mining tools, the company can then interrogate these data. Intelligent interrogation provides answers to questions such as: Who are our most valuable customers? Which customers have the highest propensity to switch to competitors? Which customers would be most likely to respond to a particular offer?

Analytical CRM has become an essential part of effective CRM implementation. Operational CRM struggles to reach full effectiveness without analytical information on the value of customers. Customer value drives many operational CRM decisions, such as:

- Which customers shall we target with this offer?
- What is the relative priority of customers waiting on the line, and what level of service should be offered?
- Where should I focus my sales effort?

From the customer's point of view, analytical CRM can deliver better, more timely, even personally customized, solutions to the customer's problems, thereby enhancing customer satisfaction. From the company's point of view, analytical CRM offers the prospect of more powerful cross-selling and up-selling programmes, and more effective customer retention and customer acquisition programmes. Retailer Wal-Mart uses analytical CRM. It collects data from its 1200 stores to identify which segments are shopping, what they are buying and which promotions are most effective. It constantly tries to improve average basket value through effective analytical CRM.

Case 1.2 shows how a UK based business-to-business (B2B) catalogue operation found that analytical CRM improved its performance on a

Case 1.2

Analytical CRM at UK Business Direct

	CRM	Traditional
Number of catalogues mailed	1000	5000
Mailing cost	£3000	£15 000
New customers obtained 1998	65	45
Conversion rate new customers	6.5%	0.09%
Initial sales per new customer	£180	£120
Total new initial sales revenues	£11 700	£5400
Acquisition cost per customer	£46.15	£333.33
Average customer sales 1998–2001	£7500	£2200
2 year gross margin (40%)	£3000	£880
1998 customers still active in 2001	80%	35%

number of metrics such as cost of customer acquisition, initial sales per customer, average customer value and customer retention, in comparison to what it normally achieved without the analytical insight provided by CRM.

Misunderstandings about CRM

This confusion about CRM has given rise to a number of misunderstandings that are challenged below.

Misunderstanding 1: CRM is database marketing

Database marketing is concerned with the development and exploitation of customer data for marketing purposes. Companies collect data from a number of sources. These data are verified, cleaned, integrated and stored on computers, often in data warehouses or data-marts. They are then used for marketing purposes such as market segmentation, targeting, offer development and customer communication.

Historically, most companies were located close to the markets they served and knew their customers intimately. Very often there would be face-to-face, even day-to-day, interaction with customers in which their knowledge of customer requirements and preferences grew. However, as companies have grown larger, they have become more remote from the customers they serve. The remoteness is not only geographical; it may also be cultural. Even some of the most widely admired American companies have not always understood the markets they served. Disney's development of a theme park near to the French capital, Paris, was not an initial success because they failed to deliver to the value expectations of European customers. For example, Disney failed to offer visitors alcohol onsite. Europeans, however, are accustomed to enjoying a glass or two of wine with their food.

Whereas most large and medium-sized companies do indeed build and exploit customer databases, CRM is much wider in scope than database marketing. A lot of what we have described earlier as analytical CRM has the appearance of database marketing. However, the issues described under strategic or operational CRM do not figure in database marketing.

Misunderstanding 2: CRM is a marketing process

At first pass, this would appear to be true, particularly for those who take CRM to mean customer relationship marketing. Indeed, CRM applications can be used for many marketing activities: market segmentation, customer acquisition, customer retention, customer development (cross-selling and up-selling), campaign management, and opportunity management, for example.

At a strategic level, however, CRM can be used as a core technology to support a company's mission to become more customer-centric. The customer data supporting a CRM strategy can be shared more widely throughout the enterprise than the marketing function alone. Operations management can use the customer data to produce customized products and services. People management (human resources) can use customer preference data to help to recruit and train staff for the front-line jobs that interface with customers. Research and development management can use customer data to focus new product development.

Customer data can not only be used to integrate various internal departments, but can also be shared across the extended enterprise with outside suppliers and partners. For example, Tesco, the international supermarket operation, has a number of collaborative new product development relationships with key suppliers. Tesco also partners with a major bank to offer financial services to Tesco customers. Both activities require the sharing of information about Tesco customers with supplier and partner.

Clearly, there is more to CRM than a marketing process.

Misunderstanding 3: CRM is an IT issue

Many of the early CRM implementations were seen as IT initiatives. Most CRM implementations require the creation of high-quality customer databases and the deployment of IT solutions. However, this should not be misread. Customer relationship management is generally aimed at creating better value for customers and company. This aim is simply made possible by IT. To say that CRM is about IT is like saying that gardening is about the spade or that art is about the paintbrush. Since IT is an enabler of business objectives, it is therefore at most a part of the CRM effort.

Not all CRM initiatives involve IT investments. The focus of CRM is on better management of customer relationships. This may involve behavioural changes in store employees, education of call-centre staff, and a focus on empathy and reliability from salespeople.

Misunderstanding 4: CRM is about loyalty schemes

Loyalty schemes are commonplace in many industries, such as car hire, airlines, food retail, hotels. Customers accumulate credits, such as air-miles, from purchases. These are then redeemed at some future point. Most loyalty schemes require new members to complete an application form when they join the programme. This demographic information is typically used together with purchasing data to help companies to become more effective at their marketing communication and offer development. Whereas some CRM implementations are linked to loyalty schemes not all are.

Loyalty schemes may play two roles in CRM implementations. First, they generate data for the customer database that can be used to guide customer acquisition, retention and development activities. Secondly, loyalty schemes may serve as an exit barrier. Customers who have accumulated credits in a scheme may be loathe to exit the relationship. The credits accumulated reflect the value of the investment that the customer has made in the scheme, and therefore in the relationship.

Loyalty schemes are discussed in more detail in Chapter 9.

Misunderstanding 5: CRM can be implemented by any company

Strategic CRM can, indeed, be implemented in any company. Every organization can be driven by a desire to be more customer-centric. Chief executives can establish a vision, mission and set of values that bring the customer to the heart of the business, and CRM technology may play a role in that transformation. Some attempts are certainly more successful than others. The banking industry has implemented CRM very widely, yet there are significant differences between the customer satisfaction ratings and customer retention rates across the industry.

Any company can also try to implement operational CRM supported by CRM technology. Any company with a sales force can automate its selling, lead management and contact management processes. The same is true for marketing and service processes. The CRM technology can be used to support marketing campaigns across the customer base. It also can be used to support query handling, problem resolution and complaints management. However, operational CRM can be much better focused if supported by analytical CRM. For example, the selling approach may differ between different customer groups. Customers with higher potential value may be offered face-to-face selling; lower value customers may experience telesales.

Analytical CRM is based on customer data. Data are needed to identify which customers are likely to generate most value in the future, and to divide the customer base into segments having different requirements. Different offers are then communicated to each customer group to optimize company and customer value over the long term. If these data are missing then analytical CRM cannot be implemented. Neither will support be made available for operational CRM implementations.

What is a relationship?

The 'R' in CRM stands for 'relationship'. But what do we really mean by the expression relationship? What is a relationship between a customer and supplier?

Thinking in terms of a dyadic relationship, that is a relationship between two parties, we can define a relationship as follows:

A relationship is composed of a series of episodes between dyadic parties over time.

Each episode in turn is composed of a series of interactions. Episodes are time bound (they have a beginning and an end) and nameable. Episodes such as making a purchase, enquiring about a product, putting together a quotation, making a sales call, dealing with a complaint and playing a round of golf make up a relationship. Business relationships are made up of task and social episodes. Task episodes are focused on the business side of the relationship, whereas social episodes are not. Within each episode, each participant will act towards, and interact with, the other. The content of each episode is a range of communicative behaviours including speech, deeds (actions) and body language. The parties within the dyad may have very different ideas about whether they are in a relationship. Buyers may think they are being tough and transactional. Sellers may feel that they have built a relationship.

Relationships are dynamic

Relationships change over time. They evolve. Dwyer identified five general phases through which relationships can evolve:[12]

1 Awareness
2 Exploration
3 Expansion
4 Commitment
5 Dissolution.

Awareness is when each party comes to the attention of the other as a possible exchange partner. Exploration is the period of investigation and testing during which the parties explore each others' capabilities and performance. Some trial purchasing takes place. If the trail is unsuccessful the relationship can be terminated with few costs. The exploration phase is thought to comprise five subprocesses: attraction, communication and bargaining, development and exercise of power, development of norms, and development of expectations. Expansion is the phase in which there is increasing interdependence. More transactions take place and trust begins to develop. The commitment phase is characterized by increased adaptation and mutually understood roles and goals. Purchasing processes may become automated.

Not all relationships reach the commitment phase. Many are terminated before that stage. There may be a breach of trust that forces a partner to reconsider the relationship. Perhaps the requirements of the customer change. The supplier is no longer needed. Relationship termination can be bilateral or unilateral. Bilateral termination is when both parties agree to end the relationship. They will probably want to retrieve whatever assets they invested in the relationship. Unilateral termination is when one of the parties moves to end the relationship. Customers may exit relationships for many reasons, such as repeated service failures or changed product requirements. Suppliers may choose to exit relationships because of their failure to contribute profit. A prior option may be to reduce cost-to-serve.

This model of relationship development highlights two attributes of highly developed relationships: trust and commitment. Trust and commitment have been the subject of a considerable amount of research.[13–16]

Trust

Trust is focused. That is, although there may be a generalized sense of confidence and security, these feelings are directed. One party may trust the other's:

- **benevolence**: a belief that one party will act in the interests of the other
- **honesty**: a belief that the other party will be credible
- **competence**: a belief that the other party has the necessary expertise.

The development of trust is an investment in relationship building which has a long-term payoff. Trust emerges as parties share experiences, and interpret and assess each other's motives. As they learn more about each other, risk and doubt are reduced.

When trust exists between partners, both are motivated to make investments in the relationship. These investments, which serve as exit barriers, may be either tangible (e.g. property) or intangible (e.g. knowledge). Such investments may or may not be retrievable when the relationship dissolves.

If trust is absent, conflict and uncertainty rise, while co-operation falls.

It has been suggested that as relationships evolve over time so does the character of trust:[17]

- **Calculus-based trust** is present in early stages of the relationship and related to economic value. The outcomes of creating and sustaining the new relationship are weighed against those of dissolving it
- **Knowledge-based trust** relies on the individual parties' interactive history and knowledge of each other, allowing each to make predictions about the other
- **Identification-based trust** happens when mutual understanding is such that each can act as substitute for the other in interpersonal interaction. This is found in the later stages of relationship development.

Commitment

Commitment is an essential ingredient for successful, long-term, relationships. Morgan and Hunt define relationship commitment as:

> an exchange partner believing that an ongoing relationship with another is so important as to warrant maximum effort to maintaining it; that is, the committed party believes the relationship is worth working on to ensure that it endures indefinitely.[13]

Commitment arises from trust, shared values and the belief that partners will be difficult to replace. Commitment motivates partners to co-operate in order to preserve relationship investments. Commitment means that partners eschew short-term alternatives in favour of more stable, long-term benefits associated with current partners. Where customers have choice, they make commitments only to trustworthy partners, because commitment entails vulnerability, leaving them open to opportunism.

Evidence of commitment is found in the investments that one party makes in the other. One party makes investments in the budding relationship and if the other responds, the relationship evolves and the partners become increasingly committed to doing business with each other. Investments can include time, money and the demotion of current relationships. A partner's commitment to a relationship is directly influenced by the size of the investment in the relationship, since these represent termination costs. Highly committed relationships may have very high termination costs, since some of these relationship investments may be irretrievable. In addition, there may be significant costs incurred in switching to an alternative supplier, such as search costs, learning costs and psychic costs.

Why companies want relationships with customers

The fundamental reason for companies wanting to build relationships with customers is economic. Companies generate better results when they manage their customer base in order to identify, satisfy and retain their most profitable customers. This is a key objective of CRM strategies.

Improving customer retention rates has the effect of increasing the size of the customer base. Figure 1.4 compares two companies. Company A has a churn rate (customer defection rate) of 5 per cent per annum; company B's churn rate is 10 per cent. Put another way, their respective customer retention rates are 95 and 90 per cent. Starting from the same position and acquiring an identical number of new customers each year,

Year	Company A (5% churn)			Company B (10% churn)		
	Existing customers	New customers	Total customer base	Existing customers	New customers	Total customer base
1998	1000	100	1100	1000	100	1100
1999	1045	100	1145	990	100	1090
2000	1088	100	1188	981	100	1081
2001	1129	100	1229	973	100	1073
2002	1168	100	1268	966	100	1066

Figure 1.4 Effect of customer retention on customer volume

company A's customer base is 19 per cent larger than company B's after 4 years: 1268 customers compared with 1066 customers.

Churn rates vary considerably. For example, after deregulation, about 25 per cent of UK utility customers changed suppliers within 24 months. The industry had been expecting 5–10 per cent churn. Most switched for better prices and to achieve a dual-fuel (gas and electricity) discount There is little merit in growing the customer base aimlessly. The goal must be to retain existing, and recruit new, customers who have future profit potential, or are important for other strategic purposes.[ii] Not all customers are of equal importance. Some customers may not be worth recruiting or retaining at all: those who have a high cost-to-serve, or are debtors, late payers or promiscuous in the sense that they switch frequently between suppliers.

Other things being equal, a larger customer base delivers better business performance. Similarly, as customer retention rates rise (or defection rates falls) so does the average tenure of a customer, as shown in Fig. 1.5. Tenure is the term used to describe the length of time a customer remains a customer. The impacts of small improvements in customer retention are hugely magnified at the higher levels of retention. For example, improving the customer retention rate from 75 to 80 per cent increases average customer tenure from 10 years to 12.5 years. Managing tenure by reducing defection rates can be critical. For example, it can take 13 years for utility customers to break even. In the UK, the average profit per household customer is £3 to £5, and the average customer acquisition cost is £40. A customer who defects after one year generates a loss of some £35.

Benefits from customer retention

Managing customer retention and tenure intelligently generates two key benefits.

First, the company's marketing costs are reduced. Fewer dollars need to be spent replacing lost customers. For example, it has been estimated that it costs an advertising agency at least 20 times as much to recruit a new client as to retain an existing client. In the UK, major agencies can spend up to £2 million on research, strategic analysis and creative work in pitching for one major client, with up to four creative teams working on different executions. An agency might incur these costs several times over as it pitches to several prospective clients to replace the lost client.[18] In addition to reducing the costs of customer recruitment, costs-to-serve existing customers also tend to fall over time. Ultimately, as in some B2B markets, the relationship may become fully automated. Some supply-chain relationships, for example, use electronic data interchange (EDI) that fully automates the ordering, inventory and invoicing processes, or develop portals that allow customers to manage their own purchasing arrangements.

Secondly, as tenure grows, suppliers better understand customer requirements. Customers also come to understand what a company can do

[ii] The idea of strategic significance is discussed in Chapter 4.

Customer retention rate (%)	Average customer tenure (years)
50	2
67	3
75	4
80	5
90	10
92	12.5
95	20
96	25
97	33.3
98	50
99	100

Figure 1.5
Retention rate and average customer tenure

for them. Consequently, suppliers become better placed to identify and satisfy customer requirements profitably, selling more product and service to the customer. Over time, as relationships deepen, trust and commitment between the parties are likely to grow. Under these circumstances, revenue and profit streams from customers become more secure. One study, for example, shows that the average online clothing customer spends 67 per cent more in months 31–36 of a relationship than in months 0–6. In the grocery market customers spend 23 per cent more over the same time differential. The same study also shows that the average clothing customer takes four purchases (12 months) to recover the costs of their acquisition; grocery customers take 18 months to break even.[19]

In sum, both the cost and revenue sides of the profit equation are impacted by customer retention.

Some companies use a model that has been variously known as a value ladder[20] or value staircase[21] to help them to understand where customers are positioned in terms of their tenure with the company. You may imagine a seven-stage customer journey from suspect status to advocate status, as follows.

1 **Suspect**: could the customer fit the target market profile?
2 **Prospect**: customer fits the profile and is being approached for the first time.
3 **First-time customer**: customer makes first purchase.
4 **Repeat customer**: customer makes additional purchases.
5 **Majority customer**: customer selects your company as supplier of choice.
6 **Loyal customer**: customer is resistant to switching suppliers; strong positive attitude to your company.
7 **Advocate**: customer generates additional referral dollars.

As in the Dwyer model cited earlier, not all customers progress uniformly along the path from 'never-a-customer' (suspect) to 'always-a-customer' (advocate). Some will have a long maturity phase (i.e. loyal customer); others will have a shorter life, perhaps never shifting from first-timer to repeat customer; others still might never convert from prospect to first-timer.

CRM software allows companies to trace where customers are on this journey and to allocate resources intelligently to advance suitable customers along the value path.

Costs and revenues vary from stage to stage. In the early stages, a company may invest significant sums in converting a prospect into a first-time customer. The investment in relationship building may not be recovered for some time. Reichheld and Sasser show that it takes a credit-card company almost two years to recover the costs of customer acquisition.[22]

This leads to the core CRM idea that a customer should be viewed not as a set of independent transactions but as a lifetime income stream. In the car industry, for instance, it is estimated that a General Motors retail customer is worth US$276 000 over a lifetime of purchasing cars (11 or more vehicles), parts and service. Fleet operators are worth considerably more.[23] When a GM customer switches to Ford, the revenue streams from that customer may be lost for ever. Case 1.3 illustrates the use of customer lifetime value in the telecommunications market.

Despite the financial benefits that accrue from a relationship there are sometimes clear disincentives for companies entering into relationships with their customers, particularly in the B2B context.

1 **Loss of control**. Relationships are bilateral arrangements, and therefore they involve giving up unilateral control over resources. Relationship partners have expectations of what activities should be performed and

Case 1.3

Optus estimates customer lifetime value in the mobile phone market

Like other telecommunications providers in the competitive mobile phone market, Optus was faced with a large percentage of their mobile phone customers switching to another carrier once their 12, 18 or 24 month contract had ended.

In an effort to reduce customer churn, Optus estimated the value of its various customer segments to ascertain which offered the highest lifetime value potential. Many factors were considered, such as the total spend on phone calls, SMS and information services over a contract period, the cost of servicing the customer and the probability of retaining the customer after the expiry of the initial contract.

The findings indicated that females aged between 20 and 25 had the highest value in the consumer market and tradesmen operating their own business had the highest value in the business market.

resources deployed both by themselves and the other party. It is not necessarily easy or cost-effective to exit a relationship. Sometimes, investments that are made in a relationship are not returned when a relationship breaks down.

2 **Resource commitment**. Relationships require the commitment of resources such as people, time and money. Companies have to decide whether it is better to allocate resources to customer management or to some other area of the business such as operations or people development.

3 **Opportunity costs**. If resources are committed to one customer, they cannot be used for another. Relationships carry with them high opportunity costs. If you commit resources to customer A, you may have to give up the possibility of a relationship with customer B, even if that seems to be a better proposition.

Customer satisfaction, loyalty and business performance

The rationale for CRM is that it improves business performance by enhancing customer satisfaction and driving up customer loyalty, as shown in Fig. 1.6. There is a compelling logic to the model, which has been dubbed the 'satisfaction–profit chain'.[24] Satisfaction increases because customer insight allows companies to understand their customers better, and create improved customer value propositions. As customer satisfaction rises, so does customer repurchase intention.[25] This in turn influences actual purchasing behaviour, which has a significant impact on business performance.

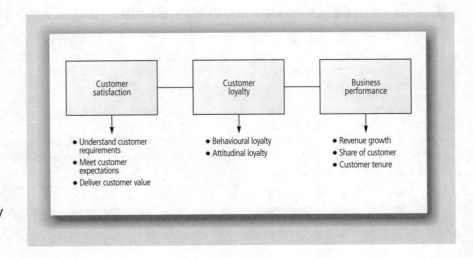

Figure 1.6
Customer satisfaction, loyalty and business performance

The variables and linkages between them will be examined. First, the major variables customer satisfaction, customer loyalty and business performance will be described.

Customer satisfaction has been the subject of considerable research, and has been defined and measured in many ways.[26] It may be defined as follows:

> Customer satisfaction is the customer's fulfilment response to a consumption experience, or some part of it.

Customer satisfaction is a pleasurable fulfilment response. Dissatisfaction is an unpleasurable fulfilment response. The 'experience, of some part of it' component of the definition allows the satisfaction evaluation to be directed at any or all elements of the customer's experience. This can include product, service, process and any other components of the experience.

The most common way of operationalizing satisfaction is to compare the customer's perception of an experience, or some part of it, with their expectations. This is known as the expectations disconfirmation model of customer satisfaction. Basically, the model suggests that if customers perceive their expectations to be met, they are satisfied. If their expectations are underperformed, this is negative disconfirmation, and they will be dissatisfied. Positive disconfirmation occurs when perception exceeds expectation. The customer might be pleasantly surprised or even delighted. This model of customer satisfaction assumes that customers have expectations, and that they are able to judge performance. A customer satisfaction paradox has been identified by expectations disconfirmation researchers. At times, customers' expectations may be met but the customer is still not satisfied. This happens when the customer's expectations are low: 'I expected the plane to be late. It was. I'm unhappy!'

Many companies research requirements and expectations to find out what is important for customers, and then measure the customers' perception of their performance compared with the performance of competitors. The focus in CRM is on the elements of the value proposition that create value for customers. Companies have to do well at meeting these important value producers.

Customer loyalty has also been the subject of considerable research. There are two major approaches to defining and measuring loyalty, one based on behaviour, the other on attitude.

Behavioural loyalty is measured by reference to customer purchasing behaviour where it is expressed in continued patronage and buying. There are two behavioural dimensions to loyalty. First, is the customer still active? Secondly, have we maintained our share of customer spending? In portfolio purchasing environments, where customers buy products and services from a number of more-or-less equal suppliers, the share of customer spending question is more important. Many direct marketing companies use RFM measures of behavioural loyalty. The most loyal are those who have high scores on the three variables: recency of purchases (R), frequency of purchases (F) and monetary value of purchases (M). The variables are measured as follows:

R = time elapsed since last purchase
F = number of purchases in a given period
M = monetary value of purchases in a given period

Attitudinal loyalty is measured by reference to components of attitude such as beliefs, feelings and purchasing intention. Those customers who have a stronger preference for, involvement in or commitment to a supplier are the more loyal in attitudinal terms.

Recently, researchers have combined both views into comprehensive models of customer loyalty. The best known is Dick and Basu's model, as shown in Fig. 1.7.[27]

These authors identify four forms of loyalty according to relative attitudinal strength and repeat purchase behaviour. The true loyals are those who have high levels of repeat buying and a strong relative attitude. High repeat purchase not associated with strong attitude may reflect inertia, high switching costs or indifference. Latent loyalty exists when a strong attitude is not accompanied by repeat buying. Perhaps this is a question of distribution and convenience.

From a practical point of view, the behavioural definition of loyalty is attractive because sales and profits derive from actions not attitudes. An attitudinal approach can help managers to understand what needs to be done to build high levels of commitment that are resistant to competitor actions. However, it is not clear from this model whether attitude

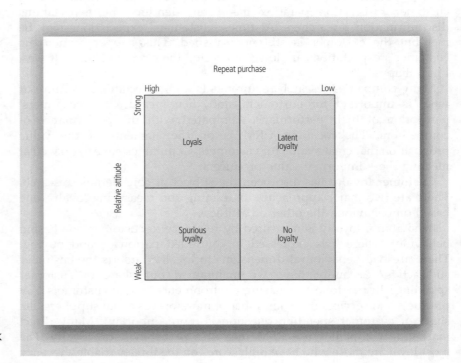

Figure 1.7
Two-dimensional model of customer loyalty (Source: Dick and Basu[27])

precedes behaviour or behaviour precedes attitude. Researchers accept that causation may be circular rather unidirectional. In other words, each may precede and reinforce the other.

Business performance can be measured in many ways. The recent trend has been away from simple short-term financial measures such as return on investment (ROI) or earnings per share. Leading companies are moving towards a more rounded set of performance indicators, such as represented by the balanced scorecard.[28] This approach uses four sets of linked key performance indicators (KPI): financial, customer, internal, and learning and growth. The implied connection between these indicators is that people (learning and growth) do things (internal) for customers (customer) that have effects on business performance (financial). The KPIs that can be customized for each organization include:

- finance
  - return on investment
  - earnings per share
  - economic value added
- customer
  - customer satisfaction
  - customer retention
  - customer acquisition
  - customer loyalty
  - customer tenure
  - sales per customer
  - revenue growth
  - market share
  - share of customer: as indicated in Fig. 1.8, share of customer focuses on winning a greater share of targeted customers' or segments' spending, rather than share of a less well-specified market
- internal
  - quality conformance
  - manufacturing cost
  - cycle times
  - speed to market
  - inventory management
  - customer information system downtime
  - on time, in full, no error (OTIFNE) logistics performance
- learning and growth
  - employee satisfaction
  - employee retention
  - employees cross-trained
  - employee productivity.

The balanced scorecard is highly adaptable to CRM contexts. Companies need to ask the following questions. What customer outcomes drive our financial performance? What internal outcomes drive our customer performance? What learning and growth outcomes drive our internal performance? Figure 1.6 shows that the customer outcomes of satisfaction and loyalty drive business performance. Another business model that is supported by many CRM practitioners in the service sector links all four

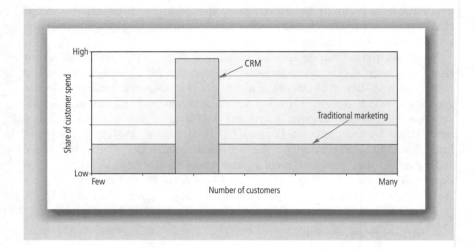

Figure 1.8
Share of market versus share of customer

classes of performance indicator. They believe that satisfied employees perform internal processes well to create value for customers who in turn become loyal and produce a strong profit performance for the company.[29]

What does the evidence show?

Research into the links between customer satisfaction, loyalty and business performance is now discussed. Analysis has been done on international data, national data, industry data and corporate data.

The European Customer Satisfaction Index is a tool that models the relationship between a number of relationship variables, including customer perceived value, customer satisfaction and customer loyalty at the international level. The model has not yet been extended to include business performance. However, researchers have found a strong relationship between value perceptions, satisfaction levels and loyalty.[30] At the national level, customer data from the Swedish Customer Satisfaction Barometer (SCSB) have been correlated with corporate profit performance. A lagged relationship was established, indicating that current customer satisfaction levels impact on tomorrow's profit performance.[31] The SCSB database matches customer-based measures with traditional financial measures of business performance, such as productivity and return on investment (ROI). SCSB researchers telephone-interview 35 000 individuals who have recently experienced a product or service and produce an annual assessment of their satisfaction levels across nine different industry sectors. The SCSB is one of several such national indices. There are others in Germany, Switzerland and the USA. A similar study, using data from the American Customer Satisfaction Index (ACSI) also found that customer satisfaction had a considerable effect on business performance, although there was variation across sectors.[32]

A number of studies in different industries and companies – including telecommunications, banking, airline and automobile distribution – support the relationship between customer satisfaction, loyalty and business performance.

- **Telecommunications**. One study of the telecoms industry found that a 10 per cent increase in a customer satisfaction index predicted a 2 per cent increase in customer retention (a behavioural measure of loyalty) and a 3 per cent interest in revenues (a business performance measure). The authors concluded that customer satisfaction was a lead indicator of customer retention, revenue and revenue growth.[33]
- **Banking**. Another study found that customer satisfaction in retail banking correlated highly with branch profitability. Highly satisfied customers had balances 20 per cent higher than satisfied customers and, as satisfaction levels went up over time, so did account balances. The reverse was also true: as satisfaction levels fell, so did account balances.[34]
- **Airlines**. A study in the airline industry examined the link between customer dissatisfaction, operating income, operating revenue and operating expense. The study identified the drivers of dissatisfaction as high load factors, mishandled baggage and poor punctuality. The study concluded that as dissatisfaction rose, operating revenue (an indicator of customer behaviour) fell, operating income fell and operating expenses rose.[35]
- **Car distribution**. A study of Volvo cars owners examined the links between customer satisfaction with three attributes – car purchase, workshop service and the vehicle itself – and loyalty and dealer business performance. The results indicated that a one scale-point increase in overall customer satisfaction was associated with a 4 per cent increase in dealer profitability at next car purchase.[36]

According to one review, there is 'growing evidence that the links in the satisfaction–profit chain are solid.'[24] However, the relationships can be both asymmetrical and non-linear. The asymmetric nature of the relationships is found by comparing the impact of an increase in one variable with an equivalent decrease. For example, a one scale-point shift up in customer satisfaction (say from 3 to 4 on a five-point scale) may not

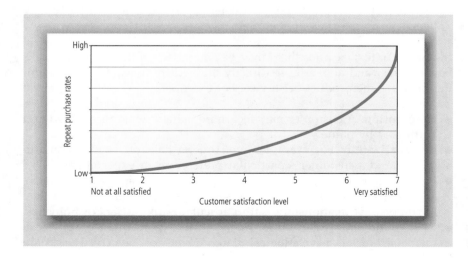

Figure 1.9
Increasing returns from investments in customer satisfaction

have a comparable impact on customer retention rates to a one-scale point downward shift (say from 3 to 2 on the same five-point scale). In addition, links can be non-linear. Non-linearity is sometimes reflected in diminishing returns, other times in increasing returns. For example, increasing returns may be obtained in customer retention as customers progress up the customer satisfaction scale, as shown in Fig. 1.9. Diminishing returns may set in if customer expectations are already largely met. Investments in increasing customer satisfaction at already high levels of performance do not have the same impact as investments at lower levels of performance.

But, do customers want relationships with companies?

Although it is clear that companies want relationships with customers, it is far less clear that customers universally want relationships with their suppliers.

There are a number of circumstances when a B2B customer may want a long-term relationship with a supplier. These include when:

- the product or its applications are complex, for example, networking infrastructure
- the product is strategically important or mission-critical, for example, core raw materials supply for a manufacturer
- there are downstream service requirements, for example, for machine tools
- financial risk is high, for example, in buying large pieces of capital equipment
- reciprocity is expected. A financial audit practice may want a close relationship with a management consultancy, so that each party may benefit from referrals by the other.

In a B2C context, relationships may be sought when the customer seeks benefits over and above those directly derived from acquiring, consuming or using the product or service. For example:

- **Recognition**. A customer may feel more valued when recognized and addressed by name.
- **Personalization**. For example, over time, a hairdresser may come to understand a customer's particular preferences or expectations.
- **Power**. Some of the power asymmetry in relationships between banks and their customers may be reversed when customers feel that they have personal relationships with particular bank officers or branches.
- **Risk reduction**. Risk takes many forms: performance, physical, financial, social, psychological. High levels of perceived risk are

uncomfortable for many customers. A relationship can reduce, or even perhaps eliminate perceived risk. For example, a customer may develop a relationship with a garage to reduce the perceived performance and physical risk attached to having a car serviced. The relationship provides the assurance that the job has been skilfully performed and that the car is safe to drive.

- **Status**. Customers may feel that their status is enhanced by a relationship with an organization, such as an elite health club.
- **Affiliation**. People's social needs can be met through commercially based, or non-commercially based, relationships. Many people are customers (members) of professional or community associations, for example.

Customer segments vary in their desire to have relationships with suppliers. In the banking industry, for example, large corporations have their own treasury departments and often obtain little value from a bank relationship; small private account holders have no need for the additional services that a relationship provides; small and medium-sized business and high net-worth individuals may have most to gain from a closer relationship.

CRM constituencies

Several constituencies, which together comprise the CRM ecosystem, have an interest in CRM:

- **Companies implementing CRM**. Many companies have implemented CRM strategies. The market for CRM software is thought to be mature in the largest CRM marketplace, the USA. Large companies in mature industries were the first to adopt CRM. They were followed by medium-sized companies. There is still potential for the CRM message to reach smaller companies, other worldwide markets and new business start-ups.
- **Customers and partners of those companies**. The customers and partners of companies that implement CRM are a particularly important constituency. If CRM does as is intended it will deliver improved customer experience. This, in turn, should result in a higher level of satisfaction, and the possibility of stronger commitment and loyalty to the supplier.
- **Vendors of CRM software**. Vendors of CRM software include companies such as Siebel, PeopleSoft, Pivotal, Oracle, SalesLogix and Salesforce.com. Some of these vendors offer CRM systems in which modules can be switched on or off according to customer needs. For example, Siebel offers a number of different service automation modules: call centre, web service and field service. Not all of these modules are relevant in all implementations. Other vendors offer specialized CRM applications, for example, for SFA only.

- **Vendors of CRM hardware and infrastructure**. Hardware and infrastructure vendors provide the technological foundations for CRM implementations. They supply technologies such as servers, computers, handheld devices, call-centre hardware and telephony systems.
- **Consultancies with a diverse range of capabilities such as strategy, business, application and technical consulting**. Consultants have benefited hugely from CRM implementations. They have helped companies implementing CRM in several ways: choosing between different vendors, developing implementation plans, and project management as the implementation is rolled out. Most CRM implementations are composed of a large number of smaller projects; for example, systems integration, data quality improvement, market segmentation, process engineering and culture change. The major consultancies such as Accenture, McKinsey, Bearing Point, Braxton and CGEY all offer CRM consultancy. Smaller companies sometimes offer specialized expertise. Peppers and Rogers provide strategy consulting. SAS and MicroStrategy focus on the statistical analysis of customer data. DunnHumby is known for its expertise in data mining for segmentation purposes.

As mentioned earlier, there is little consensus on what constitutes CRM. The CRM vendors and consultants may see the core of CRM as consisting of three major elements: a customer database, some data-mining capability, and a suite of front-end applications covering marketing, sales and customer service functions operating across all channels and touch-points. Companies implementing CRM may see it as something more rudimentary and fundamental, such as way of doing business that focuses on the customer. Within companies, different functional groups may have different perspectives: IT may see it as a systems implementation, whereas marketing may see it as a better way to run campaigns.

Why do companies implement CRM?

Companies are motivated to adopt CRM for both defensive and offensive reasons. Offensive motivations are associated with a desire to improve profitability by reducing cost, and increasing revenues through improved customer satisfaction and loyalty. Defensive motivations arise when leading competitors have adopted CRM successfully, and a company fears losing customers and revenue.

Companies thinking of adopting CRM face a significant problem. They need to know whether CRM pays. Investment in CRM may cost many millions of dollars. The typical investment of a Global 3500 company in CRM technology (software and services) is estimated at US$15 million to US$30 million annually. Over three years, the company will spend over

US$75 million.[37] In contrast, a small company can buy a CRM package off the shelf for US$1000 per seat (i.e. licensed user), costing it no more than US$10 000 a year.

Technology, however, is not the only cost of CRM. A CRM project can take between three and five years to implement fully. The technology costs tend to cluster at the front of the project. As project time moves on, people and process costs become larger. Front-office processes such as marketing and selling might need to be re-engineered. Back-office processes such as operations and finance might also be changed to suit the new focus on customers. People on the current payroll might need to be reskilled or retrenched. New talent with CRM-useful skills, such as customer analytics, may need to be recruited. The organization structure might need to be overhauled, perhaps by shifting it from a product-centric to a customer-centric structure. Technology will typically account for only one-fifth to one-third of total CRM project costs. Many companies now consider the total cost of ownership (TCO) – all people, IT and process costs – in computing returns on investment.

In early CRM implementations there was not much evidence to support CRM investment decisions. Early adopters bought CRM because they felt it made sense to understand and satisfy their customers better. Vendors and consultants sold CRM on the promise of greater customer retention and profitability. Today, vendors use evidence in selling to new customers: ROI models and case histories of successful implementations support the selling effort.

In recent years there has been much comment on the effectiveness of CRM. Gartner Research estimated that the failure rate is 65 per cent and that it may escalate to 80 per cent,[38] and that 'there is a growing view among organizations adopting CRM that their projects are not delivering the hoped-for value'.[39]

An Internet survey of some 2200 CRM clients, including many who had installed GoldMine, Onyx, Oracle, PeopleSoft, Pivotal, SalesLogix, SAP and Siebel products, concluded that customer satisfaction with the CRM product was 'very low indeed'.[40] The average customer satisfaction index score across all vendors was 63.1 out of 100, lower than reported in studies of other comparable IT sectors. The survey measured five attributes: ease of implementation, customer focus, price satisfaction, support and functionality. Ease of implementation scored lowest, at 55, whereas functionality scored highest, at 68, across all vendors. A key finding was that clients do not want 'out-of-the-box functionality', but adaptation to their own requirements.

While there has been client-side concern about CRM's performance, vendors and consultancies are, perhaps unexpectedly, more bullish. A report from Accenture claimed that a 10 per cent improvement in the top 21 CRM capabilities, including customer service and turning customer information into insight, could boost profits in a $1 billion business unit by $40–50 million. They found that between 28 and 60 per cent of the variance in companies' return on sales was due to CRM performance.[41] Fred Reichheld from Bain and Company has famously claimed that a 5 per cent improvement in customer retention, a key objective of many

CRM strategies, can enhance profit by between 45 and 95 per cent across a variety of industries.[42]

Although there is some evidence supporting CRM's delivery of a worthwhile ROI, other research suggests that up to 45 per cent of companies are unable to compute ROI from their CRM investments.[43] Only one-third of companies in a Cap Gemini Ernst and Young (CGEY) survey could provide any estimate of their expected return on CRM investments.[44]

Efforts to compute ROI from CRM investments are dogged by three questions:

1 What counts as an investment in CRM?
2 What counts as a return on that investment?
3 Over what period should the return be measured?

What counts as an investment in CRM?

Companies adopting the CRM way of doing business are likely to incur costs in a number of areas. Some of these may be capital costs; some may be expenses. They largely fall into three major categories: IT, people and process costs.

Information technology costs include investments in IT infrastructure and hardware, database development and software. The cost of hardware and software is falling. Software may be purchased outright or licensed. Several software components may be required for a large-scale CRM investment. This might include SFA, sales management automation, contact-centre automation, MA, e-commerce functionality and knowledge management.

People costs include recruitment, redeployment and training costs. The cost of IT professionals is dependent upon the supply of talent. During periods of talent shortage, IT people costs rise dramatically. Process costs may also be significant. Current working practices and workflow may need to re-engineered. Project management, change management and consultancy costs can add considerably to the final bill.

What counts as a return on investment?

At the level of strategic CRM, the executive team would want to know how much additional profit an investment in CRM would yield. For complex, long-term, multiphase projects this is an impossible question to answer. To compute the gain associated with a CRM initiative would require all other variables impacting the profit equation to be held constant, or an experimental design to be constructed. Large-scale implementations take up to five years to accomplish. During that time, the competitive environment may have changed dramatically, with new players entering, mergers and acquisitions, new products on the market, and customer expectations lifted.

Despite the expectation of shareholders that boards will measure performance against a set of hard financial indicators, senior management is also likely to employ some very soft indicators of CRM's impacts. One survey suggests that 'customer-centric visioning, in which executives develop an enterprise view of their strategy from the customer perspective' is the most valuable CRM outcome.[44] Clearly, this outcome is difficult to measure in hard numbers.

As noted earlier, every large-scale implementation is composed of a number of smaller projects. Each of these will have cost profiles and time-scales. However, not all generate revenue streams. Investments in database development and market segmentation, for example, typically represent sunk costs without which it would be impossible to run CRM-driven marketing and sales campaigns. They are necessary costs that enable CRM to function.

With small-scale implementations the task of measuring return is easier. If only a single function is automated, it is possible to establish clear performance targets. For example, it may be possible to measure the number of proposals written before SFA with the number written afterwards, or the number of prospects converted into first-time customers, or the number of quintile two customers who are migrated to quintile one.[iii] Even so, without appropriate controls in place, management could not be sure that the cause of the change is the CRM investment.

As large projects are broken down into smaller units (the operational and analytical perspectives in Fig. 1.1) it becomes easier to set some very specific KPIs which measure CRM's impact on one or both sides of the profit equation: revenues or costs. Operational KPIs may include greater sales force productivity, reduced service costs, and increased share of customer spend. Analytical KPIs may include reduced customer acquisition costs, improved productivity from direct marketing campaigns, and higher rates of multiple product ownership. Banks, for example, can improve the chances of customers becoming more profitable by having them buying several products such as savings accounts, investment accounts and insurance policies. Customers who only have a current account (checking account) are notoriously unprofitable.

Many CRM implementations use even more indirect measures of the impact of CRM upon ROI. These measure neither cost nor revenue. Rather, they measure a driver of either or both; for example, customer satisfaction or customer retention. Anderson, Fornell and Lehmann are clear that high levels of customer satisfaction drive profitability.[31] Reichheld is equally clear that customer retention drives profitability.[42] Both are elements of the satisfaction–profit chain that was examined earlier.

[iii] Many companies divide their customer into quintiles. The top 20 per cent of customers (quintile one) generally represents a higher contribution to sales and/or profit than lower quintiles. CRM strategies may focus on migrating customers from lower quintiles into higher quintiles, i.e. making customers more valuable in terms of sales and/or profit.

Over what period should the return be measured?

For many companies CRM is a long-term investment that is expected to pay off over periods of up to five or more years. As the perspective on CRM shifts from strategic to operational to analytical, the time frame over which performance is measured becomes shorter. Whether an organization becomes more customer-centric following the adoption of CRM practices is a question that can only be answered over the long term. However, it is certainly possible to measure the costs and revenue impacts of CRM-enabled marketing campaigns over a matter of weeks, if not days.

Contexts of CRM

There is wide variety in the contexts in which CRM is practised and in the relationship issues that companies face in those contexts. Customer relationship management takes many forms and addresses many relationship issues. Four contexts will be considered: banks, automobile manufacturers, high-tech companies and consumer goods manufacturers.

- **Banks** and the telecommunication firms deal with individual consumers or customers. They want CRM for its analytical capability to help them to manage customer defection (churn) rates and to enhance cross-sell performance. Data-mining techniques can be used to identify which customers are likely to defect, what can be done to win them back, which customers are hot prospects for cross-sell offers, and how best to communicate those offers. Banks and telecommunication companies want to win a greater share of customer spend (share of wallet). In terms of operational CRM, they are both transferring service into contact centres in an effort to reduce costs.
- **Automobile manufacturers** deal with distributor/dealer networks. They have little contact with end-users. They want CRM for its ability to help them to develop better and more profitable relationships with their networks. Being physically disconnected from drivers, they have built websites that enable them to interact with these end-users. This has improved their knowledge of customer requirements. Ultimately, they hope that CRM will enable them to win a greater share of end-user spend across the car purchase, maintenance and replacement cycle.
- **High-tech companies** manufacture complex products that are generally sold by partner organizations. For example, small innovative software developers have traditionally partnered with companies such as IBM to obtain distribution and sales. However, companies such as Dell have innovated channels. They go direct-to-customer (DTC). These DTC companies may use CRM to collect customer information, segment their customer base, automate their sales processes with product configurator software and deliver their

customer service online. They have also developed automated relationships with suppliers, so that they carry no or low levels of inventory, which are replenished frequently in rapid response to order patterns.

- **Consumer goods manufacturers** deal with the retail trade. They use CRM to help them to develop profitable relationships with retailers, and to understand costs-to-serve and customer profitability. Key account management practices are applied to strategically significant customers. Purchasing processes enabled by IT deliver higher levels of accuracy in stock replenishment. Manufacturers can run CRM-enabled marketing campaigns which are highly cost-effective.

The not-for-profit context

Most of this chapter has been concerned with CRM applications in the for-profit context. However, CRM can also be found in the not-for-profit context. Some of the basic skills of database development and exploitation, and customer lifecycle management, are equally relevant to not-for-profit organizations (see Case 1.4).

The Salvation Army uses CRM capability to solicit contributions, using event-based fundraising. The Army also knows the value of different donor segments, and works at retaining their high value donors and at migrating casual donors up the value ladder towards bequest status.

Universities have deployed CRM to manage their student and alumni relationships. Today's students are thought to represent considerable

Case 1.4

Not-for-profit operational CRM at the city of Lynchburg

The city council of Lynchburg, VA, USA, sought to improve the levels of information and services that it provided to its 69 000 citizens. The 'Citizens First Program' involved the design and implementation of an operational CRM strategy to open the lines of communication and to automate many services between the city council's 1100 employees, municipal departments and the citizens of Lynchburg. The project comprised the establishment of a website to provide citizens with 24/7 access to information concerning the city's services and facilities, and enabling citizens to make requests for information, enquiries and complaints. Supporting the website was CRM software and a linked call centre, providing personalized follow-up and ongoing support.

Since implementation in 1999, many benefits have been seen, namely:

- There has been a 50% reduction in the time taken to respond to citizens' enquiries.
- Citizens can track the progress of requests for service, enquiries, etc.
- The city council can measure and report on organizational performance.
- Levels of communication within the city council and between municipal departments have improved.

potential lifetime value to universities. For example, students who enjoy their experiences at a graduate school of business may return there for executive education. They may recommend the institution to their personal networks, or when they reach an appropriate level of seniority commission the school to consult or deliver customized training and development to their companies. Schools as eminent as Harvard Business School have been hugely successful at fundraising from their alumni networks.

Defining CRM

Against this background of three levels of CRM, misunderstandings about CRM, differing constituency viewpoints, and contexts of implementation, it is no easy matter to settle on a single definition of CRM. However, we can identify a number of core CRM attributes, and integrate them into a definition that underpins the rest of this book.

> CRM is the core business strategy that integrates internal processes and functions, and external networks, to create and deliver value to targeted customers at a profit. It is grounded on high-quality customer data and enabled by IT.

This definition certainly has a for-profit context. If the not-for-profit community were to replace the words business, customers and profit with appropriate equivalents, then it would apply equally well in that context.

Summary

In this chapter you have learned that CRM has a variety of meanings. It can be considered at three levels: strategic, operational and analytical. There are many misunderstandings about CRM. For example, some people wrongly equate CRM with loyalty programmes, whereas others think of CRM as an IT issue. Different constituencies such as CRM consultancies, CRM software vendors, CRM hardware and infrastructure vendors, companies that are implementing CRM, and their customers in turn, may have very different perspectives on CRM. The implementation of CRM may cost many millions of dollars, and management is increasingly demanding evidence that CRM investments will produce a satisfactory return. Although CRM is generally thought of as a business practice it also has application in the not-for-profit context.

Finally, we have produced a definition that underpins the rest of this book. We define CRM as the core business strategy that integrates internal processes and functions, and external networks, to create and deliver value to targeted customers at a profit. It is grounded on high-quality customer data and enabled by IT.

References

1. Gamble, P., Stone, M. and Woodcock, N. (1999) *Customer Relationship Marketing: Up Close and Personal.* Kogan Page.
2. See for example http://customermanagementgurus.com
3. Hennig-Thurau, H. and Hansen, U. (eds) (2000) *Relationship Marketing: Gaining Competitive Advantage Through Customer Satisfaction and Customer Retention.* Springer.
4. Gummesson, E. (2000) *Total Relationship Marketing.* Butterworth-Heinemann.
5. Kotler, P. (2000) *Marketing Management: The Millennium Edition.* Englewood Cliffs, NJ: Prentice-Hall International.
6. Rogers, E. M. (1962) *Diffusion of Innovations.* New York: Free Press.
7. Deshpandé, R. (1999) *Developing a Market Orientation.* London: Sage.
8. http://www.huthwaite.com
9. http://www.siebel.com/services/multichannel/tas.shtm
10. Page, R. (2001) *Hope is Not a Strategy: The 6 Keys to Winning the Complex Sale.* Nautilus Press.
11. Heiman, S. E., Sanchez, D. and Tuleja, T. (1998) *New Strategic Selling.* Warner Books.
12. Dwyer, F. R., Schurr, P. H. and Oh, S. (1987) Developing buyer–seller relationships. *Journal of Marketing*, Vol. 51, pp. 11–27.
13. Morgan, R. M. and Hunt, S. D. (1994) The commitment–trust theory of relationship marketing. *Journal of Marketing*, Vol. 58(3), pp. 20–38.
14. Rousseau, D. M., Sitkin, S. B., Burt, R. S. and Camerer, C. (1998) Not so different after all: a cross-discipline view of trust. *Academy of Management Review*, Vol. 23(3), pp. 393–404.
15. Selnes, F. (1998) Antecedents of trust and satisfaction in buyer–seller relationships. *European Journal of Marketing*, Vol. 32(3/4), pp. 305–22.
16. Shepherd, B. B. and Sherman, D. M. (1998) The grammars of trust: a model and general implications. *Academy of Management Review*, Vol. 23(3), pp. 422–37.
17. Harris, S. and Dibben, M. (1999) Trust and co-operation in business relationship development: exploring the influence of national values, *Journal of Marketing Management*, Vol. 15, pp. 463–43.
18. Ang, L. and Buttle, F. A. (2002) ROI on CRM: a customer journey approach. *Proceedings of the Inaugural Asia-Pacific IMP Conference*, Perth, December 2002.
19. Bain & Co/Mainline (1999) *Customer Spending On-line.* Bain & Co.
20. Christopher, M., Payne, A. and Ballantyne, D. (1991) *Relationship Marketing.* Oxford: Butterworth-Heinemann.
21. Gordon, I. (1998) *Relationship Marketing.* Ontario: John Wiley.
22. Reichheld, F. and Sasser, W. E., Jr (1990) Zero defections: quality comes to services. *Harvard Business Review*, September/October, pp. 105–11.
23. Ferron, J. (2000) The customer-centric organization in the automobile industry – focus for the 21st century. In: Brown, S. (ed.). *Customer Relationship Management: A Strategic Imperative in the World of e-Business.* Toronto: John Wiley, pp. 189–211.

24. Anderson, E. W. and Mittal, V. (2000) Strengthening the satisfaction–profit chain. *Journal of Service Research*, Vol. 3(2), pp. 107–20.

25. Anderson, E. W. (1994) Cross category variation in customer satisfaction and retention. *Marketing Letters*, Vol. 5, Winter, pp. 19–30.

26. Oliver, R. L. (1997) *Satisfaction: A Behavioural Perspective on the Consumer*. Singapore: McGraw-Hill International

27. Dick, A. S. and Basu, K. (1994) Customer loyalty: towards an integrated framework. *Journal of the Academy of Marketing Science*, Vol. 22(2), pp. 99–113.

28. Kaplan, R. S. and Norton, D. P. (1996) *The Balanced Scorecard*. Boston, MA: Harvard Business School Press.

29. Heskett, J. L., Jones, T. O., Loveman, G. W. and Schlesinger, L. A. (1994) Putting the service profit chain to work. *Harvard Business Review*, March/April, pp. 164–74.

30. Cassel, C. and Eklof, J. A. (2001) Modeling customer satisfaction and loyalty on aggregate levels: experience from the ECSI pilot study. *Total Quality Management*, Vol. 12(7/8), pp. 834–41.

31. Anderson, E. W., Fornell, C. and Lehmann, D. R. (1994) Customer satisfaction, market share and profitability: findings from Sweden. *Journal of Marketing*, July, Vol. 58, pp. 53–66.

32. Yeung, M. C. H. and Ennew, C. T. (2001) Measuring the impact of customer satisfaction on profitability: a sectoral analysis. *Journal of Targeting, Measurement and Analysis for Marketing*, Vol. 19(2), pp. 106–16.

33. Ittner, C. D. and Larcker, D. F. (1998) Are non-financial indictors of financial performance? An analysis of customer satisfaction. *Journal of Accounting Research*, Vol. 36 (Suppl. 1998), pp. 1–46.

34. Carr, N. G. (1999) Marketing: the economics of customer satisfaction. *Harvard Business Review*, Vol .77(2), March–April, pp. 15–16.

35. Behn, B. K. and Riley, R. A. (1999) Using non-financial information to predict financial performance: the case of the US airline industry. *Journal of Accounting, Auditing and Finance*, Vol. 14(1), pp. 29–56.

36. Gustaffson, A. and Johnson, M. D. (2002) Measuring and managing the satisfaction–loyalty–performance links at Volvo. *Journal of Targeting, Measurement and Analysis for Marketing*, Vol. 10(3), pp. 249–58.

37. http://www.forrester.com/ER/Report/Summary/0,1338,11224,00.html

38. Gartner Research (2001), cited on http://www.crm-forum.com/cgi-bin/item.cgi?id = 50092

39. Forsyth, R. (2001) Delivering value from CRM: Forsyth, Gartner et al. tell you how. http://www.crm-forum.com/cgi-bin/item.cgi?id= 64511

40. Forsyth, R. (2001) How satisfied are clients with CRM software packages? http://www.crm-forum.com/cgi-bin/item.cgi?id = 59744

41. Accenture (2001) How much are CRM capabilities really worth? What every CEO should know. http://www.crm-forum.com/

42. Reichheld, F. (1996) *The Loyalty Effect*. Boston, MA: Harvard Press.

43. Helms, C. (2001) Promising ROI keeps CRM expenditures high. http://www.1to1.com/inside1to1/19763.html

44. Cap Gemini Ernst and Young (2001) CGEY and Gartner share secrets of ROI. http://www.crm-forum.com/library

Chapter 2
The customer relationship management value chain

By the end of the chapter, you will understand:

1 the five primary stages of the CRM value chain
2 the basic role of customer portfolio analysis, customer intimacy, network development, value proposition development and managing the customer lifecycle in CRM strategy development and implementation
3 the four supporting conditions of the CRM value chain
4 why culture and leadership, data and IT, people, and process are important contributors to CRM strategy development and implementation.

Introduction

Chapter 1 showed that there are many different views about customer relationship management (CRM). There are strategic, operational and analytical viewpoints. In addition, different constituencies such as CRM software vendors, hardware and infrastructure vendors, consultancies and companies implementing CRM, and their customers, may have different opinions about the function and content of CRM.

We integrated these viewpoints into the following definition of CRM:

> CRM is the core business strategy that integrates internal processes and functions, and external networks, to create and deliver value to targeted customers at a profit. It is grounded on high-quality customer data and enabled by information technology.

This chapter presents a model that takes this definition as its point of departure. The model provides a 'helicopter view', giving an overview of the CRM landscape.

The CRM value chain sets out a five-step process for developing and implementing CRM strategy (Fig. 2.1). Each of the five primary steps is performed with the deployment of a number of tools and processes. These are explored in more detail later in the book. The model also identifies a number of supporting conditions that facilitate successful implementation. We explore those conditions in this chapter.

The goal of CRM

Broadly speaking, the general aim of any CRM strategy is to develop more profitable relationships with customers. Some companies do this by taking cost out of the relationship; for example, by shifting customers to

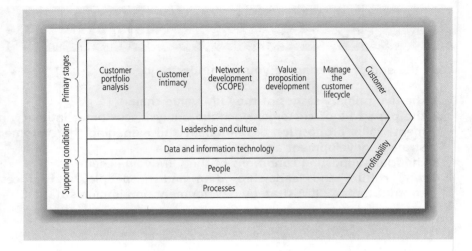

Figure 2.1
The CRM value chain

web-based self-service. Others do this by increasing the revenue earned from a customer relationship; for example, by selling customers additional products and services. Most companies use both of these approaches. This core CRM objective is noted in the arrowhead at the right end of the CRM value chain: customer profitability. In a not-for-profit context, you would work towards different CRM objectives, such as operational efficiency or increased client satisfaction.[i]

Measuring customer profitability implies that an organization must be able to trace revenues and costs to customers, either at a segment or at an individual level. Most business-to-business (B2B) companies can trace revenues to customers. Invoicing databases contain these data. Fewer B2B companies can trace costs to customers; for example, costs of customer acquisition and costs-to-serve. In business-to-consumer (B2C) CRM implementations, costs and revenues are more likely to be allocated at a segment level, since there are many more customers.

The primary stages of the CRM value chain

The model identifies five key steps in the development and implementation of a CRM strategy.

In brief, the five steps are as follows.

1 **Customer portfolio analysis**: this involves an analysis of the actual and potential customer base to identify which customers you want to serve in the future. Top of the list will be strategically significant customers, including those that will generate profit (value) in the future.

[i] These were the objectives of a CRM project for a non-government organization.

2 **Customer intimacy**: you will get to know the identity, profile, history, requirements, expectations and preferences of the customers that you have chosen to serve
3 **Network development**: you will identify, brief and manage relationships with your company's network members. These are the organizations and people that contribute to the creation and delivery of the value proposition(s) for the chosen customers. The network can include external members such as suppliers, partners and owners/investors, as well as one important internal party, employees.
4 **Value proposition development**: this involves identifying sources of value for customers and creating a proposition and experience that meet their requirements, expectations and preferences.
5 **Manage the customer lifecycle**: the customer lifecycle is the customer's journey from 'suspect' towards 'advocate status'. Managing the lifecycle requires attention to both process and structure:
   - **process**: how will the company go about the important processes of customer acquisition, customer retention and customer development, and how will it measure the performance of its CRM strategy?
   - **structure**: how will the company organize itself to manage customer relationships?

These five primary stages of the CRM value chain represent three main sequential phases of CRM strategy: analysis, resource development and implementation.

Customer portfolio analysis (CPA) and customer intimacy (CI) are primarily analytical activities. CPA involves using customer and market data to decide which customers to serve; CI involves getting to understand customers and their requirements. Network development and value proposition development are focused on building or acquiring resources to create and deliver value to customers. Managing the customer lifecycle is about implementing CRM by acquiring and retaining customers, and developing their value.

These steps are iterative and reflexive. They are iterative in the sense that the five-step process is repetitive and continuous. It is not a one-time process that leads to a strategy that is serviceable for ever. For example, in a dynamic environment in which competitors keep improving their value proposition it is important to review periodically which customers to serve, what to serve them and how to deliver the value.

The process is reflexive in the sense that there is backwards and forwards interdependence between the five stages. For example, analysis at stage 1 (customer portfolio analysis) leads to a decision about which customers the company will serve. This decision determines the composition of the value proposition (stage 4). If the company does not have the competencies to deliver, either alone or in partnership with other organizations, the proposition that customers want, then the company will need to review its target market decision.

At each step several tools and processes are used for analytical, planning, implementation or control purposes. These are detailed in Fig. 2.2.

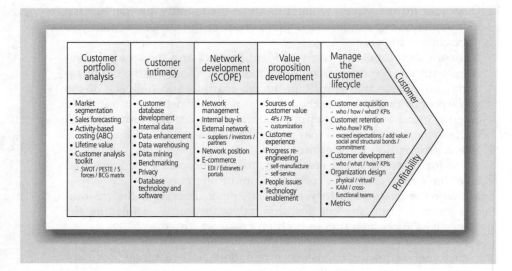

Figure 2.2
Tools and processes on the CRM value chain

The five steps, and the associated tools and processes, are described in more detail in future chapters. The sequence of the chapters follows the CRM value chain:

- Chapter 3: Information technology for customer relationship management
- Chapter 4: Customer portfolio analysis
- Chapter 5: Customer intimacy
- Chapter 6: Creating and managing networks
- Chapter 7: Creating value for customers
- Chapter 8: Managing the customer lifecycle: customer acquisition
- Chapter 9: Managing the customer lifecycle: customer retention and development
- Chapter 10: Organizing for customer relationship management.

The supporting conditions of the CRM value chain

This section will focus on the four conditions that support the development and implementation of the CRM strategy. These are

- leadership and culture
- data and information technology (IT)
- people
- processes.

These four conditions influence each of the five primary stages of the CRM value chain. If the conditions are not supportive of the CRM strategy then its implementation is less likely to succeed. Each of them is summarized in turn.

Leadership and culture

Both leadership and organizational culture can influence the outcomes of CRM strategies.

Leadership

Leadership is very important to the success of CRM implementations for a number of reasons.

Leadership decides whether CRM is focused on strategic, operational or analytical goals.

At the level of strategic CRM, leadership is needed to set out whether a customer (market) orientation, sales, product or production orientation will guide the company into the future. These different business orientations were discussed in Chapter 1. Companies that commit to CRM are more likely to have a marketing or sales orientation than a product or production orientation.

If marketing issues lie at the heart of the implementation, the broad CRM goals are likely to be expressed in terms of improved business performance through higher levels of customer satisfaction and retention. If sales goals underpin the CRM investment, the objectives are likely to be expressed in terms of improved sales effectiveness (e.g. higher sales per customer) or greater sales efficiency (e.g. reduced costs-to-serve).

The mission, vision and values of an organization will be derived from, or be reflected in, the adopted business orientation. Selfridges provides an illustration. This European upmarket fashion retailer has the following mission.

> *Our mission is to become Europe's best and most exciting department store chain by meeting customers' needs in a unique and theatrical way, whilst, at the same time maximising operational efficiency.*

This mission clearly identifies

- the strategic group within which the company operates: European department stores
- its business orientation: customer orientation, 'meeting customers' needs'
- the product: a 'unique and theatrical' shopping experience
- its values: differentiation, excellence, customer focus, operational efficiency.

These commitments form the basis of and rationale for Selfridges CRM programme. They define who the company will serve and how they will be served.

CRM can be expensive to implement

Operational and analytical CRM implementations can be expensive. Companies will be investing significantly in IT, process engineering and people development. Leadership needs to be committed to the project to ensure that an optimal level of funding is made available and appropriately deployed.

Leadership is needed to prioritize the CRM programme

Leadership will help to prioritize the CRM project. It is not uncommon for companies to be involved in a number of large-scale projects simultaneously, as well as running the everyday business. Will CRM take priority over an acquisitions project, or a corporate university project? Prioritizing major projects such as these is a high-level decision.

Leadership provides oversight

As we have seen, CRM projects can last for a considerable length of time, and involve a number of component projects, such as a data quality project, market segmentation project and sales automation project. These projects need to be scheduled, delivered and integrated to deliver the desired CRM benefits. High-level ownership or sponsorship of the CRM project gives an overview of the progress of the overall project and the timeliness and contribution of the components.

Leadership breaks down the functional silo walls

Leadership is needed at a high level because CRM projects are cross-functional. They may involve the full complement of IT, marketing, sales, service, operations and finance departments. Many projects are initiated in marketing or sales departments. Then IT becomes involved because of the automation of processes within these departments. The success of CRM projects is intimately connected to the company's change management expertise. Customer relationship management may require far-reaching changes to the company's culture, processes, resources, organizational structure, technology, objectives and measurements, and its people's skill base. A multidisciplinary team should be better placed to identify barriers to change, and impediments to successful implementation.

Whilst establishing a cross-functional implementation team is regarded as essential to successful CRM projects, high-level ownership can ensure that a strategic organization-wide overview is given to the project.[1] It has been suggested that 'getting the support of a top-level sponsor [for CRM] – preferably at the very top of the enterprise – will help to overcome many of the resistances that might be encountered. Either the vision of the business leader will persuade others to adopt the project or it will act as a subtle threat that unless they adopt it, they will not find life in the business comfortable'.[1] Despite this, it is estimated that only one in three companies have a board-level executive responsible for CRM.

The Royal Bank of Canada, winner of the large corporates section of the first international CRM excellence awards, certainly saw the merit of appointing a senior sponsor. Having decided to commit to CRM, they appointed a high-level vice president to champion the change process. They saw this as being an essential step to successful roll-out and implementation of the strategy.

In general, leadership research provides 'consistent and compelling evidence that individual leaders do make a difference' to organizational performance.[2] Research in a field that has some similarities with CRM illustrates this specifically. The Baldrige award is a business excellence programme that links business performance enablers such as leadership, process management, people management and strategic management to business performance outcomes such as customer satisfaction and retention, employee satisfaction and return on investment. A detailed statistical study of linkages between the Baldrige criteria concluded overall that leadership drives the system that leads to organizational performance.[3] In other words, the impact of leadership is indirect, ensuring that processes and people, strategy and information are managed appropriately, in turn leading to better customer outcomes and financial results. These words are equally appropriate to the significance of leadership to CRM performance.

Organizational culture

The idea of organizational culture has been around for many years. In everyday language, organizational culture is what is being described when someone answers the question 'what is it like working here?' More formally, organizational culture can be defined as:

> A pattern of shared values and beliefs that help individuals understand organizational functioning and thus provide them with the norms for behavior in the organization.[4]

Essentially, organizational culture is understood to comprise widely shared and strongly held values. These values are reflected in patterns of individual and interpersonal behaviour, including the behaviour of the business leaders, and expressed in the norms, symbols, rituals and formal systems of the organization.

There are various ways of classifying and measuring organizational culture. O'Reilly et al. identified seven dimensions of organizational culture using an instrument they developed, the Organizational Culture Profile (OCP): innovation, stability, respect for people, outcome orientation, detail orientation, team orientation, and aggressiveness.[5] The existence of these seven dimensions has been confirmed in several studies across a number of industries.[6] Several studies indicate that organizational culture affects performance.[7]

The presence of a customer-centric organizational culture makes the introduction of a CRM strategy much less threatening to the company's people. Many companies claim to be customer centric, but few are. A customer-centric firm will be resourced and organized to understand and satisfy customer requirements profitably. Typically, this will involve many attributes that are also characteristic of CRM implementations:

- identifying which customers to serve
- understanding customers' current and future requirements
- obtaining and sharing customer knowledge across the company
- measuring customer results: satisfaction, retention, future buying intention, referral behaviours (word-of-mouth), share of wallet

- designing products and services that meet customers' requirements better than competitors
- acquiring and deploying resources (information, materials, people, technology) that create the products and services that satisfy customers
- developing the strategies, processes and structure that enable the company to meet customer requirements.

Research suggests that a customer's experience of doing business with a company is influenced by a number of factors, including the company's products, services, processes, communications, reputation and people.

The behaviours of people at the interface with customers, in marketing, selling and service, can have a major impact on a customer's sense of satisfaction and value, and their future buying intentions. The model in Fig. 2.3 illustrates this phenomenon.[8] It shows that the behaviours of employees in customer-facing positions is linked to their experience in the workplace.

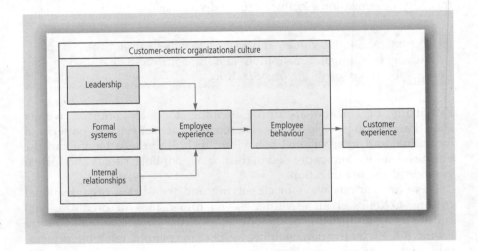

Figure 2.3
A model of customer-centric culture (© courtesy of Frost Rowley)

The model suggests that the degree to which an organizational culture is customer centric is expressed in leadership behaviours, formal systems and internal relationships. These, in turn, largely determine the experience of employees in the company (what is it like working here?), which in turn is reflected in their behaviour when interacting with customers.

In a customer-centric culture you would expect positive answers to the following questions about leadership, formal systems and internal relationships.

Leadership

- Is leadership determined to make a positive difference to customer experience?
- Does leadership provide a 'customer first' role model that employees want to follow?

- Does leadership act like it believes customers are important?
- Does leadership provide the resources necessary for customer contact people to deliver excellent service?

Formal systems

- Does the reward and recognition system acknowledge distinction in producing excellent customer experience?
- Does the company measure customer outcomes such as customer satisfaction and retention?
- Are new recruits inducted into the 'customer first' way of doing business?
- Are customers invited to take part in front-line staff appraisals?

Internal relationships

- Is customer information shared across work groups?
- Do colleagues from different functions get together to identify how to improve customer experience?
- Do we celebrate the success of colleagues in creating exceptional customer experience?

Data and information technology

The second major supporting condition for CRM implementations is data and information technology. IT is discussed in Chapter 3. Here, we want to examine the role of data in CRM.

Our definition of CRM stresses the importance of high-quality customer data. Acquiring, storing, enhancing, maintaining, distributing and using customer information are critical elements of CRM strategies. The data requirements of a CRM strategy are determined by the decisions made and the activities undertaken in the five main stages of the CRM value chain.

The task at the **customer portfolio analysis** (CPA) stage is to identify those customers that you want to serve in the future. These will be customers that are strategically significant, including those that will be profitable in the future. You can make one of two assumptions: the future will be largely the same as the past, or the future will vary significantly from the past. With the former assumption it may be possible to use historical data to estimate the future; under the latter assumption, new models will need to be devised which predict future purchasing behaviour.

Several specific activities are undertaken during CPA:

1 identification of existing and potential customers at the individual or segment level
2 tracing of historical costs and revenue to each of these segments/individuals. This tells you how profitable each customer (group) has been in the past
3 prediction of future costs of keeping and developing the value of existing customers
4 prediction of future costs of winning and keeping new customers
5 estimation of gross margin (or sales) from these customers in the future.

These activities require significant amounts of data about markets, customers, competitors and internal processes, for example:

- How do we, and our competitors, segment the market?
- How else can the market be segmented?
- Which segments are growing or declining?
- What are our costs of customer acquisition (marketing, advertising, selling, sales promotion, database costs, credit scoring)?
- What are our costs-to-serve customers (selling, service, complaint management)?
- What are our sales volumes to each segment/customer?
- What is our share of customer wallet?
- What are our gross margins on these sales?
- Will gross margins be different in the future?
- What is each customer's (or segment's) intention to buy in the future?
- What share of customer spending are we likely to lose to competitors in the future?

At the **customer intimacy** stage of the CRM value chain, the task is to obtain data about the customers you have chosen to serve that will help you to build closer and longer relationships with them. This will include, but not be limited to:

- Who plays a role in the buying processes? (Who identifies the need? Who is the specifier? Who decides? Who buys? Who uses the product? Does anybody act as gatekeeper, monitoring the volume and sources of information that reach the deciders?)
- What are the contact details on the customer side (names, addresses, phones, fax, e-mail)?
- Why do they buy from us? (What is our share of wallet? Is this declining or growing? Which other competitors are in their choice set?[ii] What do customers perceive to be our strengths and weaknesses?)
- What is the customer's buying history?
- What are the preferred communication channels for selling and service (face-to-face, phone, web self-service)?
- What parts of our value proposition are most and least valued by the customer?
- How satisfied is the customer?
- How willing is the customer to refer others to us?
- How does the customer use our product/service?
- What are the customer's future plans? (What influence will those plans have on sales volumes and customer profitability?)

[ii] Choice set refers to the alternative suppliers that a customer considers when making a purchase. Most customers buy on a portfolio basis, that is, they have several alternative suppliers who are more or less equal members of the choice set.

- What are the preferred channels for marketing communication (mail, e-mail, fax, phone, SMS)? In which contexts are each of these preferred?
- What are the preferred forms of address (familiar, formal)?

In **network development**, the task is to identify, brief and co-ordinate the business's network, including suppliers, partners and employees, to ensure that they contribute to the value creation and delivery process. Each of these network members is both a generator and a user of information for CRM.

Suppliers provide inputs for the creation of the value proposition. Suppliers can provide data such as: current and future costs, quality conformance reports, future product availability and logistics performance reports. Suppliers may also be a good source of ideas for new or improved products and cost reduction proposals for the future.

If suppliers are to understand their role in delivering value to their customer's customers they might find it useful to know who is the customer's customer, what that customer expects, what quality standards that customer wants, how competitors are trying to meet that customer's needs, and how that customer's needs might change in the future.

Partners are companies such as joint venture collaborators, franchisees, licensees and alliance partners that contribute towards the creation of value of the CRM implementer's customers. For example, Dunkin' Donuts' franchisees contribute importantly to the creation of value for the parent company's customers. They have access to the end consumer and can provide head office with information on changing customer profiles, customer expectations, or sources of customer satisfaction and dissatisfaction. They might also be able to identify untapped opportunities in underdeveloped franchise areas, or better ways to present the merchandise at point-of-sale. For the franchisees to do their jobs better, the parent can provide information on target customer profiles, batch manufacturing processes, customer service standards and product quality standards.

Employees, particularly those who interact with customers at the various touchpoints (e.g. contact centre, sales presentation, service delivery), are in an excellent position to obtain and feed customer information back to the CRM strategists. They can provide insight into how customer needs and expectations are changing, the sources of satisfaction and dissatisfaction and competitors' offerings. Where employees are in a position to have a major influence on customer perceptions, expectations and behaviours, they need to have access to a significant volume of customer information, including what was detailed earlier under customer intimacy. This information will enable them to tailor their service performance and selling efforts to the particular customer or segment requirements.

Customer data are needed for successful **development of value proposition(s)** for the selected customers. The value proposition is the offer that the company assembles, together with its network partners, to win and keep the selected customers. Most companies will design a number of related value propositions for different customer segments. The composition of the proposition might be customized at segment or individual level. Dell Computers and Levi Strauss both offer individually tailored value propositions, computers and jeans, respectively. Information about the customer's needs, preferences and expectations are important contributors to the creation and delivery of the right offer. The customer's buying history might provide useful insight into how the customer might buy in the future. Historical data on complaints, service calls and product defects allow the value proposition to be continuously improved.

Managing the customer lifecycle involves a set of customer management tasks including identifying prospective customers, recruiting those customers, selling them their first product, managing their migration up the value ladder, developing and implementing retention plans and winning back valued customers should they defect, taking some or all of their business to competitors.

Customer data enable these tasks to be performed more intelligently. For example, customer data could tell you how the costs of customer acquisition vary across channels, and how the value of customers varies across channels. This is extremely useful information for developing an intelligent customer acquisition strategy. Similarly, customer win-back strategies can be focused where they reap the greatest reward. Two important pieces of customer information can be used to guide win-back efforts: What is a customer's value in the future? What is the cost of winning back that customer? When migrating customers up the value ladder, companies can use segmentation and profiling data to identify cross-selling and up-selling opportunities. For example, a home shopping company may learn that customers who bought baby clothes in January are buyers of toddler's clothing 18 months later. This will guide the target, timing and content of the offer.

Sales and service efforts can be prioritized in real time, based on customer data. Sales priorities can be driven by the probability of closing the sale, the value of the sale, the relative importance of the product (is it under incentives this period?) and customer ranking. Service priorities can be determined by historical value, potential future value, current service level agreement and problem severity.

People

People are the third supporting condition for successful CRM implementation. Many commentators believe that people are the most important element in the performance of a CRM strategy.[1] Why is this so?

- People develop the CRM strategy
- People select the IT solution
- People implement and use the IT solution
- People co-ordinate with each other across functions to make CRM work
- People create and maintain the customer database
- People design the marketing, selling and service processes
- People may need to change established work practices
- People contribute importantly to customer satisfaction and retention when they interact with customers.

If people don't want CRM to work, it won't. According to one authority, it is essential for companies to 'listen to the people who will be affected [by CRM]' in order to win their support.[1] A sales force automation project needs to start with an understanding of existing selling practices to identify what is done, what works well and what does not. The input of salespeople to this assessment and redesign of the selling process can be critical (see Case 2.1). Without this, a new sales methodology may not be applied universally or consistently across the sales team, making it useless for sales forecasting and sales management.

Given that there are three forms of CRM, strategic, operational and analytical, it is important for CRM champions to be located at different levels in the organization. Strategic CRM needs championing at CEO level. Operational CRM needs champions at senior functional management level; for example, chief marketing officer and director of sales. Analytical CRM needs champions at lower levels yet. In general, CRM champions tend to reside in marketing, sales or service functions, since this is where most customer relationship matters are addressed. If IT people champion CRM, there is a danger that it will be seen as an IT implementation exclusively. The potential business benefits of CRM may not be achieved.

People's skills, knowledge and attitudes required for successful CRM performance may need review and upgrading. These will vary according to the level of CRM implementation: strategic, operational or analytical. Many analytical CRM projects involve experimenting with different offers to subsets of customers. The knowledge and skills required include how to segment customers, design experiments and interpret experimental data using statistical procedures. People may need to be trained in these and other competencies.

Processes

Processes are the fourth and final supporting condition for CRM delivery. Processes are the way in which things are done by the company. From a

Case 2.1

Internal marketing of the CRM strategy at Crown Relocations

Crown Relocations, a leading global relocation organization, found that implementing a CRM strategy required a great deal of participation, understanding and reinforcement among employees.

Before the strategy was finalized, the organization extensively tested the new sales force automation system among employees involved in sales and customer service, seeking their opinions about the features they felt should be included and how it would be used.

After the trial period, the system was successfully employed in many of Crown's markets and has been widely adopted by sales staff, where the new CRM system has been credited with lifting the sales performance of sales representatives by over 80%. The company believes this is largely attributable to the initial involvement they had in designing the system.

CRM perspective, processes need to be designed and operated so that they contribute to the creation of value, or at least do not damage the value being created, for customers. This implies both efficiency (low cost) and effectiveness (delivers the desired outcomes).

Processes can be divided into several categories: vertical and horizontal; front-office and back-office; primary and secondary.

Vertical processes are those that are located entirely within a business function. For example, the customer acquisition process may reside totally within the marketing department. **Horizontal** processes are cross-functional. The new product development process may involve sales, marketing, finance, and research and development groups.

Front-office (or front-stage) processes are those that customers encounter. The complaints management process is an example. **Back-office** (or back-stage) processes are hidden from customers; for example, the procurement process. Many processes straddle both front and back offices: the order-fulfilment process is an example. The order-taking part of that process sits in the front office. The production scheduling part is back office.

A distinction can be made between primary and secondary processes. **Primary** processes have major cost or revenue implications for companies. The logistics process in courier organizations, from picking up a package through moving the package to delivering the package, constitutes about 90 per cent of the cost base of the business. The customer may have a different perspective on what is important. Customers typically do not care about back-office processes. They care about the processes they touch. In the insurance industry these are the claims process, the policy renewal process and the new policy purchase process. In the courier business it is the pick, delivery and tracking process. **Secondary** processes have minor cost or revenue implications.

Strategic CRM aims to build an organization that is designed to create and deliver customer value consistently better than competitors. Designing processes that create value for customers is clearly part of the task. The company 3M's mission is 'to solve unsolved problems innovatively'. It does this in part through new product development processes that are designed to identify good ideas and bring them to the market quickly.[9] For 3M, the innovation process is a primary process that enables the company to differentiate from competitors.

The main role of operational CRM is the automation of the company's selling, marketing and service processes. Analytical CRM employs a number of processes, including the customer profiling process, opportunity management process and campaign management process. Figure 2.4 shows how First Direct, the telephone and Internet bank, has mapped its campaign management process. It shows that the propensity of a customer to open a high-interest savings account is determined by a scoring process, based on demographic and transactional data. The process is designed to enable customers to open an account either on the phone or by mail.

It is important to identify the key processes from a CRM perspective and to design these processes so that they contribute to the CRM objectives. These objectives may include customer satisfaction, customer

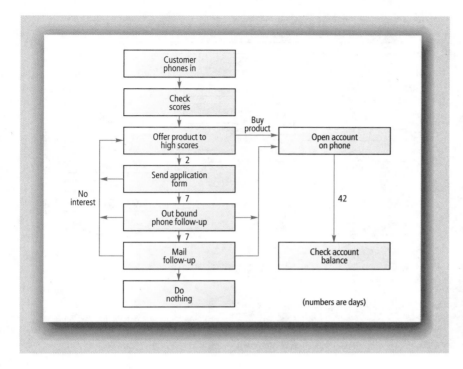

Figure 2.4
Campaign
management
process for high-
interest savings
account

retention, reduced costs-to-serve, product ownership per customer, marketing campaign effectiveness and sales-force efficiency.

Flowcharting, which is also known as blueprinting and process mapping, is a tool that can be used to make processes visible. The flowchart sets out the steps involved in performing the process. It may also identify the people (or roles) that contribute to the process, and the standards by which the process is measured, such as time, accuracy or cost. Processes always have customers. These may be internal customers (colleagues at work) who co-operate in the performance of the process, or internal or external customers who receive the final output of the process. Figure 2.5 shows the order-fulfilment process for an exporter. The flowchart shows that the process is cross-functional, and is completed by a number of internal supplier–customer relationships in series.

Software such as Visio and ABC Flowcharter is readily available to help to generate flowcharts. Flowcharts can be used to identify fail points where a process frequently breaks down, redundancies and duplications. They can also be used for induction and training of new people, and for illustrating internal customer–supplier relationships.

From a CRM perspective, process design raises a number of questions:

- What are the important processes from a CRM point of view?
- How is the present process designed?
- What does it contribute to the achievement of CRM objectives?
- What do its customers, internal and/or external, receive from and think about the process?

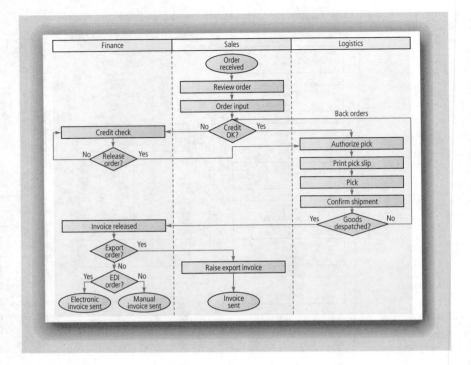

Figure 2.5
Order fulfilment:
cross-functional
process flowchart

● What process performance measures are in place (cost, time, accuracy, satisfaction)?
● Can the process and its outcomes be improved?

Processes can be rated according to the degree to which they can be improved. It has been suggested, for example, that processes be rated according to the criteria in Fig. 2.6.

	Process rating
Best practice (superiority)	The process is substantially defect-free and contributes to CRM performance. Process is superior to comparable competitors and other benchmarks
Parity	A good process that largely contributes to CRM performance
Stability	An average process that meets expectations with no major problems but that has major opportunities for improvement
Recoverability	The process has identified weaknesses that are being addressed
Criticality	An ineffective and/or inefficient process in need of immediate remedial attention

Figure 2.6
Evaluating
processes[10]

It is not just front-office processes that have an impact on CRM performance; the same is true of back-office processes. If procurement people do not know the quality requirements of the value proposition demanded by customers, they may source inputs of too high or too low quality. Similarly, if operations people are not aware of the quality expectations of customers, they may manufacture to tolerances that are unacceptable. If design people do not understand the features required by customers they may overengineer products with features that are of no value to the customer. It is also possible to underengineer products for the same reasons of inadequate understanding of customer requirements.

It is important to acknowledge that CRM can have an impact across the entire enterprise. Consequently, processes may need to be evaluated and remapped in and across all functions of the business.

Summary

In this chapter you have read about the CRM value chain, the model that underpins this book. The model consists of five primary stages and four supporting conditions. The primary stages are customer portfolio analysis, customer intimacy, network development, value proposition development and managing the customer lifecycle. These will be discussed further in upcoming chapters. The supporting conditions that are discussed in this chapter are leadership and culture, data and IT, people, and processes. Given the right sort of support from these enabling conditions, the CRM strategy can function more effectively.

References

1. Business Intelligence (2000) *Developing and Implementing a CRM Strategy.* London: Business Intelligence.
2. Thomas, A. B. (1988) Does leadership make a difference to organizational performance? *Administrative Science Quarterly*, Vol. 33(3), pp. 388–401.
3. Wilson, D. D. and Collier, D. A. (2000) An empirical investigation of the Malcolm Baldrige National Quality Award causal model. *Decision Sciences*, Vol. 3(2), pp. 1–30.
4. Deshpandé, R. and Webster, F. E., Jr (1989) Organizational culture and marketing: defining the research agenda. *Journal of Marketing*, Vol. 53 (January), pp. 3–15.
5. O'Reilly, C., Chatman, J. A. and Caldwell, D. (1991) People and organizational culture: a Q-sort approach to assessing person–organization fit. *Academy of Management Journal*, Vol. 34 (September), pp. 487–516.

6. Webster, C. and Sundaram, D. S. (undated) Exploring the relationships among organizational culture, customer satisfaction, and performance. http://marketing.byu.edu/htmlpages/ccrs/proceedings99/webster.htm

7. Deshpandé, R., Farley, J. U. and Webster, F. E., Jr (1993) Corporate culture, customer orientation, and innovativeness in Japanese firms: a quadrad analysis. *Journal of Marketing*, Vol. 57 (January), pp. 23–37.

8. For more details visit the website http://www.frostrowley.co.uk/ (used with permission).

9. Treacy, M. and Wiersema, F. (1995) *The Discipline of Market Leaders*. London: Harper Collins.

10. Adapted from Jones, P. A. and Williams, T. (1995) *Business Improvement Made Simple*. Northampton: Aegis.

Chapter 3
Information technology for customer relationship management

Chapter objectives

By the end of the chapter, you will understand:

1 the origins of CRM technology
2 the size and dynamics of the market for CRM application software
3 the structure of the CRM ecosystem
4 the most important attributes of an effective technology architecture for CRM
5 the main application areas of CRM
6 the role that analytics plays in CRM technology
7 how IT supports the primary stages of the CRM value chain.

Origins of CRM technology

The building blocks of today's customer relationship management (CRM) technology have been in place for several decades. Customer relationship management has evolved from a range of stand-alone technologies including call centres, sales force automation systems and customer information files, some of which date back to the 1970s and beyond.

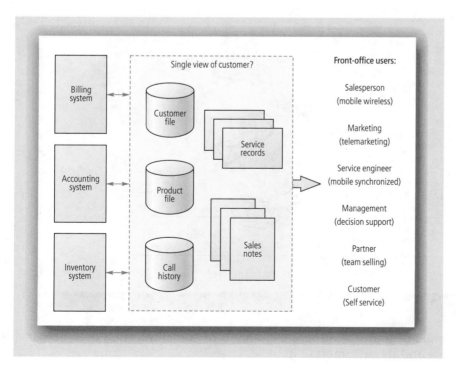

Figure 3.1
A single view of the customer for front-office applications

In the late 1980s, some organizations attempted to consolidate some of these disparate technologies. For example, the customer information file (CIF) that was central to many insurance companies and banks started to be seen as a source of marketing information, rather than a basic record of a customer's accounts. Call centres began being used for outbound calls such as up-selling customers rather than just responding to inbound service calls. The customer started to be recognized as a single entity across all customer-facing departments, leading to the idea of a 'single view of the customer' (Fig. 3.1).

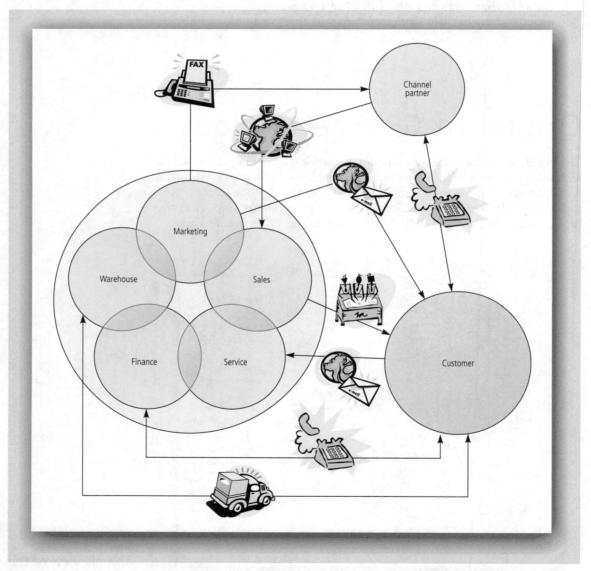

Figure 3.2(a) The challenge of multiple disparate channels of communication between an organization, its partners and its customers

Customer expectations played a direct role in the emergence of CRM technology as well. As customers moved from one industry to the next ('I am recognized by my airline, so I expect to be recognized by my energy utility') they took their increased expectations with them. Customer relationship management spread rapidly from the early adopter industries such as banks and telecommunications companies to consumer goods and healthcare. Organizations started to realize that they needed a central view of the customer, and an understanding of the value of the customer, if they were to compete effectively.

These early attempts at the creation of a consolidated customer view were often internally focused, rather than aimed at improving the customer experience. The ultimate goal became 'multichannel CRM', whereby customer contact channels such as sales, partners, marketing and the service centre were consolidated into a single view of the customer, across all communication media including face-to-face, voice telephony, e-mail, web and wireless (Figs 3.2a and b). Customers, after all, expect a continuous, consistent dialogue with a company, irrespective of the systems and departments within.

Multichannel CRM presented a significant technical challenge. The technology required to support remote field sales people is very different to the technology required to support a large, high-volume call centre. This technical challenge made it difficult to build all of the customer channels in one system.

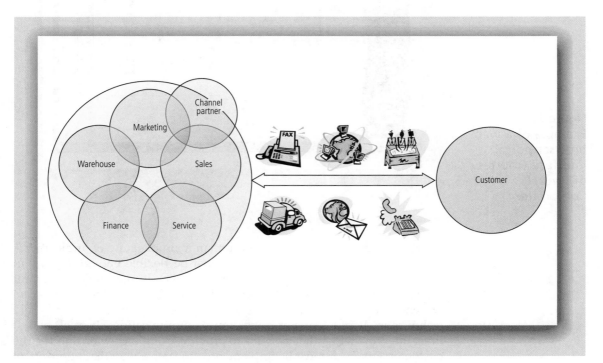

Figure 3.2(b) The customer expectation: consolidation of channels into a single, consistent dialogue (courtesy of Customer Connect Australia[1])

The emphasis on obtaining a single view of the customer is dependent on the effective deployment of operational-level CRM. Recently, the emphasis has moved towards understanding the value of the customer, and increasing the value of each interaction to the customer. This requires sophisticated analytical tools, hence the recent focus on analytical, rather than operational CRM.

Web technologies also had a significant role to play in the emergence of a broader conception of CRM, encompassing users other than direct employees (customers, partners, investors). Web browsers allowed these external users to access and share information without requiring specialist software to be installed on their own computers, leading to 'extra-enterprise CRM' functions such as customer self-service, partner portals and investor portals (Fig. 3.3).

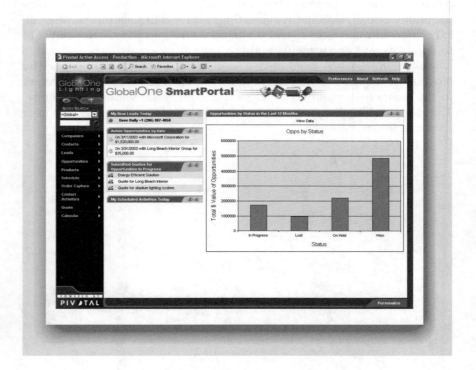

Figure 3.3
Example of a web browser portal interface (courtesy of Pivotal Corporation[2])

CRM technologies are much more than a simple suite of applications. Customer relationship management must be flexible enough to stay in touch with a changing audience (the customer). It must reflect different requirements in different industries. It must be accessible to external stakeholders and mobile professionals such as salespeople and field technicians. It must operate over any communication channel, and it must integrate with other systems to provide a single view of, and for, the customer. Finally, it must be implemented in such a way that appropriate work practices and skills are deployed, as many of the requirements of CRM cannot be solved by technology alone.

In the rest of this chapter, therefore, we address the following major topics:

- the CRM marketplace
- CRM architecture (the technical foundation on which CRM is built)
- CRM applications, including industry-specific applications
- technology for the CRM value chain.

The CRM marketplace

Market structure

The CRM market has grown dramatically since the early 1990s. Growth rates and penetration vary across different software segments, different geographies and different industries.

Software

The CRM software market is part of a worldwide market in enterprise application software (EAS), encompassing three main application suites: supply chain management (SCM), enterprise resource planning (ERP) and CRM.

During the 1980s and 1990s ERP became mainstream, accounting for over 80 per cent of the EAS market. During this time, CRM and to a lesser extent SCM were a small proportion of the overall market, but enjoyed a high growth rate. In CRM's case, compound annual growth rates exceeded 50 per cent for most of the 1990s. Since the mid-1990s, CRM technology has grown from less than one-eighth of the overall EAS market to over one-third.

In recent years, the overall EAS market has, however, contracted. The explosive growth seen in CRM in the 1990s had ceased. Year 2001 saw a drastic reduction in CRM technology expenditure. Growth is expected to recover gradually over the next few years. By 2005 CRM is expected to equal ERP and remain significantly ahead of SCM (Fig. 3.4).[3]

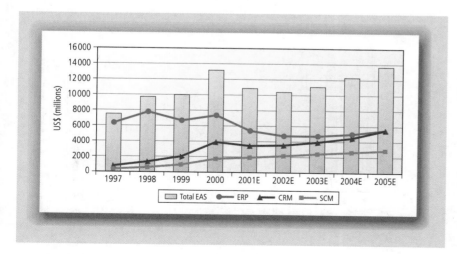

Figure 3.4
Worldwide EAS licence revenue forecast
(Source: Gartner Dataquest)

Early CRM software implementations focused on delivering uniform customer communication across sales and service, and more recently marketing. These areas, in particular sales force automation and the traditional call centre, are now reaching market maturity in the dominant US market. Future growth is expected to come from a renewed focus on contact centres (as an extension of the traditional call centre), marketing automation and analytics, and customer service automation across multiple channels (Fig. 3.5). The rapid growth in customer-facing web applications that accompanied the dot-com bubble is expected to subside before it continues at a flat growth rate.

Geography

The US market was the main driver for the growth during the 1990s, although Europe has taken an increasingly important role. These two regions account for 80–90 per cent of global CRM software

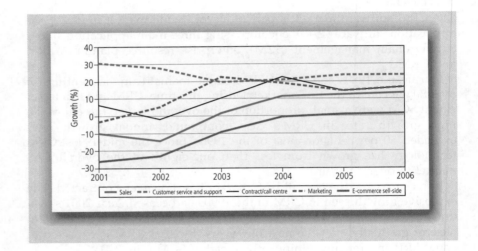

Figure 3.5
CRM application software segment growth forecast (Source: Gartner Dataquest)

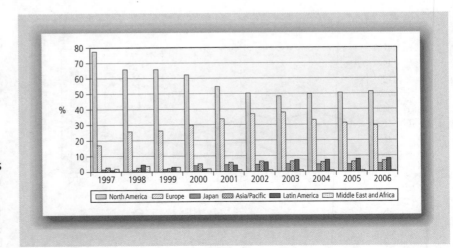

Figure 3.6
Geographical trends in CRM application software new licence revenue (Source: Gartner Dataquest)

revenue sales. Projections by Gartner Dataquest indicate that these two regions will continue to play a dominant role in total revenues, although the highest growth rates are now expected to come from Latin America and Asia (Fig. 3.6).

Industry

Early adopter industries (banking, finance, telecommunications) are expected to experience moderate growth of around 10 per cent per year from 2002 to 2006. The highest growth industries are expected to be other service industries that are yet to implement CRM on a broad scale, such as wholesalers, transportation, warehousing and professional services. Moderate growth is expected in the public sector, utilities and process manufacturing (particularly consumer goods) (Fig. 3.7).

Vertical Industry	2000	2001	2002	2003	2004	2005	2006	CAGR (%) 2002–2006
Mining	1	1	1	2	2	3	4	26.9
Utilities	135	193	276	293	308	327	346	12.4
Construction	3	3	3	3	3	3	4	5.5
Manufacturing discrete	1105	810	608	547	552	569	618	−5.3
Manufacturing process	363	424	487	567	663	743	847	14.9
Trade: wholesale	39	61	82	104	134	167	199	26.5
Trade: retail	139	100	88	86	94	99	106	1.3
Transportation and warehousing	17	45	67	114	194	245	296	46.1
Information/telecommunications	725	697	670	770	921	1087	1250	12.4
Finance and insurance	806	747	716	826	966	1111	1311	11.9
Professional, scientific and technical services	30	39	51	67	87	107	129	26.9
Educational services	9	8	8	8	8	9	9	0.9
Healthcare and social assistance	137	124	121	128	139	153	170	6.5
Public administration	132	143	151	163	181	207	237	10.7
Others	351	339	333	349	377	402	439	5.3
Total CRM	3992	3734	3662	4027	4629	5232	5965	9.8

Figure 3.7
CRM application software licence revenue by industry (US$ millions) (Source: Gartner Dataquest)

Market participants

The CRM ecosystem comprises software vendors, hardware and infrastructure vendors, and service providers (Fig. 3.8).

Software vendors

The best known participants in the CRM market are the software vendors. Specialist CRM vendors such as Siebel, Kana, E.piphany and Chordiant compete with traditional ERP vendors that have either developed a CRM product (SAP, Oracle) or acquired a CRM product (PeopleSoft with the Vantive acquisition, Nortel with the Clarify

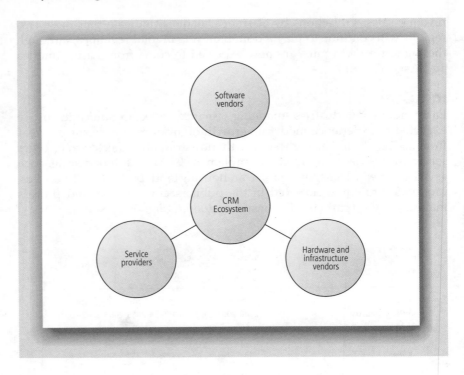

Figure 3.8
The CRM ecosystem

acquisition), or both. Recent entrants compete on differentiated value propositions, such as taking an analytical approach to CRM (E.piphany and SAS Institute), or focusing on a specific industry [Chordiant in business-to-consumer (B2C), financial services]. In terms of revenue performance, the top ranking CRM vendors in 2001 were:

1 Siebel (CRM specialist)
2 SAP (Enterprise suite)
3 Oracle (Enterprise suite)
4 PeopleSoft (Enterprise suite).[4]

The most significant change here is the rise of the enterprise suite vendors. In 2000, the top four CRM vendors contained three CRM specialists and one enterprise suite vendor. As indicated above, this reversed in 2001. This reflects the increased investment of the enterprise suite vendors in CRM, and the appeal that 'pre-integrated' suites have for customers. The appeal of pre-integrated suites is that back-office applications, such as general ledger and warehouse management, are integrated with front-office CRM applications by the software vendor, thus removing a layer of technical complexity from the implementation project.

Many of the large CRM vendors provide both large-enterprise and mid-market CRM solutions. Vendors such as PeopleSoft, Siebel, Onyx and Pivotal are examples. Some CRM vendors provide industry-specific libraries for their products; StayinFront, for example, focuses on pharmaceutical healthcare and consumer goods. There are also a number of vendors that target small-to-medium businesses specifically, such as FrontRange Solutions (GoldMine FrontOffice), Microsoft (MSCRM), Salesforce.com and Saleslogix.

The software vendors, however, are only a small proportion of the overall CRM ecosystem. The CRM software must run on hardware such as Unix or Intel-based computers. It must integrate with communications infrastructure such as telephony and e-mail systems. It must be implemented, often with the involvement of systems integrators and consultants.

Hardware and infrastructure vendors

The architectural and performance imperatives of CRM result in a high level of emphasis on hardware and infrastructure. Call centres, for example, need tight integration between the software on the customer service agent's desktop, and the automated call distributor (ACD) or switch hardware. Calls may need to be prioritized and routed based on CRM metrics such as customer value or propensity to churn. Handheld devices carried by the sales people need to be synchronized with the central CRM database. Hardware vendors such as IBM and Hewlett-Packard (recently merged with Compaq) provide a range of solutions across the hardware spectrum, while infrastructure providers such as Avaya, Genesys and Siemens provide telephony and CRM-related infrastructure solutions.

Service providers

The services component of the CRM ecosystem is the largest, and is the least clearly defined. Directly related service costs, such as for CRM implementation and technology services, are typically in the order of three times the cost of application software. Indirectly related services, however, such as business process re-engineering and strategy consulting, can lift this ratio to around 5:1, or even higher, making a

Service	Details	Examples of service providers
Strategy consulting	Consulting support for the formulation of customer strategy, contact strategy, channel strategy, CRM strategy	McKinsey, Peppers and Rogers
Business consulting	Services around business process re-engineering, process improvement and best practices for CRM	Accenture, Bearing Point, CGEY, Del Ditte
Application consulting	Design and development of application modifications, project management of software package implementation and training	CRM vendors, Accenture, CGEY, Bearing Point, IBM
Technical consulting	Design and implementation of technical infrastructure, and integration of this infrastructure with the existing business processes and applications	Unisys, IBM, Logica
Outsource service providers	Technology outsourcers and business process outsourcers.	EDS, IBM, CSC, Acxiom

Figure 3.9 CRM service providers

comprehensive CRM strategy implementation very expensive. The use of service providers in a CRM implementation is often a critical factor in overall success. Much of the CRM journey involves changes to strategy, business processes, organizational structures, skills and technical infrastructure, and good external advice can make the difference between success and failure. Furthermore, some aspects of the front office, such as the call centre, may be outsourced either technically, or as an entire business process.

Service providers for CRM can be segmented as shown in Fig. 3.9.

CRM architecture

A key consideration in effective CRM is the way in which the system is constructed, or the 'architecture'. Unlike purely internal systems, CRM systems must be able to operate in the office, out of the office and over the web. They must tie together multiple communication channels each using very different technologies (web, e-mail, telephone). And they must perform well enough and be flexible enough to suit a constantly changing, potentially growing user community.

Not only does the CRM architecture have to deal with communication and performance issues, it also had to support the relationship focus of CRM. While it is relatively straightforward to model the relationships between warehouse and production floor in the back office, the relationship modelling challenges of CRM are far more complex. How does one model an environment where a partner who is teaming with your organization on one opportunity is competing actively against you

Challenge	Architecture solution
Single customer view across the organization	Multichannel CRM across a single database
Suitability for customer-facing situations	Usable, flexible, high-performing architecture
Complex, many-to-many relationships, varying across customers and industries	Flexible data modelling
Deployment to field operations (sales, service)	Mobile and wireless
Efficient changing and upgrading of the system	Business rules repository (metadata)
Unstructured, widely dispersed information	Knowledge management
Deployment outside the organization	Web browsers
Effective modelling of customer-facing processes	Workflow and assignment
Information flow with the back office and infrastructure	Integration

Figure 3.10
Challenges to be addressed by CRM architecture

in another? This is frequently found in the information technology (IT) sector where companies like IBM and Oracle both co-operate with, and compete against, the same organization in different markets.

Furthermore, as the CRM system is modelling a constantly changing environment (the market and the customer), all of the data and process models that are built in to the system must be able to be changed quickly and efficiently. This environment also differs from one industry to the next, requiring different data models to be implemented. Finally, very few CRM implementations stand alone; they are nearly always integrated with other in-house systems.

The challenges faced by the CRM architecture, therefore, are significant (Fig. 3.10). The CRM architecture can become a major limiting factor in delivering the outcomes of a CRM project. Selection of a CRM solution must consider architectural issues, as it is very difficult, perhaps impossible, to change the architecture of a system once it has been installed.

Multichannel CRM

Two perspectives on multichannel CRM have developed since the early 1990s:

● multiple communication technology channels
● multiple organizational touch points.

In both cases, the CRM technology is aimed at consolidating these channels into a single view. The challenge here is that customers may choose to browse your website for information, e-mail you for pricing and call you to discuss discounts, expecting consistency across the whole dialogue. Multichannel technology is necessary to deliver to the customer a feeling of recognition, and consistency of service over all stages of the communication process.

Communication technology channels

Whether the customer chooses to communicate with the organization by telephone, e-mail, webchat or face-to-face, CRM is designed to track and manage a consistent dialogue that reflects the value of the customer. Strategically significant customers may expect to be given priority irrespective of the communication channel they choose; their e-mails should go to the top of the list, as should their inbound telephone calls. To achieve this, in particular where e-mails from high-value customers take priority over telephone calls from lower value customers, requires a central CRM database, and technology known as universal queuing. Universal queuing prioritizes all communications in a single queue, irrespective of their origin or technology medium, and can then prioritize response based on customer value or some other variable. To be effectively implemented, universal queuing requires the integration of the communications infrastructure (telephone, e-mail and web systems) with the CRM application (source of customer value metrics).

Case 3.1

Contact management for improved customer profitability

The National Australia Bank (NAB) was an early adopter of CRM, with the bank designing a formal system for developing relationships with customers. It knew the profitability of customers as early as 1988. Since this time the bank has shifted its focus to become more customer centred and build more profitable relationships with customers.

In achieving this goal the NAB has undertaken a series of CRM initiatives, such as segmenting its business and consumer customers into six segments and implementing a technology called 'Relationship Optimiser' developed by NCR to manage the frequency, content and channels of interaction with its customers. These initiatives have proven to be successful. The bank reports that five of the six segments became more profitable within the first 18 months of implementing these initiatives.

Organization touch points

The communications with a customer take place not only over different technology media, but also with different people within the organization. Marketing send out an offer in the mail; this must be known to the sales person before calling on a customer to discuss pricing. Similarly, when a customer calls the service desk for assistance, this marketing offer should be visible in order for the customer service agent to treat the customer correctly. This is even more important if the service desk is to perform a blended function, and cross-sell the customer to an offer at the end of the service call. Finally, partners must be included in the communication loop if channel conflict over pricing, leads and commissions is to be avoided. The technology solution for multiple contact channels includes an integrated suite of applications for all departments, customer and external partner web portals, universal implementation across the organization, synchronization technology (to get the information into the field), and a central knowledge base for products, pricing and customer activity. While the technological challenges here are significant, the most difficult aspect of multiple contact channels is often the implementation of business processes across the departments, and externally, to allow a consistent customer dialogue (Fig. 3.11, Case 3.2).

Usable, flexible, high-performing, scalable architecture

Front-office applications have a direct bearing on the customer's experience. Software applications that are difficult to navigate or configure, or that are slow to respond, leave the customer painfully aware of the limitations of your company's customer management. Furthermore, once an application has been published on the web, performance and usability issues are directly visible. Usability, performance, flexibility and scalability are key considerations in delivering a favourable customer experience.

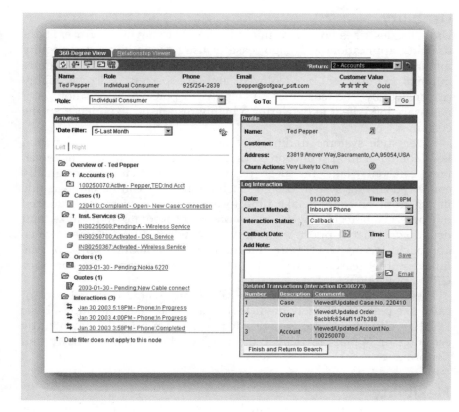

Figure 3.11
A 360 degree (multichannel) view of the customer (courtesy of PeopleSoft[5])

Case 3.2

Channel integration at Dow Chemical

Dow Chemical, a leading science and technology organization, handles tens of thousands of customer enquiries each day across a large number of channels such as face-to-face, telephone, e-mail and the Internet. However, customer information being received through these channels was rarely consolidated, and without a comprehensive view of its customers Dow had difficulty in delivering consistent levels of service and in cross-selling other products and services.

To address this problem Dow implemented a major CRM strategy utilizing Siebel software in conjunction with a new call centre. The implementation of the strategy involved substantial redesign of Dow's operations and IT infrastructure. The management consulting firm Accenture was also involved in implementing the strategy, which took 18 months to complete.

Usability

Usability describes how easy an application is to navigate or use. High-usability applications (i.e. high 'ease of use') are intuitive and require minimal effort to reach the desired outcome. Such applications require minimal training to be deployed and are perceived to be highly responsive by the customer. A highly responsive application is a necessary ingredient in delivering a highly responsive experience for the customer.

Older style systems traditionally used menu systems and function keys for navigation. Function keys can be very fast to use; however, they can only take the user through a flow that was originally conceived during system design. Such approaches can be cumbersome in the front office, and take time to arrive at the customer's desired outcome. Web technologies, in contrast, incorporate hyperlinks and drill-downs that support an intuitive, 'go where the customer wants' approach. If you want more information on something, click on the link. For this reason, a web-style interface has become the norm for CRM applications.

The only caveat to this is in the call centre, where high volumes of calls take place in a largely predictable manner. In these situations, basic HTML web technologies are not adequate, and must be augmented by scripting or applets to deliver the required level of interactivity and performance.

Flexibility

Responsiveness can be 'hard wired' by pre-empting all of the processes that a customer may require, and implementing these in the application in advance. The difficulty with this approach is that customers do not always follow your script. An application's flexibility determines how many alternatives are available to the user at any given time; these alternatives are often implemented through hyperlinks, buttons or screen tabs. A highly flexible application will have many such links, and will not require specific processes to be followed. The customer will not be told 'I'm sorry, but I can't do A until I do B'.

High performance

Performance is a function of many technologies; all must be in alignment to deliver a highly performing system. A CRM application running on an extremely fast network will still be slow if the database is overloaded. Performance of the overall system is often determined by the performance of the weakest link. Aspects of perceived performance include usability and flexibility as discussed above, network performance, database performance and server performance. Most CRM applications separate the application server from the database server, to improve performance.

Performance is also determined by integration and synchronization technologies. A CRM application will appear slow if the user has to wait for an automatic e-mail to be created and sent via the e-mail interface. Remote users will perceive the system as slow if they have to wait more

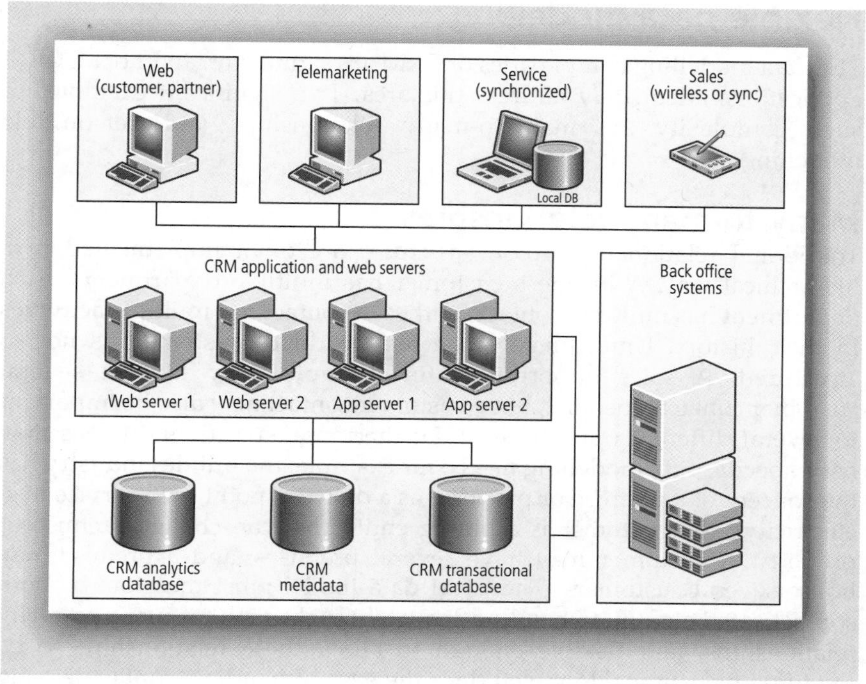

Figure 3.12
Typical CRM
architecture,
showing web, back-
office integration
and mobile:
database tier
(bottom),
application server
tier (middle), and
user interface tier
(top)

than a few minutes for their daily synchronization to their laptop. These
processes can be some of the longest in the whole system, and have a
dramatic effect on system acceptance and uptake.

An important characteristic of a high-performing architecture is the
ability to separate high-load areas such as the database and application
servers, and the ability to expand the application and web server tier by
adding more servers as required. This is shown in Fig. 3.12.

Scalability

As the CRM system grows, and is used by more internal and external
people, the scalability of the system becomes important. Acceptable
performance with 100 call centre users may become unacceptable once
the customers are online and hitting the website, or the sales people start
synchronizing across all territories at the same time. Customer relationship management applications should be assessed based on proven
numbers of users and types of users (concurrent on the web, synchronization, full load call centre, etc.) in order to assess their ability to scale.

Finally, it should be recognized that highly performing CRM systems
require investment to keep them performing. It is most important that the
CRM application be constantly monitored against predefined performance targets to ensure that performance remains acceptable. This is
particularly the case in high-turnaround areas where the customer is
involved, such as the call centre and website, and where high loads take
place at the same time, such as the afternoon synchronization run or back-
office integration run.

Flexible data modelling

The data modelling complexities of CRM are significant, and not all CRM applications adequately address this area. Two significant examples of such complexity are many-to-many relationships and person/role modelling.

Many-to-many relationships

Traditional relational database structures are often implemented in a hierarchical way. A business customer has multiple departments, each department has multiple contacts and each contact has multiple activities in their history. Unfortunately, the real world of customers is not so structured. A sales opportunity, for example, may involve several customer contacts (people), but a customer contact may also be important to several different opportunities. Furthermore, specific industries may have specific data modelling needs; for example, the utilities industry has the concept of a premise or property as a delivery point for a service (e.g. electricity); the customer is a billing entity that can change premise or property. A customer may have several premises, and a premise may house several customers. The CRM data model must therefore be both sophisticated enough to handle adequately such complex, many-to-many relationships, and flexible enough to allow these relationships to be modified over time. How well does the system handle a contact leaving one organization, and joining another, for example?

Person/role modelling

People can have a number of different roles within an organization. In a business-to-consumer (B2C) environment, customers are often also employees (e.g. the employees of a bank have their own bank accounts, often with their employer). Partners are often also customers (e.g. a reseller of computer equipment uses this equipment themselves). In these situations, the CRM data model must be able to represent the employee/customer/partner concerned as a single entity, with a single view of history, a single profile, and so on. Furthermore, the role of an entity may change depending on the situation, as is the case with an existing customer who may be a competitor on one opportunity, a partner on another and a customer on a new on-sell opportunity. The technological requirement here is for a data model that has been designed with these relationships in mind. The relationships between entities, and the roles they play, must be fluid enough so that they can adequately represent the customer situation. Only through adequate definition of requirements, and thorough scenario analysis before selecting the technology, can problems around entities and roles be avoided (Fig. 3.13).

Mobile and wireless

Many businesses go to the customer's premises, rather than waiting for the customer to come in to a store or call them. Such businesses typically employ mobile professionals, such as sales people and service techni- cians. These people are an integral part of the overall customer

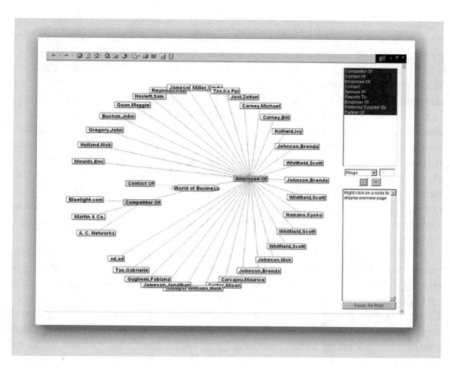

Figure 3.13
Relationship modelling diagram, showing customer, competitors and employees (courtesy of Oracle Corporation[6])

experience, and as such should be equipped with the latest customer and product information. The two main technologies that are available to support such mobile professionals are mobile (synchronized) and wireless (online).

Mobile synchronized solutions include a handheld or laptop device, with a small resident database that is a replica of the particular individual's information in the main CRM system. These systems are not 'online' or permanently connected, but rely on sophisticated synchronization

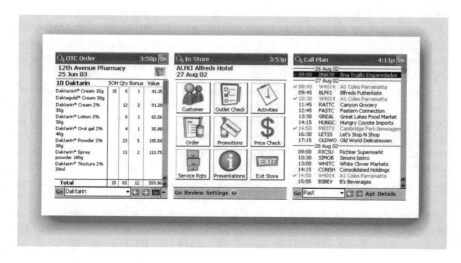

Figure 3.14
Sample handheld screen views (×3) (courtesy of O_4[7])

technology to filter the information that flows onto the relatively small handheld device. The user synchronizes the device when convenient, for example before leaving home or the office in the morning (Fig. 3.14).

The advantage of such systems is that they operate in environments that could not otherwise sustain a permanent connection, such as aeroplanes, remote areas and shopping centres. Mobile CRM clients, furthermore, are often as functional as their connected in-the-office counterparts. The disadvantage of mobile is that the synchronization process can be complex and unreliable, or may not scale well to large numbers of users with some vendor technologies. The mobile client may employ different technology to the connected client, and so may be functionally inferior. Another disadvantage is that information is only as current as the last time it was synchronized. Despite this, the mobile synchronized solution is currently the most widespread and accepted for mobile professionals.

Wireless online solutions typically involve a handheld device; however, this device is connected to the main system using a wireless connection such as a mobile phone unit or card. New technologies such as Bluetooth promise to streamline further the wireless online experience. Currently, wireless CRM clients are somewhat limited in their functional capabilities compared with their mobile synchronized and in-the-office counterparts, owing to the cost and bandwidth limitations of the wireless medium. The advantage of being continuously online, with all the ensuing benefits of data currency, is offset by the connection problems and performance limitations.

Business rules repository (metadata)

The advent of CRM, with its constantly changing landscape driven by the customer, has highlighted the inadequacies of traditional application development techniques. These techniques historically have involved extensive programming of source code in long sequences and subroutines. Unfortunately, the result of this approach is that the business logic that is built into these programs is stored in a complex, difficult to change medium. While this may suffice for the rules for debiting and crediting a ledger, it does not suffice for business processes that change regularly. Furthermore, modifications to programs are difficult to track, and even more difficult to upgrade.

Modern CRM systems, therefore, do not use this approach. These modern systems store business logic in a database that is external to the core processing logic of the application. The core processing logic is intelligent enough to know how to construct a screen with a list of records, but it does not know what the actual content or layout of the final screen will be. The content, including the layout of the columns, rules for validation, lists of values, even the processes to be represented in the view, are all stored in the associated database. This database contains metadata ('data about data'). The final result on the screen, therefore, is a combination of the core processing logic, the metadata (business rules) and the data themselves (the list of customer records).

The metadata repository is typically modified using a set of tools, provided by the CRM software vendor. Examples of such tools include PeopleTools (PeopleSoft), Siebel Tools, and Studio (E.piphany). These tools can typically perform the majority of customization functions through changes in the metadata. More complex customization normally requires the use of programming through HTML (hypertext markup language), Java or other languages.

Metadata-based applications allow an organization to change the business rules with minimal effort. New process flows, screen layouts, selection values, business processes and validation rules can be constructed without programming. More importantly, when the customer-driven process needs to be changed, this can be done quickly with minimal effort going into testing and implementation. Finally, when a new version of the core application is released, routines can be run to compare the metadata of the new release with the (modified) metadata of the customized old release, to streamline the upgrade process.

Knowledge management

A central element to effective CRM is storing and leveraging knowledge about the customer. This knowledge can take the form of structured, transactional data such as contact history and account balances, as well as unstructured information such as letters and faxes from the customer, and notes on telephone conversations. The success of CRM depends largely on how well this information is converted into enterprise-wide knowledge, and finally customer insight. This depends on the completeness, currency, accessibility and relevance of the information.

Complete customer information includes data from all contact channels. Marketing offers, sales opportunities, service calls, inbound e-mails, customer-volunteered information and website activity must be stored and presented in a format that allows the next stage of the ongoing dialogue to proceed effectively. This requires true multichannel integration and sophisticated document management capabilities for the unstructured data in the repository.

For information to be current, it must be stored in the knowledge base as soon as possible after it has been collected. Mobile solutions, wireless technology and real-time integration technologies are required to achieve high levels of information currency. Internally published information, such as product manuals and pricing, must be managed through a revision control process that only releases information that has been approved. This is a particular challenge in managing the information that is available on a company's website, giving rise to specialist content management applications designed for this purpose.

Accessible information must be available to the customer-facing employee at the time and place that the customer interaction takes place. In call centres, this relies on integration with telephony infrastructure, to support 'screen pops' based on the inbound caller ID. For field personnel, mobile and wireless technologies are required. Furthermore, with global organizations, the CRM system must support multiple languages and multiple time zones.

For information to be relevant it must take into account the context of the situation (e.g. the customer's profile, the nature of the transaction). This is achieved in CRM through personalization. Personalization technologies analyse the current dialogue context (the call centre agent's experience level and authority level, the customer value profile and history) to filter the information provided. Furthermore, once a personalization rule has been established (e.g. offer mortgage insurance to customers who have purchased a mortgage in the past three months, over $100 000), it should apply to all communication channels (website, call centre, helpdesk)

The CRM knowledge base does not only have to include customer information. Another significant knowledge management challenge is product and solution information. Without a central knowledge base, service people may resolve an issue but never share this solution with others. A key element in being able to solve future customer issues is a way of storing symptoms versus resolutions, and categorizing service requests so that they can be filtered and analysed. This knowledge base can be used for solution searching and issue resolution in the future, by service agents, partners and customers over the web.

Web browsers

Web browser technology has become an essential ingredient of modern CRM systems (Fig. 3.15). Much of the success of these systems depends on their accessibility to customers and channel partners. Conventional client/server technologies are not suitable for customers or partners, as they require the customer or partner client personal computer (PC) to have CRM software installed on it. An organization can neither expect, nor support, large numbers of customers having to install and maintain the company's CRM software. Browser-based systems, in contrast, require only a standard browser (perhaps of a certain release level) to be installed on the client machine. The CRM application then typically communicates with the web browser using HTML or dynamic HTML (DHTML).

HTML and DHTML, however, cannot support all the richness of interaction that is available in a full client/server software application. This normally means that a compromise must be reached between the level of interactivity that the web browser application supports and the need to download program components (such as Javascript or web applets) onto the client PC. The download process is seen as a negative, as it takes time and network bandwidth. The positive, however, is that these applets and scripts then allow the web browser to respond in a more interactive, sophisticated way. Each CRM vendor, therefore, has developed their own mix of technologies and languages to deploy on the web browser; resulting in varying levels of usability, interactivity and bandwidth requirement.

Browser technologies have other benefits that are important to CRM. The hyperlink-driven user interface is ideal for the loosely structured flow of most customer-facing dialogues. The ubiquitous nature of the web also makes it relatively easy for people to learn how to navigate in

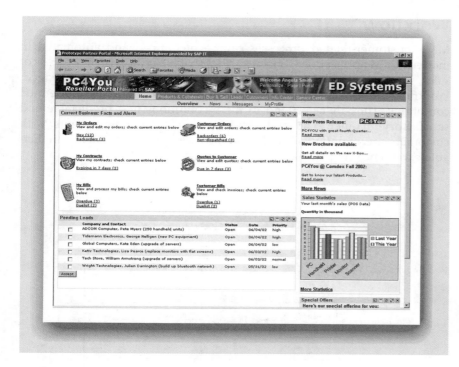

Figure 3.15
External partner portal using web browser technology (courtesy of SAP[8])

such an application. This is particularly important with customer- and partner-facing applications.

Web technologies also play an important role in integration and mobile solutions. Extensible markup language (XML), a standard, flexible format for the description of documents over the web, is becoming a standard language for integration between applications. The CRM application may communicate with the accounting system, for example, using XML. Wireless mobile solutions also typically are implemented using web servers and WML (a compact, wireless form of HTML) as a means of transferring information to and from the mobile device.

The use of the web as a means of marketing to, selling to and servicing customers has also led to the development of specialist web-based applications such as configurators and advisors. These CRM modules allow an organization to build a model of their products, product components and pricing. This model is then used to determine the products or services that are eventually offered to the customer on the web, based on the responses that the customer has given to a series of questions. For example, many PC manufacturers now allow customers to configure their own PCs on the web, including processor, memory, disk, sound, operating system and warranty options. While not immediately evident to the customer, the process behind their selections is determining a valid configuration at all times, for example, to ensure that the maximum number of card slots is not exceeded with the final configured product.

Workflow

Many customer-related processes can be predefined and automated in modern CRM applications. Business rules that are critical to the success of sales, marketing and service no longer need to be manually managed. Workflow technologies can be programmed to monitor for predefined conditions. They then respond to these conditions in a predictable and satisfactory manner. The end result is that service agreements with customers are maintained, and customers receive a consistent, predictable experience (Fig. 3.16).

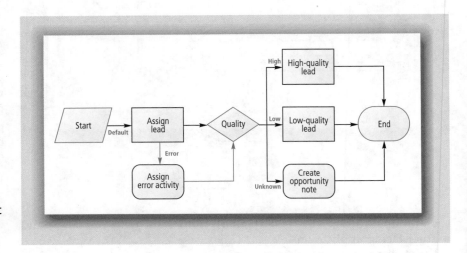

Figure 3.16
Example of a workflow process for lead assignment (courtesy of Siebel Systems[9])

Examples of workflow include:

- **escalation**: 'if a service call is 20 hours old and is high severity, and is for a high value customer, and the status is not resolved, page the service manager'
- **process automation**: 'when an e-mail comes in from a customer in southern region, automatically respond with the following . . . '
- **assignment**: 'when a lead comes in from the website, look at the product being offered, the territory, and the current workloads of my salespeople, and assign the lead to the best person'
- **dialogue scripting**: 'when a customer calls in, prompt the call centre agent with a standard welcome script. Register the customer's response, then determine the best course of action, and offer the agent a script accordingly. Continue this process to increase the chance of up-selling the customer'
- **process navigation**: 'if the customer does not offer their password, automatically navigate the user to the customer identification screen'
- **integration**: 'if the customer submits a confirmed order, automatically post it to the fulfilment system for verification and dispatch'

Integration

Integration is a major IT topic in its own right. Specialist integration middleware providers such as Webmethods, IBM (MQSeries), SeeBeyond, Vitria and Tibco play an essential role in large-scale, complex CRM projects. Not all integration requirements are complex, however; the integration challenge is largely a function of the complexity of the applications environment and the need for timeliness of information transfer. This gives rise to the two main types of integration: batch and real time.

Batch processing is technically simpler than real time, and can handle larger volumes with less impact on system performance. Batch processing stores information up in a file or batch, then moves the information across the interface into the destination system in one go. The cost, however, is the delay in moving the information. Many batch processes only run overnight, meaning that the information is always a day old in the destination system. International organizations that trade across time zones face a more complicated task in that batch processing has to be synchronized with night-time in different geographies. In general, it is preferable to use batch integration where it will suffice; for example, when transferring information that does not change often, such as part number details.

Some integration situations require real-time integration. Real-time integration takes place immediately; for example, once a customer record is updated in one system, the change is immediately reflected in the destination system. The integration process can be managed and assured using verification or queuing management technology, to ensure that integration messages are not lost. Some forms of integration, such as telephony integration, must always be real time, as the customer is on the phone at the time.

Whatever the integration technology, however, CRM generally requires up to four areas of integration: application, telephony, e-mail and web integration.

Application integration

Application integration ties together the CRM system, and other business systems such as accounting, billing, inventory and human resources. Transactions include customer orders, general ledger journals and incentive payments. This type of integration can be either batch (e.g. all changed records at the end of day) or real-time (when an order comes in, put it through to the warehouse immediately).

Application integration can be provided as standard by the CRM or other system vendors; however, in most cases this standard integration requires modification. Integration can also be hand-built, however this becomes costly over time, as the interface must be rebuilt each time a software upgrade is performed. Complex integration situations, where there are many applications requiring integration, normally require specialist integration middleware solutions that handle the flow of information or messages between applications, such as the vendors mentioned above. These solutions typically deploy standard connectors for the most common applications.

Telephony integration

Telephony integration ties the CRM application in to the telephone system, allowing inbound calls to be routed to the right person based on caller details, and outbound calls to be automatically made from the call-centre desktop (Fig. 3.17). At the financial services organization Capital One, this has meant that calls from customers who have not used their credit card for the past two months are routed to a customer retention specialist. At Qantas Airlines, if the call is from a customer who has recently made a booking, it is routed to reservations; otherwise, it goes to general customer service. The effectiveness of the integration solution for telephony is essential to the success of large-scale contact centres. In addition, technologies such as universal queuing and predictive dialling can be deployed to refine further the contact handling process.

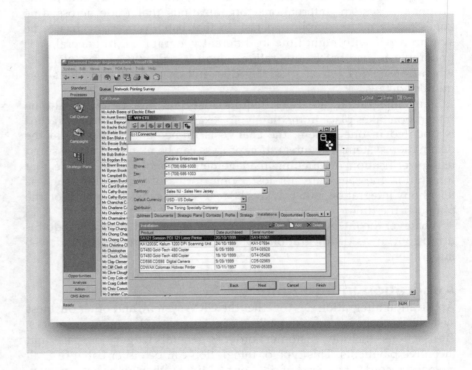

Figure 3.17
Outbound
telemarketing
call-centre
application with
telephony
integration
(courtesy of
StayinFront Inc[10])

Predictive dialling technologies are aimed at optimizing the call rates of call-centre agents. These technologies monitor the call times and predict when an agent is likely to complete the current call. The system will then dial the number of the next call, anticipating a pick-up by the customer at the precise moment that an agent will complete the current call, hence minimizing unproductive time. While these systems can increase call rates, they must be carefully managed to ensure that the quality and effectiveness of the customer interaction are satisfactory, and that agents do not suffer burnout from the increased workload.

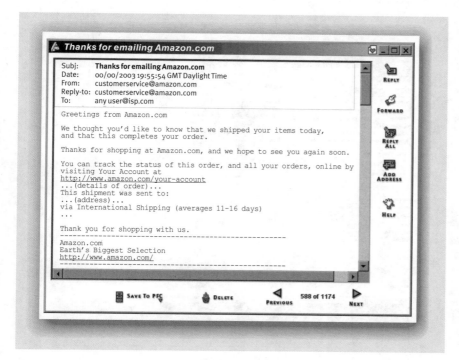

Figure 3.18
Example of an automated shipment confirmation message received by the author from Amazon.com

E-mail integration

This is a similar form of integration to telephony in that it streamlines the communication process with the customer; however, it normally requires quite different technologies to be deployed. E-mail integration can involve both the generation of e-mails as a result of an internal workflow process (e.g. once an order is ready for shipment, automatically e-mail the customer to advise dispatch details) and automated e-mail response (Figs 3.18 and 3.19).

E-mail response applications have developed quite sophisticated capabilities. Simple applications include automatic acknowledgements, such as responding to an inbound e-mail to the service desk, advising that the e-mail has been received, and the associated service request tracking number. More sophisticated applications can be designed to read inbound e-mails, search for key phrases (such as product descriptions) and automatically respond with the most likely answer. These systems can learn over time. However, they present challenges to customer satisfaction when the customer receives a response that does not address their issue.

Web integration

A significant challenge for many organizations implementing CRM is the integration of the website. Most organizations today already have a website, and this website contains large amounts of content that is duplicated in the CRM system (customer registration details, solution knowledge base, product information, pricing information, etc.). The

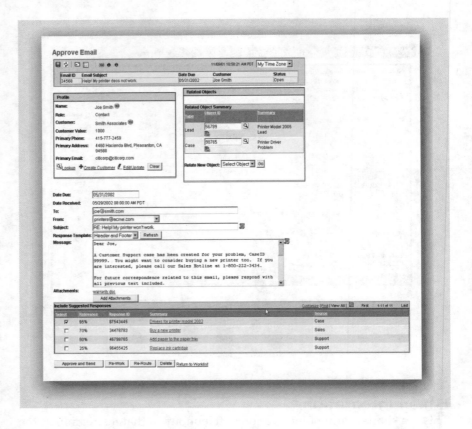

Figure 3.19
E-mail response
Courtesy of
PeopleSoft

ideal outcome is for the website to draw this information from the CRM system, using integration technologies, or for the web application to be part of the core CRM system. Any unnecessary duplication of information is likely to result in errors and increased work, not to mention an unsatisfactory experience for the customer when, for example, the call centre advises a different price to the one on the website.

Web integration may also involve webchat or web collaboration. These technologies allow an organization to assist the customer over the web, without them having to leave the web page they are in. Examples include a simple callback over a telephone line, using a number provided by the customer, web text chat, whereby the customer and the agent can have a dialogue over the web using chat windows, and interactive collaboration where the agent can effectively take control of the customer's mouse pointer, and help them to fill in a form or find a document.

CRM applications

Customer relationship management applications are generally organized into the primary functions of marketing, sales and service. These traditional business functions, however, are no longer adequate to describe fully the scope of CRM. For example, marketing, selling and servicing through partners or channels requires partner relationship management (PRM). Customer and product management, including the structure and relationships of these important elements, requires a suite of dedicated functions and modules that sit across sales, marketing and service. Finally, CRM analytics are often regarded as a separate suite of applications, with specialist solutions and vendors.

The following sections outline the main elements of each of these application areas. It should be noted that modern CRM applications have developed to be extremely rich in features and functions, far beyond what could be practically represented here. The following descriptions and diagrams, therefore, should be seen as an overview only.

Customer and product management

Customer and product management may be separate areas of a CRM application, or they may be built in to sales, service or marketing. In either case, it is essential that products and customers be adequately modelled in the application. Business-to-business (B2B) customers may have complex buying organizations and structures, or consumers (B2C) may live in, and move, households. Products may either be simple retail items or require complex configuration rules (e.g. an automobile with certain engine options, colour schemes, tyre options and accessories).

Figures 3.20 and 3.21 show the typical relationships and attributes of customer and product information.

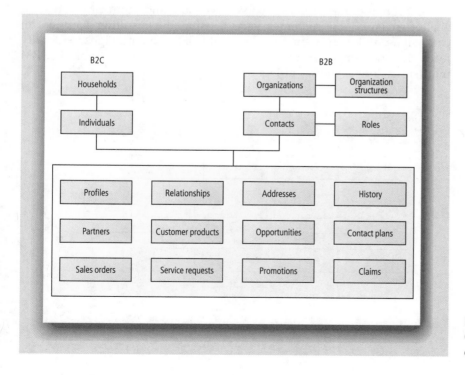

Figure 3.20
CRM components: customers

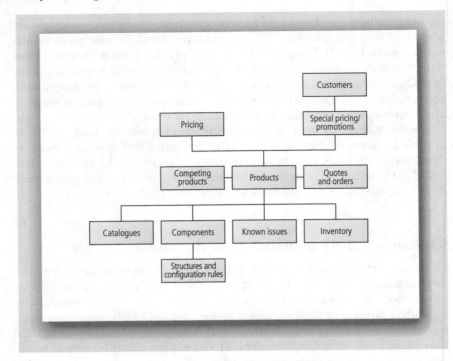

Figure 3.21
CRM components: products. These areas of a CRM application are often industry or even company specific

Marketing

The CRM marketing process involves assessing and segmenting customers (often based on customer value), using the resulting lists to run campaigns, and then evaluating the results of these campaigns to identify leads for the ongoing marketing and sales effort. A typical CRM marketing flow is shown in Fig. 3.22.

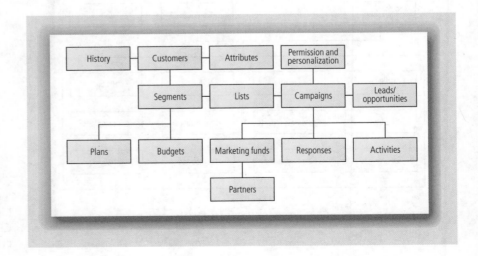

Figure 3.22
CRM components: marketing automation

This process involves a number of related CRM functions, such as managing marketing budgeting and funding, loyalty programmes and marketing through partners.

Marketing applications must also deal with the many different channels for customer communication. These include e-mail marketing, newsletters, telemarketing, conventional direct mail and web marketing. In all cases, the CRM focus on segmenting and personalizing the marketing effort is made possible by the sophistication of the underlying applications and availability of customer data.

Sales

Customer relationship management sales applications typically support many different styles of selling: B2B complex selling, B2C telesales, and so on. These may involve team selling, partner selling, specific sales methodologies and territory management. In most industries the focus is on the sales opportunity. The opportunity tracks the sale as it progresses along the sales pipeline, and allows quotes, orders and forecasts to be generated from a single source (Fig. 3.23).

A key technology to support selling processes is mobile synchronization or wireless solutions, allowing sales people access to the CRM system while on the road.

The implementation of salesforce automation technology is often accompanied by the implementation of a sales methodology. This is needed because the technology does not impose process management and standardization. Without a methodology, salespeople will all use the system differently. This makes sales management and prioritization of resources very difficult. Various sales methodologies are available; however, many of them were developed before the emergence of CRM, and are internally, rather than customer focused.

Selling over the web also presents a unique set of challenges. It requires some specialist applications such as shopping carts, storefronts, graphical

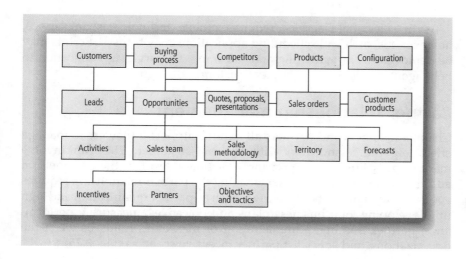

Figure 3.23
CRM components: sales force automation

catalogues and secure checkout. The emergence of product configurators has made it possible to sell complex products over the web.

Finally, selling often involves complex incentive and commission schemes, and these can be modelled in the CRM application to allow sales people to see the impact of winning a sale on their own personal compensation structure.

Service and support

Service and support applications in CRM are also highly variable. Servicing complex industrial products often requires field service engineers, while servicing a consumer with a complaint requires centralized teleservicing and a current knowledge base. The central element in CRM service is the service request or trouble ticket. This is used to track the service event through to completion, including service orders and resolutions (Fig. 3.24).

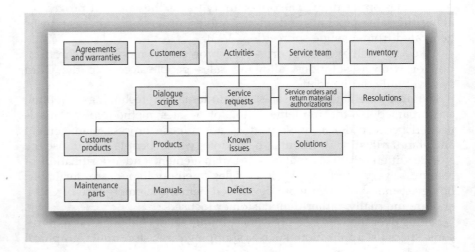

Figure 3.24
CRM components:
service automation

As in sales, field service requires mobile technologies; in service, however, dispatch and scheduling applications may be used. Scripts may be deployed (as in marketing and sales) in a teleservicing application to help agents to deliver a consistent customer dialogue.

Partner relationship management

Channel members and partners all require support if they are to manage effectively the relationship with the end-customer. This can involve marketing, selling and servicing functions through the channel. In addition to these applications, managing the partner relationship requires specialist functions to be supported, such as partner qualification and sign up, developing joint business plans and objectives, measuring performance, partner training, administration of marketing funds between the organizations, and specialist partner incentive schemes (Fig. 3.25).

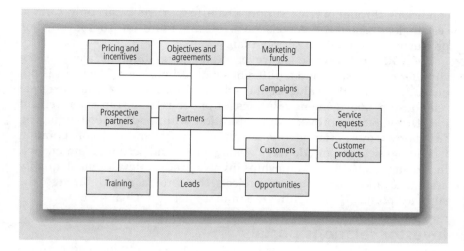

Figure 3.25
CRM components: partner relationship management

PRM most often requires a portal to be established to give partners access to the CRM system in a controlled, secure, yet collaborative way. Data security and administration are also important functions, to ensure that competing partners cannot see each other's opportunities, and that individual partners can administer their own users through the portal.

Other stakeholders

Relationship management applications extend beyond the customer, channel and partner domains. Other stakeholders in CRM include employees, investors and suppliers.

Employee relationship management

Customers deal with employees, and therefore effective CRM requires effective, well-informed employees. Employee relationship management [ERM; also known as business-to-employee (B2E)] applications provide the supporting functions to ensure that employees are knowledgeable, well equipped and well motivated. These include news, objectives, training, performance, rostering, knowledge management and incentive functions, typically presented in an employee portal. These technologies allow management to formalize the expectations, outcomes and performance of people within the organization, to align more closely the resources of the organization with the business goals.

Supplier relationship management

Traditionally, supplier management systems have focused on the transactional side of the relationship. Purchasing, receiving and payment systems have been around for some time. More recently, a focus on improving the efficiency of the supply chain has led to the implementation of technologies such as constraint-based optimization for the supply chain. These technologies seek to remove all violations of conditions throughout the supply chain (e.g. a truck can only carry a certain load and only travels on a certain route on Tuesdays), thus producing an optimized supply plan.

The CRM perspective, however, leads to a different view of the supplier relationship, and a different set of technologies. The focus is not on cost, but on the value of the relationship. As with other external relationship management solutions, supplier relationship management (SRM) involves improved communication with, and understanding of, suppliers. It most often involves a supplier portal and web collaboration technologies, order and delivery management, and account maintenance. Increasingly, supplier relationships involve product development, quality assurance and cost-reduction projects that are managed through the supplier portal. This is addressed in more detail in Chapter 6.

Investor relations portals

Just as web technologies have allowed customers, suppliers and partners to operate as an extension of an organization's CRM system, so too have investor portals led to unprecedented levels of access across the investor relationship. Many organizations today operate an investor website, allowing access to important information such as company overviews, mission and vision, strategy, financial reports, publications and presentations, statutory filings, analyst views and market assessments. Investors are able to register with the website, request information, sign up for mailing lists and provide feedback.

CRM analytics

Over the past few years CRM analytics has grown in importance. Organizations have realized that merely streamlining the customer-facing operations is not enough; an analytical view of the customer is required to understand key CRM metrics such as customer value, satisfaction and propensity to churn. The three levels of analysis in today's CRM systems, in increasing order of complexity, are standard reporting, online analytical processing (OLAP) and data mining.

Standard reporting

Customer relationship management reporting is essential to an effective CRM system. The foundation for CRM is an understanding and differentiation of customers, something that depends on good customer, and internal, information. Reporting can take the form of simple lists of information such as key accounts and annual revenues, or more sophisticated reports that embody a certain sales methodology or performance metric.

Reporting can be standardized (predefined) or query based (ad hoc). Standardized reports are typically delivered with the CRM software application, but often require work to be tailored to suit the needs of the organization. Some customization of the report can be done when it is run; for example, in selecting options or filtering criteria, but the end result is limited to what the report designers envisaged.

Query-based reporting presents the user with a selection of tools, which can then be used to construct the report that is currently required. This is far more flexible, but is not suitable for the regular, standard operational level reporting owing to the time required to set up the request for information. This is a powerful tool in the right hands, however, as it allows specific enquiries to be made; for example, 'show me all of the customers that have expired on their maintenance agreement, in my territory, with annual revenues above a certain amount'.

As the requirement for analysis grows, the standard transactional information in the core CRM database may not be structured to deliver the best results; for this reason, OLAP has become an essential part of CRM.

Online analytical processing

OLAP technologies allow information to be transformed into a format that suits analysis and ad hoc inquiry, and stored in a data warehouse. This information is often summarized in such a way that it supports rapid slicing and dicing, allowing users to drill down on graphs and tables to analyse where a certain figure or problem may have arisen. The format used is known as a star schema. It contains a central fact table surrounded by several dimension tables, giving it the appearance of a star. A data warehouse will typically contain several star schemas, such as:

- customer schema
- opportunity schema
- service request schema
- activity schema
- marketing response schema.

The customer schema, for example, may contain information such as customer sales revenue figures, volumes, cost of sales, profit margins, discounts and promotional expense. Users then perform analysis

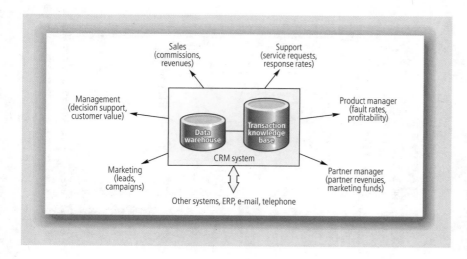

Figure 3.26 OLAP technology for CRM users (courtesy of Customer Connect Australia)

against one or more schemas, to arrive at the desired outcome. The schema format lends itself to ad hoc analysis, allowing the user to drill down on summarized information to investigate the underlying detail, seeking out the cause of a problem. This allows a wide range of analyses to take place, achieving high performance using relatively few schemas (Fig. 3.26).

Sales people can analyse their territory to determine revenue and profitability by customer. Service people can analyse call response rates and times. Partner managers can analyse the performance of partners by marketing fund approvals and partner-generated revenues.

Analysis tools can also support decisions in real time. For example, an organization may require customer scoring or predictive measures to be delivered to the call-centre agent while the customer is on the telephone. This allows a tailored offer to be made that is more likely to receive a positive response from the customer. The result is real-time CRM, an approach advocated by vendors such as E.piphany (Fig. 3.27).

An important element in CRM analytics is the information delivery mechanism. Information can be made available on the desktop, in a web browser interface with graphical layout and drill-down. This approach requires the user to search for a result. Another method of delivery involves setting trigger points (e.g. when a customer logs more than a certain number of service calls in a month). The analytics application then pushes the related information to the user via e-mail or another alert mechanism. This approach, also known as 'publish and subscribe', is a powerful management tool.

Figure 3.27
Real-time CRM analytics (courtesy of E.piphany[11])

Data mining

Data mining is an important CRM analytical capability in some industries. Banking, telecommunications, insurance, public sector, retail and utilities all require analysis of huge volumes of consumer data, a task that is very difficult without data mining. The data-mining process seeks to identify patterns and relationships in the data, using selection, exploration and modelling processes. The results include, for example, churn scoring (likelihood that the customer will leave), fraud detection, customer value scoring and campaign effectiveness scoring.

Several CRM vendors specialize in advanced analytical and mining applications. SAS Institute, for example, positions an 'Intelligence Architecture', which comprises:

- data warehousing (storage),
- business intelligence (delivery)
- analytical intelligence (data mining, predictive modelling, forecasting, simulation and optimization).

Analytical applications such as these are important in CRM, as even such simple terms as customer profitability can be hard to define, and harder to measure accurately. These applications often work alongside operational CRM applications and perhaps an activity-based costing (ABC) system, extracting information, then performing analysis for later use. The operational CRM applications can then draw on customer value or churn scores during the customer dialogue, to assist in targeting and prioritizing customer activity. Vendors such as SAS and Siebel offer prebuilt integration between their applications, for this purpose.

Activity-based costing

Traditional standard costing systems are typically product centric, and are therefore not detailed enough to allow costs to be analysed by channel and customer. However, CRM depends on an understanding of the profitability of customers, a calculation that requires costing information at the customer level. As many customer-related costs are activity based (e.g. sales effort, service calls), ABC is required to achieve a suitably accurate assessment of customer profitability.

Since ABC projects require significant revision to cost accounting processes, they may not be implemented across an entire organization. In this case, ABC analysis can be done on a project basis for a given business process or department, then discontinued until such time that this process or department has changed significantly. Companies normally start with the activity that they think accounts for a significant portion of customer-related costs; for example, selling

The ABC systems may be stand-alone or integrated with the CRM suite. Some CRM vendors regard ABC as an integral part of CRM, as it is necessary to arrive at the core concept of customer profitability and customer value. PeopleSoft's Enterprise Performance Management (EPM) product, for example, uses ABC to calculate customer profitability.

Using ABC technology, traditionally indirect costs (e.g. marketing expenses and sales time) can be traced back to customers or segments. In effect, this converts indirect costs to direct costs. The traceability requires activities, resources and cost drivers to be identified and linked back to the cost object (customer) being analysed.

Technology for the CRM value chain

The CRM value chain draws on the technologies described in this chapter in a systematic way, to deliver high levels of customer satisfaction and profitability (Fig. 3.28).

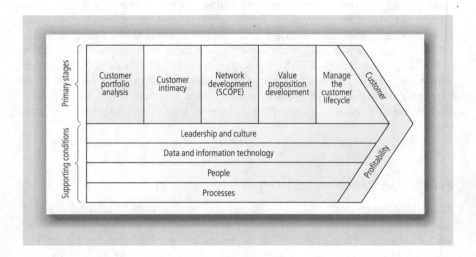

Figure 3.28
The CRM value chain

The CRM application areas discussed in this chapter can be applied at various points along the value chain, as shown in Fig. 3.29. Marketing technology, for example, can support customer portfolio analysis (segmentation), customer intimacy (customer needs analytics), network development (partner marketing funds) and managing the customer lifecycle (campaigns and events). Data mining is useful at three stages: customer portfolio analysis, customer intimacy and managing the customer lifecycle. Mining techniques can be used to identify the customers that are most profitable and to explore what they have in common. It can also be used to produce propensity-to-buy scores so that campaigns can be targeted at them.

	Customer portfolio analysis	Customer intimacy	Network development	Value proposition development	Manage the customer lifecycle
Customers and products	Customer structures	Customer profiles	Customer management	Product and pricing definition. Customer expectations	Defect tracking
Marketing	Segmentation	Predictive modelling	Partner marketing development funds	Competitive positioning, promotions, customization	Campaign management, event management, e-mail marketing
Sales	Forecasting	Historical data, revenue analytics	Partner sales analytics	Sales methodology	Order entry, order configurator, enterprise selling, web shopping
Service	Cost-to-serve	Historical data, complaint tracking, customer satisfaction analytics	Partner self service	Service level agreements	Service request management, service orders, self service, field service
PRM	Partner recruitment	Partner portal	Partner management	Marketing development funds	Partner team selling
Other stakeholders			ERM, SRM, Investor portal		Performance review
Analytics	Customer life-time value, acquisition costs, retention costs	Customer needs, customer preferences, customer satisfaction	Partner performance	Pricing, profitability and incentives	Sales performance, service performance, balanced scorecard
Data mining	Customer profitability analysis	Customer insight	Partner analysis		Churn scoring, propensity-to-buy scoring
Activity-based costing	Cost modelling				Cost actuals

Figure 3.29 How CRM capabilities map onto the CRM value chain

Summary

The CRM IT market has grown rapidly since its inception in the early 1990s. To date, this growth has been led by the CRM software application vendors. This growth is expected to continue, albeit at a slower rate, into the future.

Effective deployment of CRM in an organization requires the appropriate supporting CRM IT to be in place. Customer relationship management IT forms a foundation on which the customer value chain is built, and includes a flexible, high-performing architecture across multiple channels of communication, accessibility to the technology, mobile and web technologies, customer knowledge management and analytics, process automation and escalation workflow, integration with other systems and technologies, and a broad suite of applications, including marketing, sales, service and partners, allowing for industry-specific requirements.

References

1. www.customerconnect.com.au
2. www.pivotal.com
3. Nelson, S. Wecksell, J. and Frey, N. (2002) *2002 CRM Survey Points to Solid Demand and Modest Growth*. Strategic Analysis Report, 24 May, Gartner.
4. Topolinski, T., Eschinger, C. and Kumar, P. (2002) *Outlook for the CRM Software Market: Trends and Forecast*. 21 October, Gartner.
5. www.peoplesoft.com
6. www.oracle.com
7. www.o4corporation.com
8. www.sap.com
9. www.siebel.com
10. www.StayinFront.com
11. www.epiphany.com

Chapter 3 is contributed by John Turnbull, Managing Director of Customer Connect Australia Pty Ltd.

Chapter 4

Customer portfolio analysis

By the end of this chapter, you will understand:

1 why customer portfolio analysis is necessary for CRM implementation
2 that there are a number of disciplines that contribute to customer portfolio analysis (CPA): market segmentation, sales forecasting, activity-based costing and lifetime value estimation
3 how the CPA process differs between business-to-consumer and business-to-business contexts
4 how to use a number of business-to-business portfolio analysis tools
5 the role of data mining in CPA.

What is a portfolio?

The use of the term 'portfolio' in customer portfolio analysis (CPA) indicates that the outcome of this process is a classification of customers into different groups that are then managed on a portfolio, or collective, basis. One of the fundamental propositions of customer relationship management (CRM) is that not all customers should be managed in the same way. This is largely because they represent different revenue and cost profiles for the company. Some customers might be offered customized product and face-to-face account management; others might be offered standardized product and web-based self-service. If the second group were to be offered the same service levels as the first, they might end up being profit-takers rather than profit-makers for the company.

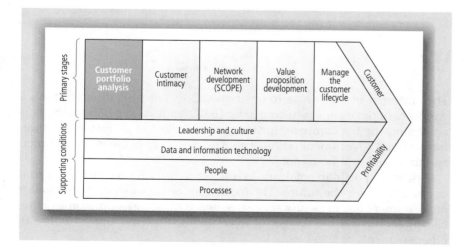

Figure 4.1
CRM value chain

Case 4.1

CRM in NatWest Corporate Banking Services

- Corporate Banking Services has three tiers of clients ranked by size, lifetime value and credit worthiness.

  - The top tier numbers some 60 multinational clients. These have at least one **individual relationship manager** attached to them.
  - The second tier, numbering approximately 150, have **individual client managers** attached to them.
  - The third tier, representing the vast bulk of smaller business clients, have access to a **'Small Business Advisor'** at each of the 100 business centres.

Customer portfolio analysis aims to optimize profit-performance across the entire customer base by offering differentiated value propositions to different segments of customers. For example, the UK-based NatWest Bank manages its business customers on a portfolio basis. It has split customers into three segments based on their size, lifetime value (LTV) and creditworthiness. As Case 4.1 shows, each group in the portfolio is treated to a different value proposition. When companies deliver tiered service levels such as this, they face a number of questions. Should the tiering be based on current or future customer value? How should the sales and service support vary across tiers? How can customer expectations be managed to avoid the problem of low-tier customers resenting not being offered high-tier service? What criteria should be employed to migrate customers up and down the hierarchy? Finally, does the cost of managing this additional complexity pay off in customer retention, additional revenues and profit?

What is a customer?

The customer in a business-to-business (B2B) context is different from a customer in the business-to-consumer (B2C) context. The B2B customer is an organization: a company (producer or reseller) or an institution (not-for-profit or government body). The B2C customer is the end consumer: an individual or a household.

Customer portfolio analysis investigates markets to identify profit opportunities for the future. The focus may be on existing customers or on customers not presently served. When CPA focuses only on existing customers there is the danger of overlooking attractive opportunities in other segments or markets.

Market segmentation

Customer portfolio analysis starts with a discipline that is routinely used by marketing management: market segmentation. Market segmentation is the process of dividing up a market into more-or-less homogeneous subsets for which it is possible to create a different value proposition. At the end of the process the company can decide which segment(s) it wants to serve. If it chooses, each segment can be served with a different value proposition.

What differentiates market segmentation in a CRM sense is a very clear focus on customer value. The outcome of this segmentation process should be the identification of the value potential of each identified segment. The company will want to identify and target those customers that can generate profit in the future: these will be the customers that the company and its network[i] are better placed to serve and satisfy than competitors.

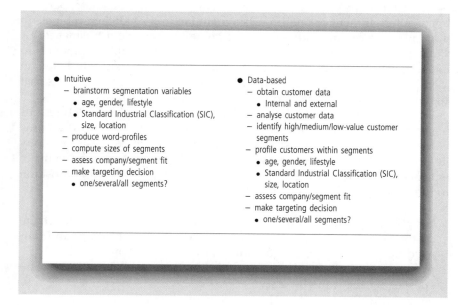

Figure 4.2
Intuitive and data-based segmentation processes

Market segmentation in many companies is highly intuitive. The marketing team will develop profiles of customer groups based on their insight and experience. This is then used to guide the development of marketing strategies across the segments. In a CRM context, market segmentation is highly data dependent. The data might be generated internally or sourced externally. Internal data from marketing, sales and finance records are often supplemented with external data from external sources such as marketing research companies, partner organizations in the company's network and data specialists (Fig. 4.2).

---

[i] Refer to Chapter 6 for more information on networks.

The market segmentation process can be broken down into a number of steps:

1 identify the business you are in
2 identify relevant segmentation variables
3 analyse the market using these variables
4 assess the value of the market segments
5 select target market(s) to serve.

Identify the business you are in

This is an important strategic question to which many, but not all, companies have an answer. Ted Levitt's classic article 'Marketing myopia' warned companies of the dangers of product-oriented answers to the question.[1] He wrote of a nineteenth century company that defined itself as being in the buggy-whip industry. It has not survived. It is important to consider the answer from the customer point of view. For example, is Blockbuster in the video-rental business, or some other business, perhaps home entertainment or retailing? Is a manufacturer of kitchen cabinets in the timber-processing industry or the home-improvement business?

A customer-oriented answer to the question will enable companies to move through the market segmentation process because it helps to identify the boundaries of the market served, it defines the benefits that customers seek and it picks out the company's competitors.

Let's assume that the kitchen furniture company has defined its business from the customer's perspective. It believes it is in the home value improvement business. It knows from research that customers buy its products for one major reason: they are home owners who want to enhance the value of their properties. The company is now in a position to identify its markets and competitors at three levels:

1 **benefit competitors**: other companies delivering the same benefit to customers (e.g. window-replacement companies, heating and air-conditioning companies and bathroom renovation companies)
2 **product competitors**: other companies marketing kitchens to customers seeking the same benefit
3 **geographical competitors**: benefit and product competitors operating in the same geographical territory.

Identify relevant segmentation variables and analyse the market

Many variables are used to segment consumer and organizational markets. Companies can enjoy competitive advantage through innovations in market segmentation. For example, before Häagen-Dazs, it was known that ice-cream was a seasonally sold product aimed primarily at children. Häagen-Dazs upset this logic by targeting an adult consumer group with a different, luxurious product, and all-year-round purchasing potential. We will look at consumer markets first.

Consumer markets

Consumers can be classified according to a number of shared characteristics. These can be grouped into user attributes and usage attributes, as summarized in Fig. 4.3.

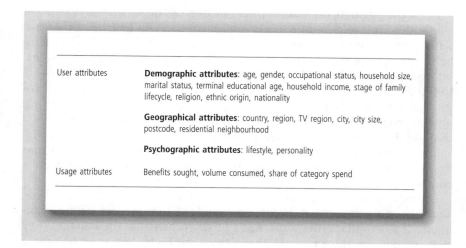

User attributes	**Demographic attributes**: age, gender, occupational status, household size, marital status, terminal educational age, household income, stage of family lifecycle, religion, ethnic origin, nationality
	Geographical attributes: country, region, TV region, city, city size, postcode, residential neighbourhood
	Psychographic attributes: lifestyle, personality
Usage attributes	Benefits sought, volume consumed, share of category spend

Figure 4.3
Criteria for segmenting consumer markets

In recent years there has been a trend away from simply using demographic attributes to segment consumer markets. The concern has been that there is too much variance within each of the demographic segmentation variables to regard all members of the segment as more-or-less homogeneous. For example, some 30–40-year-olds have families and mortgaged homes; others live in rented apartments and go clubbing at weekends. Some members of a religious group may be traditionalists; others may be progressives.

The family lifecycle (FLC) idea has been particularly threatened. The FLC traces the development of a person's life along a straight path from young and single, through married with no children, married with young children, married couples with older children, older married couples with no children at home, empty nesters still in employment, retired empty nester couple, to sole survivor working or not working. Life for many, if not most people, does not follow this path. It fails to take account of the many and varied life choices that people make: never marrieds, late marriers, childless couples, gay and lesbian partnerships, extended families, single-parent households and divorced couples, for example.

Let's look at some of the variables that can be used to define market segments. Occupational status is widely used to classify people into social grades. Systems vary around the world. In the UK, the JICNARS social grading system is used. This allocates households to one of six categories (A, B, C1, C2, D and E) depending on the job of the head of household. Higher managerial occupations are ranked A; casual, unskilled workers are ranked E. Media owners often use the JICNARS scale to profile their audiences.

A number of companies have developed geodemographic classification schemes. CACI, for example, has developed A Classification of Residential Neighbourhoods (ACORN), which allocates homes into one of the six categories shown in Fig. 4.4, and beyond into over 50 subcategories. ACORN data suggest that households in a group exhibit similar buying behaviours.

Lifestyle research became popular in the 1980s. Rather than using a single descriptive category to classify customers, as had been the case with demographics, it uses multivariate analysis to understand buying behaviour. Lifestyle analysts collect data about people's activities, interests and opinions. A lifestyle survey instrument may require answers to 400 or 500 questions, taking several hours to complete. Using analytical processes such as factor analysis and cluster analysis, the researchers are able to produce lifestyle or psychographic profiles. The assertion is made that we buy products because of their fit with our chosen lifestyles. Lifestyle studies have been done in many countries, as well as across national boundaries. Many companies conduct lifestyle research on a commercial basis and sell the results to their clients.

Usage attributes can be particularly useful for CRM purposes. Benefit segmentation has become a standard tool for marketing managers. It is axiomatic that customers buy products for the benefits they deliver, not for the products themselves. Nobody has ever bought a 5 mm drill bit because they want a 5 mm drill bit. They buy because of what the drill bit can deliver: a 5 mm hole. Practitioners of CRM need to understand the benefits that are sought by the markets they serve. The market for toothpaste, for example, can be segmented along benefit lines. There are three major benefit segments: white teeth, fresh breath, and healthy teeth and gums. When it comes to creating value propositions for the chosen customers, benefit segmentation becomes very important.

The other two usage attributes, volume consumed and share of category spend, are also useful from a CRM perspective. Many companies classify their customers according to the volume of business they produce. For example, in the B2C context, McDonald's USA found that 77 per cent of their sales are to males aged 18–34 who eat at McDonald's three to five times per week, despite the company's mission

A.	Thriving	19.8%
B.	Expanding	11.6%
C.	Rising	7.5%
D.	Settling	24.1%
E.	Aspiring	13.7%
F.	Striving	22.8%

Figure 4.4
Geodemographics,
ACORN

to be the world's favourite family restaurant. Assuming that they contribute in equal measure to the bottom line, these are customers that the company must not lose. The volume they provide allows the company to operate very cost-effectively, keeping unit costs low.

Companies that rank customers into tiers according to volume, and are then able to identify which customers fall into each tier, may be able to develop customer migration plans to move lower volume customers higher up the ladder from first-time customer to repeat customer, majority customer, loyal customer, and onwards to advocate status.

This makes sense when the lower volume customers represent an opportunity. They are an opportunity if they buy products from other suppliers in the category. This means that the company's share of customer spend is less than 100 per cent. For example, customer Jones, who buys five pairs of shoes a year, but only buys one of those pairs from 'Shoeless' retail outlets, represents a greater migration opportunity than customer Smith, who buys two pairs a year, but both of them from Shoeless. Shoeless has the opportunity to win four more sales from Jones, but none from Smith.

Whether this means that Jones is more valuable than Smith depends on the answer to other questions. First, how much will it cost to switch Jones from her current shoe retailer(s), and what will it cost to retain Smith's business? Secondly, what are the margins earned from these customers? If Jones is very committed to her other supplier, it may not be worth trying to switch her. If Smith buys high-margin fashion and leisure footwear and Jones buys low-margin footwear, then Smith might be the better opportunity despite the lower volume of sales.

Most segmentation programmes use more than one variable. For example, a chain of bars may define its customers on the basis of geography, age and music preference. Figure 4.5 shows how the market for chocolate can be segmented by usage occasion and satisfaction. Four major segments emerge from this bivariate segmentation of the market.

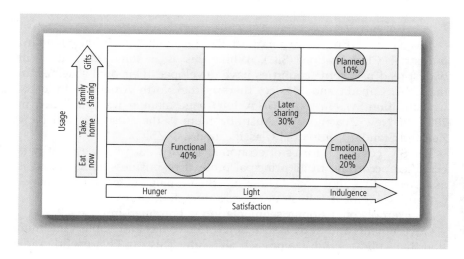

Figure 4.5
Bivariate segmentation of the chocolate market (Source: Mintel 1998)

Business markets

Business markets can also be segmented in a number of ways, as shown in Fig. 4.6.

Business market segmentation criteria	Illustration
Standard Industrial Classification	An internationally agreed standard for classifying goods and service producers
Dispersion	Geographically concentrated or dispersed
Size	Large, medium, small businesses: classified by number of employees, number of customers, profit or turnover
Account status	Global account, national account, regional account, A or B or C class accounts
Account value	<$50 000, <$100 000, <$200 000, <$500 000
Buying processes	Open tender, sealed bid, internet auction, centralized, decentralized
Buying criteria	Continuity of supply (reliability), product quality, price, customization, just-in-time, service support before or after sale
Propensity to switch	Satisfied with current suppliers, dissatisfied
Share of customer spend in the category	Sole supplier, majority supplier, minority supplier, non-supplier
Geography	City, region, country, trading bloc (ASEAN, EU)
Buying style	Risk averse, innovator

Figure 4.6
How business markets are segmented

The basic starting point for most B2B segmentation is the Standard Industrial Classification (SIC). While this is a standard that is in widespread use, some countries have developed their own schemes. In the USA, Canada and Mexico, there is the North American Industry Classification System (NAICS). A 1400 page manual was published in 2002. In New Zealand and Australia there is the Australia and New Zealand Standard Industrial Classification (ANZSIC).

The SIC covers all forms of economic activity. Each business entity is classified according to its principal product or business activity, and is assigned a five-digit code. These are then amalgamated into 92 major categories. Figure 4.7 illustrates several five-digit codes.

An example of customer segmentation is presented in Case 4.2.

Governments and trade associations often collect and publish information that indicates the size of each SIC code. This can be a useful guide

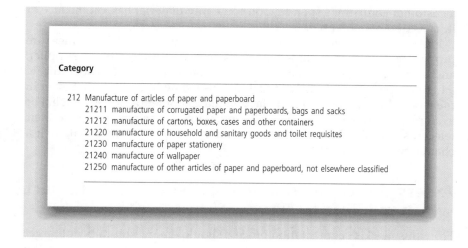

Figure 4.7
SIC examples

when focusing the CRM strategy. However, segmentation in the B2B context is often conducted not at the aggregated level of the SIC, but at an individual account level. The question is not so much, 'Do we want to serve this segment?' as much as 'Do we want to serve this customer?'

Several of these account-level segmentation variables are specifically important for CRM purposes: account value, share of category spend and propensity-to-switch.

Most businesses have a scheme for classifying their customers according to their value. The majority of these schemes associate value with some measure of sales revenue or volume. This is not an adequate measure of value, because it takes no account of the costs required to win and keep the customer. This issue is addressed later in the chapter.

Share of category spend gives an indication of the future potential that exists within the account. A supplier that only has a 15 per cent share of

Case 4.2

Customer segmentation at Dell Computer

Dell was founded in 1984 with the revolutionary idea of selling custom-built computers directly to the customer. Dell has grown to become one of the world's larger PC manufacturers and continues to sell directly to individual consumers and organizations.

The direct business model of Dell and the focus on serving business customers have resulted in the organization investing heavily in developing an advanced CRM system to manage its clearly segmented customers. Dell has identified eight customer segments: Global Accounts, Large Companies, Midsize Companies, Federal Government, State & Local Government, Education, Small Companies and Consumers. Dell has organized its business around these eight segments, where each is managed by a complete business unit with its own sales, finance, IT, technical support and manufacturing arms.

a customer company's spending on some raw material has, on the face of it, considerable potential.

Propensity-to-switch may be high or low. It is possible to measure propensity-to-switch by assessing satisfaction with the current supplier, and by computing switching costs. Dissatisfaction alone does not indicate a high propensity-to-switch. Switching costs may be so high that even in the face of high levels of dissatisfaction the customer does not switch. For example, customers may be unhappy with the performance of their telecoms supplier, but not switch because of the disruption that such a change would bring about.

Assess the value in a market segment and select which markets to serve

From this market segmentation process should emerge a number of target market alternatives. The potential of these to generate value for the company will need to be assessed. The potential value of the segmentation opportunities depends on the answers to two questions:

- How attractive is the opportunity?
- How well placed is the company and its network to exploit the opportunity?

Figure 4.8 identifies a number of the attributes that can be taken into account during this appraisal. The attractiveness of a segment is related to a number of issues, including its size and growth potential, the number of competitors and the intensity of competition between them, the barriers to entry and the propensity of customers to switch from their existing suppliers. The question of company fit rotates around the issue of the relative competitive competency of the company and its network members to satisfy the requirements of the segment.

- Segment attractiveness
  - Size of segment, segment growth rate, price sensitivity of customers, bargaining power of customers, customers' current relationships with suppliers, barriers to segment entry, barriers to segment exit, number and power of competitors, prospect of new entrants, potential for differentiation, propensity for customer switching

- Company and network fit
  - Does the opportunity fit the company's objectives, mission, vision and values? Does the company and its network possess the operational, marketing, technological, people and other competencies, and liquidity to exploit the opportunity?

Figure 4.8
Evaluating segmentation alternatives

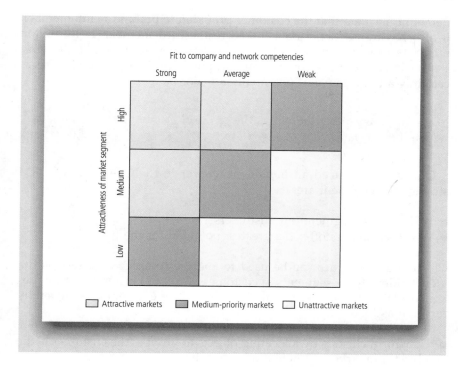

Figure 4.9
McKinsey/General
Electric customer
portfolio matrix

In principle, if the segment is attractive and the company and network competencies indicate a good fit, the opportunity may be worth pursuing. However, companies may find that they need to select from several opportunities. Some kind of scoring process needs to be developed. The McKinsey/General Electric matrix in Fig. 4.9 maps market attractiveness against business strengths, reflecting the two questions above.[2]

To use the matrix, companies need to identify attributes that indicate the attractiveness of a market segment (some are listed in Fig. 4.8), and the competencies of the company and its network. An importance weight is agreed for each attribute. The segment opportunity is rated against each attribute and a score is computed. The opportunities can then be mapped into Fig. 4.9.

Data mining for market segmentation

Data mining can be used for market segmentation and customer valuation purposes. It has particular use when there are large volumes of data that need to be analysed. This is true of B2C contexts such as retailing, banking and home shopping.

An international retailing operation such as Tesco has 14 million Clubcard members in its UK customer base. The company has the demographic data that the customer provided to become a club member. It also has transactional data linked to the card member. If 10 million members use Tesco in a week and have an average basket of 30 items, Tesco's database grows by 300 million pieces of data per week. This is certainly a huge cost, but potentially a major benefit.

> Data mining can be defined as the creation of intelligence from large quantities of data.

Questions that need an intelligent answer in the CPA stage of CRM strategy development are:

- How can we segment our customers?
- Which customers offer the greatest potential for the future?

Clustering techniques can be used to analyse complex data sets with a view to identifying segments of customers. Various clustering techniques are available for the segmentation task.[3] These techniques generally function as follows.

- They form clusters by allocating objects to groups (the customer is the 'object' in market segmentation research).
- The composition of a group is relatively homogeneous.
- An object is allocated to a group because it possesses attributes that are more closely associated with that group than any other group.

Once clusters have been formed they need to be given a CRM interpretation. Lifestyle market segments are outputs of cluster analysis on large sets of data. Cluster labels such as 'Young working-class families' or 'Wealthy suburbanites' are often used to capture the essence of the cluster.

Given the availability of transactional data, it is certainly possible to segment according to historical value. Transaction data can be converted into revenue or margin data. Customers can be segmented into quintiles or deciles according to the revenue or margin value of the purchases they make. In general, it is assumed that the cost-to-serve is standard across all customers, so no further analysis is done to convert margin data into true customer profit data. In principle, some customers do have a higher cost-to-serve because, for example, they make more demands on the contact centre. In practice, in B2C markets it is often too difficult and costly to introduce procedures that trace costs to customers. Each decile or quintile will include different customer types. Two customers with the same historical value may have generated that value in very different ways. One may have made multiple repeat purchases of household staples; the other may have made a couple of high-priced speciality purchases.

Customer relationship management strategists are more interested in what future value a customer (segment, cohort or individual) can yield. This is determined by their propensity to buy products in the future. Data mining expertise can be used to build predictive models. Data miners examine historical data sets to generate predictive models about future behaviour. Predictive models can be generated to identify:

- which customer (segment) is most likely to buy a given product
- which customers are likely to default on payment
- which customers are most likely to defect (churn).

Predictive models are built using data from the past. The data include predictors and outcomes, both of which are known. This is called 'training the model'. When the model seems to be working well, it is run on contemporary data, where the predictor data are known but the outcome data are not. This is called 'scoring'.

Predictive modelling is based on three assumptions, each of which may be true to a greater or lesser extent.[4]

- The past is a good predictor of the future . . . BUT, this may not be true. Sales of many products are cyclical or seasonal. Others have fashion or fad lifecycles.
- The data are available . . . BUT, this may not be true. Data use to train the model may no longer be collected. Data may be too costly to collect, or may be in the wrong format.
- The database contains what you want to predict . . . BUT, this may not be true. The data may not be available. If you want to predict which customers are most likely to buy mortgage protection insurance and you only have data on life policies, you will not be able to answer the question.

Two tools that are used for predicting future behaviours are decision trees and neural networks.

Decision trees

Decision trees are so called because the graphical model output has the appearance of a branch structure. Decision trees work by analysing a data set to find the independent variable that, when used to split the population, results in nodes that are most different from each other with

Name	Debt	Income	Married?	Risk
Joe	High	High	Yes	Good
Sue	Low	High	Yes	Good
John	Low	High	No	Poor
Mary	High	Low	Yes	Poor
Fred	Low	Low	Yes	Poor

Figure 4.10
Credit risk training set (Source: Brand and Gerritsen[5])

respect to the variable you are tying to predict. Figure 4.10 contains a set of data about five customers and their credit risk profile.[5]

A decision tree can be constructed to develop credit risk profiles of customers. This will be useful in determining whether they represent good or bad value.

In the analysis we treat Risk as the dependent column, also called the target variable. The other columns are independent columns. It is unlikely that the customer's name is a predictor of Risk, so we will use three other pieces of data as independent variables: debt, income and marital status. In the example, each of these is a simple categorical item, each of which only has two possible values. As you examine the data, as re-presented in the cross-tabulation of the dependent variable and all the independent variables in Fig. 4.11, you will see that the best split is income (four instances highlighted in bold on the diagonal: two high income/good risk plus two low income/poor risk). Debt and marital status each score 3 on their diagonals.

Predicted risk	High debt	Low debt	High income	Low income	Married	Not married
Good	1	1	2	0	2	1
Poor	1	2	1	2	2	1

Figure 4.11
Cross-tabulation of dependent and independent variables

Once a node is split, the same process is performed on each successive node, until either no further splits are possible or a managerially useful model has been reached.

The graphical output of this decision-tree analysis is shown in Fig. 4.12. Each box is a node. The top node is the root node. The data from the root node are split into two groups based on income. The right-hand, low-income box, does not split any further because both low-income customers are classified as poor credit risks. The left-hand, high-income box does split further, into married and non-married customers. Neither of these splits further because the one unmarried customer is a poor credit risk and the two remaining married customers are good credit risks.

As a result of this process the company knows that customers who have the lowest credit risk will be high income and married. They will also note that debt, one of the variables inserted into the training model, did not perform well. It is not a predictor of creditworthiness.

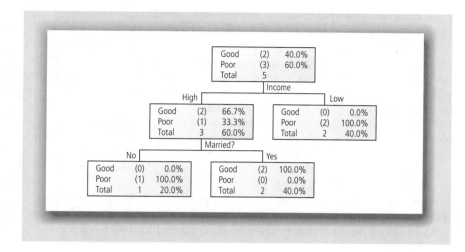

Figure 4.12
Decision-tree
output

Several software packages, such as CART (Classification and Regression Trees) and CHAID (Chi-squared Automatic Interaction Detection), perform decision-tree analysis.

Neural networks

Neural networks are another way of fitting a model to existing data for prediction purposes. The expression 'neural network' has its origins in the work of machine learning and artificial intelligence researchers who were trying to understand and learn from the natural neural networks of living creatures.

Neural networks can produce excellent predictions, but they are neither easy to understand nor straightforward to use. Neural networks represent complex mathematical equations, with many summations, exponential functions and parameters.[4]

Neural networks need to be trained to recognize patterns in sample data sets. Once trained, they can be used to predict customer behaviour from new data. They work well when there are many potential predictor variables, some of which are redundant.

Customer portfolio analysis tools

Since the early 1980s a number of tools has been specifically designed for assessing companies' customer portfolios (reviewed by Zolkiewski and Turnbull[6]). For the most part, these tools have been developed with a clear focus on the B2B context. They generally classify existing customers using a matrix and measurement approach. Many of these contributions have their origins in the work of the IMP (Industrial Marketing and Purchasing) group.[ii]

Cunningham and Homse[9] were among the first to develop the concept of a customer portfolio, which they suggested was useful for improving the allocation of resources between customers and for ensuring that relationships with key customers were managed more effectively. Their recommendations were based on over 800 interviews in 160 companies.

They discovered that sales volume was not the only criterion that companies regarded as an important attribute of a customer. Many companies valued what the researchers called technical development customers. These are customers who are active partners in product development and beta testing.

Fiocca advanced customer portfolio theory[10] when he developed a two-step customer portfolio model.

At the first step customers are classified according to:

- the strategic importance of the customer
- the difficulty of managing the relationship with the customer.

The strategic importance of a customer is determined by:

- the value/volume of the customer's purchases
- the potential and prestige of the customer
- customer market leadership
- general desirability in terms of diversification of the supplier's markets, providing access to new markets, improving technological expertise and the impact on other relationships.

The difficulty of managing the customer relationship is a function of:

- product characteristics such as novelty and complexity
- account characteristics such as the customer's needs and requirements, customer's buying behaviour, customer's power, customer's technical and commercial competence and the customer's preference to have many suppliers
- competition for the account, which is assessed by considering the number of competitors, the strength and weaknesses of competitors and competitors' position vis-à-vis the customer.

Fiocca then constructed a two-dimensional matrix, as in Fig. 4.13. The second step involves further analysis of the key accounts, in the left-hand cells of Fig. 4.13. They are classified according to:

- the customer's attractiveness
- the relative strength of the buyer/seller relationship.

[ii] The IMP is a coalition of researchers that have been examining B2B relationships from a relational perspective. Among their key concepts are relationships, networks and interaction. The group's work is discussed in Ford.[7] See also the previous edition of Ford's work.[8]

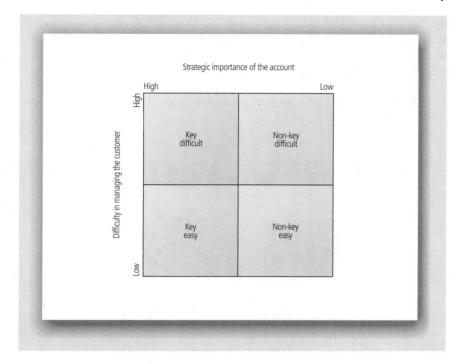

Figure 4.13
Fiocca's CPA model:
step 1

The attractiveness criteria suggested by Fiocca are conditions in the customer's market. These are classified into market factors, competition, financial and economic factors, technological factors and sociopolitical factors, as detailed in Fig. 4.14.

The strength of the customer relationship is determined by:

- the length of relationship
- the volume or dollar value of purchases
- the importance of the customer (percentage of supplier's sales accounted for by this customer)

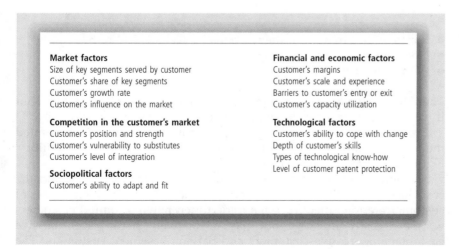

Figure 4.14
Factors influencing the customer's attractiveness (Fiocca's model)

- personal friendships
- co-operation in product development
- management distance (language and culture)
- geographical distance.

The data from this second step are then entered into a final nine-cell matrix, as shown in Fig. 4.15.

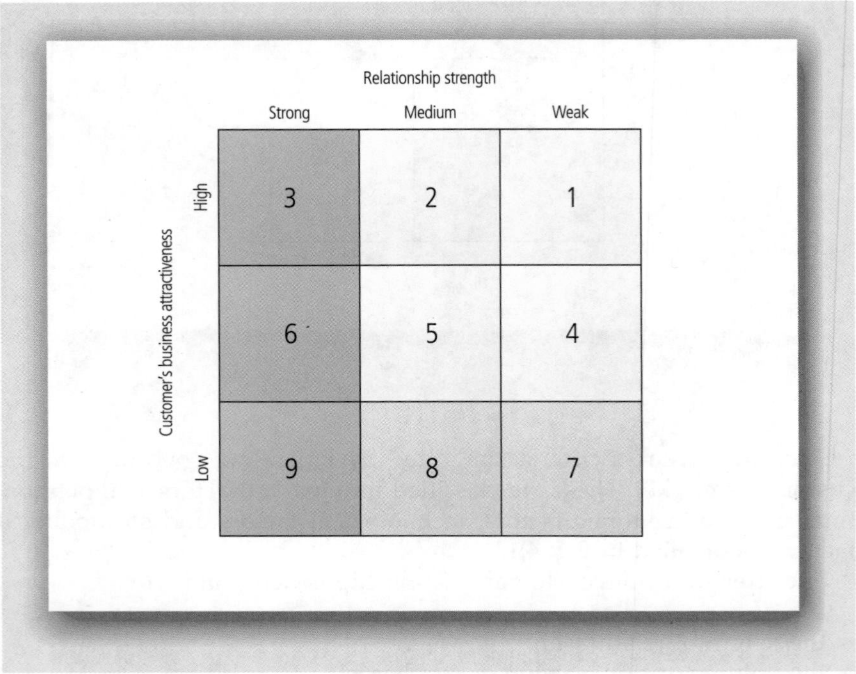

Figure 4.15
Fiocca's CPA model: step 2

Fiocca picks out three main strategies than can be used across the portfolio.

- Improve the strength of the relationship (cells 1, 2, 4 or 5).
- Hold the position (cells 3, 6 or 9).
- Withdraw (cells 7 and 8).

There have been a couple of published validations of this model,[11,12] but it has been criticized for its failure to consider customer profitability.

The CPA model presented by Shapiro et al. importantly incorporated the idea of cost-to-serve into the evaluation of customer profitability.[13] Figure 4.16 presents the matrix they developed.

Customers can be classified according to the price they pay and the costs incurred by the company to acquire and serve them. Four classes of customer are identified: carriage trade (often newly acquired customers who are costly to serve but pay a relatively high price), passive customers, aggressive customers and bargain-basement customers. The

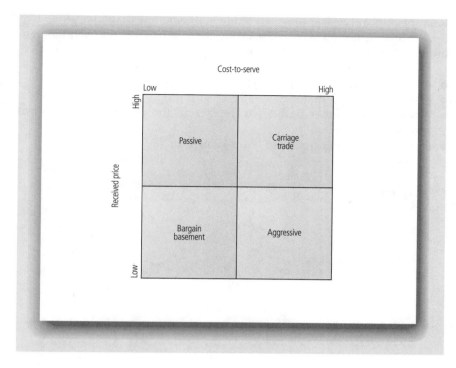

Figure 4.16
Customer
classification matrix
(Source: adapted
from Shapiro et al.[13])

important contribution from this work is that it recognizes that costs are not evenly distributed across the customer base. Some customers are more costly to win and serve and, if this is accompanied by a relatively low received price, the customer may be unprofitable. Figure 4.17 shows how costs can vary before the sale, in production, in distribution and after the sale.

Recently, Turnbull and Zolkiewski[14] developed a three-dimensional tool (Fig. 4.18) for conducting CPA. The dimensions they propose are cost-to-serve, net price and relationship value. The first two variables are adopted from the Shapiro model. Relationship value, the third dimension, allows for other strategic issues to be taken into account.

Presale costs	Production costs	Distribution costs	Postsale costs
Geographical location: close vs distant	Order size	Shipment consolidation	Training
Prospecting	Set-up time	Preferred transportation mode	Installation
Sampling	Scrap rate	Back-haul opportunity	Technical support
Human resource: management vs reps	Customization	Location: close vs distant	Repairs and maintenance
Service: design support, applications engineering	Order timing	Logistics support, e.g. field inventory	

Figure 4.17 How costs vary between customers

Relationship value is 'softer' or more judgemental than the other two dimensions. Among the questions considered when forming a judgement on relationship value are the following.

● Are the goods or services critical to the customer?
● Is the customer a major generator of volume for the supplier?
● Would the customer be hard to replace in the event of switching to another supplier?
● Does the customer generate cost savings for the supplier?

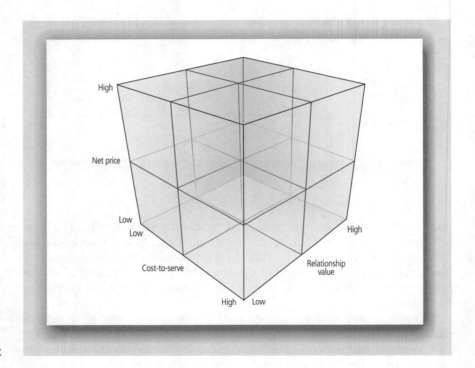

Figure 4.18
Turnbull and Zolkiewski's three-dimensional customer classification matrix

In some industries it has been impossible or too costly to find out how much it costs to win and serve customers. In this case CPA is based on revenue data only. Tesco (Case 4.3) is an illustration of this.

Sales forecasting

One major problem with all these models is that they generally take a historical or, at best, a present-day view of the customer portfolio. They identify those customers that are presently important for sales, profit or other strategic reasons. If management believes the future will be the same as the past, this presents no problem. However, if change is imminent, then there is a problem: none of the models attempts to forecast future sales to customers and the associated costs-to-serve.

Case 4.3

Customer Portfolio Analysis at Tesco

Tesco, the largest and most successful supermarket chain in the UK, has developed a CRM strategy that is the envy of many of its competitors. Principally a food retailer, in a mature market that has grown little in the past 20 years, Tesco realized that the only route to growth was taking market share from competitors. Consequently, the development of a CRM strategy was seen as being imperative.

In developing its CRM strategy. Tesco first undertook customer portfolio analysis (CPA) to examine its customer base. In a typical store it found that the top 100 customers were worth the same as the bottom 4000. It also found that the bottom 25 per cent of customers represented only 2 per cent of sales, and that the top 5 per cent of customers were responsible for 20 per cent of sales.

The results of this analysis were used to segment Tesco's customers and to develop its successful loyalty programmes.

Sales forecasting, some argue, is a waste of time, because the business environment is rapidly changing and unpredictable. Major world events such as terrorist attacks, war and drought, and market-based changes such as new products from competitors or high-visibility promotional campaigns can make any sales forecasts invalid.

However, several sales forecasting techniques can be applied. They fall into three major groups:

- **qualitative methods**:
  - customer surveys
  - sales team estimates
- **time-series methods**:
  - moving average
  - exponential smoothing
  - time-series decomposition
- **causal methods**:
  - leading indicators
  - regression models.

Qualitative methods are probably the most widely used forecasting methods. Customer surveys ask consumers or purchasing officers to give an opinion on what they are likely to buy in the forecasting period. This makes sense when customers forward-plan their purchasing. Data can be obtained by inserting a question into a customer satisfaction survey. For example, 'In the next 6 months are you likely to buy more, the same or less from us than in the current period?' And, 'If more, or less, what volume do you expect to buy from us?' Sometimes, third party organizations such as industry associations or trans-industry groups such as the Chamber of Commerce, the Institute of Directors or the

Confederation of British Industry collect data that indicate future buying intentions or proxies for intention, such as business confidence.

Sales team estimates can be useful when salespeople have built close relationships with their customers. A key account management team might be well placed to generate several individual forecasts from the team membership. These can be averaged or weighted in some way that reflects the estimator's closeness to the customer.

Operational CRM systems support the qualitative sales forecasting methods, in particular the sales team estimate. The CRM system takes into account the value of the sale, the probability of closing the sale and the anticipated period to closure. Many CRM systems also allow management to adjust the estimates of their sales team members, to allow for overly optimistic or pessimistic salespeople.

Time-series approaches take historical data and extrapolate them forward in a linear or curvilinear trend. This approach makes sense when there are historical sales data and the assumption can be safely made that the future will be the same as the past. The moving average method is the simplest of these. This takes sales in a number of previous periods and averages them. The averaging process reduces or eliminates random variation. The moving average is computed on successive periods of data, moving on one period at a time, as in Fig. 4.19. Moving averages based on different periods can be calculated on historical data to generate an accurate method.

A variation is to weight the more recent periods more heavily. The rationale is that more recent periods are better predictors. In producing an estimate for year 2002 in Fig. 4.19, one could weight the previous 4 years' sales performance by 0.4, 0.3, 0.2 and 0.1, respectively, to reach an estimate. This would generate a forecast of 5461. This approach is called exponential smoothing.

The decomposition method is applied when there is evidence of cyclical or seasonal patterns in the historical data. The method attempts to separate out four components of the time series: trend factor, cyclical factor, seasonal factor and random factor. The trend factor is the long-term direction of

Year	Sales volumes	2-year moving average	4-year moving average
1995	4830		
1996	4930		
1997	4870	4880	
1998	5210	4900	
1999	5330	5040	4960
2000	5660	5270	5085
2001	5440	5495	5267
2002		5550	5410

Figure 4.19
Sales forecasting using moving averages

the trend after the other three elements have been removed. The cyclical factor represents regular long-term recurrent influences on sales; seasonal influences generally occur within annual cycles.

It is sometimes possible to predict sales using leading indicators. A leading indicator is some contemporary activity or event that indicates that another activity or event will happen in the future. At a macro level, for example, housing starts are good predictors of future sales of kitchen furniture. At a micro level, when a credit-card customer calls into a contact centre to ask about the current rate of interest, this is a strong indicator that the customer will switch to another supplier in the future.

Regression models work by employing data on a number of predictor variables to estimate future demand. The variable being predicted is called the dependent variable; the variables being used as predictors are called independent variables. For example, if you wanted to predict demand for cars (the dependent variable) you might use data on population size, average disposable income, average car price for the category being predicted and average fuel price (the independent variables). The regression equation can be tested and validated on historical data before being adopted. New predictor variables can be substituted or added to see whether they improve the accuracy of the forecast. This can be a useful approach for predicting demand from a segment.

Customer portfolio toolkit

In addition to specifically designed CPA tools, several other tools are in common use for planning corporate strategy. These are very useful for CRM applications. These tools, however, operate at a company-specific level. This means that a CRM strategist would apply the tools to a specific company to help in the assessment of the customer's future value. The tools include:

- SWOT analysis
- PESTE analysis
- five-forces analysis
- BCG matrix analysis.

These are introduced here in brief. For a fuller report you are advised to refer to any basic corporate strategy or marketing strategy book. Five-forces and BCG matrix analyses have both been subject of considerable criticism.

SWOT and PESTE

SWOT is an acronym for strengths, weaknesses, opportunities and threats. SWOT analysis explores the internal environment (S and W) and the external environment (O and T). The internal (SW) audit looks for strengths and weaknesses in the business functions of sales, marketing, operations, finance and people management. It then looks cross-functionally for strengths and weaknesses in, for example, cross-functional processes (such as new product development) and organizational culture.

The external (OT) audit analyses the macro- and microenvironments in which the company operates. The macroenvironment includes a number of broad conditions that might impact upon a company. These conditions are identified by a PESTE analysis. PESTE is an acronym for political, economic, social, technological and environmental conditions. An analysis would try to pick out major conditions that impact on a business, as illustrated below.

- **Political environment**: demand for international air travel contracted as worldwide political stability was reduced after September 11, 2001.
- **Economic environment**: demand for mortgages falls when the economy enters recession.
- **Social environment**: as a population ages, demand for health care and residential homes increases.
- **Technological environment**: as more households become owners of computers, demand for Internet banking increases.
- **Environmental conditions**: as customers become more concerned about environmental quality, demand for more energy-efficient products increases.

The microenvironmental part of the external (OT) audit examines relationships between a company and its immediate external stakeholders: customers, suppliers, business partners and investors.

A CRM-oriented SWOT analysis would be searching for customers or potential customers that emerge well from the analysis. These would be customers that:

- possess relevant strengths to exploit the opportunities
- are overcoming weaknesses by partnering with other organizations to take advantage of opportunities
- are investing in turning around the company to exploit the opportunities
- are responding to external threats in their current markets by exploiting their strengths for diversification.

Five forces

The five-forces analysis was developed by Porter.[15] He claimed that the profitability of an industry, as measured by its return on capital employed relative to its cost of capital, was determined by five sources of competitive pressure. These five sources include three horizontal and two vertical conditions. The horizontal conditions are:

- competition within the established businesses in the market
- competition from potential new entrants
- competition from potential substitutes.

The vertical conditions reflect supply and demand chain considerations:

- the bargaining power of buyers
- the bargaining power of suppliers.

Porter's basic premise is that competitors in an industry will be more profitable if these five conditions are benign. For example, if buyers are very powerful, they can demand high levels of service and low prices, thus negatively influencing the profitability of the supplier. However, if barriers to entry are high, say because of large capital requirements or dominance of the market by very powerful brands, then current players will be relatively immune from new entrants and enjoy the possibility of better profits.

Why would a CRM strategist be interested in a five-forces evaluation of customers? Fundamentally, a financially healthy customer offers better potential for a supplier than a customer that is financially stressed. The analysis points to different CRM solutions.

- Customers in a profitable industry are more likely to be stable for the near term, and are better placed to invest in opportunities for the future. They therefore have stronger value potential. These are customers with whom a supplier would want to build an exclusive and well-protected relationship.
- Customers in a stressed industry might be looking for reduced cost inputs from their suppliers, or for other ways that they can add value to their offer to their own customers. A CRM-oriented supplier would be trying to find ways to serve this customer more effectively, perhaps by stripping out elements of the value proposition that are not critical, or by adding elements that enable the customer to compete more strongly.

BCG matrix

The Boston Consulting Group (BCG) matrix was designed to analyse a company's product portfolio with a view to drawing strategy prescriptions. The analysis takes into account two criteria, relative market share and market growth rate, to identify where profits and cash flow are earned. Figure 4.20 is a sample BCG matrix. The BCG believes that the best indicator of a market's attractiveness is its growth rate (hence the vertical axis of the matrix) and that the best indicator of competitive strength is relative market share (the horizontal axis). Relative market share, that is the market share of the business unit relative to the largest competitor, is claimed to improve the relative cost position due to the experience curve.

The matrix categorizes products in a portfolio into one of four boxes and prescribes certain strategies: milk the cows, invest in the stars, ditch the dogs and sort the question marks into products that you want to support as they become stars, and those that you expect to convert into dogs.

A balanced portfolio of products contains question marks, stars and cash cows. Cash cows generate the cash flow that supports the question marks. As the question marks grow their relative market share, and

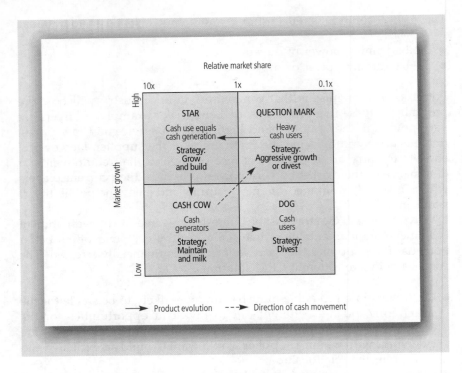

Figure 4.20
BCG matrix

become stars, they are establishing a position in the market that will eventually yield very strong positive cash flows. This happens when a leading product maintains that position in a mature market.

From a CRM perspective, a customer with a balanced portfolio of products of its own has greater lifetime potential for a supplier than a customer with an unbalanced portfolio. A company with no new products in the pipeline (these are the question marks) will struggle to remain viable when the existing cash cows dry up. This happens as competitors fight to win market share and substitutes emerge.

Activity-based costing

Many companies, particularly those in a B2B context, can trace revenues to customers. In a B2C environment, it is usually only possible to trace revenues to customers if the company operates a billing system requiring customer details, or if there is a membership scheme of some kind, such as a storecard or a loyalty programme, in place.

In a B2B context, revenues can be tracked in the sales and invoicing databases. Costs are an entirely different matter. If a company is to understand which of its customers is most profitable, it has to be able to trace costs as well as revenues to customers.

Costs vary from customer to customer, as we have seen in some of the portfolio models earlier in this chapter. There are variances within several categories of cost:

- **customer acquisition costs**: some customers require considerable sales effort to shift them from prospect to first-time customer status: more sales calls, visits to reference customer sites, free samples, engineering advice, guarantees that switching costs will be met by the vendor
- **terms of trade**: price discounts, advertising and promotion support, slotting allowances (cash paid to retailers for shelf-space), extended invoice due-dates
- **customer service costs**: handling queries, claims and complaints, demands on salesperson and contact centre, small order sizes, high order frequency, just-in-time delivery, part-load shipments, breaking bulk for delivery to multiple sites
- **working capital costs**: carrying inventory for the customer, cost of credit.

Traditional product-based or general ledger costing systems do not allow this level of analysis. Product costing systems track material, labour and energy costs to products, often comparing actual to standard costs. They do not, however, cover the customer-facing activities of marketing, sales and service. General ledger costing systems do track costs across all parts of the business, but are normally too highly aggregated to establish which customers or segments are responsible for generating those costs.

Activity-based costing (ABC) is an approach to costing that splits costs into two groups: volume-based costs and order-related costs. Volume-related (product-related) costs are variable against the size of the order, but fixed per unit for any order and any customer. Material and direct-labour costs are examples. Order-related (customer-related) costs vary according to the product and process requirements of each particular customer.

Imagine two retail customers, each purchasing the same volumes of product from a manufacturer. Customer 1 makes no product or process demands. The sales revenue is $5000; the gross margin for the vendor is $1000. Customer 2 is a different story: customized product, special overprinted outer packaging, just-in-time delivery to three sites, provision of point-of-sale material, sale or return conditions, and discounted price. Not only that, but customer 2 spends a lot of time agreeing these terms and conditions with a salesperson who has had to call three times before closing the sale. The sales revenue is $5000, but after accounting for product and process costs to meet the demands of this particular customer, the margin retained by the vendor is $250. Other things being equal, customer 1 is four times as valuable as customer 2.

Whereas conventional cost accounting practices report what was spent, ABC reports what the money was spent *doing*. Whereas the conventional general ledger approach to costing identifies resource costs such as payroll, equipment and materials, the ABC approach shows what was being done when those costs were incurred. Figure 4.21 shows how an ABC view of costs in an insurance company's claims processing department gives an entirely different picture to the conventional view.[16]

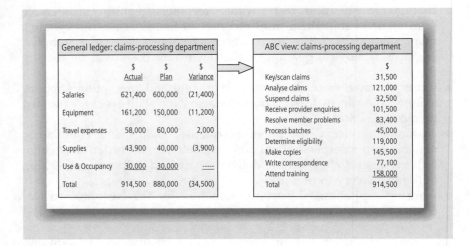

Figure 4.21
Activity-based
costing in a claims-
processing
department
(Source: adapted
from Cokins[16])

Activity-based costing gives the manager of the claims-processing department a much clearer idea of what activities create cost. The next question from a CRM perspective is 'which customers create the activity?' Put another way, which customers are the cost drivers? If you were to examine the cost item 'Analyse claims: $121 000', and find that 80 per cent of the claims were made by drivers under the age of 20, you would have a clear understanding of the customer group that was creating that activity cost for the business.

Customer relationship management needs ABC, because of its over-riding goal of generating profitable relationships with customers. Unless there is a costing system in place to trace costs to customers, CRM cannot deliver its promise.

The assumption is often made in B2B contexts that large accounts are profitable accounts. ABC tells us that this is not necessarily so. It is not uncommon to find that small customers are unprofitable because the process costs they generate are greater than the margins they generate. Similarly, many companies find that their largest accounts are also unprofitable. Why? Large accounts create more work, more activity. The work of managing the account might require the services of a large number of people: sales manager, customer service executive and applications engineer among others. The customer might demand customized product, delivery in less than container loads, just-in-time, extended due dates for payment and, ultimately, volume discounts on price. Very often it is the mid-range sales volume customers that are the most profitable.

When Kanthal, a Swedish manufacturer of electrical resistance heating elements, introduced ABC, they found that only 40 per cent of their customers were profitable. Two of their top three sales volume customers were among the most unprofitable. The most profitable 5 per cent of customers generated 150 per cent of profits. The least profitable 10 per cent lost 120 per cent of profit. The challenge for Kanthal was deciding what to do with the unprofitable customers.[17]

Overall, ABC serves CRM strategy in a number of ways.

- When combined with revenue figures, it tells you the absolute and relative levels of profit generated by each customer, segment or cohort.
- It guides you towards actions that can be taken to return customers to profit (in Kanthal's case, this involved negotiating new prices for non-standard product, and re-engineering cost-generating processes).
- It helps to prioritize and direct customer acquisition, development and retention strategies.
- It helps to establish whether customization, and other forms of value creation for customers, will pay off.

Activity-based costing sometimes justifies management's confidence in the Pareto principle, otherwise known as the 80:20 rule. This rule suggests that 80 per cent of profits come from 20 per cent of customers. ABC tells you which customers fall into the important 20 per cent. Research generally supports the 80:20 rule. For example, one report from Coopers and Lybrand found that in the retail industry the top 4 per cent of customers account for 29 per cent of profits, the next 26 per cent of customers account for 55 per cent of profits and the remaining 70 per cent account for only 16 per cent of profits.

Lifetime value

Lifetime value is an important theme in CRM. The LTV measures a customer's profit-generation for a company.

A customer's LTV can be defined as the present-day value of all net margins earned in a relationship with a customer. Historical net margins are compounded up to today's value. Future net margins are discounted back to today's value. Estimates of LTV potential look to the future only.

The focus on net margins rather than gross margins is because of the necessary inclusion of cost-to-serve considerations in computing customer profitability. Companies that do not have the costing processes in place to trace costs to customers cannot use net margin data. They must work either with gross margin or sales revenue data.

For most companies, the concern will be to identify those customers or segments that have the highest LTV potential. They are unconcerned with the past. What matters is the future.

Research by Reichheld and Sasser indicates why it is important to look forward to compute LTV.[18] Their data suggest that profit margins rise tend to accelerate over time, as shown in Fig. 4.22. This has four causes. First, revenues from customers tend to grow over time, as they buy more. In the credit-card example in Fig. 4.22, users tend to grow their balances over time as they become more relaxed about using their card for an increasing range of purchases. Secondly, existing customers are cheaper to serve, because the supplier and customer understand each other. For example, customers do not make demands on the company that it cannot

Profit (loss) per customer over time ($)						
Service	Year					
	0	1	2	3	4	5
Credit card	(51)	30	42	44	49	55
Industrial laundry		144	166	192	222	256
Industrial distribution		45	99	121	144	168
Auto servicing		25	35	70	88	88

Figure 4.22
Profit from
customers over time

satisfy. Similarly, companies do not communicate offers that have little or no value to customers. Thirdly, they generate referrals. Lexus UK, for example, believes that every retained and delighted customer generates £600 000 of referral business. Fourthly, they pay higher prices than new customers. This is partly because they are not offered the discounts that are often employed to win new customers, and partly because they are less sensitive to price offers from other potential suppliers because they are satisfied with their experience.

The computation of LTV potential is very straightforward in principle. Several pieces of information are needed. For an existing customer, you need to know the following information.

● What is the probability that the customer will buy products and services from the company in the future, period-by-period?
● What will be the gross margins on those purchases, period-by-period?
● What will be the cost of serving the customer, period-by-period?

For new customers an additional piece of information is needed.

● What is the cost of acquiring the customer?

Finally, to bring future margins back to today's value, another question needs to be answered for both existing and new customers.

● What discount rate should be applied to future net margins? (Figure 4.23 demonstrates the impact that discount rate has on customer value.)

Computation of a meaningful LTV estimate requires companies to be able to forecast customer buying behaviour, product and service costs and prices, the costs of capital (for determining the discount rate), and the costs of acquiring and retaining customers. This is very demanding, especially at the level of the individual customer.

1. Undiscounted profit earned over 5 years:

Year	
0	−$50
1	+$30
2	+$40
3	+$55
4	+$72
5	+$88
	$235

2. Discounted profit earned over 5 years (15% discount rate)

Year		
0		−$50.00
1	+$30 ÷ 1.15 =	$26.09
2	+$40 ÷ 1.15^2 =	$30.25
3	+$55 ÷ 1.15^3 =	$36.16
4	+$72 ÷ 1.15^4 =	$41.17
5	+$88 ÷ 1.15^5 =	$43.76
		$127.43

The net present value of 5-years profit earned from this customer is $127.43

Figure 4.23
Impact of discount rate on LTV

A number of companies have developed models that produce approximate LTV estimates. US Bancorp, for example, calculates a customer profitability metric called customer relationship value (CRV), in which they use historical product ownership and use to generate 'propensity to buy' indices. Overhead costs are not factored into the computation. Within their customer base, they have been able to identify four CRV segments, each having different value, cost, attrition and risk profiles:

- top tier: 11 per cent of customers
- threshold: next 22 per cent
- fence-sitters: next 39 per cent
- value destroyers: bottom 28 per cent.

Each of these segments is treated to different value propositions and customer management programmes: product offers, lending decisions, fee waivers, channel options and retention efforts. For situations where the cost of generating accurate LTV data is thought not to be prohibitive, Berger and Nasr have developed a number of mathematical models that can be used in LTV estimation.[19]

LTV can be estimated at the level of the individual customer, customer group (market segment) or cohort. A cohort of customers is a group that has some characteristic or set of characteristics in common. These might be customers recruited in a single year, or recruited though a single campaign or channel. This type of analysis is useful, for example, to find out whether certain channels are more effective or more efficient at recruiting high-value customers. A European motoring organization knows that it costs an average of $105 to recruit a new member. However, recruitment costs vary across channels. The organization's member-get-member (MGM) referral scheme costs $66, the organization's direct response TV campaign costs $300 and door-drops cost $210 per newly acquired member. The MGM scheme is most cost-effective at customer acquisition, but if these customers churn at a high rate and cost significantly more to serve, they may in fact be less valuable than customers generated at higher initial cost.[iii]

Figure 4.24 shows how to compute LTV for a cohort of customers. In year 0, the company spent $10 million in promotional campaigns to generate new customers. The result was 100 000 new customers added to the customer base at a cost of $100 per customer.

Year	$ Profit per customer	$ Net present value at 15% discount	Customer retention rate(%)	No. of customers	$ Total annual profit
0	−100			100,000	−10,000,000
1	50	43.48	60	60,000	2,608,800
2	70	52.93	70	42,000	2,223,062
3	100	65.75	75	31,500	2,071,125
4	140	80.00	80	25,200	2,016,000
5	190	94.53	85	21,420	2,024,776
6	250	108.23	90	19,278	2,086,364
7	320	120.30	92	17,736	2,133,654
8	400	130.72	94	16,672	2,179,346
9	450	127.84	95	15,838	2,024,744
10	500	123.15	96	15,204	1,872,372

Figure 4.24
Computing cohort value

In year 1 the company lost 40 per cent of these new customers, but the remaining 60 per cent each generated $50 contribution to profit. If this is discounted at 15 per cent, in year 0's currency the contribution is worth $43.48. In year 2, the retention rate rises from 60 to 70 per cent, and each of the remaining customers contributes $70 ($52.93 at discounted rate) to profit. You can see from the right-hand column in Fig. 4.24 that it takes nearly 5 years to recover the investment in acquiring this cohort. The data demonstrate a number of well-established phenomena. First, profit per customer rises over time, for reasons set out earlier in this chapter. Secondly, customer retention rate rises over time.

It is feasible to use data such as these to manage the business for improved profitability. Several strategies are available.

● Improve customer retention rate in the early periods. This will produce a larger number of customers to generate higher profits in the later periods.

[iii] In fact, customers acquired through the MGM referral scheme remain members longer, buy more and also generate word-of-mouth referrals.

- Increase the profit earned per customer by:
  - reducing cost-to-serve
  - selling additional products and services.
- Become better at customer acquisition by:
  - using more cost-effective recruitment channels
  - better qualification of prospects. Customers who defect early on perhaps should have not been recruited in the first place.

Strategically significant customers

The goal of this entire CPA process is to identify those customers that will be strategically significant for the company's future (see Case 4.4). As a result of the process you should be able to identify a number strategically significant customers (SSCs), as follows.

- **High future LTV customers**: these customers will contribute significantly to the company's profitability in the future.
- **High volume customers**: these customers might not generate much profit, but they might be of strategic value because of their absorption of fixed costs, and the economies of scale they generate to keep unit costs low.
- **Benchmark customers**: these are customers that other customers follow. For example, Japan Coin Company supplies the hardware and software for Coca-Cola's vending operation. While they might not make much margin from that relationship, it has allowed them to gain access to many other markets. 'If we are good enough for Coke, we are good enough for you', is the implied promise. Some IT companies create 'reference sites' at some of their more demanding customers.
- **Inspirations**: these are customers who bring about improvement in the supplier's business. They may identify new applications for a product,

Case 4.4

Strategically Significant Customers at Barclays Bank

Barclays is a leading UK based bank with global operations. As part of the bank's CRM strategy, it undertook customer portfolio analysis to identify which retail segments were most strategically significant. The analysis found that customers within the 25–35 year age group, who were professionally employed, and who had a mortgage and or credit card product were most strategically significant. These were the bank's most profitable customers.

The bank also found that this segment represented the highest potential lifetime value (LTV) for the bank, 12 per cent greater than any other segment. LTV is derived from the bank's estimates of future income from fees, interest and other charges over their lifetime as a customer.

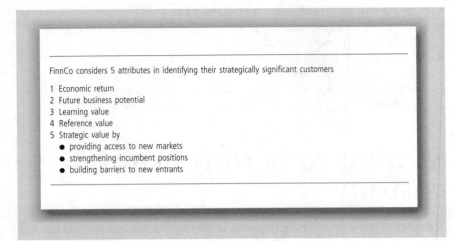

FinnCo considers 5 attributes in identifying their strategically significant customers

1 Economic return
2 Future business potential
3 Learning value
4 Reference value
5 Strategic value by
   ● providing access to new markets
   ● strengthening incumbent positions
   ● building barriers to new entrants

Figure 4.25
Strategically
significant
customers at FinnCo

product improvements or cost reductions. They may complain loudly and make unreasonable demands.

● **Door openers**: these are customers that allow the supplier to gain access to a new market. This may be done for no initial profit, but with a view to proving credentials for further expansion. This may be particularly important if crossing cultural boundaries, say between west and east.
● **Technology partners**: these customers formally co-operate with the supplier to improve the performance of the supplier's technology in return for some agreed advantages. There may be sharing of resources (people, money, knowledge) to the common goal.

One company, a Scandinavian processor of timber, has identified five major customer groups that are strategically significant (Fig. 4.25).

Customer portfolio strategies

This sort of analysis pays off when it drives the development of different strategies for different customers in the portfolio. There are several core strategies.

● **Protect the relationship**: this makes sense when the customer is strategically significant and attractive to competitors. The creation of exit barriers is discussed in the review of customer retention strategies in Chapter 9.
● **Re-engineer the relationship**: in this case, the customer is currently unprofitable but could be converted to profit if costs were trimmed from the relationship. This might mean reducing or automating service levels, or servicing customers through lower cost channels. In the

banking industry, Datamonitor reports the transaction costs detailed in Fig. 4.26. It cost 120 times more to service a customer in a branch than it does online. An Australian electricity company found that its average annual margin per customer is $60. It costs $13 to serve a customer who pays by credit card, but only 64 cents to service a direct debit customer. Each customer moved to the lower cost channel therefore produces a transaction cost saving of more than $12, which increases the average customer value by 20 per cent. Re-engineering a relationship requires attention to the activities that create costs in the relationship (see Case 4.5).

- **Enhance the relationship**: as in the strategy above, the goal is to migrate the customer up the value ladder. In this case it is done by increasing your share of customer spend on the category, and by identifying up-selling and cross-selling opportunities.
- **Harvest the relationship**: when your share of customer spend is stable, and you do not want to invest more resources in customer development, you may feel that the customer has reached maximum value. Under these conditions you may wish to harvest, that is, optimize cash flow from the customer with a view to spending the cash to develop other customers. This may be particularly appealing if the customer is in a declining market, has a high cost-to-serve or has a high propensity-to-switch to competitors.
- **End the relationship**: sacking customers is generally anathema to sales and marketing people. However, when the customer shows no sign of making a significant contribution in the future it may be the best option. Strategies for sacking customers are discussed in Chapter 9.
- **Win back the customer**: sometimes customers volunteer to take some or all of their business to other suppliers. If they are not strategically significant, it makes sense to let them go. However, when the customer is important, you may need to develop and implement win-back strategies. The starting point must be to understand why they took their business away.
- **Start a relationship**: once you have identified a prospect as having potential strategic significance for the future, you need to develop an acquisition plan to recruit the customer onto the value ladder. This issue is examined in Chapter 8.

Channel	Cost ($)
In-branch teller	1.80
ATM	0.60
Telephone	0.45
PC banking	0.30
Internet banking	0.015

Figure 4.26
Bank transaction processing costs (Source: Datamonitor, 1999)

Case 4.5

Sales support varies by segment at Syngenta

Syngenta, a leading global agribusiness organization, sought to segment the global market for crop protection products, such as herbicides and pesticides. Using qualitative and quantitative data Syngenta identified four segments amongst farmers.

1 'Professionals'. These are large spenders and keen to trial new technologies
2 'Progressives'. These have large landholdings and are early adopters of new technologies
3 'Traditionalists' are older and spend the least on crop protection products
4 'Operators' are pessimistic about farming and have difficulty in keeping up to date with new technologies and farming practices.

Syngenta now uses these four segments to guide all of its marketing activities. Service levels vary between segments. Face-to-face communications are available to Professionals and Progressives and direct mail used for Traditionalists and Operators.

Summary

In this chapter you have learned about customer portfolio analysis (CPA). The CPA process attempts to assess the value potential of each customer or customer group. It does this by estimating the revenues each customer group will generate and the costs that the company will incur in acquiring and serving those customers. Several disciplines help. Market segmentation is widely practised by marketing management. For CPA purposes, there needs to be a clear focus on customer value. A number of sales forecasting techniques can also be used to estimate what customers are likely to buy in the future. Lifetime value models can import sales forecast data to evaluate a customer's future worth to a company.

The CPA process tends to differ from B2C to B2B contexts. Several portfolio analysis tools have been developed specifically for B2B contexts. Activity-based costing can be used in B2B contexts to quantify the costs incurred in acquiring and serving customers. These need to be taken into account to understand accurately the profit contribution of a customer. Customer portfolio analysis in the B2C context tends to use data mining tools on large volumes of aggregated customer data.

The purpose of all this analysis is to disaggregate potential and current customers into subsets so that different value propositions and relationship management strategies can be developed for each group.

References

1. Levitt, T. (1960) Marketing myopia. *Harvard Business Review*, July/August, pp. 45–56.
2. Day, G. S. (1986) *Analysis for Strategic Market Decisions*. West Publishing.
3. Saunders, J. (1994) Cluster analysis. In: Hooley, G. J. and Hussey, M. K. (eds). *Quantitative Methods in Marketing*. Dryden Press, pp. 13–28.
4. Berry, M. J. A. and Linoff, G. S. (2000) *Data Mining: The Art and Science of Customer Relationship Management*. New York: John Wiley.
5. Brand, E. and Gerritsen, R. Decision Trees. Available online at http://www.dbmsmag.com/9807m05.html
6. Zolkiewski, J. and Turnbull, P. (1999) *A Review of Customer Relationships Planning: Does Customer Profitability and Portfolio Analysis Provide the Key to Successful Relationship Management?* MSM Working Paper Series. University of Manchester Institute of Science and Technology.
7. Ford, D. (2002) *Understanding Business Marketing and Purchasing* (3rd edn). Thompson Learning.
8. Ford, D. (1997) *Understanding Business Markets: Interaction, Relationships and Networks* (2nd edn). Dryden Press.
9. Cunningham, M. T and Homse, E. (1982) Controlling the marketing–purchasing interface: resource development and organisational implications. *Industrial Marketing and Purchasing*, Vol. 1(2), pp. 3–27.
10. Fiocca, R. (1982) Account portfolio analysis for strategy development. *Industrial Marketing Management*, Vol. 11, pp. 53–62.
11. Turnbull, P. W. and Topcu, S. (1994) Customers' profitability in relationship life-cycles. Proceedings of the 10th IMP Conference, Groningen, The Netherlands.
12. Yorke, D. A. and Droussiotis, G. (1994) The use of customer portfolio theory: an empirical survey. *Journal of Business and Industrial Marketing*, Vol. 9 (3), pp. 6–18.
13. Shapiro, B. P., Rangan, K. V., Moriarty, R. T. and Ross, E. B. (1987) Manage customers for profits (not just sales). *Harvard Business Review*, September/October, pp. 101–8.
14. Turnbull, P. and Zolkiewski, J. (1997) Profitability in customer portfolio planning. In: Ford, D. (ed.). *Understanding Business Markets* (2nd edn). Dryden Press, pp. 305–25.
15. Porter, M. E. (1980) *Competitive Strategy: Techniques for Analysing Industries and Competitors*. Free Press.
16. Cokins, G. (1996) *Activity-based Cost Management: Making it Work*. McGraw-Hill.
17. Kaplan, R. S. (1989) Kanthal, A., Harvard Business School Case Study No. 9–190–002.
18. Reichheld, F. and Sasser, W. E., Jr (1990) Zero defections: quality comes to the services. *Harvard Business Review*, September/October, pp. 105–11.
19. Berger, P. D. and Nasr, N. I. (1998) Customer lifetime value: marketing models and applications. *Journal of Interactive Marketing*, Vol. 12(1), Winter, pp. 17–30.

Chapter 5
Customer intimacy

By the end of the chapter, you will understand:

1 that the purpose of customer intimacy is to get to know customers better so that more intelligent CRM decisions can be made
2 the importance of high-quality data to CRM performance
3 that the customer database is the foundation for the execution of CRM strategy
4 the issues that need to be considered in developing a customer database
5 how concerned public policy makers are about data protection and privacy issues.

Introduction

In this chapter we discuss the importance of developing an intimate understanding of customers. Customer intimacy is the second of the primary phases of the customer relationship management (CRM) value chain (Fig. 5.1). Without that degree of understanding, it is impossible to create and deliver value propositions that you are confident meet customer requirements better than those of competitors. Customer insight enables more intelligent CRM decisions to be made.

For CRM to achieve its end goal of customer profitability, high-quality data need to be made available to those involved in implementing CRM at the sales, marketing and service interfaces, and to those who are responsible for developing the overall CRM strategy. Proficiency at acquiring, enhancing, storing, distributing and using customer data is critical to CRM performance. Poor-quality data produces poor-quality decisions.

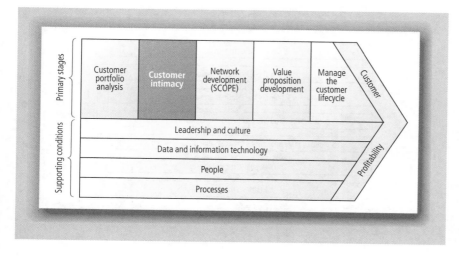

Figure 5.1
CRM value chain

The customer database is the foundation for the execution of CRM strategy.

Most databases share a common structure of files, records and fields (also called tables, rows and columns). Files (tables) hold information on a single topic such as customers, products and transactions. Each file (table) contains a number of records (rows). In the customer database, each record (row) is a unique customer. Each record (row) contains a number of elements of data such as the customer's name, address, gender, date of birth and telephone number. These elements are arranged in a common set of fields (columns) across the table. A modern customer database therefore resembles a spreadsheet.

Building a customer database

There are seven major steps in building a customer database, as shown in Fig. 5.2.[1]

Define the database functions

Customer databases generally serve two functions: operational and analytical.

The operational function of the database is to help in the everyday running of the business. For example:

- a telecoms customer service representative (CSR) needs to access a customer record when she receives a telephone query
- a hotel receptionist needs access to a guest's history so that she can reserve the preferred type of room: smoking or non-smoking, standard or de-luxe

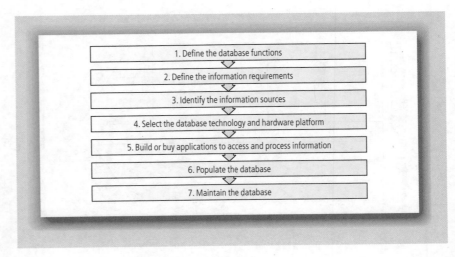

Figure 5.2
Building a customer database (based on O'Connor and Galvin[1])

1. Define the database functions
2. Define the information requirements
3. Identify the information sources
4. Select the database technology and hardware platform
5. Build or buy applications to access and process information
6. Populate the database
7. Maintain the database

- a salesperson needs to check a customer's payment history to find out whether the account has reached the maximum credit limit.

The analytical function of a database is to enable companies to optimize the value that they create for and from customers. It enables them to interrogate the data before making decisions. For example:

- the telecoms company might want to target a retention offer to customers who are signalling an intention to switch to a different supplier
- the hotel company might want to promote a weekend break to customers who have indicated their complete delight in previous customer satisfaction surveys
- the sales representative might want to compute his customer's profitability, given the level of service that is being provided.

Customer data are typically organized into two subsets, reflecting these two functions. Operational data reside in an online transaction processing (OLTP) database, and analytical data in an online analytical processing (OLAP) database. The information in the OLAP database is normally a summarized extract of the OLTP database, enough to perform the analytical tasks. The analytical database might also draw in data from other internal sources, such as billing data.

Define the information requirements

The fundamental issue that companies have to ask is: what information do we need in our database so that we can intelligently develop and implement our CRM strategy? The answer depends on the sorts of operational and analytical decisions that need to be made as the strategy is designed and implemented. Some important questions follow.

- Who are our current customers?
- What are their contact details?
- What do they buy?
- What is their payment history?
- Who else do they buy from?
- What are our customers' requirements, expectations and preferences across all components of the value proposition, including product, service, channel, and communication?
- Which prospects should we target? What does it cost to recruit new customers? Do these costs vary across different channels?
- What does it cost to serve customers?
- Which customers should we develop? What offers should we make to these customers?
- Which customers should we retain? Which should we sack?

The people best placed to answer the question 'what information is needed?' are those who interact with customers, and those who have to make strategic CRM decisions. For example, a direct marketer who is planning an event-based campaign might want to know response rates to previous mailings broken down by customer group, the content of those offers, sales achieved by these mailings and the number of items returned unopened. She would also want to know the names and addresses of her selected target, their preferred method of communication (Mail? E-mail? Phone?), their preferred form of salutation (First name? Mr? Ms?) and the types of offer that have been successful in the past. She might have a particular offer in mind and want to identify and profile the customers most likely to respond. Operational and analytical needs such as these define the contents of the database.

A useful distinction can be made between 'need-to-know' and 'like-to-know'; that is, between information needed for operational and analytical purposes, and information that might be useful at some future point. Given the costs of developing and maintaining the database, companies need to be rigorous in screening data requirements.

With the advent of packaged CRM applications, much of this design work has been done by the software vendors. Although it is unlikely that a generic CRM application will have all of the information required for a specific company's CRM efforts, the availability of industry-specific applications, with their corresponding industry-specific data models, allows for a much closer fit. The database design process for both operational and analytical CRM applications becomes one of implementing exceptions that have been overlooked by the generic industry model. Some CRM vendors have also designed the extract, transform and load processes to move information from OLTP to OLAP databases.

Customer information fields

Within the CRM databases, several fields (columns) of information about customers are important: contact data, contact history, transactional history, intentions, needs, benefits, expectations, preferences and benchmarks.

Contact data: who is the main contact (name), and who else (other names) is involved in buying decisions. What are their roles: decision-maker? Buyer? Influencer? Initiator? Gatekeeper? What are the customer's invoice addresses, delivery addresses, phone numbers, fax numbers, e-mail addresses, street addresses, postal addresses?

Contact history. Outbound: who has communicated with the customer, when, about what, and with what outcome? **Inbound**: with whom has the customer initiated communication? When, about what and with what outcome?

Transactional history: what items has the customer bought, and when? What has been offered to the customer but not been bought?

Intentions: whereas 'history' looks backwards, 'intentions' looks forwards. What does the customer intend to buy? It is helpful to attach probabilities to future purchases, particularly as salespeople guide customers through their buying process towards closure. Is there a 10 per cent, 20 per cent . . . 90 per cent chance of making a sale? Alternatively, you could attach labels such as 'possible' or 'probable', or colours such as red, amber and green.

Intentions describe not only individual purchase possibilities, but also the broader plans of your customer. In a business-to-business (B2B) context, if your customer is planning to modify an existing product, launch a new product, supply a new segment of customers or enter new geographical markets, this will almost certainly have implications for your business. Plans of this kind signal a 'new task' buy, one that the customer has not made before, or a 'modified re-buy' where the customer changes one or more parts of their buying process. Perhaps they will develop a new specification or put together a new shortlist of possible suppliers; they may request proposals from this shortlist, set a new price limit or request technical input to help them with the development process.

Needs: the word 'need' implies a deficit of something. A manufacturer needs raw materials for its operations; it needs a logistics system to ensure orders are fulfilled on time, in full and with no error. Without these it cannot remain in business. In a business-to-consumer (B2C) context, needs can be thought of as 'the requirements of a particular social life'.[2] A 15-year old might need a skateboard and a mini-disc player to remain a credible member of his chosen social group.

To understand needs you have to understand the customer's reasons for buying. Purchasing motivations can be split into 'because of' and 'in order to' motivations.

- 'Because of' motivations are linked to some prefigurative force. The motivation to buy or consume is driven by some pre-existing condition. For example, a company buys spare parts for its equipment because of a history of down-time in operations.
- 'In order to' motivations have a future perspective. Purchasing behaviours are performed now in order to achieve some future condition. A private individual might buy a second home in order to enjoy the tranquillity of its rural location.

If you understand the source of and content of the customer's needs you are much better placed to serve them. When a need is driven by a problem, the size of the problem determines the significance of the need. For this reason, information about needs should be accompanied by information about the problem that has given rise to the need. For example, a consumer may have suffered frequent breakdowns with their previous car, making them very mindful of the need for reliability with the next purchase.

Benefits: customers buy products to experience the benefits they create. For example, one customer might buy from you because of your consistent product quality, which enables them to run their manufacturing processes with fewer disruptions; another might buy the same product because of its variety of applications, thereby eliminating the requirement to maintain and manage complex inventory. These customers have different needs that are met by the benefits they find in your products. Some companies find it helpful to produce an exhaustive checklist of the benefits that customers experience. They can then note which benefits are particularly valued by each customer.

Expectations: expectations act as comparison standards when the customer has used or consumed your product.

There have been a number of attempts to classify expectations. Miller, for example, produced a four-level hierarchy:[3]

- the ideal level: 'what can be'
- the predicted level: 'what will be'
- the minimum tolerable: 'what must be'
- the deserved level: 'what should be'. This is the level that customers think is equitable or fair given what they have invested in finding and buying the product.

Parasuraman and his colleagues suggested that customer expectations fall within a zone of tolerance, ranging from 'what must be' (minimum tolerable) to 'what can be' (desired level).[4] Woodruff's group of researchers suggested that customers are willing to accept a level of performance that falls within a zone of indifference. This zone ranges around the customer's judgement of what is a reasonable expectation of the supplier.[5] Oliver integrated these levels and zones of expectation into the framework shown in Fig. 5.3.[6]

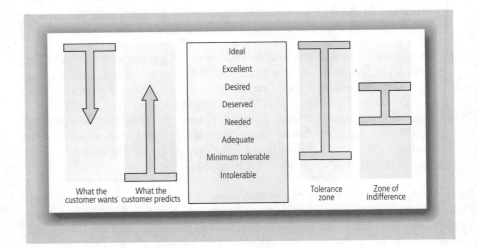

Figure 5.3
Customer expectations hierarchy (Source: Oliver[6])

The figure suggests that customer expectations can be classified in a number of ways. What customers **want** ranges from what they 'need' to what they regard as 'ideal'. What customers **predict** they will experience is generally set at a lower level of expectation from the intolerable to the desired.

Customer expectations may be the outcome of a number of influences. Clearly, previous experience with your company and your competitors can be important. Promises made by your salespeople and service representatives and in your advertising can be influential. Customers' needs may be active in forming expectations. If the customer needs spare parts to avoid down-time in operations, their expectations will surely fall within the zone of indifference. As long as there are sufficient parts to ensure continuity of production then they will probably be satisfied.

Word-of-mouth is another influence on expectations. Referrals or recommendations from friends and colleagues are particularly influential because of the impartiality and independence of the source. If expectations are then underperformed, the future buying behaviour of both the referrer and the referred may be at risk.[7]

This body of research into expectations is important for a number of lessons it provides CRM practitioners.

- Customers may use a number of reference points to evaluate the performance of a supplier: ideal, desired, deserved and adequate, for example. From a CRM perspective it is important to understand which level of expectations is operating. In one unpublished study, customers of a chain of auto service stations were asked about their car servicing expectations. Most customers said they expected to have their car serviced within 2 days of calling for an appointment (this expectation was based on the norm for the industry). Another group of customers said they expected their cars to be collected at the end of their working days, serviced overnight and delivered to their homes in time for the morning commute. Clearly, this expectation was based on a view of what was 'ideal'. If CRM practitioners are to understand and meet customer expectations it may be necessary to conduct fundamental research into customer expectations. Some customers may be able to identify different expectation standards. For example, a customer may feel that it is adequate for an order to be fulfilled within 48 hours, but that the ideal would be overnight replenishment.
- Expectations change over time. If your industry standard has been order fulfilment within 48 hours and one of your competitors introduces just-in-time replenishment, customer expectations are likely to change. What used to delight customers last year may be the norm this year.
- It is important to understand the focus or the content of the expectation. Suppliers need to know the attributes of their offer that are subject to customer expectations. These attributes may be objective or subjective. A personal computer (PC) brand expects its component suppliers to supply defect-free parts. It therefore selects suppliers that manufacture to Six Sigma standards.[i] A bank customer might be more subjective, having expectations of courteous service, knowledgeable employees and convenient ATM locations.
- Customers usually have expectations of a number of attributes. Not all of these attributes are equally important. For example, a hotel guest may expect the room to be quiet and the TV to receive CNN. The room expectation is a 'must be' expectation. It is a critical attribute. The TV expectation is a desired attribute but not critical. Practitioners of CRM must understand what is important and what is not important to customers.

---

[i] Six Sigma was Motorola's quality policy when it won the Malcolm Baldrige national quality award in 1988. Six Sigma sets defect tolerance levels at a maximum of 3.4 defects per million opportunities.

- Expectations act as the basis for satisfaction judgements. In general, if expectations have been met you can expect the customer to be satisfied. An exception is when the customer's expectations are at the bottom of the hierarchy and fall into the intolerable category. Customers would rarely say, 'I expected your service to be appalling. My expectations have been met, it was appalling and I am therefore satisfied!'
- Suppliers need to understand the limits to each customer's tolerance zone and zone of indifference. Customers are likely to vary in their tolerance levels, for a number of reasons. Some customers are more risk averse, for example, and are unable to tolerate large variances from expectation. It is also important to understand the customer's context. When the context is important to the customer, the expectations are likely to be firmer. A prospective father-in-law booking a hotel for a wedding reception is more likely to have highly rigorous expectations than the same person booking a casual table in the restaurant at the same hotel.

Preferences: it is helpful to understand customer preferences. What is the preferred medium of communication: mail, telephone, e-mail, etc.? If it is e-mail, is plain text or HTML preferred? What is the preferred salutation? And the preferred contact time and location? Customers may prefer you to contact them by phone for some communications (e.g. an urgent product recall), by mail for others (e.g. invoicing) and face-to-face for other reasons (e.g. news about new products). Figure 5.4 shows the results of some research into customer preferences. When a customer's preferences are employed in CRM applications, it may be taken as evidence that the company really does know the customer well.

Benchmarks: it is also useful to understand how customers form judgements about your company's performance.

Customers will often use some form of informal benchmarking process in which they compare your performance with the performance of others. They may compare you with others in your industry, or laterally against performance in the other industries, as the following illustrations show.

	In writing	Phone	E-mail
When sending a bill	90	6	1
To advise special offers	75	10	6
When sending a reminder	70	20	4
When finding out more about the customer	55	18	4
When company has made a mistake	50	20	6
Just to say hello	40	40	6

Figure 5.4
Preferred customer communication (per cent) (Source: Henley Centre, 2001; based on a sample of 2000)

Customers who receive unconditional service guarantees from mid-market hotel chains may wonder why upmarket chains are unable or unwilling to guarantee their performance. Customers used to experiencing perfect performance from courier service suppliers that always get packages to the right destination within the prescribed time limit, might wonder why airlines still lose their bags. Customers may benchmark nationally or internationally, depending on their awareness of points of comparison.

Desirable data attributes

The data that support CRM decision-making should satisfy a number of criteria. They should be shareable, transportable, accurate, relevant, timely and secure.[8] The desirable data attributes can be remembered through the mnemonic STARTS. These augment the desirable attributes of CRM architecture that were discussed in Chapter 3. If data are to be shareable, transportable, timely and secure, the CRM architecture of the CRM system must enable this.

Data need to be *shareable* because several users may require access to the same data at the same time. For example, profile information about customers who have bought annual travel insurance might need to be made available to customer service agents in several geographical locations simultaneously as they deal with customer enquiries in response to an advertising campaign.

Data need to be *transportable* from storage location to user. Data need to be made available wherever and whenever users require. The user might be a hot-desking customer service representative, a delivery driver en route to a pick-up, an independent mortgage consultant or a salesperson in front of a prospect. Today's international corporations with globally distributed customers, product portfolios across several categories and multiple routes to market face particularly challenging data transportation problems. Electronic customer databases are essential for today's businesses, together with enabling technologies such as data synchronization, wireless communications and web browsers to make the data fully transportable.

Data *accuracy* is a troublesome issue. In an ideal world it would be wonderful to have 100 per cent accurate data. However, data accuracy carries a high level of cost. Data are captured, entered, integrated and analysed at various moments. Any or all of these processes may be the source of inaccuracy. Keystroke mistakes can cause errors at the point of data entry. Inappropriate analytical processes can lead to ill-founded conclusions. In CRM, data inaccuracy can lead to undue waste in marketing campaigns, inappropriate prospecting by salespeople, and generally suboptimal customer experience. It also erodes trust in the CRM system, thus reducing usage. This leads to further degrading of data quality. To counter this, usage volumes and data quality should be monitored. Data need to be entered at source rather than second hand; user buy-in needs to be managed; data-quality processes such as de-duplication need to be introduced. Newsagency and book retailer WH Smith attributes high response rates of CRM-enabled direct marketing to the accuracy of its database. For example, an offer of Delia Smith's *How to Cook* book achieved an 8 per cent response rate, significantly more than was the norm before their data-quality project was implemented.

Relevant data are pertinent for a given purpose. To check a customer's credit worthiness you need their transaction and payment histories, and their current employment and income status. To flag customers who are hot prospects for a cross-sell campaign, you need their propensity-to-buy scores. In designing a data management system to support a CRM strategy, relevance is a major issue. You need to know what decisions will be made and what information is needed to enable them to be made well.

Timely data are data that are available as and when needed. Data that are retrieved after a decision has been made are unhelpful. Equally, decision-makers do not want to be burdened with data before the need is felt. Bank tellers need to have propensity-to-buy information available to them as the time a customer is being served.

Data *security* is a hugely important issue for most companies. Data, particularly data about customers, are a major resource and a source of competitive advantage. They provide the foundation for delivery of better solutions to customers. Companies need to protect their data against loss, sabotage and theft. Many companies regularly back up their data. Security is enhanced through physical and electronic barriers such as firewalls. Managing data security in a partner environment is particularly challenging, as it is essential that competing partners do not see each other's sales lead and opportunity information, despite being signed into the same CRM system through the same portal.

Identify the information sources

Information for the database can be sourced internally or externally. Before building the database it is necessary to audit the company to find out what data are available. Internal data are the foundation of most CRM programmes, although the amount of information available about customers depends on the degree of contact that the company has. Some companies sell through partners, agents and distributors, and have little knowledge about the demand chain beyond their immediate contact.

Internal data can be found in various functional areas.

Marketing might have data on:

- market segmentation
- customer profiles
- customer acquisition channels
- promotional campaign responses
- product registrations
- product warranties
- requests for product information.

Sales might have records on:

- customer purchasing history, including recency, frequency, monetary value
- buyers' names and contact details

- account number
- SIC code
- important buying criteria
- terms of trade: discounts, payment period
- potential customers (prospects)
- responses to proposals
- competitor products and pricing
- customer requirements and preferences.

Finance may have:

- credit ratings
- payment histories.

Customer service might have records of:

- customer satisfaction levels
- customer complaints, resolved and unresolved
- communication history: dates and issues
- loyalty programme membership and status
- service histories
- service requirements.

In the UK, the high-street retailer Boots has shifted away from traditional marketing research as a means of understanding its customers. These days it relies heavily on data generated by its loyalty card. This provides both demographic and transactional data about its customers. The company has 20 full-time analysts working to extract meaning from the data.[9]

Enhancing the data

External data are used to enhance the internal data and can be brought into the database from a number of sources, including market research companies and marketing database companies. The business intelligence company Claritas, for example, offers clients access to their Behaviourbank and Lifestyle Selector databases. These databases are populated with data obtained from many millions of returned questionnaires. Experian, another intelligence company, provides geodemographic data to its clients. External data can be classified into three groups:[10]

- compiled list data
- census data
- modelled data.

Compiled list data are individual-level data assembled by list bureaux or list vendors. They build their lists from a variety of personal, household and business sources. They might use local or council tax records, questionnaire response data, warranty card registrations or businesses' published annual reports.

If you were a retailer thinking of diversifying from leisurewear into dancewear and had few relevant customer data of your own, you might be interested in buying or renting data from an external source. Data could have been compiled by the bureau or vendor from a variety of sources, such as:

- memberships of dance schools
- student enrolments on dance courses at school and college
- recent purchasers of dance equipment
- lifestyle questionnaire respondents who cite dance as an interest
- subscribers to dance magazines
- purchasers of tickets for dance and musical theatre.

Census data are obtained from government census records. In different parts of the world, different information is available. Some censuses are unreliable; others do not make many data available for non-governmental use.

In the USA, where the census is conducted every 10 years, you cannot obtain census data at the household level, but you can at a more aggregated geodemographic level, such as zipcode, block group and census tract. Census tracts are subdivisions of counties. Block groups are subdivisions of census tracts, the boundaries of which are generally streets. In the USA there are about 225 000 block groups, with an average of over 1000 persons per group. Census data available at geodemographic level include:

- median income
- average household size
- average home value
- average monthly mortgage
- percentage ethnic breakdown
- marital status
- percentage college educated.

For the UK census, there are 155 000 enumeration districts, each comprising about 150 households and 10 postcodes. The enumeration district is the basis for many geodemographic data.

Individual-level data are better predictors of behaviour than are geodemographic data. However, in the absence of individual-level data, census data may be the only option for enhancing your internal data. For example, you could use census data about median income and average household size to predict who might be prospects for a car reseller's promotion.

Modelled data are generated by third parties from data that they assemble from a variety of sources. You buy processed, rather than raw data from these sources. Often they have performed clustering routines on the data. For example, Claritas has developed a customer classification scheme called PRIZM. In Great Britain, PRIZM describes the lifestyles of people living in a particular postcode. Every postcode is assigned to one of 72 different clusters on the basis of their responses to a variety of lifestyle and demographic questions. Eighty per cent of the data used in the clustering process is less than 3 years old.

Figure 5.5 provides the PRIZM profile of residents of one postcode in the London suburb of Twickenham. They are assigned to PRIZM code A101, which applies to about one-third of one per cent of households in the country. The figure profiles their occupational status, living accommodation, car ownership, holidaying behaviour and media consumption.

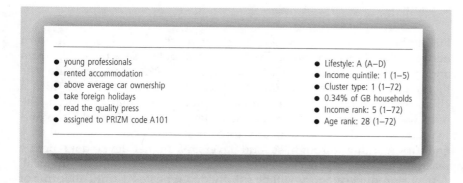

- young professionals
- rented accommodation
- above average car ownership
- take foreign holidays
- read the quality press
- assigned to PRIZM code A101

- Lifestyle: A (A–D)
- Income quintile: 1 (1–5)
- Cluster type: 1 (1–72)
- 0.34% of GB households
- Income rank: 5 (1–72)
- Age rank: 28 (1–72)

Figure 5.5
PRIZM analysis of
TW9 1UU, UK

If you want to use external data to enhance your internal data, you will need to send a copy of the data that you want to enhance to the external data source. The source will match its files to yours using an algorithm that recognizes equivalence between the files (often using names and addresses). The source then attaches the relevant data to your files and returns them to you.

Secondary and primary data

Data are either secondary or primary. Secondary data are data that have already been collected, perhaps for a purpose that is very different from the CRM requirement. Primary data are data that are collected for the first time, either for CRM or for other purposes.

Primary data collection through traditional means such as surveys can be very expensive. Companies have therefore had to find relatively low-cost ways to generate primary customer data for their CRM strategies. Among the data-building schemes that have been used are:

- **competition entries**: customers are invited to enter competitions of skill, or lotteries. They surrender personal data on the entry forms
- **subscriptions**: customers may be invited to subscribe to a newsletter or magazine, again surrendering personal details
- **registrations**: customers are invited to register their purchase. This may be so that they can be advised on product updates
- **loyalty programmes**: many companies run loyalty programmes. These enable companies to link purchasing behaviour to individual customers and segments. When joining a programme, customers complete application forms, providing the company with personal, demographic and even lifestyle data. These are covered further in Chapter 9.

Select the database technology and hardware platform

Data can be stored in a database in a number of different ways:

- hierarchical
- network
- relational.

Hierarchical and network databases were the most common form between the 1960s and 1980s. The hierarchical database is the oldest form and not well suited to CRM applications. You can imagine the hierarchical model as an organization chart or family tree, in which a child can have only one parent, but a parent can have many children. The only way to obtain access to the lower levels is to start at the top and work downwards. When data are stored in hierarchical format, you may end up working through several layers of higher level data before reaching the data you need. Product databases are generally hierarchical. A major product category will be subdivided repeatedly until all forms of the product have their own record.

To extend the family tree metaphor, the network database allows children to have one, none or more than one parent. Before the network database had the chance to become popular, the relational database superseded it, eventually becoming an American National Standards Institute (ANSI) standard in 1971.

Relational databases are now the standard architecture for CRM databases. Relational databases store data in two-dimensional tables comprised of rows and columns. In a customer database, each row is a unique customer and each column contains some attribute of that customer. Each customer is given a unique identifying number.

Companies also have other databases for sales, service, inventory, payments and so on. The customer's unique identifying number enables linkages to be made between the various databases. These linkages can be:

- **one-to-one**: each record in one database can be linked to one other record in another database
- **one-to-many**: each record in one database can be linked to many records in another database
- **many-to-many**: each record in one database can be linked to many records in another database, and each record in that database can, in turn, be linked to many records in the first.

Let's imagine you are a customer of an online retailer. You buy a book and supply the retailer with your name, address, preferred delivery choice and credit-card details. A record is created for you on the 'Customer' database, with a unique identifying number. An 'Orders Received' database records your purchase and preferred delivery choice. An 'Inventory' database records that there has been a reduction in the stock of the item you ordered. This may trigger a reordering process when inventory reaches a critical level. A 'Payment' database records your payment by credit card. There will be one-to-many linkages between your Customer record and these other databases. With the advent of enterprise suites from vendors such as Oracle, SAP and PeopleSoft, all of these databases may reside in the one system and be pre-integrated.

The choice of hardware platform is influenced by several conditions:

- **the size of the database**: even standard desktop PCs are capable of storing huge amounts of customer data
- **existing technology**: most companies will already have technology that lends itself to database applications
- **the number and location of users**: many applications are quite simple, but in an increasingly global marketplace the hardware may need very careful specification and periodic review. For example, the hardware might need to enable a geographically dispersed, multilingual, user group to access data for both analytical and operational purposes.

The selection of the CRM database can be done in parallel with the next step in this process, selection of CRM applications. Modern database applications come together with their own database schema, which predetermines the tables and columns in the database structure. Each CRM vendor then supports a specified list of database technologies, for example, Oracle or SQL Server.

Build or purchase applications to access and process the information

Users of the customer database need to be able to extract quickly the right data for any operational and analytical application. The applications include:

- marketing applications:
  - market and customer segmentation
  - campaign management
  - direct marketing
  - event-based marketing
  - multichannel marketing
- sales applications:
  - managing the sales pipeline
  - lead management
  - opportunity management
  - contact management
- sales management applications:
  - salesperson performance management
  - workload allocation
  - salesperson appraisal

- service applications:
  - contact centre management
  - customer communications
  - enquiry handling
  - helpdesk management
  - complaints management.

For each of these applications, the user of the database needs to identify what information is needed. For example, for workload assignment by sales management, the user might need to know how many accounts of each class (key account, A, B and C class accounts) are serviced by each salesperson, the number of prospects each salesperson handles, the service expectations of each customer group, the location of these customers, the expertise of each salesperson (better at generating new accounts or better at handling existing accounts), the key performance indicators for each salesperson, the salesperson's historical performance against those key performance indicators, and the selling, service and account management tasks defined in each salesperson's contract.

It may be necessary to process the data, that is, perform analytical procedures on the data before decisions can be made. Before choosing any technique to analyse the data, you will need to answer the following three questions.

1 How many variables need to be analysed at the same time?

You may want to analyse one variable (univariate analysis), two variables (bivariate analysis) or three or more variables simultaneously (multivariate analysis). 'What is the average age of our customers?' is a question requiring univariate analysis. 'Does spending varying according to age?' requires bivariate analysis. 'Can we usefully cluster our customers using demographics, lifestyle and transactional data?' needs multivariate analysis.

Most front-office people would be familiar with univariate statistics that measure central tendency within a data set (mean, mode and median) and with measures of dispersion such as the standard deviation. There will be less familiarity with bivariate statistics such as correlation, simple regression and chi-squared. Multivariate statistical processes such as multiple regression, factor analysis, cluster analysis, multidimensional scaling, analysis of variance, conjoint analysis and discriminant analysis are generally part of the specialist knowledge of operational researchers and statisticians. In designing the interface between data and users, it may be necessary to employ this type of specialist in data analysis.

2 Do you want to describe a set of data or to draw inferences about a population?

Descriptive statistics provide you with summaries of the data in your database. For example, descriptive statistics would tell you the average age of your customers, the number of customers each salesperson manages, and the association between customer complaints and products purchased.

If you want to draw inferences you will be using the data in your database to make inferences about a wider population. You will need to be competent at sampling, a practice that is based on probability theory.

3   What types of data are you analysing?

For analytical purposes data are organized into four major categories: nominal, ordinal, interval and ratio. Qualitative variables are nominal data. The other three classes of variable are forms of quantitative data.

Nominal measures are the simplest form of measure. They are used only to classify, identify or categorize customers. Customer names and identification numbers are nominal measures. Nominal measurement systems meet four criteria. There must be at least two categories; these must be distinct, mutually exclusive and exhaustive (e.g. male/female). When there are two or more categories, the names or numbers attached to each category must be distinctive to avoid confusion. The classification system must be exhaustive to capture all customers on the database, and the categories must be mutually exclusive in that any one customer should only fit in one category.

Ordinal measures are used to rank customers. If customers were ranked by annual sales you would be using an ordinal measure. Ordinal measures indicate whether one customer has more or less of some characteristic than another. Rankings do not, however, indicate the magnitude of any difference. You would know from an ordinal scale that the first ranked customer had more of the measured characteristic than the second ranked, but you would not know whether the latter ranked a close or distant second.

Interval measures remedy the 'order of magnitude' problem associated with ordinal measures. Interval measures identify not only rank order, but also the distance between rankings. Most customer satisfaction questionnaires use five-, seven- or nine-point interval scales. An interval measure like this tells you how much difference there is between observations. However, in interval scales there is no fixed zero point. You would not be able to claim that customers at point 2 on the satisfaction scale were twice as satisfied as customers at point 1. Because of this you cannot perform division or multiplication on the data.

Ratio measures have all the properties of nominal, ordinal and interval measures but, unlike interval measures, ratio measures also have a fixed and absolute zero point. Therefore, it is possible to classify customers, rank them and compare differences. Customer spending is measured on a ratio scale. Because of the fixed zero point you can claim that a customer spending $14 million is seven times the size of a customer spending $2 million. Whereas only addition and subtraction are possible on interval data, multiplication and division are possible on ratio data.

Until you have answered these three questions you will be unable to choose the correct analytical procedure.

Customer relationship management questions that need analytical power range from the relatively straightforward to the complex, for example:

- What sales have been made to a given customer in the last 5 years?
- Why do our customers defect to competitors?
- What is the average length of time that it takes to process a customer's request for information?
- Do we sell more to older customers than younger?
- What has been the sales trajectory in our various customer segments over the past 4 years, and what sales are forecast for the future?
- Given the data we have, what is the optimal way to segment our customers to predict future profit streams?

Populate the database

Having decided what information is needed, how to store it and how to use it, the next task is to obtain the data and enter them onto the database. Customer relationship management applications need data that are appropriately accurate. We use the 'appropriately' because the level of accuracy depends on the function of the database. Operational CRM applications generally need more accurate and contemporary data than do analytical applications.

You may be one of the many who have experienced the results of poor-quality data. Perhaps you have been invited to become a donor to a charity to which you already donate direct from your salary. This could have happened when a prospecting list that has been bought was not checked against current donor lists. Perhaps you have been addressed as Ms when you prefer Mrs. This is caused because the company has either not obtained or not checked your preferences.

The main tasks in ensuring that the database is populated with appropriately accurate data are:

1 verify the data
2 validate the data
3 de-duplicate the data
4 merge and purge data from two or more sources.

Verification: this task is conducted to ensure that the data have been entered exactly as found in the original source. This can be a very labour-intensive process since it generally involves keying the data in twice, with the computer programmed to flag mismatches. An alternative is to check visually that the data entered match the data at the primary source.

Validation: this is concerned with checking the accuracy of the data that are entered. There are several common inaccuracies, many associated with name and address fields: misspelt names, incorrect titles, inappropriate salutations. A number of processes can improve data accuracy:

- range validation: does an entry lie outside the possible range for a field?
- missing values: the computer can check for values that are missing in any column
- check against external sources: you could check postcodes against an authoritative external listing from the mail authorities.

De-duplication: also known as de-duping. Customers become aware that their details appear more than once on a database when they receive identical communications from a company. This might occur when external data are not cross-checked against internal data, when two or more internal lists are used for the mailing or when customers have more than one address on the database. There may be sound cost reasons for this (de-duplication does cost money), but from the customer's perspective it can look wasteful and unprofessional. De-duplication software is available to help in the process.

The de-duplication process needs to be alert to the possibility of two types of error:

1 removing a record that should be retained. For example, if a property is divided into unnumbered apartments, and you have transactions with more than one resident, then it would be a mistake to delete any record. Similarly, you may have more than one customer in a household, bearing the same family name or initials
2 retaining a record that should be removed. For example, you may have separate records for a customer under different titles such as Mr and Dr.

Merge and purge: also known as merge–purge. This is a process that is performed when two or more databases are merged. This might happen when an external database is merged with an internal database, when two internal databases are merged (e.g. marketing and customer service databases), or when two external lists are bought and merged for a particular purpose such as a campaign. There can be significant costs savings for CRM-based marketing campaigns when duplications are purged from the combined lists.

Merge–purge can also operate at the level of the individual customer record. For example, two salespeople may have been working on the same customer in different locations. The CRM system should then support a merge–purge process to create a single master record from the two.

Maintain the database

Customer databases need to be updated to keep them useful. Consider the following statistics.

- 19 per cent of managing directors change jobs in any year.
- 8 per cent of businesses relocate in any year.
- In the UK, 5 per cent of postcodes change in an average year.
- In western economies about 1.2 per cent of the population dies each year.
- In the USA, 43 million people change addresses each year.

It does not take long for databases to degrade. Companies can maintain data integrity in a number of ways.

- Ensure that data from all new transactions, campaigns and communications are inserted into the file immediately. You will need to develop rules and ensure that they are applied.
- Regularly de-duplicate the database.
- Audit a subset of the files every year. Measure the amount of degradation. Identify the source of degradation: is it a particular data source or field?
- Purge customers who have been inactive for a certain period of time. For frequently bought products, the dormant time period might be 6 months or less. For products with a longer repeat purchase cycle, the period will be longer. It is not always clear what is a suitable dormancy period. Some credit-card users, for example, may have different cards in different currencies. Inactivity for a year only indicates that the owner has not travelled to a country in the previous year. The owner may make several trips in the coming year.
- Drip-feed the database. Every time there is a customer contact there is an opportunity to add new or verify existing data.
- Get customers to update their own records. When Amazon customers buy online, they need to confirm or update invoice and delivery details.
- Remove customers' records when they request this.
- Insert decoy records. If the database is managed by an external agency, you might want to check the effectiveness of the agency's performance by inserting a few dummy records into the database. If the agency fails to spot the dummies, you may have a problem with their service standards.

Data integration

So far in this chapter we have assumed that companies have a single customer database. In most companies there are several customer databases, maintained by sales, marketing and service functions. There might also be customer data in other databases, for example, product or production databases. In companies that have several routes to market, there will probably be a considerable amount of information in the various channel databases, as suggested in Fig. 5.6. External data from suppliers, business partners, franchisees and others may also need to be integrated (see Case 5.1).

Companies often face the challenge of synchronizing and integrating data from several sources into a coherent single view of the customer. When Dun & Bradstreet was integrating data from several sources to create a marketing database it found 113 different entries for AT&T alone. These included ATT, A.T.T., AT and T and so on.

Failure to integrate databases may lead to inefficiency and damaged customer relationships. For example, you may have bought an item online, and later be offered the same item through a different channel of the same company, home shopping perhaps.

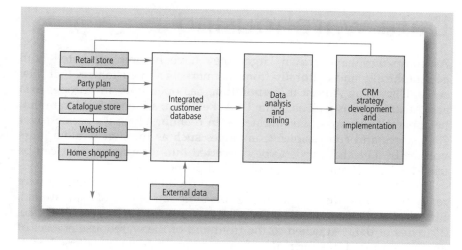

Figure 5.6
A single view of the customer

Data integration at the American Heart Association

The American Heart Association (AHA) is a not-for-profit US health organization dedicated to reducing disability and death from heart attack, stroke and related cardiovascular disorders.

One of the AHA's major goals has been improving its relationships with stakeholders, including many thousands of volunteers conducting unpaid work for the organization, donors, businesses and the media. However, a challenge facing the AHA in achieving this goal was integrating the organization's data, which were previously located in over 150 separate databases, often geographically isolated and specific to certain departments within the organization. These provided a fragmented view of customers' profiles and history of activities.

AHA chose to implement a CRM software system across the organization to integrate all existing databases. Since implementation, the AHA has found that its staff are far more productive, and it is able to respond to customers more quickly and provide more personalized service. Donations from customers have increased by over 20 per cent, using the system to contact potential donors compared with previous activities.

One solution to the problem of database integration is to convert from legacy systems (older mainframe systems) to newer systems with a centralized database that can accept real-time inputs from a number of channels.[10] Where there is considerable investment in legacy systems and huge numbers of records are held in the database, this may not be a cost-effective solution. Legacy systems are typically batch-processing systems. In other words, they do not accept real-time data. Many technology firms have developed software and systems to allow companies to integrate databases held on different legacy systems.

Data warehousing

As companies have grown larger they have become separated both geographically and culturally from the markets and customers that they serve. Disney, an American corporation, has operations in Europe, Asia and Australasia, as well as in the USA. Benetton, a French fashion brand, has operations across five continents. In retailing alone it operates over 7000 stores and concessions. Companies such as these generate a huge volume of data that needs to be converted into information that can be used for both operational and analytical purposes.

The data warehouse is a solution to that problem. Data warehouses are really no more than repositories of large amounts of operational, historical and customer data. Data volume can reach terabyte levels, i.e. 2^{40} bytes of data. Attached to the front end of the warehouse is a set of analytical procedures for making sense out of the data. Retailers, home-shopping companies and banks have been early adopters of data warehouses.

Watson[8] describes a data warehouse as being:

- **subject-oriented**: the warehouse organizes data around the essential subjects of the business (e.g. customers) rather than around applications (e.g. car insurance)
- **integrated**: it is consistent in the way that data from several sources are treated (e.g. coding conventions are standardized: M = male, F = female)
- **time-invariant**: data are organized by various time periods (e.g. months)
- **non-volatile**: the warehouse's database is not updated in real time. There is periodic bulk uploading of transactional and other data. This makes the data less subject to momentary change.

There are several steps and processes in building a warehouse. First, you must identify where the relevant data are stored. This can be a challenge. When the Commonwealth Bank opted for a CRM approach to its retail banking business, it found that relevant customer data were resident on over 80 separate systems. Secondly, data must be extracted from those systems. It is probable that when these systems were developed they were not expected to align with other systems.

The data then need to be transformed into a standardized, consistent and clean format. Data in different systems may have been stored in different forms, as Fig. 5.7 indicates. Also, the quality of data from different parts of the business may vary. The culture in sales may be highly driven by quarterly performance targets. Getting sales reps to maintain their customer files may be not straightforward, as much of their information may be in their heads. In contrast, direct marketers may be very dedicated to keeping their data in good shape.

After transformation, the data need to be uploaded into the warehouse. Archival data that have little relevance to today's operations may be set aside, or only uploaded if there is sufficient space. Recent operational and

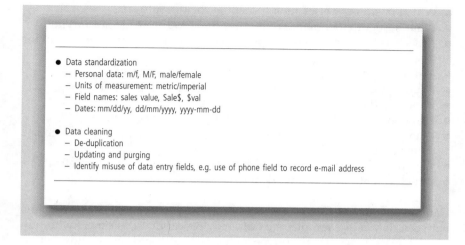

Figure 5.7
Data
transformation

transactional data from the various functions, channels and touchpoints will most probably be prioritized for uploading.

Refreshing the data in the warehouse is important. This may be done on a daily or weekly basis depending on the speed of change in the business and its environment. If this were the case, CRM practitioners would need to rely on operational databases rather than the warehoused data for day-to-day decision-making.

Data marts

A data mart is a scaled down version of the data warehouse. Some warehousing projects have taken years to implement and have yielded few measurable benefits. Data mart project costs are lower because the volume of data stored is reduced and the number of users is capped. Technological requirements are less demanding.

Data mining

Data mining, as noted in Chapters 3 and 4, is the search for meaning within large volumes of data. Although data mining can be performed on operational databases, it is essential given the volumes of data held in data marts or warehouses. Higher processing speeds and reduced storage costs have made data mining more economical.

Data mining can provide answers to questions that are important for CRM strategy development and implementation. For example:

- How can our market and customer base be segmented?
- Which customers are most valuable?

- Which customers offer most potential for the future?
- What sorts of customers are buying our products? Or not buying?
- Are there any patterns of purchasing behaviour in our customer base?
- Should we charge the same price to all these segments?
- What is the profile of customers who default on payment?
- What are the costs of customer acquisition?
- What sorts of customer should be targeted for acquisition?
- What offers should be made to specific customer groups to increase their value?
- Which customers should be targeted for customer retention efforts?
- Which retention tactics work well?

Data mining helps CRM in a number of ways. It can find **associations** between data. For example, the data may reveal that customers who buy low-fat desserts are also big buyers of herbal health and beauty aids, or that consumers of wine enjoy live theatre productions. One analyst at Wal-Mart, the American retailer, noted a correlation between nappy sales and beer sales, which was particularly strong on Fridays. On investigating further he found that fathers were buying the nappies and picking up a six-pack at the same time. The company responded to this information by locating these items closer to each other. Sales of both rose strongly.[11]

Sequential patterns often emerge from data mining. Data miners look for 'if . . . then' rules in customer behaviour. For example, they might find a rule such as 'If a customer buys walking shoes in November, then there is a 40 per cent probability that they will buy rainwear within the next 6 months', or 'If a customer calls a contact centre to request information about interest rates, then there is a 50 per cent probability the customer will defect in the next 3 months'. Rules such as these enable CRM people to implement timely tactics. In the first instance, there is an opportunity for cross-selling. In the second, there may be an opportunity to retain the customer.

Data mining also works by **classifying**. Customers can be classified into mutually exclusive groups. Market segmentation and customer portfolio analysis are illustrations of classification schemes.

For example, you might be able to segment your existing customers into groups according to the value they produce for your company. You can then profile each group. When you identify a potential new customer you can judge which group the prospect most resembles. That will give you an idea of the prospect's potential value.

You could also classify customers into quintiles or deciles in terms of important transactional information such as the recency, frequency and monetary value of the purchases they have made. This is called RFM analysis. Then you can experiment with different treatments, making different offers and communicating in different ways, to selected cells of the RFM matrix (see Fig. 5.8). You can expect to find that customers who have bought most recently or frequently or spend most with you are the most responsive in general terms.

Another approach in data mining is **clustering**. This was mentioned in the discussion of market segmentation in Chapter 4. Practitioners of CRM

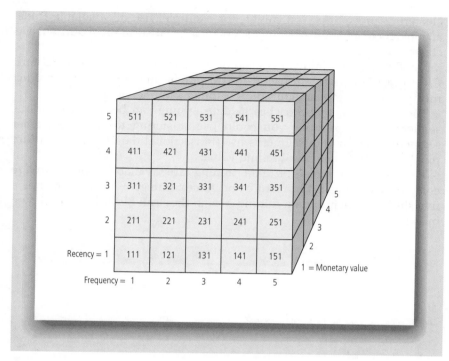

Figure 5.8
A recency–
frequency–
monetary value
matrix

Case 5.2

Data mining at Marks & Spencer

Data mining has proven to be a successful strategy for the UK retailer Marks & Spencer (M&S). The company generates large volumes of data from the 10 million customers per week it serves in over 300 stores. The organization claims that data mining lets it build one-to-one relationships with every customer, to the point that whenever individual customers come into a store the retailer knows exactly what products it should offer in order to build profitability.

Marks & Spencer believes that two factors are important in data mining. First is the quality of the data. This is higher when the identity of customers is known, usually as a result of e-commerce tracking or loyalty programme membership. Second is to have a clear business goal in mind before starting data mining. For example, M&S uses data mining to identify 'high-margin', 'average-margin' or 'low-margin' customer groups. The company then profiles high-margin customers. This is used to guide customer retention activities with appropriate targeted advertising and promotions. This technique can also be used to profile average-margin or low-margin customers who have the potential to be developed into high-margin customers.

attempt to cluster customers into groups. The general objective of clustering is to minimize the differences between members of a cluster while also maximizing the differences between clusters. Clustering techniques work by using a defined range of variables to perform the clustering procedure. You might, for example, use all available transaction data to generate customer segments. A statistical procedure such as cluster analysis finds the hidden clusters.

Finally, data mining can contribute to CRM by **making predictions**. CRM practitioners might use historical purchasing behaviour to predict future purchasing behaviour and customer lifetime value.

These five major approaches to data mining can be used in various sequences. For example, you could use clustering to create customer segments, then within segments use transactional data to predict future purchasing and customer lifetime value.

The analytical tools for data mining are available from software companies such as SAS Institute and MicroStrategy. SAS recommends a five-step approach to data mining, which they call SEMMA. It is shown in Fig. 5.9.

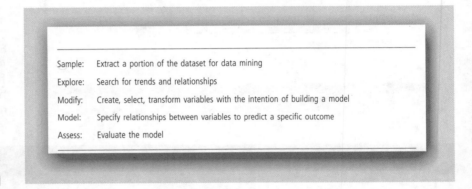

Figure 5.9
SEMMA: the SAS
data mining model

Privacy issues

Privacy and data protection are major concerns to legislators around the world. Customers are increasingly concerned about the amount of information that commercial organizations have about them, and the uses to which that information is put. In fact, most consumers are not aware of just how much information is available to companies. When you use the Internet, small programs called cookies are downloaded onto your hard disk from the sites you visit. A very small number of websites obtain permission from their site visitors prior to the download; most do not.

There have been two major responses to the privacy concerns of customers: self-regulation and legislation. The first is self-regulation by companies and associations. For example, many companies publish their privacy policies and make a commercial virtue out of their transparency. Professional bodies in fields such as direct marketing, advertising and market research have adopted codes of practice that members must abide by.

In 1980, the Organization for Economic Cooperation and Development (OECD) developed a set of principles that has served as the foundation for personal data protection legislation around the world.[12] These principles are voluntary guidelines that member nations can use when framing laws to protect individuals against abuses by data gatherers. The principles are as follows.

- **Purpose specification**: at the time of data collection, the consumer should be provided with a clear statement of the purposes for which the data are being collected.
- **Data collection processes**: data should be collected only by fair and lawful means.
- **Limited application**: data should be used only for valid business purposes.
- **Data quality**: personal data should be relevant for the purposes used and kept accurate, complete and up to date.
- **Use limitation**: personal data should not be disclosed, sold, made available or otherwise used for purposes other than as specified at the time of collection unless the consumer gives consent or as required by law. Consumer consent can be obtained through either an opt-in or opt-out process. Opt-in means than consumers agree that their data may be used for a particular purpose. Opt-out means that consumers prohibit use for that purpose.
- **Openness**: consumers should be able to receive information about developments, practices and policies with regard to their personal data. They should be able to find out what data have been collected and the uses to which they have been put. Consumers should have access to the data controller.
- **Access**: consumers should be able to access their data in readable form, to challenge the data and, if the challenge is successful, have the data erased, corrected or completed.
- **Data security**: personal data should be protected against risks such as loss, unauthorized access, destruction, use, modification or disclosure
- **Accountability**: a data controller should be accountable for compliance with these measures.

Legislation has been enacted at a number of levels. In 1995, the Council of the European Union issued Directive 95/46/EC on the 'Protection of Individuals with Regard to the Processing of Personal Data and on the Free Movement of Such Data'. This applies to all forms of data and information processing, including e-commerce. It required all member states to upgrade their legislation to a common standard by 1998. Companies are now only allowed to process personal data where the individual has given consent or where, for legal or contractual reasons, processing is necessary. EU countries are not allowed to export personal data to countries where such exacting standards do not apply. Legislation guarantees certain rights to citizens of the EU:

- **notification**: individuals are to be advised with without delay about what information is being collected, and the origins of the data, if not from the individual

- **explanation** of the logic behind the results of automated decisions based on customer data (e.g. why a credit application was rejected)
- **correction/deleting/blocking** of data that do not comply with legislation
- **objection**: individuals can object to the way in which their data are processed (opt-out). Where the objection is justified, the data controller must no longer process the information.

Data controllers are also required to comply with certain obligations, including the following.

- Only collect and process data for legitimate and explicit purposes.
- Only collect personal data when individual consent has been granted, or is required to enter into or fulfil a contract, or is required by law.
- Ensure that the data are accurate and up to date.
- At the point of data collection, advise the individual of the identity of the collector, the reason for data collection, the recipients of the data, and the individual's rights in respect of data access, correction and deletion.
- Ensure that the data are kept secure and safe from unauthorized access and disclosure.

The USA has not adopted these legislative standards, but in order to enable US companies to do business with EU organizations, the US Commerce Department has devised a set of 'Safe Harbor' principles. US organizations in the Safe Harbor are assumed to adhere to seven principles regarding notice (as in notification, above), choice, onward transfer (disclosure to third parties), security, data integrity, access and enforcement (accountability). US companies obtain Safe Harbor refuge by voluntarily certifying that they adhere to these principles. This enables data transfers to be made to the USA. Two areas of difference between the EU Directive and these seven principles are in access and enforcement. The Safe Harbor wording for access is weaker. The Safe Harbor principle states that 'individuals must have *reasonable* access to personal information about them that an organization holds, and to be able to correct or amend the information *where it is inaccurate*'. The enforcement principle is unclear about sanctions should a company breach the standard and it allows no possibility of enforcement by government agencies.

In the USA, there is a tendency to rely on self-regulation by individuals or associated companies, rather than legislation at state or federal level. For example, the World-Wide Web Consortium (W3C) has developed a Platform for Privacy Preferences (P3P) standard for improving privacy protection in e-commerce. This comprises three major elements.

- A personal profile: each Internet user creates a file consisting of personal data and privacy rules for use of that data. Personal data might include demographic, lifestyle, preference and click-stream data. Privacy rules are the rules that the user prescribes for use of the data, e.g. opt-in or opt-out rules, and disclosure to third parties. The profile is stored in encrypted form on the user's hard drive, can be updated at any time by the users and is administered by the user's web browser.

- A profile of website privacy practices: each website discloses what information has been accessed from the user's personal profile and how it has been used.
- Automated protocols for accessing and using the user's data: these allow either the user or the user's agent (perhaps the web browser) automatically to ensure that the personal profile and the privacy rules are being complied with. If compliance is assured, then users can enter websites and transact without problems.

This is now being complemented by a more rigorous approach to legislation. In Australia, privacy legislation has been enacted at state and federal levels.

Summary

This chapter has discussed the development and exploitation of customer databases for CRM functions. These functions can be classified as operational or analytical. Customer databases need to be constructed with a very clear idea of the applications for which the data are needed. These applications range across the full territory of CRM strategy development and implementation. Customer data can be used to answer strategic questions such as 'Which customers should we serve?' and tactical questions such as 'What is the best day to communicate with a given customer?'

We described a seven-step approach to developing a high-quality customer database, and identified the columns of information that are usefully maintained on the customer record: contact data, contact history, needs, benefits, expectations, preferences and benchmarks. Compiled list data, census data and modelled data can be used to enhance the basic data available in company-maintained customer databases, most of which adopt the standard relational architecture. Attached to the front end of many databases are data mining systems that allow users to make sense of the data for analytical CRM applications. The chapter ended by looking at data integration, data warehouses and data marts, and privacy issues.

References

1. O'Connor, J. and Galvin, E. (2001) *Marketing in the Digital Age* (2nd edn). *Financial Times*/Harlow: Prentice Hall.
2. Buttle, F. (1989) The social construction of needs. *Psychology and Marketing*, Vol. 6(3), Fall, pp. 197–210.
3. Miller, J. A. (1977) Studying satisfaction, modifying models, eliciting expectations, posing problems and making meaningful measurements. In: Hunt, H. K. (ed.). *Conceptualization and Measurement of Consumer Satisfaction and Dissatisfaction.* Cambridge, MA: Marketing Science Institute, pp. 77–91.

4. Parasuraman, A., Berry, L. L. and Zeithaml, V. A. (1991) Understanding customer expectations of service. *Sloan Management Review*, Vol. 32 (Spring), pp. 39–48.

5. Woodruff, R. B., Cadotte, E. R. and Jenkins, R. L. (1983) Modelling consumer satisfaction processes using experience-based norms. *Journal of Marketing Research*, Vol. 20, August, pp. 296–304.

6. Oliver, R. L. (1997) *Satisfaction: A Behavioural Perspective on the Consumer.* New York: McGraw-Hill.

7. Buttle, F. A. Word-of-mouth: understanding and managing referral marketing. *Journal of Strategic Marketing*, Vol. 6, pp. 241–54.

8. Watson, R. T. (1999) *Data Management: Databases and Organisations.* New York: John Wiley.

9. Ross, L. (1999) IBM case study: Boots the Chemist. *International Journal of Customer Relationship Management*, Vol. 2(2), Sept./Oct., pp. 133–40.

10. Drozdenko, R. G. and Drake, P. D. (2002) *Optimal Database Marketing: Strategy, Development and Data Mining.* Thousand Oaks, CA: Sage.

11. Dempsey, M. (1995) Customers compartmentalised. *Financial Times*, 1 March.

12. Swift, R. S. (2001) *Accelerating Customer Relationships using CRM and Relationship Technologies.* Upper Saddle River, NJ: Prentice Hall.

Chapter 6
Creating and managing networks

By the end of the chapter, you will understand:

1 how networks contribute to the achievement of CRM objectives
2 the composition of a business network
3 the SCOPE network model of CRM
4 the major classes of network membership: supplier, partner, owner/investor and employee
5 the concepts of network, network position, activity link, actor bond, resource tie, internal marketing, empowerment and service–profit chain.
6 trends in supplier–relationship management
7 the roles of partners in value creation and value delivery.

Introduction

This chapter focuses on the third primary phase of the customer relationship management (CRM) value chain (Fig. 6.1): network development. The basic claim in this chapter is that the achievement of CRM objectives requires companies to develop and manage a business network comprising suppliers, partners, investors and employees. Companies do not exist in splendid isolation. They are positioned within a network, and it is the performance of the network that determines whether companies achieve their goals. Customer relationship management performance is more assured when the resources of the network are aligned and co-ordinated to contribute to the creation and delivery of value to the focal company's customers.

This chapter emphasizes that the achievement of customer-oriented CRM objectives such as customer acquisition, customer retention and share of wallet relies on the performance of a company in managing its other network relationships. Imagine a retailer that has developed a relationship with a bank to offer a financial services product to the retailer's customers. This is an arrangement that blurs the conventional distinctions between retailer and bank. Each partner needs to understand the other's competencies, to share customer information, to align their technologies and to be clear about the goals of the partnership. If the relationship between the retailer and bank is poorly managed, value will neither be delivered to customers nor created for the partners. Liberating the potential value in customer relationships hinges on companies effectively managing their non-customer network relationships as well.

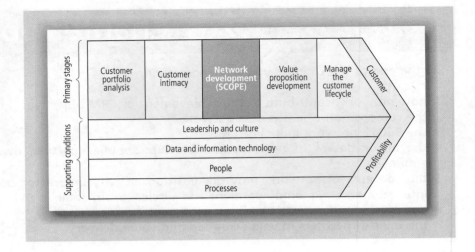

Figure 6.1
CRM value chain

Competition for the customer's dollar is changing. In the past, competition has been head to head between independent companies. Today, competition is increasingly between networks. A good illustration of this is the motor industry. In the 1920s Ford not only assembled cars, it also owned steel mills, coal mines, iron ore mines, steam ships, rubber plantations, sheep farms and railroads. It was standard practice for companies to own and manage as many factors of production as they could. Today is different. In the year 2000, Ford only produced about 50 per cent of the value of their cars. The rest was outsourced to members of their supplier network. In Ford's competitive group, General Motors produces 70 per cent of the value of its cars, Chrysler 30 per cent and Toyota only 20 per cent.

Conventionally, it has been the manufacturer or service provider that dominates the network through their brand power. Examples are IBM, GE (General Electric), UPS (United Parcel Service) and AMP (Australian Mutual Provident). This is changing. Sometimes members of the supply chain can be so powerful that they call the shots. Intel and Microsoft carry so much weight that computer manufacturers such as Dell, Toshiba and Compaq take great risks if these components are not part of the finished product.

Members of the demand chain can also wield significant power and influence. A high percentage of sales in some retail categories are retailer brands (own brands). Wal-Mart and Tesco both specify precisely what they require from their own-brand manufacturers. Sometimes manufacturers have a role in helping to determine the specification, but ultimately it is clear where the final decision rests: with the retailer. Multiple retailers also have sufficient power to expect compliance from manufacturers of major brands. Even Procter and Gamble, Unilever and General Foods are not exempt from their influence. Wal-Mart, however, does claim to want closer relationships based on open dialogue and information exchange with key vendors (Fig. 6.2).

- Wal-Mart looks for a very close relationship and strong commitment from its key vendors like Warner-Lambert. Highly valued: trust and integrity

- Wal-Mart is willing to listen to new solutions, opinions and ideas. Don't be afraid to contribute

- Analytical skills are essential when dealing with Wal-Mart. We will give you access to all kinds of data. Use the data to build a win-win relationship

- Wal-Mart is hungry for consumer insight. We place great value on any information that can improve our understanding of the people who shop in Wal-Mart stores

- Prepare to engage management. Wal-Mart management is as keen as anyone to hear what business partners have to say. Don't feel bound by hierarchy or categories

Figure 6.2
Wal-Mart's commitments to key vendors

What is a network?

A network is a coalition of organizations that works collectively, and sometimes collaboratively, to create value for the customers of a focal organization. The focal firm is the firm whose network we are considering. Sometimes that coalition is loosely connected; at other times, it is tightly defined, as in the relationship between Dell Computers and its component suppliers. In most networks, companies will do business with companies other than the focal firm. Networks supply the material inputs, service and knowledge for value creation. There is growing recognition that the resources within networks need to be actively co-ordinated and managed. A focal organization must take responsibility for managing its network so that it creates and delivers sustainable value to customers. Failure by any network member can threaten the performance of the focal organization.

The need to manage networks is recognized in modern CRM systems, with the move towards extra-enterprise CRM. Customer relationship management systems now include applications for managing relationships with partners (PRM), the integration of websites for investor relations, the management of employees (ERM) and, through integration with enterprise resource planning (ERP), the management of suppliers.

Principles of network management

In this section we set out a number of principles of network management. These are largely derived from the work of the IMP (Industrial Marketing and Purchasing) group of researchers.[1–5]

A network consists of a wide range of companies – suppliers, joint venture (JV) partners, contractors, distributors, franchisees, licensees, and so on – that contribute to the focal firm's creation and delivery of value to its customers. However, this is not the boundary of the network. Each of these companies, in turn, will have its own set of business relationships. Relationships between companies in the network both constrain and enable focal companies in the achievement of their goals. For example, a supplier might introduce the focal firm to another of its customers, enabling them to work on a project of shared interest. Alternatively, a supplier might choose to withdraw from a relationship with the focal firm in order not to endanger a relationship with a bigger, more profitable customer.

Most companies operate within and through two major forms of network: supplier networks and distribution networks. These are examined in the following sections.

Supplier networks

As mentioned earlier, Toyota only manufactures about 20 per cent of the value of its cars. It relies on a network of approximately 50 000 supplier relationships to create and supply the inputs required for car manufacture. This is not to say that Toyota tries to manage 50 000 relationships. The company has a number of critical relationships with tier one suppliers (Fig. 6.3); these in turn have a number of important

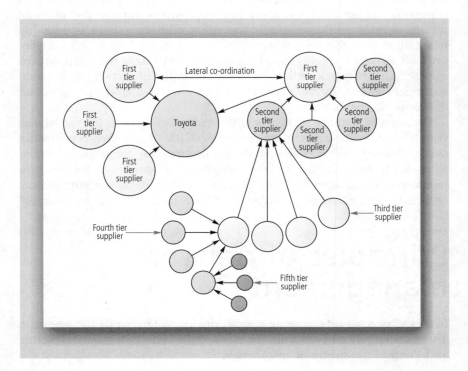

Figure 6.3
Toyota's supplier network
(Source: adapted from Ford et al[1])

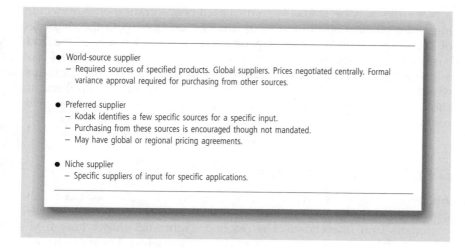

- World-source supplier
  - Required sources of specified products. Global suppliers. Prices negotiated centrally. Formal variance approval required for purchasing from other sources.

- Preferred supplier
  - Kodak identifies a few specific sources for a specific input.
  - Purchasing from these sources is encouraged though not mandated.
  - May have global or regional pricing agreements.

- Niche supplier
  - Specific suppliers of input for specific applications.

Figure 6.4
Kodak's supplier classification

relationships that enable them to create and deliver what Toyota wants; these have relationships with third tier companies that enable them to meet their customers' requirements, and on.[6]

Toyota regards these tier one suppliers as 'systems suppliers'. This means that they not only supply the parts that they manufacture but are also responsible for managing the contributions of a network of lower tier suppliers. This is much the same idea as the 'category captain'. Some large supermarket operators have appointed category captains to work co-operatively with them to create profitable product categories. A category is a class of product such as men's shaving supplies, hosiery or ice-cream. The category captain is responsible to the retailer for assembling a network of complementary lower tier suppliers that contribute to the category performance.

This illustrates a number of features of networks. Unlike single supplier–customer relationships, networks consist of a large number of indirect relationships. They also demand careful co-ordination. Toyota needs to work closely with tier one suppliers so that they know exactly what Toyota wants and when. Many of these tier one suppliers will have their own CRM systems to manage their relationships with Toyota. Tier one, in turn, needs to co-ordinate with tier two suppliers. There might also need to be lateral co-ordination between suppliers at any tier. For example, this might be needed when Toyota's tier one suspension subassembly manufacturer needs to co-ordinate with Toyota's tier one braking system subassembly manufacturer.

Large companies within networks can exert considerable influence on the overall structure and performance of the network. Toyota might, for example, insist on specific product quality standards, not only from tier one suppliers, but also from tier two, three or four suppliers. It might also require a tier three supplier to stop purchasing from a tier four supplier, if that supplier also supplies a competitor. Toyota tries to influence suppliers up to three tiers away.

Networks may be global. With increased concentration of manufacturing and globalization of brands, companies are faced with the challenge of sourcing inputs that are of a universal standard whether the end-customer is in America or Azerbaijan, Sydney or Shanghai. Kodak has addressed this problem by classifying its suppliers into three groups, world source suppliers, preferred suppliers and niche suppliers, as shown in Fig. 6.4. This enables Kodak managers to purchase with confidence.

Distribution networks

All companies have demand chains. Demand chains comprise the customers of the focal firm, their customers, and the customers of these customers until the end user is reached. Figure 6.5 shows how IBM's demand chain moves computers so that they reach end users in Italy.[7]

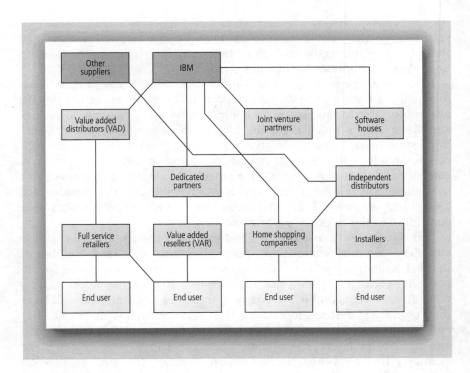

Figure 6.5
IBM's distribution network
(Source: adapted from Ford et al[1])

This network illustrates a number of other features of business networks. Networks comprise a variety of organizations that contribute in different ways to the performance of the network. Companies bring different competencies, resources, relationships, management styles and histories to the network. Quite possibly, each company will have been established and developed for different purposes, and may be working towards objectives that are in conflict with the focal firm. There is often potential for conflict in the relationships of customers and the focal firm. In this illustration, IBM supplies home shopping companies directly, thus denying its other first tier customers the opportunity to develop their own relationships with these catalogue companies.

Not all relationships are alike

On examining the character of relationships between businesses linked in dyads or networks it becomes clear that there is a huge amount of variability. Relationships vary in terms of their importance, intensity, closeness, strength, adaptation and commitment.[8]

Not all relationships are equally important. Some assume more importance because of their implications for value creation or value destruction. A relationship that is difficult and costly to manage may be important because it is a value destroyer. In contrast, a relationship with a strategically significant supplier assumes importance because of the value it produces. Relationship intensity is expressed in the number, frequency and level of contacts between the companies. In a close relationship there would be sharing of information, joint problem solving and commitment of resources by both partners, and trust would evolve over time. Closeness does not necessarily imply a lack of conflict. Conflict and co-operation can coexist in strong relationship; they are not necessarily mutually exclusive.

Some relationships are stronger than others. They are more able to withstand challenges to the bonds that tie them. These bonds may be social or structural. Structural bonds are present in the investments that one party makes in the other, and in the adaptations that one party makes for the other. These are harder to break than social bonds. When the investments are mutual this is evidence of bilateral relational commitment. These issues are explored in greater detail in Chapter 9.

Activity links, resource ties and actor bonds

Researchers have identified three attributes that help them to make sense out of business-to-business (B2B) relationships: activity links, resource ties and actor bonds, whether at the level of a bilateral relationship or a network.[4] These attributes may be remembered through the mnemonic BRA, where B = Bonds, R = Resources and A = Activities.

Relationships exist because at least one party performs activities for the other. These may be manufacturing or service activities, core or peripheral to the parties involved. Manufacturing may involve complete or partial processing of material inputs. Business-to-business services cover an enormous range of activities: accounting, advertising, book-keeping, consultancy, design, and so on. Suppliers have to decide what services they want to perform for their customers; customers, in turn, have to decide what they want to do in-house or to outsource.

Resource ties also connect network neighbours. Companies may dedicate resources to perform the activities that link the firms. The resources may include people, knowledge, equipment and money. Utilities companies sometimes employ independent customer contact firms to manage their customer relationships. For the contact centre, the dedicated headcount and technology is a resource tie that binds them to their customer. A chemicals supplier manages the inventory of a major customer by installing a telemetry monitoring system at the customer's premises.[9] This is a major investment in the relationship, and one that is unlikely to be recovered if the relationship breaks down. It acts as a structural bond between the two companies.

The actors within networks are both companies and individuals. Bonds exist at both levels. Actor bonds at a corporate level may be based on culture, values, law, geography, power or equity.

Cultural bonds are very strong among Japanese companies. In general, they prefer to deal with each other rather than with non-Japanese alternatives. This has made it very difficult for foreign companies to enter the Japanese market. Large companies prefer to deal with other large companies. For example, it is almost unheard of for a big-spending advertiser to work with a small advertising agency. Small and medium-sized enterprises (SMEs) generally develop strong relationships with other SMEs to help each other to compete against the might of the larger companies.

Some companies are renowned for their strong **values**. The Co-operative Bank is known for its pro-environment, ethical stance. It bonds closely with other companies, such as investment houses, that adopt the same position. It refuses to invest in companies that have poor environmental records.

Legal bonds tie companies together too. These may be contracts to supply goods at fixed prices. Even if there is no longer commercial value in a deal, the legal bond ensures that obligations are met.

Geographical bonds exist when companies in a trading area – street, city region or country – create a buyer–seller–referral network that supports all members of their group. In the UK, retailers in Leamington Spa have combated out-of-town developments by creating a loyalty programme in which customers can collect and redeem loyalty credits at any member store.

Power-based bonds are found when there is an asymmetry in the power relations between two companies. Sometimes the power resides in the bigger organization, particularly when one player has the advantage of monopoly or monopsony. Small suppliers to major retail chains complain about the retailer being demanding in terms of price. However, given the market access that these retailers provide, suppliers often accede to their demands. At other times power resides in the player with scarce, sought-after resources, such as knowledge, talent, connections and money.

Equity bonds are established when one party takes an ownership interest in another, perhaps by buying a block of shares, or by direct investment into a JV.

Actor bonds at an interpersonal level are social bonds. As the number of transactions and episodes linking firms grows, the interpersonal relationships between actors on the supplier and customer side begin to mature. Typically, levels of mutual understanding grow, problem-solving becomes joint, trust develops and there is commitment to the continuance of the relationship. A danger that companies must address is the loss of innovation as relationships become routinized and institutionalized. The social links between people are important dimensions of a network relationship, but are generally easier to break than activity links and resource ties.

There is dynamic interplay between these BRA components. As the range of activities grows, so does the variety of resource ties and interpersonal bonds. If someone quits a job, this may bring to an end or reconfigure the activities linking two organizations.

From dyad to network

Whereas BRA is helpful to understanding the relationship between members of a single supplier–customer dyad, at the level of the network there is an added level of complexity. It has been suggested that managers think about the larger context by considering three BRA issues.[1]

- The **activity pattern** of the network: what are the activities connecting the many dyads (or larger groups) in the network? In addition to customer–supplier relationships, the network may contain JVs, partnerships, licensing and franchising relationships. Is it possible to eliminate, reassign or integrate activities to make the network more effective or efficient?
- The **resource constellation** of the network: this is the sum of resources that are invested in interfirm relationships across the network as a whole. In a complex network, there will almost certainly be both underemployed resources and resource shortages. Are there ways in which the resources of the network could be better allocated for improvements in effectiveness or efficiency? For example, does the focal company need to run its own fleet of vehicles when a network member has spare capacity in logistics? Must the focal company set up a retail sales force if another network member can perform the same function on a commission basis?
- The **web of actors** in the network: intercompany and interpersonal relationships within a network form a complex social structure. This happens in many ways. Equity stakes in companies make for complex patterns of ownership and influence. Company A has a stake in company B; company B has a stake in companies A and C. Company

C has stakes in companies A and D. Directors have multiple memberships of network companies' boards. Marketers meet up at branch meetings of their professional organizations. Salespeople organize social events for their key accounts. Personal relationships contribute to the atmosphere of a business relationship, making it close or distant, friendly or antagonistic, open or closed. Established interpersonal relationships both enable and constrain the development of other interpersonal relationships.

Several different managerial roles have been identified in business networks.[10]

- The network **architect** designs a network for a given purpose. This might, for example, be the leader of a JV across international borders, involving several companies. Typically, architects are senior management with strategic responsibility. For example, when companies adopt CRM as their basic business strategy, a senior manager often acts as architect specifying the various network tasks that need performing as the CRM project takes shape. The architect may identify a number of roles for network partners: systems integrators, CRM software vendors, data analytics companies and so on (Fig. 6.6).
- The **lead operator** introduces particular businesses or individuals into the network.
- The **caretaker** takes an overview of the performance of the network, perhaps suggesting ways in which the network resources could be better deployed.

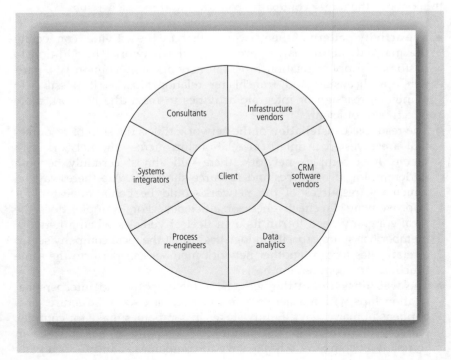

Figure 6.6
Technology partners for CRM implementations

Network position

A network is a coalition of organizations that are connected to each other through activity links, resource ties and actor bonds. Every company in the network occupies a particular position in relationship to other members. This is called network position, and can be defined as follows:

> A company's network position is the sum total of a company's network relationships and all the activity links, resource ties and actor bonds that these relationships contain.

A company's network position is a resource that can create competitive advantage. Networks supply the resources and perform the activities that enable the focal company to deliver value to the selected customers. Network positions are dynamic. Members adapt their network positions as they work to ensure their survival and prosperity. They look for opportunities to exploit: relationships that can be used to lift sales or reduce costs. Avon Rubber plc, for example, manufactures engine mounts for the car industry and counts Ford as one of its strategically significant customers. It leveraged its relationship with this reference customer to win business from Saab, and to enable it to present its credentials to other car manufacturers.

Skilful management of the company's network position can realize several benefits. Toyota uses its network position to enhance its cars' reliability, economy and design. Toyota works with and through its network members to keep costs low, while ensuring that product quality is high. Every company's network position is subject to a set of relational obligations and restraints among network members. For example, in the Toyota example the company expects tier one suppliers to develop and strengthen their relationships with tier two suppliers to ensure that Toyota obtains the quality it wants. Tier two suppliers expect tier one suppliers to maintain a good relationship with Toyota to ensure that they have ongoing access to a strategically significant customer.

It is unlikely that all the potential for competitive advantage that is contained in a network is presently exploited. Focal companies may not be fully aware of the opportunities that exist for co-operation and rationalization between network members. For example, there may be opportunities to bring together the innovation competencies of one network member, the manufacturing expertise of another and the marketing know-how of a third company, to create and launch success-ful new products. Or there may be opportunities to develop joint purchasing arrangements. Perhaps it might be possible to eliminate some processes that are duplicated. For example, a supplier may have a quality assurance programme in place; the supplier's customer may not need a quality control programme based on inspection of that supplier's products.

Network management and CRM

This brief review of network management contains a number of lessons for CRM practitioners. They fall into three major categories: identify network requirements, acquire network expertise and manage network performance.

Identify network requirements

You should identify the business functions that need to be performed to create and deliver value to your customers: these may be functions performed by suppliers, distributors, franchisees, contractors or business partners, for example. Some of these will be critical to value creation and delivery; others will not. You will need to find ways to bond more closely with the critical network members. This may involve improved communication and collaboration.

Acquire network expertise

You will need to evaluate your current network position to identify current network members and assess whether they have the resources and commitment to perform the activities required. If the present network is inadequate you will need to extend your network to find the resources to perform the activities that are required. Effectively, what you will be doing is leveraging existing, or developing new, actor bonds at the organizational or interpersonal level to improve network performance.

New network members are critical for winning a higher share of customer wallet. Tesco, for example, partners with a number of organizations, including Royal Bank of Scotland and General Motors, as

Case 6.1

Partnering at Tesco

Tesco has actively sought to create partnering programmes with other organizations. Partners have included:

- Lunn Poly, one of the UK's multiple travel agencies, to offer a discounted travel service to its customers
- B&Q, a major home improvement chain, to offer discounted 'do-it-yourself' and homeware products
- Royal Bank of Scotland, to offer banking and other financial services
- Direct Line, to offer household insurance products
- General Motors, to enable customers to buy cars at discounted prices.

The objective of all these programmes has been to win a greater share of customer spend.

shown in Case 6.1. It has developed a number of other JVs where it does not have the competencies itself to exploit opportunities.

Manage network performance

You will need to brief network members so that they understand your customers and their role in creating value for them. This may mean writing specifications, implementing common CRM applications, setting and monitoring quality standards, or designating people to take an oversight or coaching role. You should monitor how well the existing network is performing and look for ways to improve performance. Improvements can take two forms: more effective contributions or more efficient contributions from the network. Network members can contribute to CRM performance in a number of specific ways:

- offering new customer insight: they may be able to improve your understanding of your customers. In Australia, when Commonwealth Bank and Woolworths, the food retailer, created a JV to launch Ezi-Bank, the bank learned a lot more about their customers from access to Woolworth's transactional data
- value-adds for your company or customers as a result of:
  - Better cost performance at meeting your specifications
  - Improved product quality
  - Identifying new opportunities.

There is a clear danger in overspecifying network relationships. Marks & Spencer, for example, had very tight control over its supplier relationships. It established specifications and controlled design and quality rigorously. One effect was to stifle innovations. Suppliers did what they were told and failed to contribute to their full potential.

The SCOPE of CRM

There are four main constituencies of a focal organization's network: suppliers, owners/investors, partners and employees (Fig. 6.7). This figure shows the focal firm's customers at the heart of the network and the four constituencies rotating around them. The mnemonic SCOPE may be used to remember the constituencies in the network: S = Suppliers, C = the focal firm's Customers who are at the hub of the network, O = Owners/investors, P = Partners and E = Employees. The direction of the arrowhead in the outer wheel is meant to indicate that they all working towards the common goal of helping the focal firm to create and deliver value to their chosen customers.

Three of these constituencies are external to the company: suppliers, owners/investors and partners. One is internal: employees. This constituency was not considered in the discussion of network management above. One can even think of the internal constituency as being a network in its own right. Individuals within firms have formal relationships with colleagues, for example in a reporting hierarchy or cross-functional teams. They also have informal relationships that are not task oriented.

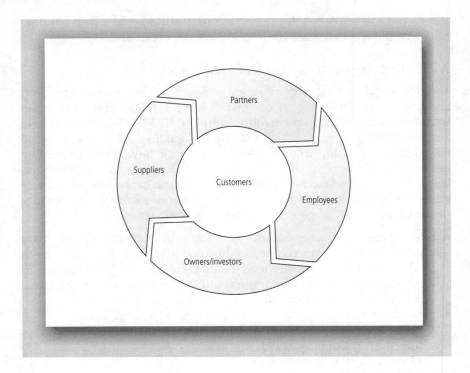

Figure 6.7
The SCOPE of CRM

The following sections look at relationships with suppliers, owners/
investors, partners and employees.

Supplier relationships

Many people claim that supplier relationship management is quite
distinct from CRM. In information technology (IT) terms, this is so.
Supplier relationship management is a back-office function managed
through ERP applications, whereas CRM is a front-office function
managed through a different set of software applications. However,
supplier relationships are discussed here because these functions can and
should be aligned and synchronized to contribute significantly to the
achievement of value for both the focal company and its customers (see
Case 6.2). Suppliers need to be briefed and managed so that they provide
the right inputs, at the right time and at the right price to enable the focal
company to serve its customers well.

Relationships with suppliers are critical to the delivery of value to both
the focal company and its customers. In 1999, General Motors spent US $62
billion and General Electric spent $24 billion on purchases. For many
companies, purchasing costs are 50 per cent or more of the total costs of the
company. There are variations between industries: in electricity and gas
utilities, input goods and services represent 10–15 per cent of sales. In
electronics it is 30–60 per cent; in chemicals it is 40–85 per cent. In 2000,

Synchronizing customer and supplier management at SEAT

Supply-chain management is synchronized with customer purchasing at Spanish auto manufacturer SEAT.

EXEL is a global leader in providing supply-chain solutions to the automotive industry. EXEL works closely with SEAT, providing an all-in-one solution for the car manufacturer and its suppliers. Essentially, EXEL manages the logistics for the just-in-time assembly line, linking the manufacturer with a network of more than 120 component suppliers.

To achieve this, EXEL manages the supply of 95 500 components every day and nearly 6500 components every hour, from the suppliers to the assembly line, where 2335 cars per day are manufactured. It takes only 105 minutes between a part being ordered by SEAT and that part being assembled in the car. To build 2335 cars per day, EXEL receives an order for a new car every 35 seconds.

Ford's purchasing bill amounted to $80 billion. A 1 per cent saving in procurement costs would lead to a direct improvement in Ford's bottom line of $800 million, doubtlessly thrilling shareholders!

Improvements in supply-network management not only offer the prospect of reductions in direct input costs.[i] Suppliers can also contribute directly to their customers' competitiveness by helping in product improvement, new product development, process improvement and quality management programmes.

The relationship between suppliers and their customers has often been portrayed as a conflicted, adversarial power struggle in which each player manoeuvres to secure a bigger share of profit. While there is still clear evidence of short-term, opportunistic behaviours on both the supplier and the customer side, in recent years there has been a trend towards a more relational approach to supplier management. This is characterized as a shift from a win–lose approach to supplier management to a win–win approach. Many companies now co-operate closely with their suppliers in a number of activities, such as product development, supplier accreditation and process alignment.

Product development

Suppliers may have ideas for product improvements or new products. Boeing, for example, co-operates with major international airlines as it develops new aircraft. This ensures that their innovations meet customer requirements, giving a strong probability that the aircraft will ultimately be adopted. Sometimes product development costs and risks are shared between customer and supplier.

---

[i] We prefer the term 'supply-network management' to the more conventional term 'supply-chain management', because it clearly acknowledges its systemic rather than linear nature.

Supplier accreditation programmes

Some purchasers have introduced supplier accreditation programmes, under which certified or preferred supplier status is granted to suppliers that meet certain quality standards. If you are not accredited you are not shortlisted to supply. Without accreditation you cannot begin to establish a relationship.

One common approach to supplier accreditation is to use international standards such as ISO 9000, which is administered by the International Organization for Standardization, based in Geneva. ISO 9000 is a family of generic quality management standards in which quality is defined as 'all those features of a product (or service) which are required by the customer.' ISO 9000 sets out principles that are designed to ensure that organizations do what is necessary to make their products and services conform to customers' requirements. The standard was first introduced in 1987 but was recently relaunched as ISO 9000:2000.

The ISO 9000:2000 family of standards is based on an international consensus about what organizations should do to satisfy customers' quality requirements consistently. ISO 9000:2000 is presented as a set of standardized requirements for a quality management system, regardless of what an organization does, its size, or whether it's in the private, or public sector. Focal companies can ensure that their suppliers are accredited to ISO 9000 standards.

The revised standard is based on eight quality management principles:

1 customer focus	5 systems approach to management
2 leadership	6 continual improvement
3 involvement of people	7 factual approach to decision-making
4 process approach	8 mutually-beneficial supplier relationships.

Standards and guidelines	Purpose
ISO 9000:2000, Quality Management Systems – Fundamentals and Vocabulary	Defines the fundamental terms and definitions used in the ISO 9000 family which help you avoid misunderstandings in their use.
ISO 9001:2000, Quality Management Systems – Requirements	This is the requirement standard that is used to assess your ability to meet customer and relevant regulatory requirements and thereby pursue customer satisfaction. It is the only standard in the ISO 9000 family against which third-party certification is available.
ISO 9004:2000, Quality Management Systems – Guidelines for Performance Improvements	This guideline standard provides guidance for continual improvement of your quality management system to benefit all parties through sustained customer satisfaction.

Figure 6.8
ISO 9000 family of quality standards

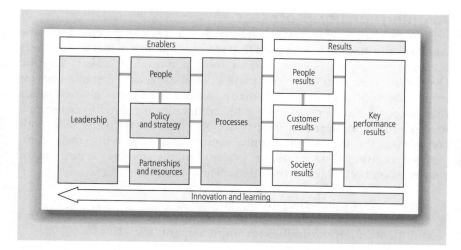

Figure 6.9
EFQM business excellence model (© European Foundation for Quality Management)

The eight principles are defined in *ISO 9000:2000, Quality Management Systems – Fundamentals and vocabulary* and in *ISO 9004:2000, Quality Management Systems – Guidelines for Performance Improvements* (Fig. 6.8).

Other companies insist that their suppliers apply for the Malcolm Baldrige National Quality Award, the European Quality Award or some other acknowledged business excellence model. The European Quality Award (Fig. 6.9), which is administered by the European Foundation for Quality Management (EFQM), assesses company performance against a non-prescriptive framework. The model's framework contains nine criteria. Five of these are 'enablers' (leadership, policy and strategy, people, partnerships and resources) and four are 'results' (customer results, people results, society results and key performance results). The 'enabler' criteria describe what an organization does. The 'results' criteria describe what an organization achieves. 'Results' are explicitly linked to 'enablers'. You will note that a number of the criteria that EFQM believe to be important to business performance also appear in our CRM value chain model: leadership, processes, partnerships, people and customer results, for example.[11]

Other companies, such as Ford and Motorola, operate their own supplier accreditation programmes. Motorola has said: 'If you're a Motorola supplier, an ISO 9000 certification won't even buy you a cup of coffee. We would never stop auditing a company with ISO 9000. It's just a fraction of what we are looking for.'[12]

Process alignment

Once customers and suppliers make a commitment to each other, they may begin to look for opportunities to align their processes. Processes alignment has the objective of reducing the costs of maintaining the relationship. Two processes are typically aligned: quality processes and the order fulfilment processes.

Aligning quality processes

Failure to comply with quality standards can be a huge cost for some companies. It has been suggested that the poor quality of incoming goods accounts for up to 70 per cent of total non-quality costs.[13] Despite Deming's injunction that companies should 'cease dependence on inspection to achieve quality',[14] many companies still use inspection for that purpose. An alternative is for the companies involved to determine together how to improve quality inputs, thereby reducing, for both companies, the cost of non-conformance, and improving their competitive position. The resulting practice might involve a number of processes on both sides of the relationship, such as:

- The customer establishes quality standards.
- The supplier benchmarks quality conformance against best-in-class and identifies opportunities for improvement.
- Supplier and customer agree strategy for quality improvement, involving *kaizen* (continuous improvement by all people involved in the process), information sharing and ongoing benchmarking.
- The supplier introduces a quality assurance programme (quality inspection programme abandoned by the customer).

Figure 6.10 shows how NCR changed its purchasing processes as it became more relationally oriented.[15] Key changes were that the company ceased the practice of inviting suppliers to tender annually, and developed a number of key supplier relationships. The quality of bought-in parts improved materially.

The order-to-cash cycle

A second process that is often redesigned as companies become closer is the order-to-cash cycle, or the order-fulfilment process. This process involves the customer establishing an acceptable inventory level and issuing an order for inventory replenishment when that limit is approached. The supplier fills the order and invoices the customer. The customer pays the invoice. Costs are removed from, and accuracy is improved in, this process by the application of two different technologies: electronic data interchange (EDI) and Extranets.

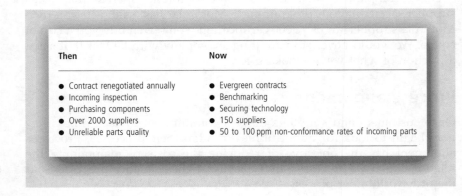

Then	Now
• Contract renegotiated annually	• Evergreen contracts
• Incoming inspection	• Benchmarking
• Purchasing components	• Securing technology
• Over 2000 suppliers	• 150 suppliers
• Unreliable parts quality	• 50 to 100 ppm non-conformance rates of incoming parts

Figure 6.10
How NCR's purchasing policies changed

Electronic data interchange enables suppliers and customer to trade electronically. It involves the interchange of unambiguously structured inventory, order and invoice data between computers according to agreed message standards. It eliminates the labour-intensive paper trail that is characteristic of many order-processing systems.

Electronic data interchange brings a number of strategic and operational benefits to companies. Operational benefits from EDI include cost savings, improved accuracy, better fulfilment performance, and improved cash flow and working capital positions.

- The need to re-enter data from paper documents can be eliminated, thus preventing clerical errors. It has been suggested that 70 per cent of all computer input has previously been output from another computer. Each re-entry of data is a potential source of error.
- Electronic processing of orders costs a fraction of paper-based systems, perhaps as little as one-tenth. This is partly because EDI reduces the need for people to be involved in order processing.
- EDI systems can reduce inventory costs. When customers submit their delivery requirements with order data, suppliers can plan production with more confidence, thus reducing inventories. Reduction in inventory can result in major savings.
- Use of EDI to transmit invoice data and payments can improve cash flow and working capital as invoices are routinely dealt with according to rules built into the system.

Strategic benefits from EDI include the following:

- it acts as a structural bond that not only symbolizes the commitment of the participants, but also acts as a barrier to exiting the relationship
- access to customer purchasing history, detailed customer management costs and payment history that can be useful when conducting customer portfolio analysis
- improved customer service (more accurate and timely fulfilment)
- better forecasting of demand coupled with the opportunity to develop new business processes such as just-in-time operations.

Other than EDI, many companies use Extranets to manage the order-fulfilment process with their customers. Extranets provide the infrastructure that enable customers to access a supplier's portal. A portal acts as a store-front. It is a company's electronic shop window. It has on display a number of products and services that are customizable for different portal visitors. The Extranet enables customers and other visitors to gain access to parts of the 'store' behind the portal store-front from outside the company. Visitors gain access by a password or security certificate. Customers can use a supplier's portal to place orders, track order progress, download training manuals, obtain price lists, access FAQ pages, and obtain invoices, brochures and collateral materials. Suppliers can use portals to service the requirements of some or of all of their customers. One of the major benefits is that portals reduce service costs by eliminating the use of more expensive communication channels such

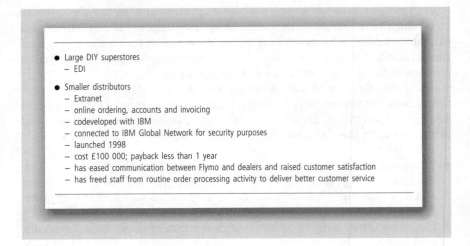

- Large DIY superstores
  - EDI

- Smaller distributors
  - Extranet
  - online ordering, accounts and invoicing
  - codeveloped with IBM
  - connected to IBM Global Network for security purposes
  - launched 1998
  - cost £100 000; payback less than 1 year
  - has eased communication between Flymo and dealers and raised customer satisfaction
  - has freed staff from routine order processing activity to deliver better customer service

Figure 6.11
Flymo's electronic customer service

as sales representatives, couriers, fax and telephone. Effectively, Extranets enable customers to serve themselves on company portals. Whether this enhances or detracts from customer satisfaction is a moot point.

Apple's Reseller Information System is a portal that allows Apple's distributors to establish inventory levels in Apple's warehouses, review process and place orders without Apple's intervention.

One company that has segmented its customer base, offering EDI to one segment and Extranet-enabled service to another, is Flymo, a manufacturer of lawnmowers available through both retail multiples and independent retailers. As shown in Fig. 6.11, Flymo services its large superstore customers by EDI, while smaller customers experience Extranet-based service.

Trends in customer–supplier relationships

Several trends in supplier management are helping companies to improve the value they create for themselves and their customers. Important among these are vendor reduction programmes, category management, product development alliances and electronic procurement.

Vendor reduction programmes

The tradition has been for companies to have many suppliers competing to supply inputs. These would be played off against each other to obtain the best deal on any particular transaction. This short-term focus is now being replaced by a relational approach to supplier management, known as strategic sourcing or supplier partnering. A main driver of this change has been recognition of the high fixed costs of supplier management.

Purchasing costs can be divided into fixed and variable. Variable costs are those that are associated with a particular transaction. These include the invoiced costs of the product and any itemized costs such as insurance and transportation.

Fixed costs are all the other costs of creating and maintaining a relationship with a supplier. These costs include:

- the costs of raising and processing each order. This may be $100 regardless of the value of the items purchased
- the time of management and staff, as they:
  - check supplier credentials and credit ratings
  - communicate with suppliers
  - audit conformance to order specification
  - identify the best deal on a transaction by transaction basis
- technology costs.

These costs are fixed regardless of the value of the items purchased, and may be greater than the invoiced value of the purchased items. Purchasers customarily try to reduce variable costs by negotiating better prices or by outsourcing specialist services such as logistics to third parties. Often, however, there are greater gains to be made from controlling fixed costs, and this generally means reducing the number of vendors with whom a company transacts.

According to consultants AT Kearney, vendor reduction programmes are accelerating. In 1999, they expected that 25 per cent of companies presently listed as suppliers would be delisted in the next 2 years.[16] Companies engaged in these programmes are pursuing a number of benefits:

- **Reduced transaction costs**: the fixed costs of purchasing are reduced when the number of vendors is reduced. This is complemented by reduced search costs. If you deal with a few regular suppliers, you spend less time and money searching for new suppliers to add to your list.
- **Additional volume discounts**: by consolidating purchases that had previously been distributed among a number of suppliers, customers place themselves in a stronger negotiating position. Dun and Bradstreet, for example, consolidated their purchasing of telecoms, IT and travel to yield annual savings of $10 million.
- **Performance compliance**: closer relationships with fewer suppliers, supported by shared information about future requirements, and enabled by IT, produces better order fulfilment. Given closer relationships with fewer suppliers, customers expect their logistics and quality standards to be met. For example, many companies have adopted an OTIFNE logistics performance standard that requires suppliers to deliver on-time (OT), in full (IF) and with no error (NE). If your supplier achieves on-time compliance of 80 per cent, in-full compliance of 90 per cent and no-error compliance of 70 per cent, overall performance compliance computes at $90\% \times 80\% \times 70\%$, or 50 per cent only.

- **Increased technical co-operation**: suppliers and customers can share customer and technical information to reduce risk, share costs and improve the probability of new product success.

Figure 6.12 sets out the benefits that the retailer Tesco believes it enjoys from its strategic sourcing programme, and Fig. 6.13 names a number of US and European companies that have pursued vendor reduction programmes. Some companies, such as British Home Stores, Ford, SEAT, Shell Retail and Xerox, have achieved significant benefits by applying vendor reduction across the entire organization. The data on Compaq and Laura Ashley indicate the economies that are feasible within a particular area such as logistics.

Category management

A number of retailers and brand manufacturers have turned to category management in recent years as a means of improving business performance. Category managers treat a group of related or substitutable products as a single strategic business unit. The focus is not on brands,

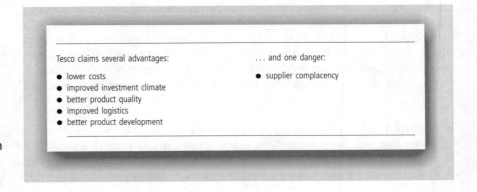

Figure 6.12
Tesco benefits from vendor reduction programmes

Tesco claims several advantages:

- lower costs
- improved investment climate
- better product quality
- improved logistics
- better product development

... and one danger:

- supplier complacency

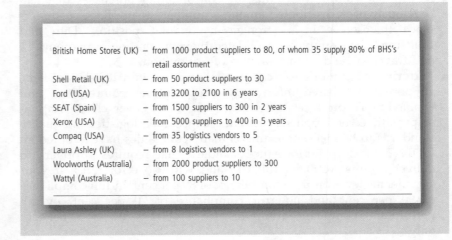

Figure 6.13
Vendor reduction programmes from around the world

British Home Stores (UK)	– from 1000 product suppliers to 80, of whom 35 supply 80% of BHS's retail assortment
Shell Retail (UK)	– from 50 product suppliers to 30
Ford (USA)	– from 3200 to 2100 in 6 years
SEAT (Spain)	– from 1500 suppliers to 300 in 2 years
Xerox (USA)	– from 5000 suppliers to 400 in 5 years
Compaq (USA)	– from 35 logistics vendors to 5
Laura Ashley (UK)	– from 8 logistics vendors to 1
Woolworths (Australia)	– from 2000 product suppliers to 300
Wattyl (Australia)	– from 100 suppliers to 10

but on categories. Category management has been described as 'a management system [that] aims to reduce the distance from supplier to customer by defining and managing product categories, rather than individual brands, in an environment of enhanced mutual trust and co-operation between manufacturer and retailer'.[17]

Retailers and their suppliers co-operate to recommend and create category assortments that suit the needs of the retailer, supplier and customers alike. The retailer will often work with a 'category captain', usually a brand leader in the category, to create the assortment plan. The captain will be responsible for assembling a network of cosuppliers to contribute to the category.

Category management requires the retailer and supplier to establish close links that enable them to agree category objectives, optimize the category assortment, introduce new products, de-list brands or items that do not contribute to category performance, and plot category of brand promotions. Category management is enabled by IT functions such as EDI, electronic funds transfer and activity-based costing.

Category management is cited as a win–win strategy for retailer and manufacturer, generating a number of benefits, as shown in Fig. 6.14.[18]

New product development alliances

It is becoming more common practice for companies to co-operate with their suppliers in product improvement and new product development programmes. Supplier competencies can be used to reduce development costs and accelerate time-to-market. For example, suppliers may

Benefits for supplier	Benefits for retailer
Increased profitability	*Financial:*
	Increased sales
Increased business knowledge	Increased margins
	Reduced costs
Improved relationships with retailers	Improved efficiency
	Increased market share
	Non-financial:
	Organizational learning
	More effective strategy implementation
	Better customer service
	Improved customer knowledge
	Understanding cost structures
	More open communications with suppliers
	Improved personal relationships
	Stability of best practice

Figure 6.14
Category management benefits

be able to advise on cheaper or better specifications for the product. They may share some of the cost burden if they are assured of being a key supplier when the product is eventually brought to market. Suppliers may even be the original source of new product ideas for their customers.

Collaboration platforms provide a set of technological tools and an information environment for collaboration between businesses developing new products. These platforms enable the alignment and integration of processes or work from geographically separated network members. For example, Boeing has established virtual design teams with its suppliers to work on aircraft design projects. Technology companies working on systems integration projects for clients that have multinational sites are also linked by these collaborative platforms.

E-purchasing

Another trend in customer–supplier relationships is for customers to buy online. Disintermediation, the elimination of one or more intermediaries from the supply chain, has the effects of reconfiguring the cost structure and redistributing margins among channel members. Banking was the first industry to go direct-to-consumer (DTC).

Suppliers adopt DTC marketing because it offers the prospect of two benefits: reduced customer management costs and enhanced control over the customer experience. The investment company Fidelity, for example, charges 3.25 per cent of the value of a purchase when a retail customer uses a standard paper-based application form to buy shares in mutual funds; when the purchase is made online the charge is only 1 per cent. In the travel business, distribution costs for a £300 package holiday are £45 if sold through a travel agent and £10 if sold direct over the Internet.[19]

This has been happening in both B2B and B2C contexts.

B2C e-commerce

Although the volume of consumer purchasing made online varies from country to country, and from product to product, the USA is still the marketplace in which online purchasing is at its most advanced. According to the US Census Bureau, e-purchasing by consumers has now exceeded 1 per cent of total consumer spending for the first time ($8700 million in the last quarter of 2000). The trend is upward as consumers become more confident in their remote shopping behaviours. Forecasting consumer spending on the Internet is a dangerous occupation. In 1998, for example, it was forecast that 7 per cent of consumer expenditure would be online by the end of the century.[20] It did not happen. Research tells us that consumers adopt innovations when they feel that the innovation offers a relative advantage over existing solutions, is compatible with their values and lifestyle, is relatively simple to understand and use, can be tried on a limited basis to reduce risk, and has benefits that are readily observable.[21] It is doubtful whether consumers regard these attributes as true of the Internet.

The categories that dominate consumer spending are travel, books, and computer hardware and software. Media products – books, music, videos and software – account for nearly 25 per cent of online sales. Airline ticketing is the single largest category, at 10 per cent. Combined with car rentals and hotel reservations, the aggregated travel category approximates 20 per cent of total spending.

Companies manage their customer interface on the Internet in different ways. Some companies only take orders online. Others receive payment online as well. A few deliver their product online too, for example, software companies.

In general, shoppers like the convenience and speed of online purchasing, and they expect to enjoy a price advantage over their bricks-and-mortar shopping. An important indicator of growing confidence is the increase in the number of customers making clothing purchases online. These are generally products that customers like to touch and try on before buying.

B2B e-commerce

Business-to-business e-commerce is a much more significant phenomenon than B2C e-commerce. Its value is difficult to pin down because there is no standard definition as to what counts as e-commerce. However, experts generally agree that the value of transactions in B2B e-commerce is about 10 times the value of B2C e-commerce. Business-to-business e-commerce is growing quickly because entry costs are very low. It can cost as little as $1000 to design a brochure-type website, with ongoing annual costs of web-hosting and site maintenance of only a few hundred dollars. In addition, unlike EDI, web-based trading employs open networks and standards delivering a much higher degree of interactivity and flexibility. The Internet is ubiquitous, accessible and cheap.

Timmers has provided a useful taxonomy of business models in B2B e-commerce.[22] Among the B2B models he recognizes are e-shops, e-procurement, e-malls, e-auctions and third-party marketplaces.

E-shops are normally associated with B2C e-commerce, but some B2B enterprises also enable customers to purchase online. Companies hope that their web presence will lead to increased demand, global presence and cost reduction in promotion and sales. Customers anticipate lower prices, better information and greater convenience. The site operator expects enhanced revenues from reduced cost, increased sales and, possibly, the sale of advertising space such as banner ads. Customers of pharmaceutical company Merck can buy laboratory equipment and products from the website www.merck-ltd.co.uk. Some company websites, such as www.dell.com, devote sections of their websites to corporate purchasing, as distinct from the household section.

E-procurement involves the electronic tendering and procurement of goods and services. Japan Airlines, for example, procures some of its supplies through its web presence. For the customer, anticipated benefits include wider choice of suppliers, lower input costs and reduced transaction costs owing to automation of the process. E-procurement may be accompanied by electronic negotiation and contracting. Customers and suppliers might also perform collaborative specification. Suppliers hope that they will have the opportunity to submit more tenders, perhaps globally, and experience lower tendering costs.

We are seeing evidence of 'co-opetition', that is co-operation between competitors, to secure better deals on input raw materials and goods. For example, keen rivals Unilever and Procter and Gamble have begun to co-operate in the procurement of raw materials for manufacturing.

An **e-mall** is a collection of e-shops on a single site. Industry.Net was established in 1990 to provide an industry marketplace for engineering and manufacturing professionals seeking access to information about products, services and suppliers. Industry.Net's revenues come from supplier membership fees and advertising. By 1999, it had 600 000 registered buyers, and 20 000 listed companies featuring 10 million products in 9500 categories. Effectively, Industry.Net has reconfigured the traditional value chain for industrial goods and services. It offers benefits to site visitors, buying members, supplier members and customers. Customers enjoy convenient access to a large amount of information from many suppliers, searchable catalogues, business and industry news, and online events such as trade shows and conferences. For suppliers, the site offers access to a global customer base, support to bring catalogues online and advertising space on the site's web-pages.

E-auctions are electronic versions of conventional auctions. They feature electronic bidding, sometimes linked with payment and delivery. Some are enhanced by multimedia presentations of the goods being auctioned. Benefits for suppliers and customers include increased efficiency in buying and selling. Infomar is a real-time information and communication system for the fishing industry. One of the system's capabilities is the electronic auction. It links fish producers to remote buyers. Fish producers enter their inventory into Infomar's database. Buyers can make offers to buy in a number of ways. They can enter the spot market, where bids are linked to an auction clock. When the clock stops the highest bidder has made the purchase. The system also enables other forms of purchasing such as tenders and options. The auction capability of Infomar is enabled by their technology partner SCS.

The JV GlobalNetXchange was established with seven equity partners from three continents, Europe, Australasia and the USA. Among them are Carrefour, Coles Myer and Sears Roebuck. Members, who now number over 1000, conduct auctions online though their website www.gnx.com (Fig. 6.15). GNX was created to drive down costs across the extended supply chain. GNX claims to be 'a secure, integrated e-business network, [it] connects global retailers and suppliers of all sizes with collaboration and buying solutions that fundamentally improve the way trading partners conduct business.'

Third-party marketplaces are buyer–seller websites that are operated by third parties. These provide an additional web-presence for many suppliers whose product catalogues appear on the site. Tradezone (www.tradezone.onyx.net) concentrates on the maintenance, repairs and operations (MRO) market. The products sold are non-strategic, time-critical consumables. Tradezone provides search-engine-enabled access

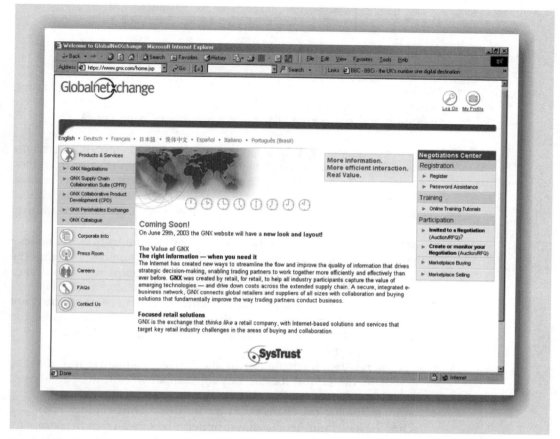

Figure 6.15 www.gnx.com

to supplier catalogues, order processing and payment processing on a secure site.

These business models show the number of electronic options that companies have to secure supplies in addition to EDI. They include e-shops, e-procurement, e-malls, e-auctions and third-party market-places. Sometimes, buyers can find out about potential suppliers by accessing the information generated by virtual communities. Virtual communities generally develop around the website of a host organization. The interaction between the members of the community is a core benefit for visitors, and the information members provide is of value in learning about suppliers. There are several industry-specific virtual communities, such as www.apparelex.com (for clothing and apparel), www.indconnect.com/steelweb (for the steel industry) and www.nano-thinc.com (for nanotechnology).

Not all of these options are necessarily relational in character. E-auctions, for example, tend be compatible with a very transactional view of supplier relationships. Each auction can be viewed as a unique event in which participants buy and sell as if there were no history linking them.

Not all customers want relationships with suppliers

Whereas many companies do believe there is value in co-operating closely with their suppliers, others have resisted this trend towards co-operation and partnering. They cite a number of concerns.[23]

- Fear of dependency: this is driven by a number of worries. Customers are concerned that the supplier might act opportunistically, once they are in a preferred position, perhaps taking the opportunity to raise prices. They also fear the reduction in their flexibility to choose suppliers. There may also be concerns over a loss of personal authority and control.
- Lack of perceived value in the relationship: customers may not believe that they will enjoy significant savings in transaction costs, or that the relationship will help them to create a superior competitive position or generate additional revenue, or that there will be any social benefits.
- Lack of credibility in the proposed partners: customers may choose not to partner because they feel that the potential partner is unreliable, too small or strategically insignificant, has a poor reputation or is insufficiently innovative.
- Lack of relational orientation in the buying company: this may be present in the culture of the buying company, its transaction-based reward systems or its organizational structure.
- Rapid technological changes: in an industry with rapidly changing technology, commitment to one supplier might mean that the company misses out on new developments available through other suppliers.

Owner/investor relationships

In the SCOPE model, the second constituency that needs to be managed so that it supports the CRM strategy comprises business owners and investors. They are the O in SCOPE. Owners and investors have expectations of a return on their investment. They expect the value of their stock price to grow and dividends to be paid. These expectations need to be managed. In general, Western investors, whether institutional or individual, take a rather short-term view of investments. They expect to see a return immediately. This short-termism is responsible for hot investment money racing from one money-making opportunity to another.

The period that it can take for CRM to show a return on investment varies according to the level of CRM that is being implemented: strategic, operational or analytical. Further, the type of evidence that signifies a return also varies with the CRM level. Investors supporting a strategic CRM project will need to have deeper pockets and more patience than investors behind an analytical CRM project. They make quite different demands on investors. Strategic CRM generally requires major changes at considerable expense and delivers returns over the medium to long term. At the other end of the spectrum, analytical CRM costs less and generates quicker returns. Investors need to understand what they are supporting and what returns to expect.

A **strategic** CRM implementation demands investments in technology, processes and people. These projects often involve major changes in corporate culture and restructuring of the business around customer groups, and might take 3–5 years to make a return. Even then, the evidence of a return may be rather soft by normal investor standards: higher levels of customer satisfaction and customer retention, or a greater share of customer spend. Employees' attitudes to customers may have changed, or the business may acquire, share and use customer information more intelligently. Over a 3–5 year term it is practically impossible to prove that any shift in sales or profit is due to CRM or, for that matter, any other type of programme.

Business performance is influenced by many conditions, a large number of which are beyond the control of any single enterprise, for example, business cycles, exchange rates, international relations, government regulations, competitor action and technological advances. Changes in these conditions over a 3–5 year term may serve to promote, counterbalance or reduce the impact of a CRM programme.

An **operational** CRM project such as sales force automation might yield a return within 12–24 months. Computer infrastructure and software has to be installed, the selling process modelled and current data transferred onto the new system, then salespeople need to be trained to work the new system. The returns on such an investment might include higher levels of salesperson productivity, such as calls made, proposals written and enquiries handled. An operational CRM project for 3Com, the company behind Palm handheld computers, involved shifting customer service from call centre to web self-service. 3Com enjoyed $16.8 million savings in year 2000 as fewer calls entered the call centre, talk times fell, call transfers fell and training costs fell. It is not reported whether customer satisfaction was influenced.

An **analytical** CRM implementation can show results almost immediately. Even a more complex project in which internal data from several databases is integrated and enhanced with bought-in data should show a return within a year.

It is often possible to conduct experiments on subsets of customers, to generate evidence that there is a return on CRM investment. You can prove CRM's value by reference to specific data such as customer acquisition costs, sales per customer, customer retention rates and customer tenure.

Reichheld claims that 'just as there are customers and employees who are right for your business there are investors who are right'.[24] The typical investor, focused on the short term, is not the right investor. He suggests that even if you are a publicly owned company you can pursue one or more of four ways to create a stable group of long-term oriented investors: educate current investors, shift the investor mix to institutions that avoid investor churn, attract the right kind of core owner, and operate as a privately owned company.

Educate current investors

Investors are justifiably sceptical of new business models. In recent years they have been promised improved profitability from business process re-engineering (BPR), ERP and total quality management (TQM). Many investors have been disappointed. Why should their response be any different with another three-letter abbreviation, CRM, particularly when various reports suggest that upwards of 60 per cent, and perhaps as many as 90 per cent of CRM implementations have failed?[25]

Investors need to understand that CRM, well implemented, does have an influence on shareholder value. One notable case is the Royal Bank of Canada (RBC), which won the first international award for CRM excellence in large corporations. RBC started its CRM initiative in 1995. To date, they have invested over $100 million. The Bank's Vice President for CRM claims: 'we no longer view CRM as a program. [It] is our core strategy. We absolutely conclude the CRM is paying us back in spades. It has enabled us to grow both top of the house revenue line and at the same time achieve huge cost savings.' Revenue growth is running at 10–15 per cent per annum, and profit growth at 25 per cent.

Investors need to understand that CRM, when well implemented, influences both sides of the profit equation: costs and revenues. Customer relationship management is very much about recruiting and retaining the right customers. These are customers who generate long-term value for the business. The long term may be several years, particularly if the repurchase cycle is extended. General Motors reckons that its customers are worth $276 000 over a lifetime of being GM customers, during which they purchase 11 GM vehicles.[26]

Finally, investors need to understand that CRM yields long-term benefits. There may be short-term results, but the true benefits may take years to deliver. Failure at CRM is indeed still an option . . . but it is not a requirement.

Shift the investor mix towards institutions that avoid investment churn

Most investors routinely churn their portfolios in search of a better return. However, some institutions are more stable investors than others, preferring to buy and hold for the long term. Low-churn investing appeals to a limited number of investment houses. Once you have identified them, it is suggested that you market your stock to them in much the same way as you market your products and service to your customers. This means segmenting the institutional investor market, targeting particular investors and positioning your stock against other stocks competing for the buying power of those chosen investors. Nike is one company that has pursued this strategy in order to maintain a stable shareholder base.

Attract the right kind of core owner

This approach is based on finding an institutional or individual investor who understands your CRM goals and is prepared to take a controlling position, and be patient for the long-term benefits. Reichheld cites Warren Buffett as the archetypal controlling investor. Buffett runs the investment company Berkshire Hathaway, where portfolio turnover is below 10 per cent. He has bought stock in very few companies over the past 20 years, and has remained loyal to those companies. He looks for companies that show high return on equity, a strong customer base, a simple business idea and an undervalued market position. Buffett is not the only investor taking the long view. Japanese and German investors typically take a much longer term view of their investments than most of their Western counterparts.

Go private

Companies that are privately owned do not need to dance to the tune of the stock market. They can take a long-term view of investments in customer management. However, private ownership is not for everybody. The level of debt that is needed to fund a CRM-based approach to business development can be very high. In fact, it may be too high a risk for most private business owners to bear.

The entrepreneur Richard Branson floated the Virgin Group on the London stock market in 1986. By October 1988 he had bought back all the distributed shares at huge personal cost. He had been unable to run the businesses under the Virgin umbrella in the way he wanted. He felt that his entrepreneurial approach to management was incompatible with the institutional demands for immediate returns on investment. The institutions would not have tolerated the results achieved by his airline, Virgin Atlantic. Established in 1984, it was in only 1995 that the airline showed a return on capital employed that would have been positive enough to please an institutional investor, 27 per cent. Just 3 years previously, the airline recorded a negative 29.7 per cent return. Branson was able to keep to his strategy of 'happy employees + customer value = business performance'.

Partner relationships

In the SCOPE model, the third constituency that needs to be managed so that it supports the CRM strategy is business partners. In general, the main function of business partners is to help to create and deliver value

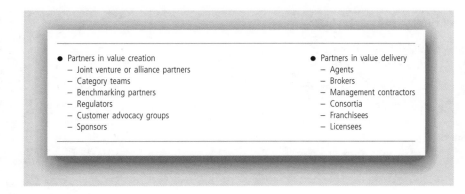

Figure 6.16
Partners in the SCOPE model

to the focal company's customers. They are the P in SCOPE. Figure 6.16 identifies a number of different types of partners, divided into groups focused either on value creation or on value delivery.

Partners in value creation

We identify a number of different types of partners in value creation: joint venture or alliance partners, category teams, benchmarking groups, regulators, customer advocacy groups and sponsors.

Strategic alliances

The terms 'joint venture', 'strategic alliance' and 'business partnership' tend to be used interchangeably. Indeed, there is no clear consensus on the differences, if any, between these business forms. However, they all feature interfirm co-operation. Partners in JVs or alliances maintain their own strategic autonomy while simultaneously establishing activity links, resource ties and actor bonds between the partner organizations for particular purposes. When British Airways and American Airlines agreed to co-ordinate routes, schedules and reservation systems, this was an alliance. It was neither a merger nor an acquisition. Both retained their autonomy. Alliances may involve two or more companies, two or more nations and two or more jurisdictions. They can be highly complex entities with no clear legal status. Equally, they can be very simple arrangements.

Case 6.3

The People's Lottery: a UK joint venture

The People's Lottery is a joint venture between nine companies. It developed and operates a national lottery in the UK. It is an unusual joint venture because there are no shareholders and no dividends, and all profits go to charity. A different group of JV partners ran the lottery previously. They were known as Camelot plc. They owned shares in the JV. A significant portion of profit was distributed among the shareholders.

Partners in the People Lottery are:

- Automatic Wagering International Inc.
- KPMG Consulting
- Energis
- Compaq
- Microsoft
- Cisco
- J Walter Thompson
- Kellogg's
- Virgin

Historically, many JVs were initiated to enable a dominant partner to enter a submissive partner's market. Essentially, the JV was an export channel. More recently, however, a new form of JV has emerged in which there is more co-operation between partners in the development of new products for sale in the partners' and third-party markets.

Not all alliances are strategic. To be so they must contribute to the strategic goals of both organizations. You would expect to find a more balanced contribution and participation in a strategic alliance.

There are several different types of alliance. Broadly, they can be classified into alliances between non-competing firms and alliances between competitors (known as co-opetition).

Alliances between non-competing firms

There are three main strategic motives behind alliances between non-competing firms. This section is largely derived from the research of Dussauge and Garrette[27].

International expansion

Renault formed a JV with DINA (Diesel Nacional, SA) to enter the Mexican market. When Procter and Gamble (P&G) decided to enter the Chinese market, they formed a JV with Guanzhou Lonkey Industrial Company (GLIC). Procter & Gamble brought its technology and manufacturing expertise to the table. GLIC brought its distribution network and local knowledge.

Vertical integration

Vertical partnerships bring together neighbours in the supply or demand chain. Aerospatiale and Thomson set up a vertical partnership called Sextant Avionique. Thomson manufactures avionics and electronic equipment used by Aerospatiale in its aircraft and helicopters. They are now involved in a 50–50 JV to manufacture and design new forms of equipment for the aerospace industry. Pepsi acquired part of Pizza Hut, KFC and Taco Bell to secure access to the restaurant market segment.

Diversification

Alliances aimed at diversification feature cross-industry agreements. BMW and Rolls-Royce got together to establish a JV to enable BMW to enter the aircraft engine market. JVs may be initiated when technologies begin to converge. Philips and DuPont have co-operated in the development of an optical disk system for data storage.

The STAR alliance has joined together 15 airlines that fly complementary routes. As shown in Case 6.4, the alliance produces benefits for both passengers and partners.

Alliances between competing firms

Alliances between competitors seem paradoxical. How can competitors co-operate? Research suggests that perhaps 70 per cent of alliances are

Case 6.4

STAR alliance

Air Canada, Air New Zealand, All Nippon Airways, Asiana Airways, Austrian Airlines, BMI, Lauda, Lufthansa, Mexicana, SAS, Singapore Airlines, Thai Airways International, Tyrolean, United Airlines, Varig

Benefits to frequent flyers:

- 688 destinations in 128 countries
- convenient booking
- more frequent flights (seamless travel)
- time saved in transit
- joint frequent flyer programmes
- more lounges

Benefits to alliance members:

- purchasing power: 'everything from toilet paper to aircraft'
- shared costs (estimated at $1 bn p.a.)
- joint IT
- shared airport positions

between competitors.[28] There are, again, three main types of alliances between competitors.

Shared supply alliances

This happens when competitors get together to experience economies of scale on the manufacture of some component or some stage of the manufacturing process. Volkswagen and Renault jointly manufacture automatic gearboxes. The European market for automatic transmission cars is only 8 per cent of the overall market. Together, because of the volumes, they generate economies that they could not enjoy independently, as they co-operate in research and development, and manufacturing.

Quasi-concentration alliances

In a quasi-concentration alliance the parties collaborate for the creation of a product that the consortium then offers to the market. In other non-consortium activities the parties compete as usual. An example is the development of the Tornado fighter plane by BAe, DASA and Alenia. Given the huge capital costs it made little sense for the three to compete in the market independently. Quite possibly none of them would have made a return on their investment in the project. Collectively, they were able to pool their resources and develop a product, the manufacture of which was shared among the three partners.

Complementary alliances

In a complementary alliance, partners bring different competencies to the alliance. Commonly, one partner has developed a new product that is distributed through the other party's distribution network. Ford sold rebadged Mazda cars, and Chrysler sold Mitsubishi cars in the USA. Chrysler only sold those models that filled gaps in Chrysler's product line.

Category teams

A category team consists of the network of brand owners that contribute to a category offer by a retailer. The retailer in partnership with the category captain decides which brands and lines to stock. The UK's confectionary market contains a number of 'must-have' brands manufactured by Mars, Nestlé and Cadbury. Whoever serves as category captain, these three manufacturers must be offered shelf-space.

Benchmarking partners

Benchmarking is defined as:

> a continuous, systematic process for evaluating the products, services, and work processes of organizations that are recognized as representing best practices, for the purpose of organizational improvement.[29]

Xerox, the copier company, is reputed to have originated benchmarking. Xerox's patents expired towards the end of the 1970s. As they did, Japanese competitors such as Canon introduced their products to the US market. To Xerox's alarm, they did so at a retail price that was lower than Xerox's manufacturing costs. Xerox began a benchmarking programme to find out what they could do to match and better the Japanese.

One of the key components of the benchmarking process is the selection of benchmarking partners (Fig. 6.17). A common misunderstanding about benchmarking is that it is simply a matter of identifying

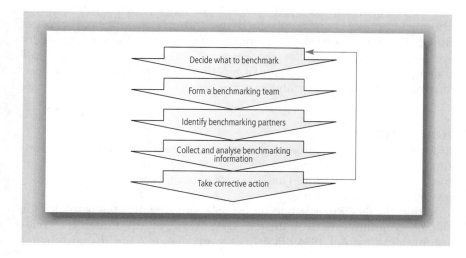

Figure 6.17
Five-step benchmarking process

and learning from best-in-class companies. It is not so. Benchmark groups are networks of companies that expect mutual gain from their participation.

The benchmarking group may be internal to a company, intra-industry or trans-industry. Each has their value, depending on the benchmarking objective. For example, a bank wanting to identify the practices that generate the highest average deposits per account would want to construct an internal benchmarking group.

An intra-industry benchmarking group has been established by 18 corporations in the telecoms industry, including AT&T, Nynex, MCI and GTE. They are learning from each other by sharing their knowledge on customer satisfaction, new product development and customer service.

A trans-industry group of benchmarking participants from FedEx, Caterpillar, Westinghouse and DuPont was established to learn from each other about best practices in the area of financial management.

Participants usually have concerns about disclosure of competitively sensitive information to their benchmarking partners. For this reason, codes of practice have been developed. These include the Benchmarking Code of Conduct of the American Productivity and Quality Centre, and the European Benchmarking Code of Conduct.[30]

Benchmarking groups can have significant impact on the creation of customer value. GPT Payphone Systems manufactures payphones, phone-cards and payphone management systems for customers in 80 countries. It set up a benchmarking programme to identify best practice in receiving and managing customer returns. As a result it set up and rolled out a barcode booking-in system for returns that also served to track repairs, and a buffer-stock system for replacing returned goods. The result was a 99.7 per cent success rate in next-day replacement, and a considerable increase in customer satisfaction.[30]

In the USA, Avon Cosmetics' immediate customers are the 450 000 sales representatives that sell Avon products to the end consumer. Fifteen per cent of this sales force generates 50 per cent of sales. Avon established an internal benchmarking study to identify and share best practice within and across the company's five geographical sales regions. The objective was to improve branch productivity through a range of process improvements. Among the outcomes were changes to the way managers were trained in the use of the company's IT system, improved call management system, and regular meetings between customer service supervisors to share ideas and experiences.

Regulators

Many industries are regulated, particularly those in which consumers are thought to be at risk either because of deregulation or because of monopolistic competition. These include financial services, telecoms, rail, gas, electricity and airlines.

In the UK, the Office of Telecommunications (Oftel) is the regulator for the telecommunications industry. Oftel was set up under the Tele-communications Act 1984. Its goal is to make sure 'you [the customers] receive the best quality, choice and value for money for all your telephone services.'[31] Oftel has three directorates: Regulatory Policy, Compliance and Business Support. Regulatory Policy Directorate is responsible for developing policies on telecommunications. Compliance Directorate makes sure that phone companies meet their obligations under telecoms and competition laws and regulations. Business Support Directorate supports the entire organization.

Oftel's duties include promoting the interests of consumers, maintaining and promoting effective competition, and making sure that telecommunications services are provided in the UK to meet all reasonable demands, including emergency services, public call boxes, directory information and services in rural areas.

A close relationship with regulators allows telecoms companies to ensure that they are not in breach of regulations or legislation, and have early knowledge of and perhaps influence forthcoming regulations or legislation. The regulator's office is also a source of useful insight into the issues that are troubling customers.

Customer advocacy groups

Customer advocacy groups (CAGs) promote and protect the interests of consumers. CAGs operate within many countries. Examples are the Consumers' Association of Canada, the Consumers' Association of Singapore and the Consumers' Association of Iceland.

In the UK, the Consumers' Association, publishers of *Which?* magazines and books, is a not-for-profit (NFP) organization which has been researching and campaigning on behalf of consumers since it was founded in 1957. With over 700 000 members, it is the largest consumer organization in Europe. Its mission is to 'empower consumers to make informed consumer decisions, and to achieve measurable improvements in goods and services.'[32]

There are some international consumer advocacy groups too. Consumers International (CI) is a federation of national consumer associations that 'defends the rights of all consumers, particularly the poor and marginalized, through empowering national consumer groups and campaigning at the international level.'[33] CI represents over 250 organizations in 115 countries. It focuses on issues such as food distribution, health care and globalization.

CAGs can have direct influence on corporate behaviour and indirect influence through lobbying activity. During the 1970s the UK's Consumers' Association (CA) developed its role as a campaigning body and lobby group. In 1972 it was instrumental in the establishment of the Office of Consumer Unions (BEUC), which lobbies consumer issues to the EC in Brussels. The CA claims responsibility for several important Acts of Parliament which have improved the position of consumers, including the Unfair Contract Terms Act 1977, the Consumer Agreements Arbitration Act 1988, the Property Misdescriptions Act 1991, the Cheques Act 1992 and the Sale and Supply of Goods Act 1994. Among the CA's more recent campaigns are improved food labelling, contaminant-free meat and better-designed pension products. They claim that 'annuities, the traditional method of guaranteeing an income in retirement, are failing to yield enough for pensioners'.[32]

Individual activists may also be worth considering as part of the P constituency of SCOPE. For example, Ralph Nader, the American lawyer and consumer activist, wields considerable influence. His 1965 book, *Unsafe at Any Speed*, detailed the carelessness of the American car industry in producing unsafe vehicles. A particular target was General Motors with its fragile Corvair. Nader wrote, 'A great problem of contemporary life is how to control the power of economic interests which ignore the harmful effects of their applied science and technology.'[34] The book led to congressional hearings and a series of automobile safety laws was passed in 1966.

Since 1966, Nader has been responsible for at least eight major federal consumer protection laws such as the motor vehicle safety laws; the Safe Drinking Water Act; the launching of federal regulatory agencies such as the Occupational Safety and Health Administration (OSHA), Environment Protection Agency (EPA) and Consumer Product Safety Administration; the recall of millions of defective motor vehicles; and access to government through the Freedom of Information Act of 1974.[35]

Some consumer advocacy groups concentrate on single industries, for example the Timeshare Consumers' Association. It aims to 'expose anti-consumer practices and organisations which operate in a manner detrimental to timeshare buyers and owners'.[36]

Case 6.5

Hoechst-Roussel aligns with patient advocacy groups

When Hoechst-Roussel Pharmaceutical launched Trental (pentoxifylline) for the treatment of intermittent claudication, an early form of peripheral arterial disease, its marketing management tried to reach senior citizens – the primary market for Trental – by launching an educational programme. Most older people did not view the major symptoms of this condition – leg cramps or pain while walking – as a disease; rather they interpreted the symptoms as a normal part of ageing and, therefore, they did not seek treatment or even tell their physicians about the problem. The programme was unsuccessful until Hoechst decided to reach the senior population in a more effective and credible way through the development of a relationship with the National Council on Ageing (NCOA), a non-profit American resource of information, training, advocacy and research on all aspects of ageing. The result was a national NCOA-sponsored public service education programme called 'Leg Alert'. At its core, Leg Alert was a medical screening programme. In the programme's first year, local Leg Alert screening events were held in communities across the nation; local cosponsors typically were an NCOA member centre, a local television station and a local shopping mall, which also hosted the screening. Local physicians directed each event and served as programme spokespersons. The programme's first-year success – measured by such criteria as number of persons screened, media impressions achieved and product sales – was so great that Leg Alert 'how-to' screening handbooks now have been developed and distributed to senior centres and hospitals.

Pharmaceutical companies work with and through Patient Advocacy Groups (PAGs) to achieve the aims of both the advocacy group and themselves (Case 6.5). PAGs are established to represent the interests of sufferers from disease, their families and carers. In the UK, for example, there are the National Schizophrenia Fellowship (NSF), Depression Alliance, SANE, Parkinson's Disease Society, British Diabetic Association, National Osteoporosis Society, Amarant Trust, Terence Higgins Trust, Women's Health Concern, Aids Treatment Project, Wellbeing, Macmillan Cancer Relief, the British Heart Foundation and many others. The relationship between the pharmaceutical company and PAG can be mutually beneficial.[37]

Sponsors

Although sponsors are generally insignificant in the for-profit context, they play a much more important role in the NFP context. Indeed, sponsors may be the principal source of income for NFP organizations.

Sponsorship can be defined as:

> The material or financial support of some property, normally sports, arts or causes, with which an organization is not normally associated in the course of its everyday business. The relationship between sponsor and sponsored is one in which the sponsor pays a cash or in-kind fee in return for access to the exploitable commercial potential associated with the property.

There has been significant growth in sponsorship in recent years. Worldwide, an estimated US$17.4 billion is being invested in sponsorship. This has been attributed to several conditions: the perceived ineffectiveness and inefficiency of advertising, government restrictions on tobacco and alcohol advertising, reduced government assistance to the arts, increased popularity and commercialism of sports and arts, the increasing trend to globalization of corporate/brand entities, and the progress of relationship marketing.[38]

Sponsors are looking for a number of commercial gains from sponsorship, including:

- increasing awareness and visibility for the product or company
- influencing consumer attitudes
- influencing consumer behaviour
- associating the product or company with a lifestyle
- entertaining key clients
- rewarding employees
- finding opportunities to launch new products
- differentiating the product or company from competitors.

For example, the cigarette manufacturer Rothmans sponsored the Williams Formula 1 team. Their objectives in sponsoring motor-sport were to increase awareness of their brands, encourage consumer trial and purchase of brands, and maintain loyalty towards their more established products.[39]

Organizations that enjoy the support of sponsors are common in the arts, sports or causes. However, trends indicate that such organizations are becoming more professional in seeking revenue streams from other sources. They are finding that they compete for limited sponsorship funds and that they must make a business case and deliver to the sponsors objectives to maintain the relationship.

Partners in value delivery

We identify a number of different types of partners in value delivery: agents, brokers, management contractors, consortia, franchisees and licensees.

These might be thought of as customers under the C of SCOPE. However, what sets this group apart from customers is that they do not take title to the products they sell. They do not therefore generate direct revenue streams for the focal company.[ii] Partners in value delivery are an integral part of many CRM implementations. In many cases, end customers regarded them as the suppliers of the goods, rather than the focal company. Customer relationship management principles therefore can be applied between partner and end customer, as well as focal company and partner. Partner relationship management (PRM) software can be used to help companies to manage these relationships: typically, PRM enables the provision of customized information to partners, distribution of product and marketing information, control of marketing funds, monitoring of activities, processing of orders and provision of leads. It is important that these partners understand and help to implement the focal company's CRM strategy.

Agents

Agents are commonly used when a business is small or geographically separated from the markets served and does not want or cannot afford to recruit and operate its own sales team. Agents do not purchase and resell; they simply represent the principals whose products they sell. They are order-getters, offering business owners the opportunity to access their established networks. Agents generally work on a commission basis. Agencies are common in the fashion industry. Apparel manufacturers broadly split into two groups. Large international, national or regional brands such as Benetton, Nike and Giordano tend to operate in the high-volume end of the fashion market. Brands such as Akira, Michelle Jank and Tea Rose tend to operate at the other extreme, selling through few outlets at higher prices. Whereas the former have their own sales teams, the latter tend to operate through agencies.

[ii] Although this is generally true, franchisees often pay a fee up-front for rights to use the business format, periodic marketing levies and training fees.

Agents representing manufacturers fall into two major categories.

- Manufacturers' agents represent two or more principals that produce complementary lines. In general, these agents agree contractual terms covering lines sold, territorial rights, prices, commissions, order-processing routines and returns policy.
- Selling agents are contracted to sell a manufacturer's entire output. Very often these are found in primary and production-oriented businesses such as mining, forestry and industrial equipment.

CRM systems can assist the manufacturer–agent relationship in several ways. They can provide a portal through which product information is published, marketing funds are approved and order progress is tracked.

Brokers

The role of the broker is to bring together buyer and seller. Brokers can be hired by either party. They assume no risk. Common examples are food brokers, real estate brokers and insurance brokers.

Management contractors

Management contractors are companies that undertake to manage some important part of a business, even the customer interface, on behalf of a principal. They are common in the hospitality industry, where the ownership and operation of hotels are separated. It is not unusual for hotels to be owned by an insurance or investment company, and for the operation of the hotel to be contracted out to a hotel management company. Contractors manage properties for well-known brand owners such as Holiday Inn, Marriott, Sheraton and Hilton. The contractor pays all the operating expenses and retains a management fee, normally between 3 and 5 per cent of gross income, remitting the surplus to the owner. The owner provides the property, fixtures and working capital, and assumes full legal responsibility. The contractor may undertake to manage the hotel under the operating standards of their own brand, or manage to the standards of another hotel brand. Sometimes hotel management companies are brought in to turnaround a struggling property.

Where a contractor is brought in to manage the customer interface, it is in a position to influence customer experience positively or negatively. It is critical that the contractor understands the experience that the principal wants its customers to enjoy. Customer relationship management systems allow principals to access detailed information about customer inter-actions, therefore enabling them to manage their contractor relationships more effectively.

Consortia

A consortium is a group of organizations that act co-operatively for mutual benefit. Often the organizations are independent of each other, as in the Best Western and Flag Hotel consortia, and the members of the SPAR group of independent grocery retailers.

Sometimes they are not independent. Kieretsu and chaebols are Asian examples. Some Japanese companies have formed into *kieretsu*. The kieretsu is a family of interlocked organizations, connected by common memberships on boards of directors, shared banking arrangements and close personal relationships. Sumitomo and Mitsubishi are examples. In Korea, some companies have formed into *chaebols*. These consortia are similar to the kieretsu but are reliant on close government connections for financial support. Daewoo and Samsung are examples.

Consortia are generally NFP organizations, built to generate economies of scale for their memberships. There are economies to be found in purchasing, marketing, training and development, and operations. Whereas a single hotel could not afford to develop and promote itself internationally, as a member of a consortium in which all members pay an advertising appropriation, it could create an international presence. Similarly, consortia can afford to invest in a centralized reservation system, which would be unaffordable to an individual member. Consortia members also operate as a cross-referral network.

Consortia management generally establish standards that members must meet in their operations. Best Western hotels reject 90 per cent of applicants. The objective is to create and deliver a consistent experience to customers wherever they encounter the consortium member. Leading Hotels of the World, for example, is a consortium that stresses excellence in service, physical structure, cuisine and guest comforts. Failure to meet the standards may result in exclusion.

Franchisees

Franchising is a rapidly growing form of business. A franchise is a licence to operate a business format for a prescribed time period within a defined geographical area. Franchisees receive training in the operational and managerial processes for running the format successfully. They gain access to a proven customer value proposition and a turn-key business operation. Typically, a franchise or investment fee is paid up front, as well as an ongoing royalty on sales. Franchise operations are among the best known in many industries, for example McDonald's, Holiday Inn, Century 21, Dunkin' Donuts, Midas and H&R Block.

The relationship between franchisor and franchisee can be conflicted. Sources of conflict are generally connected to the asymmetry of the power relationship: the sharing of revenues from the franchisee's operation, the level of franchisor support and the degree of franchisor control. The franchisor typically demands that franchisees do not depart from the approved format. They want customers to have a standard experience wherever they encounter the brand. Franchisees, in turn, may feel that they, the entrepreneurs, know more about the strengths and weaknesses of the business format than the principal. After all, they come into contact with customers and they have to run the operation. If they were drawn into changing the product offer and modifying processes, the franchisor would probably terminate the contract.

There is a growing recognition that the franchisor and franchisees together can create a mutually beneficial network through closer co-operation. Mature franchising operations such as Domino's Pizza are now committed to learning from their franchisees' experiences. They no longer believe that headquarters is the source of all innovation and knowledge about their business.

Licensees

Licences are rights granted to a business partner to exploit intangible assets such as technology, skills, designs or knowledge in exchange for remuneration such as fees or royalties. The value of US licensing arrangements was estimated at $93 billion in 2002.[40]

Licensing is commonly linked to the movie industry. Disney characters such as Mickey Mouse and Donald Duck have a long history of being licensed. Their images appear on a huge range of merchandise from pyjamas to lunch boxes and breakfast cereals. Technology is also widely licensed. When Kodak invented the disc camera, it licensed the technology to a large number of competitors, to speed up its access to world markets and inhibit competitors' investments in substitute technologies. Toshiba licenses its technology to Chartered Semiconductor Manufacturing.

Licensing has spread into the packaged goods market. Allied Domecq has licensed the use of the Kahlua brand to the company Herbal Enterprise, who have introduced Kahlua Iced Coffee into supermarkets. Jack Daniel's, the bourbon brand, is licensed for use in Jack Daniel's Grilling Sauces. Licensors seem increasingly enthusiastic about these licensing deals, which pay royalties of 1–7 per cent of retail sales, because they generate out-of-category exposure for their brands, and yield additional revenues for relatively little risk.

As with franchising, licensing arrangements can be fraught with difficulties. From the focal company's perspective it is important to ensure that licensees understand the brand values of the property they are licensed to exploit. The contract is designed to protect the property and ensure that it is used in appropriate applications. Disney would not licence Donald Duck for use in a pornographic website!

CRM systems play an important role in ensuring standards, marketing material and product specifications are well communicated and current. This relies on technologies for content management that allow companies to manage the release of information to partners and others through a formal approval and release process. Network members can then be advised when a product specification is changed or an advertising campaign is about to be released.

Employees

In our SCOPE model, the final constituency that needs to be managed so that it supports the CRM strategy is the employees. They are the E in SCOPE.

The IMP research into networks, which was discussed at the beginning of the chapter, omits reference to employees as part of the network that businesses need to manage. In the context of CRM, however, it is clear that employees can have a major impact on the creation, development and maintenance of customer relationships and satisfaction. This is particularly true in the service industries, where there is interaction between customers and employees during service encounters. Service marketing theorists call this 'inseparability'. Services are said to be inseparable because the service is produced at the same time it is consumed. Imagine you have contacted a call centre to register a complaint. The customer service agent is frustrated and angry because she has been denied a bonus she thought she was due. The competence, courtesy, empathy and responsiveness of the CSA are important contributors to your experience. Your experience may be at risk!

A number of leading CRM application suites now contain modules for managing customer relationships: employee relationship management (ERM).

Many companies intuitively recognize the importance of their people in creating value for customers and company alike. Some explicitly acknowledge the importance of people. In PepsiCo's 1998 annual report, for example, the company announced the launch of the PepsiCo Challenge:[41]

> The people who make, move, sell and service our products have the power to make customers smile. Boosting their capability, loyalty and enthusiasm will work wonders. We need to make PepsiCo an even more attractive, humanistic place to work by offering challenging jobs and pay, of course. But also, making sure we treat our frontline people with even more dignity and respect and by recognizing the enormous contribution they make to our success.

Companies need to be able to identify, recruit, develop and retain high-quality employees who can contribute effectively to the achievement of the company's CRM goals. Employee turnover is a huge cost in some industries. In food service, for example, front-line staff can turn over at 200 per cent or more each year. Turnover in senior positions can be high too. Nearly 20 per cent of managing directors change position each year. When an employee departs, a company incurs the direct costs of replacing that person: search costs, interviewing costs, relocation costs and so on. There may also be indirect costs such as business lost when customer accounts are not properly serviced. In extreme cases, employees may take customers with them when they depart. This is common in the advertising industry. When creative staff leave an established agency to set up on their own, they very often take clients with them.

Companies need to define the competencies that people should have to work successfully in defined strategic, operational and analytical CRM roles. Employees who are responsible for managing an important strategic alliance will need different competencies from employees working on the analysis of customer data using data mining tools. They, in turn, will need different competencies from those who work in the front line, interfacing with customers, perhaps in a call centre. ERM systems, therefore, contain functionality that enables companies to manage their recruitment, objective setting, performance management and training programmes.

Whatever their role, it is important that employees buy into the CRM mission and vision. They must understand what the company is trying to achieve in the markets served.

Internal marketing

The concept of internal marketing has been in existence since the 1980s, when Len Berry suggested that it made sense to apply marketing-like strategies to people management.[42] Winning and keeping good employees was thought to be much like winning and keeping good customers. Furthermore, to win employees' commitment to your CRM strategy, you are advised to market that strategy to them as if it were a product they were expected to buy. Internal marketing can be defined as:

A planned effort to overcome organizational resistance to change and to align, motivate and integrate employees towards the effective implementation of corporate and functional strategies.[43]

There is little evidence of companies writing internal marketing plans along the same lines as their external marketing plans, but it is possible to employ the same architecture to think in a structured way about how you would win your colleagues' commitment to your CRM strategy. Most marketing plans address a number of core issues: marketing objectives, market segmentation and targeting, market positioning, and marketing mix. Each of these will be explained briefly in the context of internal marketing of a CRM strategy.

Marketing objectives. These might include broad goals such as winning commitment to the CRM strategy, motivating employees to adopt new work practices, or developing a culture in which the customer's voice is central. Equally, objectives might be readily quantifiable, for example, training 100 per cent of employees to understand the concept of customer lifetime value.

Market segmentation and targeting. Segmentation involves dividing the internal market into homogeneous subsets so that each group can be targeted with a different marketing mix.

The internal marketplace most probably consists of different people with differing levels of buy-in to the CRM strategy. Winning buy-in can be a big challenge. Buy-in operates at an emotional or intellectual (rational) level. Intellectual buy-in is where employees know what has to be changed and understand the justification for the change. Emotional buy-in is where there is genuine heartfelt enthusiasm, even excitement, about the change. There is emotional commitment. The matrix in Fig. 6.18 shows the possibility of four employee segments, reflecting the presence or absence of emotional and rational buy-in. Champions are emotionally and rationally committed. Weak links are neither emotionally nor rationally committed. Bystanders understand the changes being introduced, but feel no emotional commitment to align themselves with the

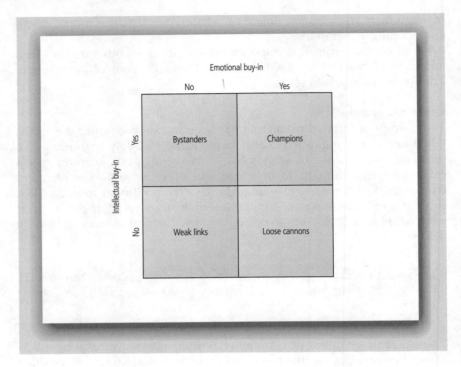

Figure 6.18
The buy-in matrix

change. Loose cannons are fired up with enthusiasm but really do not understand what they have to do to contribute to the change. All these segments will be found in major change projects such as a CRM implementation.

The CRM project needs to be marketed to each of these groups in different ways.

The challenges are to enthuse bystanders with a passion for adopting CRM practices, and to educate loose cannons on the reasoning behind CRM. Weak links can be truly problematic if they are in customer-facing roles or impact on customer experience. It has been said that it takes many years to win a customer's confidence and trust, but only one incident to break it. If efforts to win them over fail, weak links may need to be reassigned to jobs where there is no customer impact.

There may be other useful ways to segment the internal market. You might, for example, segment by the employee's degree of customer contact.[44] This has been applied to a European train operating company (Fig. 6.19). As a consequence, they identified four segments of employees in different roles in the company.

Market positioning. Positioning is concerned with how you want the CRM strategy to be perceived by each internal market segment. For some employees it may make sense to position it as a sound strategic move that will make their shareholdings more valuable; for others the positioning may be about job enrichment, work satisfaction, process simplification or anything else that the segment values. One positioning will not suit all segments.

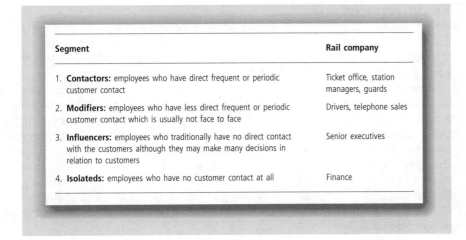

Segment	Rail company
1. **Contactors:** employees who have direct frequent or periodic customer contact	Ticket office, station managers, guards
2. **Modifiers:** employees who have less direct frequent or periodic customer contact which is usually not face to face	Drivers, telephone sales
3. **Influencers:** employees who traditionally have no direct contact with the customers although they may make many decisions in relation to customers	Senior executives
4. **Isolateds:** employees who have no customer contact at all	Finance

Figure 6.19
Segmenting the internal market by level of customer contact

Marketing mix. The marketing mix is the set of tools that marketers use to bring about the results they want in their target markets. The tools are commonly known as the 4Ps: product, price, promotion and place. An extended marketing mix with three additional Ps – people, physical evidence and process – has been developed for services marketers.[45] These ingredients are mixed in ways that the internal marketer feels will bring about the objectives. Figure 6.20 shows how the 7Ps can be use to promote buy-in to the CRM strategy. Key elements in the internal marketing mix are communication and networking.[46]

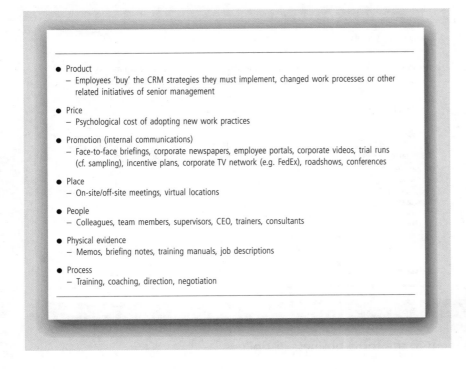

- Product
  - Employees 'buy' the CRM strategies they must implement, changed work processes or other related initiatives of senior management
- Price
  - Psychological cost of adopting new work practices
- Promotion (internal communications)
  - Face-to-face briefings, corporate newspapers, employee portals, corporate videos, trial runs (cf. sampling), incentive plans, corporate TV network (e.g. FedEx), roadshows, conferences
- Place
  - On-site/off-site meetings, virtual locations
- People
  - Colleagues, team members, supervisors, CEO, trainers, consultants
- Physical evidence
  - Memos, briefing notes, training manuals, job descriptions
- Process
  - Training, coaching, direction, negotiation

Figure 6.20
Using 7Ps as the internal marketing mix

Empowerment

Strategic CRM implementations are about creating a culture and climate in which the customer's voice is heard, valued and acted upon. Consequently, a growing number of companies are giving their customer contact staff a higher level of authority to meet, and even exceed, customer requirements. Some companies make heroes out of employees who have 'gone the extra mile'. However, empowerment is not just a matter of telling employees that they are now responsible for managing the customer relationship. Empowerment means equipping employees with the knowledge and skills to match the responsibility. For example, they need to know how to deal constructively with a customer complaint, particularly one that is objectively unjustified. This may involve scripting the dialogue in advance, providing information from a knowledge database on known problems and how they can be resolved, or providing diagnostic tools.

Empowerment ranges from total authority to do what it takes to satisfy and retain a customer, to bounded empowerment where the employee has a more limited discretion to act. The boundaries may be financial (e.g. no more than $200 per customer) or product related (e.g. domestic appliances but not financial services).

Empowerment helps to create an environment in which employees feel trusted and valued, leading to greater job satisfaction and motivation, which in turn can improve customer satisfaction and retention.[47]

	Value delivery strategies		
	Operational excellence	**Product leadership**	**Customer intimacy**
Core business processes that ...	Sharpen distribution systems and provide no-hassle service	Nurture ideas, translate them into products and market then skilfully	Provide solutions and help customers to run their businesses
Structure that ...	Has strong, central authority and a finite level of empowerment	Acts in an ad hoc, organic, loosely knit and ever-changing way	Pushes empowerment close to customer contact
Management systems that ...	Maintain standard operating procedures	Reward individuals' innovative capacity and new product success	Measure the cost of providing service and of maintaining customer loyalty
Culture that ...	Acts predictably and believes 'one size fits all'	Experiments and thinks 'out-of-the-box'	Is flexible and thinks 'have it your way'
Companies like ...	McDonald's	3M	Ritz Carlton Hotels

(row label: Company traits)

Figure 6.21 Empowerment in the three business disciplines

However, empowerment is not always an appropriate strategy. Treacey and Wiersema identified three basic marketing disciplines: operational excellence, product leadership and customer intimacy (Fig. 6.21).[48] The role of empowerment must be limited in businesses founded on operational excellence. Too much empowerment might slow down and impede the operational processes that create excellence. It is much better suited to environments dedicated to customer intimacy.

The service–profit chain

The above section introduced the link between satisfied employees and satisfied customers. Many companies believe that happy employees make happy customers make happy shareholders. Among them are Marriott Hotels and Resorts, Virgin Airline, Taylor Nelson SOFRES (market research company), Sears Roebuck and Volvo Cars. They believe that if employees are satisfied at work, they will deliver excellent experience to their internal and external customers. This, in turn, will drive up customer retention rates and improve business performance.

There is some evidence to support this claim. Some is generated by practitioners and consultants, some by academics.[iii] Schneider and Bowen have found that a climate for service and a climate for employee well-being are highly correlated with customer perceptions of service quality. Put another way, the experiences that employees have at work are associated with the experiences of customers. Sears Roebuck, the retailer, has found a high inverse correlation between customer satisfaction and employee turnover: the stores with highest employee turnover had the lowest customer satisfaction and vice versa.[50]

These connections between business performance, customer satisfaction and employee satisfaction are spelt out in the service–profit chain, a model developed by a group of Harvard professors (Fig. 6.22).[51–53]

The model suggests linkages between internal service quality (the quality of service received from colleagues in the workplace), employee satisfaction, value delivered to customers, external customer satisfaction, customer loyalty and business performance. The model does not claim cause–effect relationships between these variables. It simply finds evidence of correlation. Businesses such as AC Nielsen, the international market research company, for example, find the model very attractive. It provides them with an organizing framework for running their business. They claim: 'We live and breathe the service–profit chain, understanding our customers is fundamental to our success – satisfied employees make satisfied clients, make happy shareholders.'[54]

[iii] McCarthy's book *The Loyalty Link: How Loyal Employees Create Loyal Customers*[49] is an example of the consultant's approach. He writes, 'the abstract nature of these terms [customer loyalty and employee loyalty] makes it difficult to prove empirically that such a link exists, but there is a preponderance of indirect evidence'. He then cites many examples of associations between employee satisfaction, employee retention and customer loyalty.

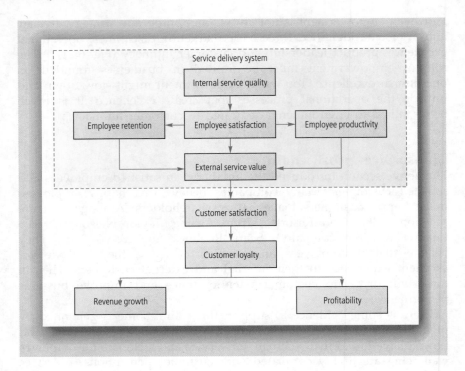

Figure 6.22
The service–profit
chain (Source:
Heskett et al.[51])

In one study at Sears, it was found that increases in employee attitude correlated strongly with increases in both customer satisfaction and revenue growth.[52] Sears developed a measurement model linking employee experience to customer experience to business performance. This they called the Total Performance Indicators (TPI) model. They reported: 'We use the TPI at every level of the company, in every store and facility; and nearly every manager has some portion of his or her compensation at risk on the basis of non-financial measures. . . . [I]n the course of the last 12 months, employee satisfaction on the Sears TPI has risen by almost 4 per cent and customer satisfaction by 4 per cent . . . if our model is correct – and its predictive record is very good – that 4 per cent improvement in customer satisfaction translates into more than $200 million in additional revenues in the past 12 months.'

Research on the linkages between components in the service–profit chain has met with mixed results. For example, one grocery retailing study found no correlation between employee satisfaction and customer satisfaction. The same study yielded a negative correlation between employee satisfaction and profit margin.[55] However, another study by the UK's Institute of Employment Studies found that employee commitment was connected to company profitability in three ways:

- directly through employee behaviours: the report suggested that a 1 per cent increase in commitment could lead to a monthly increase of up to £200 000 in sales per outlet

- indirectly through customer satisfaction
- indirectly through a reduction in staff absenteeism and turnover.[56]

Although research continues, the service–profit chain is proving to be a useful framework for many businesses.

Summary

This chapter has described the importance of managing the business network so that it helps you to create and deliver value to your selected customers. The network consists of:

- suppliers
- business owners/investors
- partners, including strategic alliance partners, category teams, benchmarking groups, regulators, customer advocacy groups, sponsors, agents, brokers, management contractors, consortia members, franchisees and licensees
- employees.

Within these networks, actors (individuals, groups, teams, organizations) deploy resources to perform activities. The challenges in network management are to identify the activities that need to be performed in order to create and deliver the value required, and to recognize, then co-ordinate and manage, the actors and resources that are best suited to perform those activities. Sometimes these will be internal to the organization; often they will be external.

References

1. Ford, D., Berthon, P., Gadde, L.-E., Håkansson, H., Naudé, P., Ritter, T. and Snehota, I. (2002) *The Business Marketing Course: Managing in Complex Networks*. Chichester: John Wiley.
2. Ford, D., Gadde, L.-E., Håkansson, H., Lundgren, A., Snehota, I., Turnbull, P. and Wilson, D. (1998) *Managing Business Relationships*. Chichester: John Wiley.
3. Gemünden, H.-G., Ritter, T. and Walter, A. (1997) *Relationships and Networks in International Markets*. Oxford: Pergamon.
4. Håkansson, H. and Snehota, I. (1995) *Developing Relationships in Business Networks*. London: International Thompson Press.
5. Naudé, P. and Turnbull, P. W. (eds) (1998) *Network Dynamics in International Marketing*. Oxford: Pergamon.
6. Blenkhorn, D. and Noori, A. H. (1990) What it takes to supply Japanese OEMs. *Industrial Marketing Management*, Vol. 19(1), pp. 21–30.

7. Ford, D. (2001) *Understanding Business Markets and Purchasing*. London: Thompson Learning.
8. Cheung, M. Y. S. and Turnbull, P. W. (1998) A review of the nature and development of inter-organisational relationships: a network perspective. In: Naudé, P. and Turnbull, P. W. (eds). *Network Dynamics in International Marketing*. Oxford: Pergamon, pp. 42–69.
9. See, for example, the 'our system' page on www.chemstation.com
10. Snow, C. C., Miles, R. E. and Coleman, H. J., Jr (1992) Managing 21st century network organizations. *Organizational Dynamics*, Winter, pp. 5–19.
11. For more information, go to http://www.efqm.org/
12. Henkoff, R. (1993) The hot new seal of quality. *Fortune*, June 28, pp. 68–71.
13. Bergman, B. and Klefsjö, B. (1994) *Quality: From Customer Needs to Customer Satisfaction*. London: McGraw-Hill.
14. Deming, W. E. (1986) *Out of Crisis*. Cambridge, MA: Cambridge University Press.
15. Cali, J. F. (1993) *TQM for Purchasing Management*. New York: McGraw-Hill.
16. Jacobs, M. (1999) Strategic procurement: the power of information. Corporate Seminar organized by SAS/D&B, Manchester, UK.
17. Hutchins, R. (1997) Category management in the food industry: a research agenda. *British Food Journal*, Vol. 99(5), pp. 177–80.
18. Hogarth-Scott, S. (1995) Shifting category management relationships in the food distribution channels in the UK and Australia. *Management Decision*, Vol. 35, pp. 310–18.
19. Wileman, A. (1999) Virtual necessity. *Management Today*, July, p. 95.
20. Phillips Traffica Limited (1998) *The Net Effect Report*. London: Phillips.
21. Rogers, E. M. (1962) *Diffusion of Innovations*. New York: Free Press.
22. Timmers, P. (2000) *Electronic Commerce: Strategies and Models for Business-to-Business Trading*. Chichester: John Wiley.
23. Biong, H., Wathne, K. and Parvatiyar, A. (1997) Why do some companies not want to engage in partnering relationships? In: Gemünden, H.-G., Ritter, T. and Walter, A. (eds). *Relationships and Networks in International Markets*. Oxford: Pergamon, pp. 91–108.
24. Reichheld, F. F. and Teal, T. (1996) *The Loyalty Effect: The Hidden Force Behind Growth, Profits, and Lasting Value*. Boston, MA: Harvard Business School Press.
25. Ang, L. and Buttle, F. (2002) ROI on CRM: a customer journey approach. ANZMAC Annual Conference, Melbourne.
26. Ferron, J. (2000) The customer-centric organization in the automobile industry – focus for the 21st century. In: Brown, S. (ed.). *Customer Relationship Management. A Strategic Imperative in the World of e-Business*. Toronto: John Wiley, pp. 189–211.
27. Dussauge, P. and Garrette, B. (1999) *Cooperative Strategy: Competing Successfully Through Strategic Alliances*. Chichester: John Wiley.
28. Morris, D. and Hergert, M. (1987) Trends in international collaborative agreements. *Columbia Journal of World Business*, Vol. 22(2), pp. 15–21.

29. Spendolini, M. (1992) *The Benchmarking Book*. New York: AMACOM.
30. Bendell, T., Boulter, L. and Goodstadt, P. (1998) *Benchmarking for Competitive Advantage*. London: FT Pitman.
31. For more details refer to http://www.oftel.gov.uk
32. For more details refer to http://www.which.net
33. For more details refer to http://www.consumersinternational.org
34. Nader, R. (1965) *Unsafe at any Speed: The Designed in Dangers of the American Automobile*. New York: Grossman (out of print).
35. For more details refer to http://www.nader.org
36. For more details refer to http://www.timeshare.org.uk
37. Buttle, F. A. and Boldrini, J. (2001) Customer relationship management in the pharmaceutical industry: the role of the Patient Advocacy Group. *International Journal of Medical Marketing*, Vol. 1(3), February, pp. 203–14.
38. Quester, P. G. and Thompson, B. (2001) Advertising and promotion leverage on arts sponsorship effectiveness. *Journal of Advertising Research*, Vol. 41(1), January/February, pp. 33–47.
39. Andrews, S. and Tucker, E. (1996) *Rothmans International: The Role of Sponsorship as a Promotional Tool*. Case No. 596–004–1. Bedford: European Case Clearing House.
40. Lauro, P. W. (2002) Licensing deals are putting big brand names into new categories at the supermarket. *New York Times*, 18 June 2002.
41. Thomson, K. (1998) *Emotional Capital*. Oxford: Capstone.
42. Berry, L. L. (1981) The employee as customer. *Journal of Retail Banking*, 3 (March), 25–8.
43. Ahmed, P. K and Rafiq, M. (2002) *Internal Marketing: Tools and Concepts for Customer-Focussed Management*. Oxford: Butterworth-Heinemann.
44. Judd, V. C. (1987) Differentiate with the 5th P: people. *Industrial Marketing Management*, 16, pp. 241–7.
45. Booms, B. H. and Bitner M.-J. (1981) Marketing strategies and organisation structures for service firms. In: Donnelly, J. H. and George, W. R. (eds). *Marketing of Services*. Chicago: AMA, pp. 47–51.
46. Gilmore, A. and Carson, D. (1995) Managing and marketing to internal customers. In: Glynn, W. J. and Barnes, J. G. (eds). *Understanding Services Management*. Chichester: Wiley, pp. 295–321.
47. Bowen, D. E. and Lawler, E. E. (1992) The empowerment of service workers: what, why, how and when. *Sloan Management Review*, Spring, 31–9.
48. Treacey, M. and Wiersema, F. (1995) *The Discipline of Market Leaders: Choose Your Customers, Narrow Your Focus, Dominate Your Market*. Reading, MA: Addison-Wesley.
49. McCarthy, D. (1997) *The Loyalty Link: How Loyal Employees Create Loyal Customers*. New York: John Wiley.
50. Schneider, B. and Bowen, D. (1993) The service organization: human resources management is crucial. *Organizational Dynamics*, Spring, pp. 39–52.
51. Heskett, J. L., Jones, T. O., Loveman, G. W., Sasser, W. E., Jr and Schlesinger, L. A. (1994) Putting the service–profit chain to work. *Harvard Business Review*, March/April, pp. 164–74.

52. Rucci, A., Kirn, S. P. and Quinn, R. T. (1998) The employee–customer profit chain at Sears. *Harvard Business Review,* January/February, pp. 82–97.

53. Loveman, G. W. (1998) Employee satisfaction, customer loyalty and financial performance. *Journal of Service Research*, Vol. (1), August, pp. 18–31.

54. For more details refer to http://www.acnielsen.com.au/

55. Silvestro, R. and Cross, S. (2000) Applying the service–profit chain in a retail environment. *International Journal of Service Industry Management*, Vol. 11(3), pp. 244–68.

56. Barber, L., Hayday, S. and Bevan, S. (1999) *From People To Profits*. Institute of Employment Studies Report 355.

Chapter 7
Creating value for customers

By the end of the chapter, you will understand:

1 the several meanings of the term 'value'
2 how customers compute 'benefits' and 'sacrifices' in the value equation
3 the sources of customer value
4 the importance of customization in creating value
5 the meaning of customer experience
6 a number of tools for mapping customer experience.

Introduction

Chapter 6 described how companies form networks that create and deliver value to customers. This chapter presents more about value, the fourth primary stage of the customer relationship management (CRM) value chain (Fig. 7.1). What do customers mean when they talk about value? What are the various elements that make up the value proposition? What is the role of 'experience' in creating value for customers?

First we examine the concept of value. Later in the chapter we turn to the concept of customer experience.

Our definition of CRM, repeated below, stresses the centrality of value creation and delivery. Customer relationship management aims to create and deliver value to targeted customers at a profit.

CRM is the core business strategy that integrates internal processes and functions, and external networks, to create and deliver value to targeted customers at a profit. It is grounded on high-quality customer data and enabled by information technology.

Understanding value

The word value has several different meanings. Valarie Zeithaml's research found that customers used the term value in four different senses.[1]

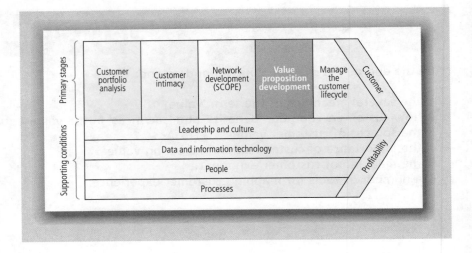

Figure 7.1
CRM value chain

- Value is 'low price'. For some customers the lowest price is the best value.
- Value is 'getting what I want from a product or service'. These customers define value in terms of the benefits they receive, rather than the price they pay.
- Value is the 'quality I get for the price I pay'. These customers regard value as a trade-off between the price they pay and the quality they experience
- Value is 'all I get for all I sacrifice'. This group of customers finds value in the relationship between every benefit they experience in purchase, ownership, use, consumption and disposal of a product or service, and the various sacrifices they make to enjoy those benefits.

These different views of value can be captured in a single definition of value.

> Value is the customer's perception of the balance between benefits received and sacrifices made to experience those benefits.

For some customers, value equates to low price, for others it is having their particular requirements met, for another group quality is the dominant concern. It is possible to present this definition in the form of an equation:

$$\text{Value} = \frac{\text{Benefits}}{\text{Sacrifices}}$$

The equation shows that you can increase the customer's perception of value in two main ways: increase the benefits they experience, or decrease the sacrifices they make.

Let's look at sacrifices.

- **Money**: the price of the offer. This may or may not be the listed price. There may be additional costs such as credit-card surcharges, interest charged on extended payments or warranty costs. There may be discounts applied for relationship customers, early payment or volume purchases.

- **Search costs**: the purchasing process may include exhaustive pre-purchase work in searching for solutions and comparing alternatives. This can take considerable time. In a business-to-business (B2B) context, a purchaser's time may have a real monetary cost. When purchasing involves several people these costs may be very high indeed. This is one of the reasons that customers are motivated to remain with existing suppliers and solutions. There may also be travel and accommodation costs as buyers visit reference customers to see solutions on site. Transaction costs are normally lower when search costs are eliminated, and purchasing processes are routinized. Some suppliers are prepared to take on the costs of managing inventory for important customers, so that they are less tempted to search for alternative solutions. Known as vendor managed inventory (VMI), it reduces search and reorder costs for customers.
- **Psychic costs**: purchasing can be a very stressful and frustrating experience. For some customers, holiday shopping at Christmas and other festivals means struggling to come up with gift ideas for relatives they rarely see, travelling on crowded public transport, pushing through throngs of shoppers, dealing with temporary sales staff who do not have enough product knowledge, paying inflated prices and carrying home arms full of heavy packages, and doing all this in bad weather! Psychic costs can be so great for some customers that they postpone purchases until a better time. Others cancel purchasing completely.

    Perceived risk is also a consideration in computing psychic cost. Perceived risk takes a variety of forms: performance, physical, financial, social and psychological. Performance risk occurs when the customer is not fully sure that the product will do what is required. Physical risk is when the customer feels that there may be some bodily harm done by the product. Financial risk is felt when there is danger of economic loss from the purchase. Social risk is felt when customers feel that their social standing or reputation is at risk. Psychological risk is felt when the customer's self-esteem or self-image is endangered by an act of purchase or consumption. When perceived risk is high, psychic cost is correspondingly high.

    Customers feel uncomfortable at higher levels of perceived risk. They act to reduce risk in a number of ways (Fig. 7.2). When customers try to reduce perceived risk, they are in effect trying to reduce the denominator of the value equation, thereby improving value. Suppliers can develop ways that help customers to reduce their levels of perceived risk. For example, performance risk is reduced by performance guarantees; financial risk is reduced by firm prices and interest-free payment plans.

Clearly, there is more to the sacrifice component of value equation than money alone. This accounts for customers buying what appear to be suboptimal solutions to their problems. Why would a customer buy a

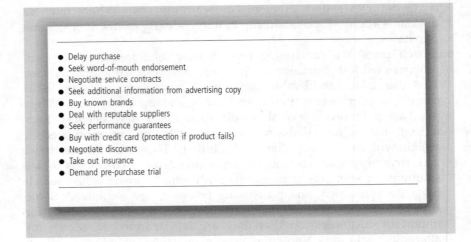

- Delay purchase
- Seek word-of-mouth endorsement
- Negotiate service contracts
- Seek additional information from advertising copy
- Buy known brands
- Deal with reputable suppliers
- Seek performance guarantees
- Buy with credit card (protection if product fails)
- Negotiate discounts
- Take out insurance
- Demand pre-purchase trial

Figure 7.2
How do customers reduce perceived risk?

printer for $500 when an identically specified machine is available for $300? Perhaps the answer lies in search and psychic costs. There is more to the benefit component than quality alone, although one expert has developed a value management methodology based on using quality as the numerator and monetary price as the denominator. This method assumes that customers will prefer the offer that delivers the best value ratio of quality against price. Gale presents this view that quality and monetary price are the basis of value computation by customers.[2]

There is a trend towards considering costs from the perspective of 'total cost of ownership' (TCO). This looks not only at the costs of acquiring products, but also at the full costs of using and servicing the product throughout its life, and ultimately disposing of the product. The process that we describe with the generic title of 'consumption' can in fact be broken down into a number of subprocesses, including search, purchase, ownership, use, consumption and disposal processes. The TCO is an attempt to come up with meaningful estimates of lifetime costs across all these subprocesses.

When customers take a TCO view of purchasing, suppliers can respond through a form of pricing called economic value to the customer (EVC). In a B2B context, EVC works by proving to customers that the value proposition being presented improves the profitability of the customer, by increasing sales, reducing costs or otherwise improving productivity. The EVC computes for customers the value that the solution will deliver over the lifetime of ownership. Suppliers can apply EVC thinking to each subprocess of the 'consumption' process described above. For example, a computer supplier may agree to provide free service, and to collect and dispose of unwanted machines after 4 years. Customers performing these tasks themselves would incur tangible costs. This is therefore the value that these activities have for customers.

Through EVC, suppliers are encouraged to customize price for customers on the basis of their particular value requirements.

Customer value researchers have developed several typologies of value. Sheth and colleagues have identified five types of value:

functional, social, emotional, epistemic and conditional.[3] In a B2B context, a distinction is made between economic value (satisfying economic needs at low transaction costs) and social value (satisfaction with the relationship with the supplier).[4]

Companies compete in a number of different ways, as indicated in Fig. 7.3.[5] In a well-regulated economy, most companies compete by trying to deliver consistently better value than competitors. This means understanding customers' requirements fully, and creating and delivering better solutions than competitors to the customer's problems. As noted in Chapter 6, this is a network achievement, guided by a focal company that is concerned to satisfy the requirements of a target market.

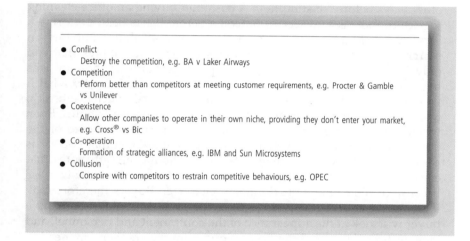

* Conflict
  Destroy the competition, e.g. BA v Laker Airways
* Competition
  Perform better than competitors at meeting customer requirements, e.g. Procter & Gamble vs Unilever
* Coexistence
  Allow other companies to operate in their own niche, providing they don't enter your market, e.g. Cross® vs Bic
* Co-operation
  Formation of strategic alliances, e.g. IBM and Sun Microsystems
* Collusion
  Conspire with competitors to restrain competitive behaviours, e.g. OPEC

Figure 7.3
How companies compete (Source: Easton et al.[5])

Value is found in the contextualized application of solutions to customer problems. A solution that works in one context is valuable; that same solution, not working in another context, has no value. In a B2C context, McDonald's may have great value as a solution to the question, 'Where shall I hold my 8-year-old daughter's birthday party?' It has less value as a solution to the question, 'Where shall I take my fiancée for her 23rd birthday?'

To create better value for the customers, companies have to reinvent the numerator (benefits) and denominator (sacrifices) of the value equation. In a B2B context, this is often done in partnership with customers, on a customer-by-customer basis. Unique solutions may be required. In business-to-consumer (B2C) contexts, solutions are segment or niche specific, and are supported by market intelligence. To win and keep customers, companies have constantly to seek to improve the value they create. This means improving the benefits or decreasing the sacrifices that customer experience. Given that this happens in a competitive environment, it is necessary not only to keep current with customer requirements, but also to stay up to date on competitors' efforts to serve these customers.

Sources of customer value

It is the job of professional marketers to develop the offers that create value for customers: the value proposition. The tools used to create value are called the marketing mix. McCarthy grouped these into a classification known as the 4Ps: product, price, promotion and place.[6] This is widely applied by goods manufacturers.

Services marketing experts have found this taxonomy inadequate because it fails to take account of the special attributes of services. Services are performances or acts that are:

- **Intangible-dominant**: services cannot be seen, tasted, or sensed in other ways before consumption. A customer buying an office-cleaning service cannot see the service outcome before it has been performed. Services are high in experience and credence attributes but low on search attributes. Experience attributes are those attributes that can only be experienced by trying out a product. Your last holiday was high in experience attributes. You were not able to judge fully what it would be like before you took the trip. Services such as health, insurance and investment advice are high in credence attributes. Even when you have consumed these services you cannot be sure of the quality of the service delivered. How confident are you that you car is well serviced by your mechanic? Search attributes are attributes that can be checked out in advance of a purchase. Services are low in these because of their intangible-dominant character. Buyers therefore look for tangible clues to help them to make sensible choices. Perhaps a buyer will look at the appearance of the equipment and personnel, and view testimonials in a 'brag-book'. Service marketers therefore need to manage tangible evidence by 'tangibilizing the intangible'.
- **Inseparable**: unlike goods that can be manufactured in one time and location and consumed at a later time in another location, services are produced at the same time and place they are consumed. Your dentist produces service at the same time as you consume it. This means that service customers are involved in and sometimes coproduce the service. This coproduction means that quality is more difficult to control and service outcomes are harder to guarantee. For example, a correct diagnosis by a doctor depends in large measure on the ability of the patient to recognize and describe symptoms. Sometimes service providers' best intentions can be undone by customer behaviour. Promoters of rock concerts where there have been riots know only too well that customer behaviour can change the fundamental character of a concert experience. Sometimes, other customers participate in the service experience, making it more, or less, satisfying. In a bar, other customers create atmosphere, adding to the value of the experience. In a cinema, ringing cell-phones and talkative patrons can spoil an otherwise excellent movie experience.
- **Heterogeneous**: unlike goods, which can be mechanically reproduced to exact specifications and tolerances, services cannot. Many services are produced by people. People do not always behave as scripted or

trained. A band can perform brilliantly one weekend but 'die' the next. Sometimes the service outcome is coproduced by customer and service provider. All of these factors make it hard for companies to guarantee the content and quality of a service encounter. Many services, for example in the financial services sector, are becoming increasingly automated to reduce the unacceptable level of quality variance that is associated with human interaction. Many customer service centres now script their interactions with customers to eliminate unacceptable customer experience.

● **Perishable**: services cannot be held in inventory for sale at a later time. A hotel room that is unoccupied on Monday night cannot be added to the inventory for Tuesday night. The opportunity to provide service and make a sale is gone forever. This presents marketers with the challenge of matching supply and demand.

Service marketing's response to these special characteristics has been to develop a new toolkit for creating customer value. It contains another 3Ps, making 7Ps in total.[7] The additional 3Ps are people, physical evidence and process (Fig. 7.4). As we shall see later, although developed for services contexts, they can provide a useful framework for the manufacturing context as well.

Before exploring each of these sources of customer value, we will look at the issue of customization.

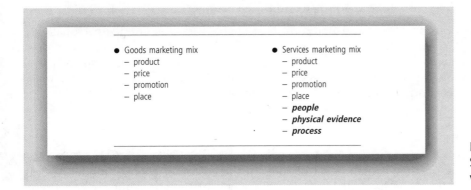

Figure 7.4
Sources of customer value

Customization

Customer relationship management aims to build mutually beneficial relationships with customers, at either the segment or individual level. A fundamental approach to achieving this goal is to customize the value proposition to attract and retain strategically significant customers. Customer relationship management aims to fit the offer to the requirements of the customer; it is not a one-size-fits-all approach.

Customization has both cost and revenue implications. It may make strategic sense because it generates competitive advantage and is appealing to customers, but there may be serious reservations because of the costs of customization. Companies need to ask whether investment in customization will generate a return higher than could be achieved through other strategies carrying a similar amount of risk.

Customization may mean the loss of economies of scale, thus increasing unit costs. There may be additional technology costs. When Dell Computers' customers are online, they are able to design their own computers. Customers interface with the front end of a technology called a Configurator. This is a rule-based system that enables or disables certain combinations of product features including chassis, hard disk capacity, memory, processor speed, software and connectivity. The technology is connected to back-office functions such as assembly and procurement. Each Dell computer is made to order. Customization means that companies have to be aware of and responsive to customers' differing requirements. Information systems designed to capture, store and distribute customer data also have a cost. (See Case 7.1.)

Case 7.1

Self manufacturing by customers at www.its4me.com

In the year 2000 www.its4me.com was formed with the ambition to create an online insurance intermediary to sell motor, home and other general insurance products over the Internet. The business sought to offer better value in terms of products and services sold directly to the customer, while reducing costs for the company and the customer.

To differentiate the business, www.its4me.com has enabled customers to personalize insurance products. A series of easy-to-use menu options is presented to customers to guide them through the process of selecting an insurance policy and various options to include in it. The company also attempts to enhance customer experience by using a webcam to show to customers the physical office and the staff working in real-time.

Configurator technologies can be quite sophisticated. In their simplest form they contain a set of rules (if the customer chooses model A, only allow one hard disk). At the other end of the spectrum are constraint-based optimization technologies similar to those employed in supply-chain optimization systems. The constraints are applied in a systematic way to ensure that the final configuration is optimum, for example, in producing least cost products.

Customization has been the norm in B2B markets for many years. Suppliers routinely make adaptations to suit the needs of customers. It is also true that customers make adaptations to suit suppliers. These adaptations serve as investments that make the relationship hard to break. Suppliers may adapt, or customize, any of the 7Ps, regardless of whether they manufacture goods or perform services. Although the additional 3Ps were developed for service companies, they also apply in the B2B manufacturing context, where they can be customized (Fig. 7.5).

- Product – Solvay Interox, a chemicals company, customizes its hydrogen peroxide product for textile industry customers
- Price – Dell Computer offers lower prices to its larger relationship customers than its small office–home office (SOHO) customers
- Promotion – Ford customizes communications to its dealership network
- Place – Procter and Gamble delivers direct to store for its major retail customers but not smaller independents
- People – Hewlett Packard creates dedicated virtual project groups for its consultancy clients
- Physical evidence – Thomson and other major tour operators overprint their point-of-sale material with travel agency details
- Process – Xerox customizes its service guarantee and recovery processes for individual customers

Figure 7.5
Customizing the 7Ps

- **People**: manufacturers can adjust the profile and membership of account teams to ensure that customers receive the service they deserve and can afford. Kraft, for example, has customer teams for major retail accounts that consist of a customer business manager (key account manager), category planner, retail sales manager, sales information specialist, retail space management and supply chain specialist. This customer-facing team can then draw on additional company expertise if needed, including brand managers and logistics specialists. The composition and membership of the team are agreed for each major retail account.
- **Physical evidence**: manufacturers use many different forms of physical evidence, such as scale models, cut-away models, product samples and collateral materials. Kitchen manufacturers provide customized swatches of worktop and cabinet colours to their major retail distributors.
- **Process**: important manufacturing industry processes are the order fulfilment process and the new product development process. Manufacturers can customize these to suit the requirements of different customers. Major fast-moving consumer goods (FMCG) manufacturers have evolved twinned new product development processes. They have their own in-house processes as well as customized processes in which they codevelop new products in partnership with major retailers.

Mass customization in B2C markets

It is in B2C markets that customization has become more widespread of late. Until recently, most consumer companies have either mass-marketed their products or developed product variants for particular niches. A growing number is now attempting to mass-customize their offers. This is enabled by customer databases that store customer preferences, Internet-enabled interactivity that permits companies to learn about changing customer requirements through improved communication, and mass-customization technologies.

Case 7.2

Tailored value propositions at Heineken Ireland

Heineken, the world's number one beer exporter, has been very successful in the Irish beer market with brands collectively capturing around 17 per cent of the total market. This success has been attributed to a deep understanding of the market, a strong portfolio of brands and a commitment to customer satisfaction. To sustain its position, Heineken sought to focus on delivering superior service to its 9000 commercial customers, namely pubs, hotels and wholesalers. To accomplish this Heineken chose to implement a CRM system with software vendor Siebel Systems.

For Heineken, one advantage of the Siebel software has been its ability to create single, comprehensive profiles of customers, which can be used to tailor product bundles and services, and to provide improved levels of customer service. Heineken believes that the CRM system provides the ability to build collaborative, higher quality relationships with customers. For example, sales representatives are able to prioritize their interactions with key customers and instantly analyse historical data to identify sales trends and buying patterns from individual customers to geographical areas, using their notebook computers while on the road.

Mass customization can be defined as:

> the use of flexible processes and organizational structures to create varied and even individually tailored value propositions, at the same cost as mass-produced, standardized offers.

This is not the same as offering customers more choice. Customers certainly want their needs to be met. They do not necessarily want choice. Giving customers' choice has been the default strategy when companies have been unable to identify and meet customers' precise requirements. Choice means work for the customer in comparing offers. Work adds to the cost of the consumption process.

Mass customization is common in service industries serving end consumers. This is largely because of the inseparability of service production and consumption. The interaction between consumers and service producers during the service encounter lets customers influence both the service process and the outcome (see Case 7.3).

Mass customization is becoming more common in manufacturing companies. Dell Computers' mass-customization model allows customers to design up to 14 000 different configurations of personal computer. Ford was able to produce 27 million different Ford Fiestas, more than were actually sold. In examples such as these, the deployment of a product configurator is essential. Without it, each combination of product options would require its own unique identification number in the information system.

Levi Strauss has three different routes to market: jeans specialists, department stores and their own Original Levis Stores. The Original Levi

Case 7.3

Mass customization at Amazon.com

Amazon.com has become the world's largest and most successful online retailer, diversifying from books and CDs into other areas such as electronics and clothing.

Much of Amazon.com's continued success has been related to its CRM strategy of retaining and gaining increased sales from its customers. To achieve this Amazon.com utilizes CRM software to customize the product offering for each customer. Based on available information such as previous purchases and products that have recently been browsed, Amazon.com's CRM software can predict a range of other products in which the customer is likely to be interested.

For example, a customer who selects to purchase a Ernest Hemingway novel may receive a recommendation to purchase another novel by the author or a DVD documentary of the author's life.

Store is where the company experimented with mass customization in the production of Levi jeans. Customer measurements were taken in store and fed into the production system. Ten days later the customer would receive a pair of customized jeans. For Levis, this differentiation allowed them to maintain a price premium that was harder to justify with a mass-production strategy. For customers there was the added value that the jeans fitted perfectly.

The following pages look at how value can be created by astute management of the marketing mix variables.

Value from products

Companies make products, but customers do not buy products. Customers buy solutions to their problems. They buy benefits, or better said, they buy the expectation of benefits. Nobody ever buys a lawnmower because they want a lawnmower; people want attractive lawns. Products are means to ends.

Products that offer better solutions to problems create more value for customers. A better solution is one in which the balance between benefits and sacrifices of the value equation is enhanced for the customer.

Marketers often distinguish between different levels of the product, sometimes known as a customer value hierarchy.[8,9] The **core** product is the basic benefit that customers buy. Companies competing for customer demand must be able to meet the core benefit requirements. MBA students typically are buying one or more of three basic benefits: salary enhancement, career development or personal growth. Schools compete in delivering the basic benefits to customers. A second level is the **enabling** product. This consists of the physical goods and service that are necessary for the core benefit to be delivered. In the MBA case, this would comprise the buildings, classroom fixtures, faculty and educational technology. A third level, the **augmented** product, consists of the factors that position and differentiate one competitor from another. In the MBA illustration this might be teaching method, for example, learning through real-life projects, or an extensive international exchange programme, or a leafy out-of-town location.

Companies offering the same core benefit have to compete to deliver value to customers through the enablers and the augmentations. As Levitt noted,

> . . . competition is not between what companies produce in their factories, but between what they add to their factory output in the form of packaging, services, advertising, customer advice, financing, delivery arrangements, warehousing, and other things that people value.[10]

Value is created for customers through:

- product innovation
- additional benefits
- product–service bundling
- branding
- product synergies.

Product innovation

Most 'new' products are modifications of existing products, cost reductions or line extensions. Very few products are 'new-to-the-world' or create new product categories. New products in all of these categories can improve customer value perceptions, but it is the dramatic ground-breaking inventions that create leaps in customer value. History is littered with them: Stephenson's locomotive, Edison's incandescent light bulb, Hargreaves' spinning jenny and Newcomen's steam engine. More recently we have had Akio Morita's (Sony) Walkman and James Dyson's Dual Cyclone vacuum cleaner, the subject of Case 7.4.

The Dyson case shows that value perceptions are not tied to price alone. The Dyson Dual Cyclone model DC01 was introduced to the market at a price well over that of the established players. It outsold competitors by 5:1, nonetheless. Dyson has also invented a number of other products: the sea-truck, the Ballbarrow (to replace the wheel-barrow), the Waterolla (a water-filled garden roller) and the Trolleyball (an application of Ballbarrow technology to boat launchers), and most recently, Dyson has launched the Contrarotator™, the world's first washing machine with two drums rotating in opposite directions.

Occasionally, old technologies provide value-creating modern-day solutions. Trevor Bayliss invented the wind-up radio after seeing a programme about the spread of AIDS in Africa. The programme highlighted the difficulty that health professionals faced in getting safe-sex messages to rural and poor areas where there were no power sources

Creating customer value through product innovation: the Dyson dual cyclone vacuum cleaner

- James Dyson's Dual Cyclone™ system was the first breakthrough in technology since the invention of the vacuum cleaner in 1901. The Dyson model replaces the traditional bag with two cyclone chambers which cannot clog with dust. After the outer cyclone has spun out the larger dust and dirt particles, the inner cyclone accelerates the air still further to remove the minute health-threatening particles.
- In 1993, the Dyson DC01 was launched in the UK, retailing at around £200, a significantly higher price than competitors. Since its introduction the DC01 has become the best-selling vacuum cleaner ever, outselling its nearest competitor by 5:1.

for conventional radios. Bayliss's first working prototype used a clockwork mechanism connected to a dynamo and ran for only 14 minutes. In 1995, BayGen Power Industries was set up in Cape Town, employing disabled workers to manufacture the Freeplay® wind-up radio. The product has two energy sources. As an alternative to the dynamo power, it is equipped with solar cells. The product has created value for all concerned: the manufacturers, investors, resellers, employees, Bayliss, who receives royalties from each manufactured unit and, of course, radio audiences. It has been very successful in South Africa and has provided vital access to the wider world for refugees from Macedonia and Albania. In 2002, the radio was selling at a rate of 120 000 units a month. The same technology is being applied to torches.

Additional benefits

Companies can create additional value for customers by attaching additional benefits to their products: a lawnmower operates more quietly; a car comes with a 5 year warranty; a fork-lift truck is supplied with a free options package.

Sometimes additional benefits are accompanied by repositioning the product is a different segment of the market. Lucozade had been glucose drink for older people and was widely associated with illness. The brand owner, GlaxoSmithKline, repositioned this product as an energy drink in the rapidly growing sports drink market, where it has enjoyed considerable success. The brand's website claims that athletes drinking isotonic Lucozade were able, in tests, to improve their athletic performance better than athletes drinking water alone.[i]

Low-involvement products have low levels of personal significance or relevance to customers. Customers feel a low sense of commitment to the brand and are therefore more likely to switch to competitors. Adding additional benefits helps brand owners to increase the level of customer involvement. There are two main approaches: product modification and

[i] For more information go to http://www.lucozadesport.com/

product association. Product modification means changing the product in some way so that it ties in more closely to the customer's needs, values and interests. Detergent manufacturers, for example, have reformulated their brands so that they are more environmentally friendly. Nappy manufacturers have resegmented the market so that there are different products for boys and girls, day and night, babies of different weights, and even 'swimmer' models. Product association means linking the brand to some issue or context that is of high importance to customers. Mobil, for example, has tied its brand to national Olympic interests. For every gallon or litre purchased, the company contributed to the fund supporting Olympic athletes.

Product–service bundling

Product–service bundling is the practice of offering customers a package of goods and services at a single price. Tour operators routinely bundle several elements of a vacation together: flights, transfers, accommodation and meal plan, for example. For the customer, bundling can reduce money, search and psychic costs. For the company, there are economies in selling and marketing.

Changing the composition of a bundle can have the impact of increasing customer perceived value. Adding and removing elements from the bundle can both have this effect. Adding elements to the bundle increases the benefits side of the value equation. In a B2C context, for example, supermarket operators can offer a bagging service at checkout at no extra cost to the customer. If the people performing this task are diverted from other tasks, then there may be no additional costs for the operator. Removing elements from the bundle enables the company to establish a new price point, therefore adjusting the value equation for customers. In a B2B context, companies often ask for elements to be removed from a bundle in return for a lower price. For example, a training college with its own information technology (IT) department may ask the supplier of its IT equipment for a lower price in return for not using the supplier's help desk and IT support facilities. If the price is reduced by $5000 and the saving to the supplier is $6000 then both parties win.

Branding

A brand can be defined as:

> any name, design, style, words or symbols that distinguish a product from its competitors.

Brands create value for customers in a number of ways, on both sides of the value equation.

- **Search costs**: brands reduce search costs by clearly identifying the product as different from others.
- **Psychic costs**: brands can reduce the psychic costs associated with purchase. Over time, brands acquire meanings that are reflected in

particular product attributes and values. If you buy a Mercedes vehicle, it may be because you understand that the brand attributes are excellence in engineering, assured quality build and high resale value. A customer who understands what the brand means is less at risk than the customer who does not understand. Brand knowledge like this is acquired from experience, word-of-mouth or marketer-controlled communication.

- **Benefit assurance**: brands offer an implicit assurance of a particular customer experience. When you buy any of the products carrying the Virgin brand it may be because you know or sense that Virgin's brand values are service excellence, innovation and good value.

Product synergies

Companies can create value for customers by finding synergies between products in the company's portfolio. For example, if you take a Virgin flight you will be offered a Virgin cola. If you buy Microsoft software, the company will offer you complementary software for related applications. These cross-selling opportunities sometimes are created not from within a single company but from a company's network.

Disney is particularly good at exploiting synergies. Disney characters such as Snow White and the Little Mermaid are created in Disney's film division. The characters then appear in theme parks around the world (USA, Paris, Tokyo, Hong Kong) in other service environments such as cruises and retail stores, and on the Disney TV network. Finally, the characters are licensed for use in other applications. For example, you will find Disney characters on lunch boxes and school bags, on clothing and shoes, and on McDonald's packaging for special movie-linked promotions.

Value from service

A service, as noted earlier, is a performance or an act performed for a customer. Service is an important part of many companies' value propositions. In most developed economies, about 70 per cent of gross domestic product is created by services organizations. For these organizations, service is the core product. Even in manufacturing firms, service is often an important part of the enabling and augmented product. For example, carpet manufacturers make floor coverings to international standards. While there is some potential to compete through product innovation, many manufacturers believe that the best way to compete is through offering better service to their distributors, and corporate and domestic customers. Typical services include stockholding, design, measurement, cutting to order, delivery and fitting. Companies need to understand that their efforts to improve service should be focused. Companies should find out what service elements are important to customers and where performance needs to be improved (see Case 7.5). If the customer's biggest problem is your failure to deliver on time, in full and with no error, it makes little sense to invest in updating the livery of your vehicles and drivers.

Case 7.5

Creating customer value from service innovation at HSBC

HSBC is one of the world's large banking groups. The organization has embraced IT to provide improvements in the quality of service it offers customers.

The organization has become a global leader in providing Internet banking services to personal and business customers and has won a number of awards in this area.

Much of the bank's success has resulted from undertaking extensive research among customers to determine how they could improve existing services and/or add new elements to the portfolio available in the Internet banking channel.

The findings led to the bank redesigning its Internet banking operations to offer faster and more secure access, as well as other services such as the ability to transfer money easily between HSBC accounts in various countries.

This section looks at a number of service-related methods for creating value: improving service quality, service guarantees, service-level agreements and service recovery programmes.

Service quality

Two major perspectives have influenced the way in which service quality is managed:

- **quality is conformance to specification**: this is consistent with Philip Crosby's view of quality.[11] In a service environment, conformance to specification might mean:
  - producing error-free invoices
  - delivering on time, in full as promised to customers
  - producing an initial response to customer complaints within 24 hours
- **quality is fitness for purpose**: Joseph M. Juran expressed this point of view, that quality means meeting customer requirements. It is the customer that decides whether quality is right.[11,12] If you are a farmer, a Land Rover is the right quality vehicle. If you are an Executive Limousine company, a Mercedes is the right quality vehicle. In a services environment, fitness for purpose might mean:
  - allowing the customer to select a preferred communication channel: phone, e-mail or postal service
  - recruiting customer contact staff who are highly empathic and responsive
  - customizing products for customers.

These perspectives on quality can happily coexist. Specifications for service performance can be based on customer expectations. The ISO 9000 quality documentation process makes companies set out on paper how they plan to achieve consistent service outputs meeting specific standards. If customers determine the standards, there need be no conflict between these two approaches.

Two service quality theories have dominated management practice as companies try to become more service oriented: the SERVQUAL gaps model and the Nordic model.

The Nordic model, originated by Christian Grönroos and developed by others, adopts a disconfirmation of expectations approach.[13] This claims that customers have certain expectations of service performance, with which they compare their actual experience. If the expectations are met, this is confirmation; if they are overperformed, this is positive disconfirmation; if they are underperformed this is negative disconfirmation. In the first two cases, service quality is deemed good or unexpectedly good; in the last, bad. Grönroos distinguishes between two sets of attributes evaluated by customers: technical and functional. Technical service quality (TSQ) focuses on *what* customers receive from a service encounter. Functional service quality (FSQ) is focused on *how* the service is delivered. TSQ questions are: Did my clothing come back from the cleaner with the grass stains removed? Has the software engineer fixed the bug on my PC? FSQ questions are: Was the help in the dry cleaner's courteous? Was the software engineer responsive? Grönroos suggests that FSQ is more important than TSQ in most product markets, the reason being that technical competence is an entry-level qualification for being a service provider in these markets.

The significance of this model is that it stresses the importance of understanding customer expectations and of developing a service delivery system that performs well in meeting customers' TSQ and FSQ expectations.

The SERVQUAL model was developed by A. 'Parsu' Parasuraman and colleagues in North America.[14–17] Like the Nordic model, SERVQUAL is based on the expectations disconfirmation approach. The model's authors identified five core components of service quality: reliability, assurance, tangibles, empathy and responsiveness, as defined in Fig. 7.6. These can be remembered through the mnemonic RATER.

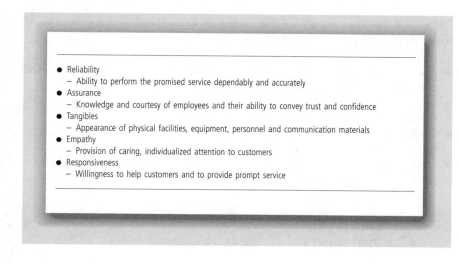

- Reliability
  - Ability to perform the promised service dependably and accurately
- Assurance
  - Knowledge and courtesy of employees and their ability to convey trust and confidence
- Tangibles
  - Appearance of physical facilities, equipment, personnel and communication materials
- Empathy
  - Provision of caring, individualized attention to customers
- Responsiveness
  - Willingness to help customers and to provide prompt service

Figure 7.6
SERVQUAL
dimensions (RATER)

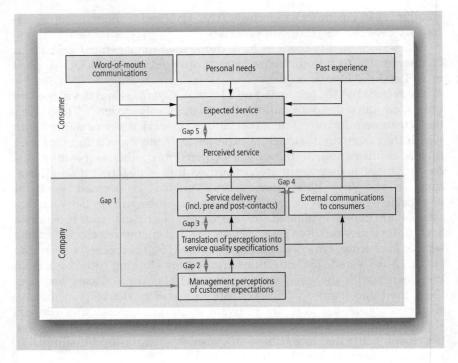

Figure 7.7
The SERVQUAL gaps model
(Source: Parasuraman et al[15])

They developed a measurement and management model to accompany the conceptual model. The measurement model is based on a 44-item questionnaire that measures customers' expectations and perceptions of the RATER variables.[15,16] The relative importance of these variables is also measured. This enables you to compute the relative importance of any gaps between expectation and perceptions. Management can then focus on strategies and tactics to close the important gaps.

The management model (Fig. 7.7), identifies the reasons for any gaps between customer expectations and perceptions (gap 5). Gap 5 is the product of gaps 1, 2, 3 and 4. If these four gaps, all of which are located below the line that separates the customer from the company, are closed then gap 5 will close. The gaps are as follows.

● Gap 1 is the gap between what the customer expects and what the company's management think customers expect.
● Gap 2 is the gap that occurs when management fails to design service standards that meet customer expectations
● Gap 3 occurs when the company's service delivery systems – people, technology and processes – fail to deliver to the specified standard.
● Gap 4 occurs when the company's communications with customers promise a level of service performance that the people, technology and processes cannot deliver.

The importance of SERVQUAL is that it offers managers a systematic approach to measuring and managing service quality. It emphasizes the importance of understanding customer expectations, and of developing internal procedures that align company processes to customer expectations. Among the strategies and tactics that might be employed to close gaps 1–4 are the following:

- Gap 1: the gap between what the customer expects and what the company's management think customers expect:
    - conduct primary research into customers' service quality expectations
    - learn from front-line customer contact staff
    - flatten the hierarchical structure
    - include expectations data in customer records.
- Gap 2: the gap that occurs when management fails to design service standards that meet customer expectations:
    - commit to the development of service standards wherever possible
    - assess the feasibility of customer expectations
    - develop a standards documentation process
    - automate processes where possible and desirable
    - outsource activities where you lack the competencies
    - develop service quality goals.
- Gap 3: the gap between service quality specifications and delivery:
    - invest in people: recruitment, training and retention
    - invest in technology
    - redesign workflow
    - encourage self-organized teams
    - improve internal communication
    - write clear job specifications
    - reward service excellence.
- Gap 4: the gap that occurs when the company promises service it cannot deliver:
    - brief your advertising agency
    - train employees not to overpromise
    - penalize employees who overpromise
    - encourage customers to sample the service experience
    - excel at service recovery
    - encourage and manage customer complaints.

There is growing evidence that investment in service quality improvements pays off in enhanced customer satisfaction and customer retention, although like other investments, there does appear to be a point at which diminishing returns set in, and gains in satisfaction and retention are much less attractive.[18,19] An example of a company's understanding of customer expectations is shown in Fig. 7.8.

The SERVQUAL model has been subjected to much criticism but it is still in widespread use in original and customized forms.[18] One criticism is that customers often do not have clearly formed expectations, and therefore that the disconfirmation approach is inappropriate. Some of these critics have developed an alternative, perceptions-only, model of service quality that they have dubbed SERVPERF.[20, 21]

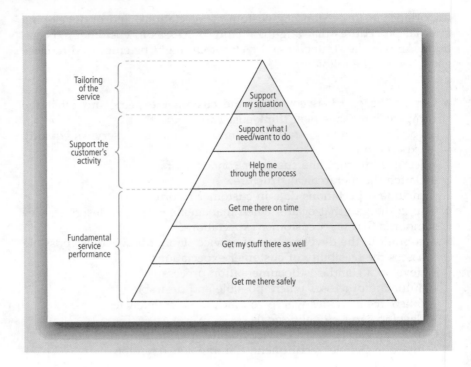

Figure 7.8
SAS airline's understanding of customer expectations

Service guarantees

A service guarantee is an explicit promise to the customer that a prescribed level of service will be delivered. Guarantees can be either specific or general. Specific guarantees focus on particular parts of the customer's experience. For example:

> Sleep tight or it's a free night. We guarantee it. (Howard Johnson's).

> Comfort guaranteed. Or you get 25 000 miles (BA).

General guarantees are limitless. For example:

> We guarantee to give perfect satisfaction in every way (LL Bean).

> Guaranteed. Period (Land's End).

Guarantees can be constructed for internal or external customers. The examples above are of external guarantees. The housekeeping supplies department at Embassy Suites guarantees that its internal customer, the housekeeping department, will receive supplies on the day requested. If not, the department pays $5 to the housekeeper.

Service guarantees can be customized for individual customers or segments. An IT service centre guarantees a 3 hour service to priority one customers and 48 hour service to all others. Should the company fail to honour these guarantees, it 'fines' itself by issuing a credit note to the customers.

From the customer's perspective, guarantees can be an effective way to reduce risk, and thereby increase value. After all, if the guarantee is unconditional, and the consequence of invoking the guarantee is that customer does not have to pay, there is effectively zero financial risk.

Service-level agreements

The purpose of a service-level agreement (SLA) is to define the mutual responsibilities of both the customer and the supplier of a given service. SLAs apply to both internal and external customer relationships. It is not uncommon for utility companies to outsource their customer contact function to a third party. An external SLA of this sort will carefully define both parties' expectations of the services to be performed, the service processes to be followed, the service standards to be achieved and the price to be paid. The SLA may well form part of an enforceable legal contract. A number of metrics are used to measure performance of the supplier and compliance with SLA service standards. These include:

- **availability**: the percentage of time that the service is available over an agreed period
- **reliability**: the percentage of time that the service is withdrawn or fails in the period
- **responsiveness**: the speed with which a demand for service is fulfilled. This can be measured using turn-around time or cycle time
- **user satisfaction**: this can be measured at the time the service is delivered or periodically throughout the agreed service period.

Many companies also have internal SLAs between service departments and their internal customers. An IT services department, for example, may establish a number of different SLAs with different customer groups. For instance, it might undertake to process payroll for the human resources department, or to maintain and service desktop devices for a contact centre. This is unlikely to be formalized in a contract.

SLAs create value for customers by reducing uncertainty about the services that will be delivered, their standards and costs. A successful SLA clarifies the boundaries and relative roles of customer and supplier. Each knows the other's responsibility.

Service recovery programmes

Service recovery includes all the actions taken by a company when there has been a service failure. Services fail for many different reasons.[22] Sometimes technical service quality fails; other times the failure is in functional service quality. Sometimes the blame lies with the company, sometimes with the customer and sometimes with a network member. Typically, customers are not concerned with who is to blame; they just want the situation resolved.

Research shows that when companies resolve problems quickly and effectively there are positive consequences for customer satisfaction, customer retention and word-of-mouth.[23] It has even been found that customers who have been let down, then well recovered, are more satisfied than customers who have not been let down at all.[24] This can perhaps be explained in terms of the RATER dimensions of service quality. Getting service right first time demonstrates reliability, but recovering well after service failure shows empathy and responsiveness. Reliability can be programmed into a company's service production and delivery processes. Empathy and responsiveness demonstrate the human attributes of concern for others and flexibility. Conversely, customers who have been let down once, only to experience a unsatisfactory recovery process, can turn into 'terrorists' who actively look for opportunities to spread bad word-of-mouth.[25]

When customers experience service failure, they have the choice of doing nothing or voicing their displeasure. A customer who chooses to voice can complain to the service provider, complain to associates and others in their personal network, or complain to a third party such as a consumer affairs organization or industry ombudsman.

Equity theory suggests that customers who complain are seeking justice and fairness. Equity theory explains that customers compare the sacrifices they make and the benefits they experience (as in the value equation) to other customers' sacrifices and benefits. When customers pay the same price but experience an unsatisfactory level of service compared with other customers, they feel a sense of inequity or unfairness. When they complain, they want the company to fix the imbalance. They want justice.

Research suggests that there are different types of justice. Figure 7.9 highlights three forms of justice that complainants seek: distributive justice, procedural justice and interactional justice.[26] Distributive justice is achieved if the customer obtains the material outcome wanted after complaint. Customers might be satisfied with an apology or a credit note against future purchases. Alternatively, a customer may want the service

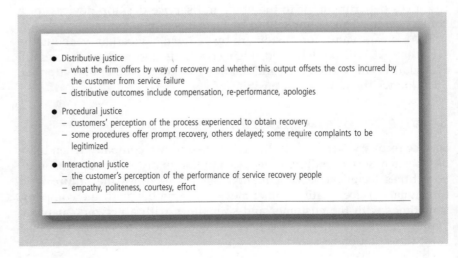

- Distributive justice
    - what the firm offers by way of recovery and whether this output offsets the costs incurred by the customer from service failure
    - distributive outcomes include compensation, re-performance, apologies

- Procedural justice
    - customers' perception of the process experienced to obtain recovery
    - some procedures offer prompt recovery, others delayed; some require complaints to be legitimized

- Interactional justice
    - the customer's perception of the performance of service recovery people
    - empathy, politeness, courtesy, effort

Figure 7.9
Service recovery
and justice seeking

to be reperformed. If distributive justice is concerned with what is received, procedural justice is concerned with the customers' evaluation of the processes and systems that are encountered during the complaints episode. Customers generally do not want to complete forms, provide difficult-to-find proofs of purchase or write formal letters confirming the complaint. These structures do not suggest that a company is organized and willing to resolve the problem quickly. Interactional justice is achieved if the customer judges that specific complaint-related inter-actions with the provider's people have been satisfactory. They want employees to be responsive and empathic.

Value from processes

In the previous section we have described some processes that help to create customer-perceived value: the service quality management process and the service recovery process. Elsewhere in the book we have touched on additional processes that impact on customers: the order-to-cash cycle, the selling process, the campaign management process, the customization process, the database development process, the benchmarking process and the innovation process, for example. A process can be defined as:

> a structured set of activities that converts one or more inputs into an output.

Thought of in this way, a process is workflow; it is how things get done. Companies are comprised of very large processes. IBM, for example, has identified 18 critical processes, Xerox 14 and Dow Chemical 9.[27] These big processes in turn are composed of smaller processes. For example, the manufacturing process takes a number of inputs – materials, technology, labour – and converts them into products. This big process is composed of several smaller processes such as machining, assembly and packing processes. Companies have thousands of processes. But processes are more than simply workflow; they are also resources that can be used to compete more effectively, to create more value for both customers and company.[27–29]

Process innovation can create significant value for customers (see Case 7.6). For example, First Direct started out as a telephone bank with no branch network. Customer management was entirely IT enabled, with customer service being delivered from a number of call centres. The bank's customer satisfaction ratings have been consistently higher than competitors' branch operations. Daewoo established a direct-to-customer distribution channel that replaced the normal distributor arrangements of other auto manufacturers. Customer experience was under better control and costs were reduced. easyJet speeded up customer service by improving plane turnaround times from 50 to 33 minutes, through improved teamwork.

Later chapters look in detail at critical CRM processes, including the customer acquisition process, the customer retention process and the

Case 7.6

Creating customer value by process reengineering at Asia Online

Asia Online, a leading ISP in the Asia-Pacific region, implemented a CRM software system to create added value for its customers by automating many services and processes.

Online bill payment and technical support services were the first processes moved from call centres to automated online processes.

The results of Asia Online's strategy have been positive. Operating costs are 35 per cent lower, attributable to the online processes, and there has been a 50 per cent decrease in customer complaints from slow customer service and incorrect billing.

customer development process. Each of these in turn could be decomposed into subprocesses. For example, the customer acquisition process could be broken down into the prospecting process, the customer contact process and the welcoming process.

Xerox's 14 key business processes are shown in Fig. 7.10. Many of these macroprocesses have an impact on customer experience or value perceptions, including the customer engagement, market management, product maintenance, and product design and engineering processes.

Complaints management

This section examines one additional process that impacts on the external customer's perception of value: the complaints management process.

Customers complain when they experience one of two conditions: their expectations are underperformed to a degree that falls outside their zone of tolerance, or they sense that they have been treated unfairly. Equity theory, described above, explains the customer's response to being treated unfairly. Customers also have a zone of tolerance for service and product performance. The range of tolerable performance will depend on the importance of the product, or the particular product attribute that is giving cause for complaint. Tolerances will be stricter for more important

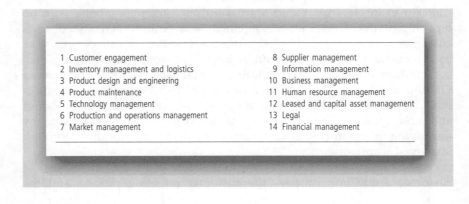

1 Customer engagement
2 Inventory management and logistics
3 Product design and engineering
4 Product maintenance
5 Technology management
6 Production and operations management
7 Market management
8 Supplier management
9 Information management
10 Business management
11 Human resource management
12 Leased and capital asset management
13 Legal
14 Financial management

Figure 7.10
Xerox's 14 key
business processes

products and attributes. For unimportant products and attributes, customers are likely to be less demanding.

No-one likes receiving complaints. However, a complaints management process needs to be developed that takes a positive view of customer complaints. Customers who complain are giving you a chance to identify root causes of problems as well as to win back customers who are unhappy, and therefore retain their future value. Worryingly, customers who do not complain may already have taken their business elsewhere.

A complaints management process should enable companies to capture customer complaints before customers start spreading negative word-of-mouth or take their business elsewhere. Research suggests that word-of-mouth can be very influential.[30] Up to two-thirds of customers who are dissatisfied do not complain to the organization.[31] They may complain to their social networks. Unhappy customers are likely to tell twice as many people about their experience than customers with a positive experience.[32]

Many customers who are unhappy do not complain, for several possible reasons.

- They feel the company doesn't care. Perhaps the company or the industry has a reputation for treating customers poorly.
- It takes too much time and effort.
- They fear retribution. Many people are reluctant to complain about the police, for example.
- They don't know how to complain.

Companies can address all of these issues by making their customers aware of their complaints policy and processes. A complaints management process that is simple and transparent should facilitate the capture of complaints.[ii] Some companies use dedicated free-phone and fax lines. Some reward complainants. Stew Leonard's, the Connecticut retailer, rewards complainants with an ice-cream. The purpose is to generate enough complaints to enable them to conduct root cause analysis and identify the causes of failure. If failures can be traced to particular people or processes, then the company is well placed to fix the cause of the problem.

Complaints enter companies at many different customer touchpoints: accounts receivable, order processing, sales engineering, logistics, customer contact centre, and so on. The system needs to collate complaints from around the business, then aggregate and analyse them to identify root causes. Software is available to help in this process. Ultimately this should enable the company to achieve a higher level of first-time reliability and reduce the amount of rework that is needed.

Experience and research suggest that customers generally want to have their complaints resolved at the first point of contact without being referred to supervisors, speedily and effectively. Figure 7.11 details some ideas for improving complaints management processes.

[ii] ISO 10018 is a new draft international standard for complaints handling. National Standards also exist in the UK (BS8600) and Australia (AS4269).

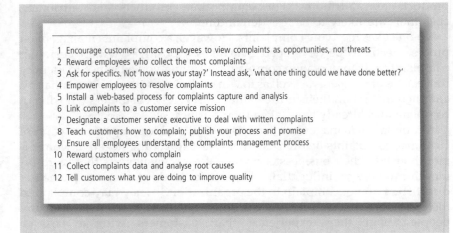

1 Encourage customer contact employees to view complaints as opportunities, not threats
2 Reward employees who collect the most complaints
3 Ask for specifics. Not 'how was your stay?' Instead ask, 'what one thing could we have done better?'
4 Empower employees to resolve complaints
5 Install a web-based process for complaints capture and analysis
6 Link complaints to a customer service mission
7 Designate a customer service executive to deal with written complaints
8 Teach customers how to complain; publish your process and promise
9 Ensure all employees understand the complaints management process
10 Reward customers who complain
11 Collect complaints data and analyse root causes
12 Tell customers what you are doing to improve quality

Figure 7.11
Improving the complaints management process

Value from people

Many companies claim that people are their key differentiators from their competitors, and a major source of customer value. This is especially so in professional services such as counselling, consulting and coaching where people are the product.

In the UK, the home improvement retailer B&Q has made a strength out of recruiting former building tradespeople such as carpenters, electricians and plumbers to help to customers diagnose their problems and choose the right products in-store. First Direct was the first UK financial institution to a offer a telephone banking service. Many other competitors now occupy the same space, so First Direct has had to reposition itself. It is no longer a technology leader. It now claims that it is a bank that can offer 'sparkling, intelligent conversation' to its customers.

There are many important roles that need to be filled for CRM strategies to work well. Some of these are customer contact roles, but many are back-office roles. People with the right SKA (skill, knowledge and attitude) profile need to be recruited, developed and retained for each position:

● back-office: data miner, systems integrator, campaign manager
● front-office: sales representative, key account manager, customer service agent.

All these roles need to have carefully constructed job descriptions that set out the objectives, responsibilities, reporting arrangements and key performance indicators for the roles.

One of the more important jobs in CRM is the customer contact role. This is a boundary-spanning role. That is, the role occupant sits in the space between an organization and its external customers. They are paid by the company, but work closely with customers. Boundary spanners have two fundamental and interdependent roles: information management and relationship management. Boundary spanners are accountable for collecting information about customers. What are the customer's requirements, expectations and preferences? What are the customer's future plans? Who is involved in the customer's buying decisions? The boundary spanner may have responsibility for maintaining the customer data on the database.

This information enables the role occupant to perform the second role, managing the customer relationship. This might involve winning, growing and maintaining the customer's business, handling customer queries and complaints, representing the customer's interests to the company, and ensuring the customer's satisfaction.

Some companies distinguish between different customer management roles. A common distinction in the sales office is between hunters and farmers. Hunters are more aggressive and are better at winning new business; farmers are more nurturing and better at growing account value. You would expect hunters to score high on ego-drive, while farmers would score higher on empathy in psychometric tests.

There is a trend towards key account management that is driven by a number of trends: global customers, consolidated purchasing, vendor reduction programmes and customers who want better service and closer relationships with their suppliers. The role of key account manager, national account manager or global account manager is extremely important. Occupants needs an advanced, and rare, SKA profile including selling skills, negotiating skills, communication skills, analytical skills, problem-solving skills, customer knowledge, market knowledge, competitor knowledge and customer orientation, as well as a detailed understanding of what their own company's network can deliver. We examine key account management in greater detail in Chapter 10.

Value from physical evidence

Some companies create value for customers by managing physical evidence. This is especially important for service industries that are intangible-dominant. Physical evidence can be defined as:

> the tangible facilities, equipment and materials that companies use to communicate value to customers.

Physical evidence includes a company's premises, and their internal and external environments, print materials, websites, corporate uniforms and vehicle livery. It makes sense for companies to audit and record their physical evidence and determine how best to manage it to create specific impressions on customers. Banks, for example, generally occupy traditional buildings with columns, portico, steps and large, heavy doors. This is designed to communicate conservative values, security and probity. McDonald's uses primary colours, bright lights and the ubiquitous golden arches in the form of the letter M. Hospitals convey impressions of hygiene and care through white uniforms, immaculately clean premises and well-maintained gardens. You only need to reflect on the traditional clothing, livery and appearance of funeral services to understand the significance of physical evidence.

Value from customer communication

Companies are now able to create value for customers from communication strategies that were impossible in earlier years. Companies are thinking about how to enable multilateral communication: company-to-customer, customer-to-company and even customer-to-customer. Customers can now communicate with companies through e-mail, websites, telephone, fax, chat rooms, contact centres, help-desks and complaints lines, as well as by old-fashioned correspondence.

Traditionally, customer communication has been one way: from companies to customers. The conventional tools for company-to-customer communication are unilateral: advertising, sales promotion, publicity, public relations and personal selling. With the exception of selling these communication channels are mediated and non-interactive. Mediated means that communication is through media or channels owned by third parties. It is not direct-to-customer (DTC).

Three processes are responsible for the enhanced power of communication to create value for customers: disintermediation, personalization and interactivity.

Disintermediation

Today, the development of new technologies has led to the emergence of many DTC communication tools, including e-mail, direct mail and cellphones. Companies are now able to get their message direct to customers.

Personalization

High-quality databases and DTC channels together enable companies to tailor offers and communications to individual customers (see Case 7.7). This is what Peppers and Rogers have called one-to-one marketing.[33-36] Data on customers' buying history and propensities-to-buy can be used to develop offers that meet with a much higher response rate and conversion rate than conventional mailings. The content, timing and delivery channels for communications can be based on customer preferences. Another form of personalization is found online. Many companies enable customers to personalize their website. Customers of www.amazon.com, for example, can enjoy a customized greeting, customized book recommendations and a self-edited customized personal profile. Customers of www.lastminute.com can personalize their

Case 7.7

Customized communication at Mercedes-Benz

Mercedes-Benz decided to launch its new M-Class off-road vehicle in the USA, knowing that it was already a crowded market. However, they accessed publicly available and corporate data to obtain details of all current owners of off-road and Mercedes vehicles. Mercedes then undertook a series of personalized direct mailings to the database with the objective of raising awareness about the vehicle. The pretext for the communication was to ask for help in the process of designing the vehicle. There was an overwhelming response and the respondents were sent questionnaires which asked for guidance on design issues.

Two months later Mercedes presold its first year sales target of 35 000 vehicles. It had been expecting to spend some US$70 million marketing the car, but by using this CRM-based approach it only needed to spend US$48 million, saving US$22 million. The programme was so successful that Mercedes is looking to use the same approach in the future with other model launches.

home page (mylastminute.com) using technology that stores their preferences. This enables the company to refine its messaging to the customer base. It claims to achieve click-through rates that are 30 per cent higher than non-targeted messaging.[37]

Personalization can also be performed on communications with employees such as customer service agents. For example, scripting and support can be tailored to enable agents unfamiliar with a product or customer group to perform competently in telephone interactions.

Interactivity

Interactive technologies have been around since the advent of the telephone. Recently, the Internet has revolutionized the scope for interactivity through two major technologies, e-mail and the world-wide web. E-mail enables customers and company to interact effectively, often in real time. For example, customers can e-mail for information that is unavailable on the frequently asked questions (FAQ) pages of corporate websites. E-mail gives customers access to a specific named person or work group such as help@ or askme@. Contact with a name gives customers the sense that they have an individual who is taking care of them.

The world-wide web is an Internet-enabled service that allows computer users globally to communicate with each other. A company can upload a website and anticipate huge reach. Websites come in a variety of forms. Some are simply electronic brochures. Others enable transactions to be made, while others are highly interactive. The financial services website www.morningstar.com allows customers to construct investment portfolios, conduct analyses using online tools and join in discussion groups. You can create your own daily newspaper at www.ft.com based on your personal interests and preferences. Some excellent websites offer an experience similar to human dialogue. Configuration engines allow the most appropriate products to be offered based on an analysis of the customer's specific needs, problem resolution logic allows customers to find the best solution to a problem, and webchat windows allow human dialogue over the web if all else fails.

To create value for customers from your communication strategies you need to understand and adapt to your customers' purchasing behaviour. You must know who is involved in the buying decision, what information they need and where they want and expect to find that information. A buying process may be quite lengthy. A company making a complex purchase for the first time might progress through a series of steps such as the following.

1 Recognize the problem: the customer acknowledges there is a problem requiring a solution.
2 Search for alternative solutions.
3 Specify the optimal solution.
4 Search for suppliers.
5 Solicit proposals from suppliers.
6 Select a supplier.
7 Establish an order routine.
8 Make a purchase.
9 Evaluate the process.

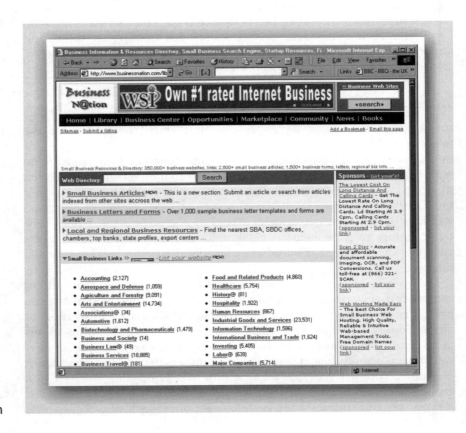

Figure 7.12
Information availability on line at www.
businessnation.com

The customer's decision-making process might involve different people using different resources at different stages of the buying process. The search for optimal solutions might involve a small group of engineers and procurement people contacting current suppliers that may be able to help, examining paper files held in the office, calling professional colleagues in non-competing organizations, visiting the websites of electronic intermediaries, or searching the Internet with the help of a search engine. You need to make the right information available at the right time to the right people.

The Internet has made available a huge amount of information to customers, resulting in their greater empowerment. For example, the website www.businessnation.com (Fig. 7.12) connects visitors to over 350 000 business websites across the full range of industries.

Value from channels

The traditional task of the distribution function is to provide time and place utilities to customers. Effectively this means getting products and services to customers when and where they want. Consumer goods companies have usually constructed channels using intermediaries such as wholesalers and retailers. Business-to-business companies have often sold direct or employed industrial distributors. The location of service providers may be critical or irrelevant to the creation of value for customers. Customers want their grocery retailers to be conveniently located, but do not care where their telecoms service provider is located.

An emerging task for intermediaries in the B2B environment is value augmentation. Channel partners in technology industries add services and complementary products that are not available from the core product manufacturer. The purchase of an enterprise resource planning (ERP) system, for example, may require implementation services, technical services, business process re-engineering, change management, customization of software or specialized hardware such as radio frequency (RF) handheld units in the warehouse. Channel partners not only distribute the ERP product, they also provide or co-ordinate others to provide these additional products and services.

Internet-enabled disintermediation has allowed many companies to bypass or supplement their traditional bricks-and-mortar channels. Many companies have elected to develop transactional websites so that they can sell direct. Others have developed brochure-ware sites that direct interested prospects to traditional channel members. One major benefit attached to this latter option is that it reduces the level of channel conflict, which can be extremely high if an intermediary believes that a supplier is attempting to sell direct to the intermediaries' customers. Additional routes to market include:

- directories such as Yahoo! and Excite
- search engines such as Alta Vista and Infoseek

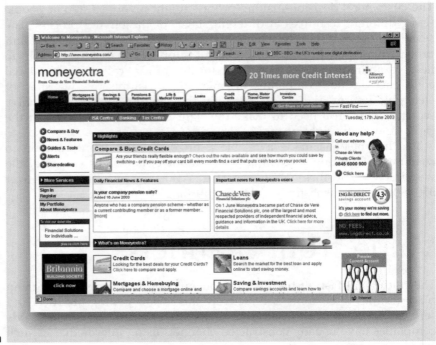

Figure 7.13
Electronic
reintermediation on
www.moneyextra.com

- e-malls such as BarclaySquare and Buckingham Gate
- virtual resellers such as Amazon and CDNow.[38]

Unless customers are committed to a small number of suppliers they may find that it is too costly and inefficient to deal with a large number of potential disintermediated suppliers. This has created opportunities for reintermediation. Reintermediation adds an electronic intermediary to the distribution channel. Examples are:

- www.internetbuydirect.com for a wide range of consumer and business-related products
- www.lastminute.com for holidays, flights, accommodation and gifts
- www.laterooms.com for discounted hotel rooms
- www.moneyextra.com for mortgages, credit cards, bank loans, insurances and pensions (Fig. 7.13).

Ultimately, companies face four options when creating value for customers from electronic channels.[39]

- No Internet sales: this might be the best option for small businesses with a local clientele. Companies on the Internet access an international audience. If they are unable to fill the demand that might arise, they are perhaps better off using traditional channels.
- Internet sales by reseller only: a reseller, selling on behalf of many companies, may be big enough in terms of customer numbers and

revenues to invest in online transactional capability. Fulfilment of orders may be performed by the reseller or the manufacturer.

● Internet sales by producer only: it would be unusual for a company selling through conventional channels to establish a web presence that is in direct competition to those channel members. This would generate significant channel conflict.

● Internet sales by all: both reseller and producer sell online.

Which of these strategies will add value for customers depends on whether customers enjoy additional time and place utility from online purchasing.

Customer experience

Companies are becoming more interested in managing and improving customer experience. For example, the mission of Amazon.com is to deliver 'high quality end-to-end, order-to-delivery customer experience'.

If you were to ask your customers, 'What is it like doing business with us?' their answers would describe their experience.

The idea of customer experience has its origins in the work of Pine and Gilmore.[40] They suggested that leading economies have shifted through four stages of economic development: extraction of commodities, making goods, delivering services and now staging experiences (Fig. 7.14).

You can buy experiences such as a white water rafting experience and a travel experience. Experiences within product categories can vary substantially. Your experience on a charter flight differs from your experience on a scheduled flight; your experience at the Hard Rock Café differs from your experience at McCafé.

The Kiwi Experience company takes customers, mostly backpackers, on bus tours around New Zealand. Unlike most bus tours, customers can

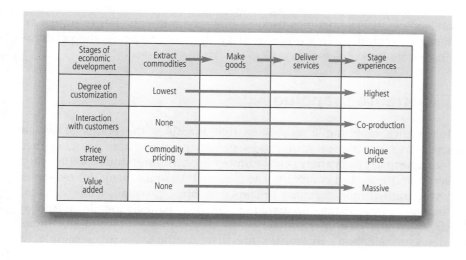

Stages of economic development	Extract commodities →	Make goods →	Deliver services →	Stage experiences
Degree of customization	Lowest			Highest
Interaction with customers	None			Co-production
Price strategy	Commodity pricing			Unique price
Value added	None			Massive

Figure 7.14
The experience economy

join, leave and rejoin the tour whenever they want. The experience incorporates accommodation, travel, entry to attractions, the company of other travellers and the leadership of the driver. Each customer's experience has the potential to be unique, even those travelling on the same tour.

Customer experience is a customer's overall cognitive and affective response to their exposure to a company's performance. For example, if you were undergoing hospital treatment, your experience would consist of your interpretations of what you encountered over a number of touchpoints: during admission, in the ward, in the theatre, after surgery and during discharge. A customer's evaluation of experience is an overall impression of a company's performance.

Although customers may report their impressions in terms of many variables, two major variables are dominant: people and processes. Customers gather a lot of personal experience about your company when they come into contact with your people and processes.

Customer experience is a major driver of word-of-mouth. One study in the hospitality industry, for example, found that 75 per cent of restaurant customers tell others about their poor service experiences; 38 per cent tell others about their excellent experiences. Improving customer experience can therefore have two benefits: it can reduce negative word-of-mouth; it can also increase positive word-of-mouth.

To improve customer experience, it is first necessary to understand it. Companies have a number of tools for improving insight into customer experience.

Mystery shopping

A number of market research companies offer mystery shopping services. Mystery shopping involves the recruitment of shoppers to report on their customer experience with the company sponsoring the research. They might also perform a comparative shop when they compare the sponsor's performance with competitors. Mystery shopping is widely used in B2C environments such as retailing, banks, service stations, bars, restaurants and hotels. It is sometimes used in B2B environments. For example, an insurance company might use mystery shopping to assess the performance of its broker network.

Experience mapping

Experience mapping is a process that identifies the points at which customers experience your processes and people. These are customer touchpoints. The variety and number of customer touchpoints vary across industry and company. The National Australia Bank, for example, has identified nine customer touchpoints: branch, e-mail, website, ATM, financial planner, Internet banking, personal banker, mobile mortgage specialist and customer contact centre. Focus groups, face-to-face interviews or telephone interviews are then conducted with a sample of

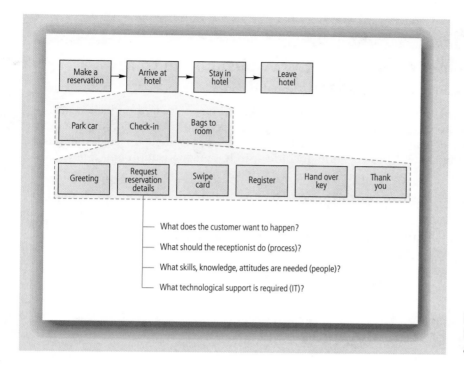

Figure 7.15
Experience map of
a hotel guest

customers to describe their experience at these touchpoints. The focus is on two important questions. What is the experience like? How can it be improved? The objective is to identify the gaps between actual experience and desired experience. Then the company can begin to focus on strategies to close the gaps. These strategies typically involve improvements to people and processes. Outcomes might be better training and reward schemes for people, or investment in IT to support process improvements. Figure 7.15 illustrates how mapping can be applied to a hotel guest's experience.

The map shows that the customer's experience consists of four primary stages. The 'arrival at hotel' stage can be decomposed into three secondary stages: parking the car, checking-in and taking bags to the room. The check-in stage is again decomposed, this time into six main steps. It is at this level that the customer experiences the hotel's people and processes. This is where opportunities for improving people and processes can focus. Every customer experience can be decomposed and redesigned in this way. However, not all customer encounters contribute equally to the overall assessment of experience. In the hospital illustration, patients are often prepared to tolerate food quality of a standard that would be utterly unacceptable for a surgical procedure. Companies are well advised to focus on the critical episodes and encounters that make up customer experience. Case 7.8 describes how the online retailer www.lastminute.com has invested in the improvement of customer experience.

Enhanced customer experience at www.lastminute.com

⟨ Quotation from www.lastminute.com's 2001 annual report ⟩

'The new technology platform went live in October 2000 and has delivered on its promises – the site is quicker, more stable and demonstrably supports scalability. Additionally we have introduced a number of new features to make the site more convenient for customers and therefore increase conversion. These benefits include search, personalisation and a new look and feel in all markets.

Customers now use an improved booking process that has been reduced from seven steps to four.

We are constantly evolving the site to make it simple for customers to buy with greater speed and efficiency.'

Process mapping

Process mapping is a form of blueprinting, a technique popularized by Shostack.[41] Blueprints are graphical representations of business processes. They are useful not only for developing ways to improve customer experience in the front office, but also for improving back-of-house internal customer–supplier relationships, setting service standards, identifying fail-points, training new people, and eliminating process redundancy and duplication. Process blueprints are generally prepared as follows.

1 Identify the process to be mapped.
2 Break down the process into its molecular elements.
3 Identify workflow within the process. In other words, detail the order in which work is done to accomplish the process's output (use arrows).
4 Identify points in the process where there is variability in the process. This might either be planned or unplanned variability. For example, unplanned variability in a service encounter occurs when a service engineer arrives on-site to fix a problem. Any number of unanticipated problems can impede service delivery. Planned variability occurs when a doctor and patient work together to identify symptoms clearly.
5 Identify the line of visibility. This is the line that separates the customer's view of the process from the company's. This line separates back-of-house from front-of-house and is the line at which customer experience happens.

Refinements to this basic procedure include identifying the people who perform different parts of the process, and setting service standards (time to complete) for different molecular elements.

The customer activity cycle

The customer activity cycle (CAC) is an attempt to understand the process that customers go through in making and reviewing buying decisions.[42] Vandermerwe broke the process into three main stages:

1 deciding what to do
2 implementing the decision
3 reviewing what was done.

Others have taken different approaches to the CAC. For example, one consultancy has divided the CAC into five stages: information acquisition, purchase, install, handle incidents and identify new needs[iii]

The CAC enables companies to break down a complex process into more basic elements and to collect data on the customer's experience throughout the process. Then companies can look for ways to improve the experience. As shown in Fig. 7.16, this might involve simplifying processes or creating a closer relationship to keep abreast of the customer's changing requirements. The figure concerns the relationship between Citibank and a customer whose needs are changing as it begins to transact across borders. The basic CAC is shown as comprising four stages: opening a bank account, using banking facilities, expanding banking needs across borders and updating banking needs. The italicized box content shows what Citibank was able to do to improve the experience of the customer at these four stages.

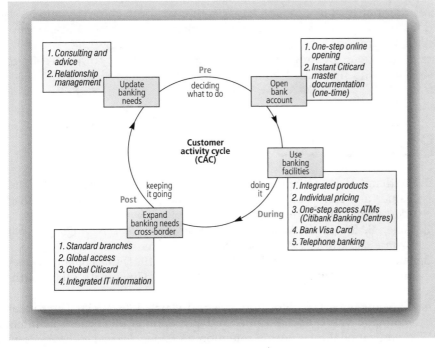

Figure 7.16 Citibank's understanding of the customer activity cycle (Source: Vandermerwe[42])

[iii] Go to www.stakeholderpower.com for more detail.

Summary

This chapter has stressed the importance of creating value for customers. Value is a term that has several meanings, but can be usefully thought of as the relationship between the benefits experienced from a product or service and the sacrifices made to enjoy those benefits. Value is therefore enhanced when sacrifices are reduced or benefits increased. Three major types of sacrifice have been identified: money, search and psychic costs. Companies can offer improved value to customers by creating and delivering better solutions to customers' problems.

The sources of customer value are represented by what marketers call the marketing mix. These are the 4Ps: product, price, promotion and place. In the services environment, the 4Ps are supplemented by three additional Ps: process, physical evidence and people. In the B2B environment, value propositions have long been customized. Customization is now emerging as a powerful force in the B2C environment too. Any of the 7Cs can be customized.

Management can create additional value by their management of the 7Ps. For example, product innovation, branding and product–service bundling are ways to create additional value. Similarly, service quality improvement programmes, service guarantees, service-level agreements and service recovery programmes may be seen as value adding.

The Internet and high-quality databases are allowing companies to tailor their customer communication strategies at segment or, often, unique customer level. Messages can be communicated directly to customers, side-stepping the media long used for broadcast advertising. They can also be personalized not only in form of address but also in content and timing. Unlike traditional media, the newer channels, including the Internet, are interactive. Companies can receive instant feedback from their customers.

Finally, we examined the emerging issue of customer experience. A growing number of companies are working to improve customer experience. Essentially, this means improving the customer interface at the moments of truth when customers come face-to-face with a company's people and process.

References

1. Zeithaml, V. A. (1988) Consumer perceptions of price, quality and value: a means–end model and synthesis of evidence. *Journal of Marketing*, Vol. 52, July, pp. 2–22.
2. Gale, B. T. (1994) *Managing Customer Value: Creating Quality and Service that Customers Can See*. New York: Free Press.
3. Sheth, J. N., Newman, B. I. and Gross, B. L. (1991) *Consumption Values and Market Choices: Theory and Applications*. Cincinnati, OH: South-Western.
4. Gassenheimer, J. B., Houston, F. S and Davis, J. C. (1998) The role of economic value, social value, and perceptions of fairness in inter-organizational relationship retention decisions. *Journal of the Academy of Marketing Science*, Vol. 26, Fall, pp. 322–37.

5. Easton, G., Burrell, G., Shearman, C. and Rothschild, R. (1993) *Managers and Competition*. Oxford: Blackwell.

6. McCarthy, E. J. (1996) *Basic Marketing* (12th edn). Homewood, IL: RD Irwin.

7. Booms, B. H. and Bitner, M.-J. (1981) Marketing strategies and organizational structures for service firms. In: Donnelly, J. and George, W. R. (eds). *Marketing of Services*. Chicago: American Marketing Association, pp. 47–51.

8. Kotler, P. (2000) *Marketing Management: The Millennium Edition*. Saddle River, HJ: Prentice Hall.

9. Levitt, T. (1980) Marketing success – through differentiation of anything. *Harvard Business Review*, January/February, Vol. 58(1), pp. 83–91.

10. Levitt, T. (1969) *The Marketing Mode*. New York: McGraw-Hill, p. 2.

11. Crosby, P. B. (1979) *Quality is Free*. New York: McGraw-Hill.

12. Juran, J. M. (1964) *Managerial Breakthrough*. New York: McGraw-Hill.

13. Grönroos, C. (1984) A service quality model and its marketing implications. *European Journal of Marketing*, Vol. 18, pp. 36–44.

14. Parasuraman, A., Zeithaml, V. A. and Berry, L. L. (1985) A conceptual model of service quality and its implications for future research. *Journal of Marketing*, Vol. 49, Fall, pp. 41–50.

15. Parasuraman, A., Zeithaml, V. A. and Berry, L. L. (1988) SERVQUAL: a multiple-item scale for measuring consumers' perceptions of service quality. *Journal of Retailing*, Vol. 64(1), pp. 22–37.

16. Parasuraman, A., Zeithaml, V. A. and Berry, L. L. (1991) Refinement and reassessment of the SERVQUAL scale. *Journal of Retailing*, Vol. 64, pp. 12–40.

17. Parasuraman, A., Zeithaml, V. A. and Berry, L. L. (1994) Reassessment of expectations as a comparison standard in measuring service quality: implications for future research. *Journal of Marketing*, Vol. 58(1), pp. 111–32.

18. Buttle, F. (1996) SERVQUAL: review, critique and research agenda. *European Journal of Marketing*, Vol. 30(1), pp. 8–32.

19. Rust, R. T. (1995) Return on quality (ROQ): making service quality financially accountable. *Journal of Marketing*, Vol. 59(2), April, pp. 58–71.

20. Cronin, J. J. and Taylor, S. A. (1992) Measuring service quality: a re-examination and extension. *Journal of Marketing*, Vol. 56, July, pp. 55–68.

21. Cronin, J. J. and Taylor, S. A. (1994) SERVPERF versus SERVQUAL: reconciling performance-based and perceptions-minus expectations measurement of service quality. *Journal of Marketing*, Vol. 58, January, pp. 125–31.

22. Keaveney, S. M. (1995) Customer switching behaviour in service industries: an exploratory study. *Journal of Marketing*, Vol. 59(2), April, pp. 71–82.

23. Tax, S. W., Brown, S. W. and Chandrashekaran, M. (1998) Customer evaluations of service complaint experiences: implications for relationship marketing. *Journal of Marketing*, Vol. 62, April, pp. 60–76.

24. Hart, C. W., Heskett, J. L. and Sasser, W. E., Jr (1990) The profitable art of service recovery. *Harvard Business Review*, Vol. 68, July/August, pp. 148–56.

25. Tax, S. S. and Brown, S. W. (1998) Recovering and learning from service failure. *Sloan Management Review*, Fall, pp. 75–88.

26. Sparks, B. and McColl-Kennedy, J. R. (2001) Justice strategy options for increased customer satisfaction in a service recovery setting. *Journal of Business Research*, Vol. 54, pp. 209–18.

27. Davenport, T. H. (1993) *Process Innovation: Reengineering Work Through Information Technology*. Boston, MA: Harvard Business School Press.

28. Hammer, M. and Champy, J. (1993) *Re-engineeering the Corporation*. New York: Harper Business.

29. Keen, P. G. W. (1997) *The Process Edge: Creating Value Where it Counts*. Harvard Business School Press.

30. Buttle, F. A. (1998) Word-of-mouth: understanding and managing referral marketing. *Journal of Strategic Marketing*, Vol. 6, 241–54.

31. Richins, M. (1983) Negative word-of-mouth by dissatisfied customers: a pilot study. *Journal of Marketing*, Vol. 68, pp. 105–11.

32. TARP (1995) *American Express – SOCAP Study of Complaint Handling in Australia*. Society of Consumer Affairs Professionals.

33. Peppers, D. and Rogers, M. (1993) *The One-To-One Future*. London: Piatkus.

34. Peppers, D. and Rogers, M. (1997) *Enterprise One-To-One*. London: Piatkus.

35. Peppers, D., Rogers, M. and Dorf, B. (1999) *The One-To-One Fieldbook*. Oxford: Capstone.

36. Peppers, D. and Rogers, M. (2000) *The One-To-One Manager*. Oxford: Capstone.

37. Lastminute.com. (2001) Annual report.

38. Sarkar, M., Butler, B. and Steinfeld, C. (1996) Exploiting the virtual value chain. *Journal of Computer Mediated Communication*, Vol. 1(3).

39. Kumar, N. (1999) Internet distribution strategies: dilemmas for the incumbent. *Financial Times*, Special issue on mastering information management, 7. www.ftmastering.com

40. Pine, B. H. and Gilmore, J. H. (1998) Welcome to the experience economy. *Harvard Business Review*, July–August, pp. 97–105.

41. Shostack, G. L. (1987) Service positioning through structural change. *Journal of Marketing*, Vol. 51, pp. 34–43.

42. Vandermerwe, S. (1993) Jumping into the customer's activity cycle: a new role for customer services in the 1990s. *Columbia Journal of World Business*, Vol. 28(2), Summer, pp. 46–66.

Chapter 8

Managing the customer lifecycle: customer acquisition

By the end of the chapter, you will understand:

1 the meaning of the terms 'customer lifecycle' and 'new customer'
2 what businesses can do to acquire new customers, including
3 which potential customers to target
4 how to communicate with them
5 what to offer them.

Introduction

This chapter and the next two chapters introduce the idea of a customer lifecycle and its management. Managing the customer lifecycle is the fifth and final primary stage of the customer relationship management (CRM) value chain (Fig. 8.1). It is at this phase of the CRM value chain that we consider the critical issues of process and structure for CRM implementation.

The core CRM processes are the customer acquisition, customer retention and customer development processes, which together make up the customer lifecycle. How can companies identify and acquire new customers, grow their value to the business and retain them for the long term? What are the key metrics or key performance indicators (KPIs) that can be used to measure a company's process performance? The issue of structure is one of organizational design. What form of organizational design enables a company to achieve its CRM objectives? The processes of customer development and retention are examined in Chapter 9, and structure is the subject of Chapter 10.

In this chapter you will find out about the important issue of customer acquisition, the first concern as you try to manage the customer lifecycle. New customers have to be acquired to build companies. Even in well-managed companies there can be a significant level of customer attrition. These lost customers need to be replaced. We look at several important matters for CRM practitioners: which potential new customers to target, how to approach them and what to offer them.

Customer lifecycles are presented in different ways by different authorities, but basically they all attempt to do the same thing. They

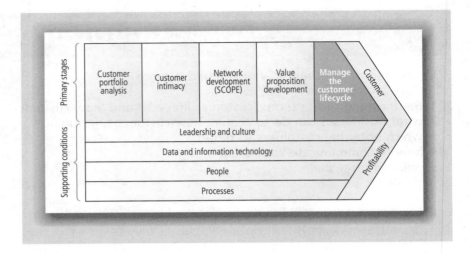

Figure 8.1
CRM value chain

attempt to depict the development of a customer relationship over time. Ford, for example, traces business-to-business (B2B) relationships through four main stages: pre-relationship, exploratory, developing and stable stages.[1] As relationships move along this trajectory, their character changes. The uncertainties that each party had about the other begin to disappear as they mutually grow in knowledge and understanding. One party, or perhaps both parties, begins to make investments in the other; they show commitment by adapting to each other. If there is no evidence of commitment, the relationship is unlikely to progress beyond the exploratory stage. If commitment is demonstrated, they will perhaps grow to trust each other and the relationship heads towards stability. This chapter focuses on the earliest stages of a customer relationship, when there is progress up the value ladder from suspect to prospect to first-time customer status.

Because we are taking a management view of customer relationships, the customer lifecycle has been collapsed into three major management activities:

- acquiring new customers
- retaining existing customers
- developing customer value.

The first task in managing the customer lifecycle is to acquire customers. Customer retention is a pointless exercise if there are no customers to retain. Customer acquisition is always the most important goal during new product launches and with new business start-ups. For small business with ambitions to grow, customer acquisition is often as important as customer retention. A one-customer company, such as BICC, which supplies copper cable to a single customer, BT, can double its customer base by acquiring one more customer. Conversely, the loss of that single customer could spell bankruptcy.

Even with well-developed and implemented customer retention plans, customers still need replacing, sometimes at a rate of 25 per cent or more a year. In a business-to-consumer (B2C) context, customers may shift out of your targeted demographic as they age and progress through the family lifecycle; their personal circumstances may change and they no longer need and find value in your product; they may even die. In a B2B context, you may lose corporate customers because they have been acquired by another company with firmly established buying practices and supplier preferences; they may have stopped producing the goods and services for which your company provided input; they may have ceased trading. Customer loss to these uncontrollable causes indicates that customer acquisition will always be needed to replace natural attrition.

Several important questions have to be answered when a company puts together a customer acquisition plan. These questions concern targets, channels and offers:

- Which prospects (potential new customers) will be targeted?
- How will these prospects be approached?
- What offer will be made?

These issues need to be carefully considered and programmed into a properly resourced customer acquisition plan. Most marketing plans do not distinguish between customer acquisition and customer retention. They are not separately funded or plotted strategies. It is recommended that companies think about these as separate, but related issues, and develop appropriate strategies.

What is a new customer?

A customer can be new in one of two senses:

- new to a product category
- new to the company.

New-to-category

New-to-category customers are customers who have either identified a new need or have found a new category of solution for an existing need. Consider the B2C context. When a couple have their first child, they have a completely new set of needs connected to the growth and nurturing of their child. This includes baby clothes, food and toys. As the child grows, the parents are faced with additional new-to-category decisions, such as preschool and elementary education. Sometimes, customers also become new-to-category because they find a new category to replace an existing solution. Mobile phones have now significantly replaced card- or cash-operated pay-phones in many countries. More environmentally friendly detergents and nappies are growing their share of market, as customers switch from current solutions.

Sometimes, customers beat marketers to the punch, by adopting established products for new uses. Marketers then catch on and begin to promote that use. Arm and Hammer baking soda was used by customers to deodorize fridges and rubbish bins, and as a mild abrasive for whitening teeth. The manufacturer Church and Dwight responded to this revelation and began to promote a variety of different applications. It is now an ingredient in toothpaste. Their website www.armhammer.com provides visitors with many other tips for baking soda applications. Auto manufacturers noticed that many utility vehicles were being bought not by tradespeople but as fun vehicles for weekend use. They began promoting this use, while at the same time trying to innovate in product design to meet the requirements of that market segment. The result has been the emergence of a completely new market segment: the market for sports utility vehicles. Several websites serve this market, www.suv.com, for example.

The same distinction between new needs and new solutions exists in the B2B marketplace. Customers can be new-to-category if they begin an activity that requires resources that are new to the business. For example, when McDonald's entered the coffee shop market, they needed to develop a new set of supplier relationships. New-to-category customers may also be customers who find a new solution for an existing problem. For example, some clothing manufacturers now use computer-operated sewing machines to perform tasks that were previously performed by skilled labour and traditional sewing machines.

New-to-category customers are sometimes expensive to recruit; sometimes they are not. For example, when children leave home for university, banks compete vigorously for their patronage. They advertise heavily in the mass media, communicate direct-to-student, and offer free gifts and low- or zero-cost banking for the duration of the studentship. In contrast, supermarket retailers incur no direct costs in attracting these same students to their local stores.

New-to-company

The second category of new customers is customers that are new to the company. New-to-company customers are won from competitors. They may switch to your company because they feel you offer a better solution or because they value variety. In general, new-to-company customers are the only option for growing customer numbers in mature markets where new-to-category customers are not entering the market. In developed economies, new players in grocery retail can only succeed by winning customers from established operators. They would not expect to convert those customers completely but to win a share of their spend by offering better value in one or more of important categories. Once the customer is in-store, the retailer will use merchandising techniques such as point-of-sale signs and displays to increase spending.

New-to-company customers can be very expensive to acquire, particularly if they are strongly committed to their current supplier. Commitment is reflected in a strong positive attitude to, or high levels of investment in, the current supplier. These both represent high switching costs. A powerful commitment to a current supplier can be difficult, and often is too expensive, to break. High potential value customers are not always the most attractive prospects because of this commitment and investment. A lower value customer with a weaker commitment to the current supplier may be a better prospect.

Portfolio purchasing

New customers can be difficult to identify in markets where customers exhibit portfolio purchasing. Customers buy on a portfolio basis when they buy from a choice set of several more or less equivalent alternatives. A customer who has not bought from one of the portfolio suppliers for a matter of months or even years may still regard the unchosen supplier as part of the portfolio. The supplier, however, may have a business rule that says: 'If a customer has not bought for 3 months, mail out a special offer.' In the UK, many grocery customers shop at both Tesco and Sainsbury's. These retailers do not simply compete to acquire and retain customers. Instead, they compete for a larger share of the customer's spending.

Retention and acquisition of customers make more sense as strategic objectives where portfolio purchasing is not a characteristic behaviour.

Strategic switching

You may encounter evidence of strategic switching by customers. These are customers who shift their allegiances from one supplier to another in pursuit of a better deal. Banks know that their promotional pricing stimulates hot money. This is money that is moved from account to account across the banking industry in search of the best rate of interest. Sometimes the money may only be in an account overnight.

The telecoms company MCI discovered that about 70 per cent of customers newly acquired from competitors stayed for 4 months or less. These customers had been acquired when MCI mailed a cheque valued at $25, $75 or more to competitors' customers. When the cheque was banked, this automatically triggered the transfer of service to MCI. A few months later these customers again switched suppliers when another deal was offered and the cheque had already been cashed. MCI fixed the problem by adjusting the promotion. Instead of mailing an immediately cashable cheque, its promotion was relaunched as a 'staged rebate' promotion. The accounts of new customers who stayed for 3, 9 and 13 months were credited with sums equivalent to the value of the cheque that would previously have been sent.[2]

Sometimes, a customer may have been regained a second or further time as a new customer. For example, if the couple mentioned previously were to have a second child after 4 years, they would most likely have been removed from the mother-and-baby databases. A new record would have to be created. The customer would need to be targeted afresh. In portfolio markets, a customer who has not purchased in quarter 1 may be treated as a new customer for promotional purposes in quarter 2, as the company attempts to reactivate the customer.

Customer value estimates

Companies must choose which of several potential customers or segments to target for acquisition. The final choice will depend on a number of considerations.

- What is the estimated value of the customer? This depends on the margins earned from the customer's purchases over a given period.
- If that customer switches, what proportion of that spending will your company earn?
- What is the probability that the customer will switch from current suppliers?

Imagine a competitor's customer who will spend $5000, $6000, $7000 and $8000 with that supplier over the next 4 years at gross margins of 40 per cent. Without discounting those future margins, the customer is worth $10 400 ($2000 + $2400 + $2800 + $3200). Let's assume that your intelligence, based on customer satisfaction and loyalty scores, suggests that you have a 40 per cent chance of converting the customer and that, once converted, you will win a 50 per cent share of the customer's available spending in that category.

The value of this customer can now be computed as follows: gross margins, multiplied by share of the customer's spending, multiplied by the probability of winning the customer's business. Using the numbers above, this customer is worth $10 400 × 0.50 × 0.40 or $2080. The question now becomes: can you recruit this customer and maintain a relationship over the next 4 years for less than $2080? If you can, then the customer will make a net contribution to your business. This simple algorithm allows you to compare different customer acquisition opportunities. Other things being equal, a customer that shows a higher potential contribution is a better prospect. The approach can be adjusted customer by customer and can take account of a number of additional factors, such as discounting future margins, producing differently costed approaches to customer acquisition, re-estimating future margins to take account of cross-selling opportunities and estimating the annualized costs of customer retention.

Hofmeyr has developed the Conversion Model™. This contains a battery of questions designed to assess whether a customer is likely to switch. His basic premise is that customers who are not committed are more likely to be available to switch to another provider. Commitment, in turn, is a function of satisfaction with the brand or offer, the attractiveness of alternatives, and involvement in the brand or offer. The Conversion Model allows customers to be segmented into four subsets according to the level of commitment: entrenched, average, shallow and convertible. Non-customers are also segmented according to commitment scores into four availability subsets: available, ambivalent, weakly unavailable and strongly unavailable. Hofmeyr claims that these scores can be used to guide both acquisition and retention strategies.[3]

A core principle of CRM is that customer knowledge is used to target acquisition efforts accurately. By contrast, poorly targeted acquisition efforts waste marketing budget and may alienate more prospects than they gain through irrelevant, inappropriate messaging.

Prospecting

The first major decision to be made for a customer acquisition plan is the identification of prospects. Prospecting is a mining term. In that context, it means searching an area thought likely to yield a valuable mineral deposit. In CRM, it means searching for opportunities that might convert into strategically significant customers.

Prospecting is an outcome of the segmenting and targeting process described in Chapter 4. Prospects are end-products of that process. Segmentation divides a heterogeneous market into homogeneous sub-sets, even down to the level of the unique customer. Targeting is the process of choosing which market segments, clusters or individuals, to approach with an offer. In Chapter 4, we identified several characteristics of the strategically significant customer. These are the attributes that companies would find most attractive in a prospect.

Business-to-business prospecting

In the B2B environment, it is very often the task of the salesperson to do the prospecting. The first step is to generate the leads. Leads are individuals or companies that might be worth approaching. The lead then needs to be qualified. The qualification process submits all leads to a series of questions, such as:

- Does the lead have a need for my company's products?
- Does the lead have the ability to pay?
- Is the lead authorized to buy?

If the answers are yes, yes, yes, the lead becomes a genuine prospect. Ability to pay covers both cash and credit. The ability to pay of prospective customers can be assessed by subscribing to credit-rating services such as Dun & Bradstreet and Standard & Poor's. Being a well-known name is no guarantee that a prospect is credit-worthy, as suppliers to Enron know. Authority to buy may be invested in a named individual, a decision-making unit composed of a group of employees, a group composed of internal employees and external advisor(s) or, in some rare cases, an external individual or group. Andersen Consulting (now Accenture) was appointed by Chrysler to act as systems integrator for a completely new robotics system. Proposals were put to a group of Andersen employees only, while Chrysler retained the power to veto any choice.

Automated lead qualification is possible in some CRM systems. Banks, for example, have rule-based algorithms for scoring the credit-worthiness of loan applicants. Models employ data such as income, tenure in job and marital status to determine risk. These models have become more

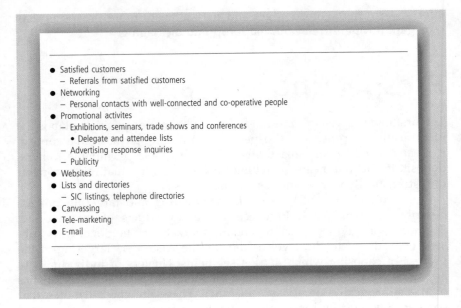

- Satisfied customers
  - Referrals from satisfied customers
- Networking
  - Personal contacts with well-connected and co-operative people
- Promotional activites
  - Exhibitions, seminars, trade shows and conferences
    - Delegate and attendee lists
  - Advertising response inquiries
  - Publicity
- Websites
- Lists and directories
  - SIC listings, telephone directories
- Canvassing
- Tele-marketing
- E-mail

Figure 8.2
Sources of business-to-business leads

sophisticated over time. Some years ago, the only question that home shopping companies would ask of customers to check their credit worthiness was 'do you have a telephone?'

Once leads have been qualified, CRM practitioners need to decide the best channels for initiating contact. A distinction can be made between direct-to-customer (DTC) channels such as salespeople, direct mail, and telemarketing and channels that are indirect, either because they use partners or other intermediaries or because they use bought time and space in media. The improved quality of databases has meant that direct channels allow access to specific named leads in target businesses.

Leads come from a variety of sources. In a B2B context this includes the sources identified in Fig. 8.2. Many companies are turning to satisfied customers who may be willing to generate personal referrals. The customer database should be designed to enable you to establish which customers are satisfied. These special customers can then be proactively approached for a referral. They may be prepared to write a letter or an e-mail of introduction, provide a testimonial or receive a call to verify the credentials of a salesperson.

Networking can be defined as:

> the process of establishing and maintaining business-related personal relationships

A network may include members of a business association, friends from university or professional colleagues in other companies. In some countries it is essential to build and maintain personal networks. In China, for example, the practice of *guanxi* means that it is almost impossible to do business without some personal connections already in place.

Referral networks are common in professional services. Accountants, banks, lawyers, auditors, tax consultants and estate agents will join together into a referral network in which they undertake to refer clients to other members of the network.

Promotional activities can also generate useful leads. Exhibitions, seminars, trade shows and conferences can be productive sources. Companies that pay to participate in these events may be able either to obtain privileged access to delegate and attendee lists, or to generate lists of their own, such as a list of visitors to their stand at a trade show.

In general, B2B marketers do little advertising, although this can generate leads. Many B2B companies think of marketing as a lead-generating activity, and sales as lead conversion activity. Most B2B advertising is placed in highly targeted specialist media such as trade magazines.

Publicity

An important activity for some B2B companies is publicity. Publicity is an outcome of public relations (PR) activity, and can be defined as:

> free editorial coverage of a story relevant to a company's interests.

Successful PR can generate publicity for your product or company in appropriate media. This coverage, unlike advertising, is unpaid. Although unpaid, publicity does create costs. Someone has to be paid to write the story and submit it to the media. Many magazines, trade papers and online communities are run on a shoestring. They employ very few staff and rely heavily on stories submitted by companies and their PR staff to generate editorial matter. Editors are looking for newsworthy items such as stories about product innovation, original customer applications or human-interest stories about inventors and entrepreneurs. Editorial staff will generally edit copy to eliminate deceptive or brazen claims.

Websites

Company websites can also be fruitful sources of new customers. Anyone with access to the Internet is a prospective customer. The Internet enables potential customers to search globally for products and suppliers. To be effective in new customer generation, websites must take into account the way in which prospects search for information. There are four main ways:[4]

- keying in a page's URL
- using search engines
- exploring directories, web catalogues or portals
- surfing.

A URL is a website address. URL stands for Uniform (or Universal) Resource Locator. By typing it into a web browser's address window, you move straight onto the website. Even if you did not know IBM's URL, you could reasonably guess that it is www.ibm.com. URLs can be saved as favourites once you are sure of the address.

Search engines provide an indexed guide to websites. Users searching for information type keywords into a web-based form. The engine then reports the number of hits, that is, webpages that feature the keyed word or words. Users can then click on a hyperlink to take them to the relevant pages. To ensure that your site is hit when a prospect is searching, you need to register with appropriate search engines. There are hundreds of search engines, but among the most well-known are Google, Infoseek, Netscape, Webcrawler, Alta Vista and Lycos. Sites such as www.search-enginewatch.com offer tips on how to benefit from website registration. There are also meta search engines. These are engines that search for keywords on other search engines. Among them are www.meta-crawler.com and www.37.com, which lets users search through 37 other search engines.

Directories or web catalogues such as Yahoo! provide a structured hierarchical listing of websites, grouped into categories such as business, entertainment and sport. Companies choose under which category to register. For example, Rolls-Royce aero engine division (www.rolls-royce.com) and seven other manufacturers can be accessed from Business_and_Economy > Business_to_Business > Aerospace > Engines on the Yahoo! directory.

Portals are websites that act as gateways to the rest of the Internet. Portals tend to be focused on particular industries or user groups and offer facilities such as search engines, directories, customizable home pages and free e-mail. For example, the portal www.CEOExpress.com provides a wealth of information and access to other sites that may be of use to busy chief executives (Fig. 8.3).

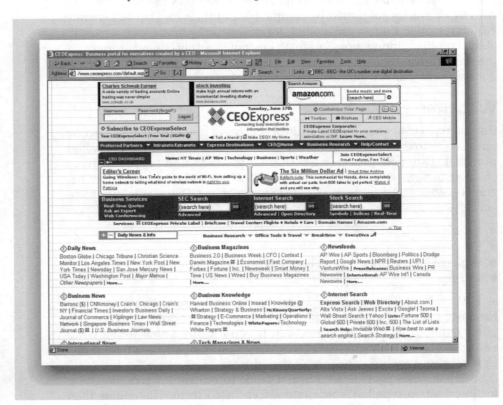

Figure 8.3
The portal
CEOExpress

Surfing is a term used to describe a more intuitive and less structured approach to website searching.

When prospective customers reach your site they need to be able to do what they want. This may mean searching for a product, registering for information (effectively enabling permission-based prospecting by supplying their name, alias or e-mail address), requesting a quotation, describing their requirements and preferences.

Lists of prospects can be developed from many sources such as telephone directories, business lists, chamber of commerce memberships, professional and trade association memberships, and magazine circulation data. Lists can also be bought ready-made from list compilers and brokers. Some of these lists will be of poor quality: out of date, containing duplications, omissions and other errors. High-quality lists with full contact details, including phone and e-mail address, tend to be more expensive. Lists can support direct marketing efforts by phone, mail, e-mail, fax or face-to-face.

Canvassing and telemarketing

Canvassing involves making unsolicited calls, sometimes known as cold calls. This can be a very wasteful use of an expensive asset: the salesperson. Some companies have banned their salespeople from cold calling. Others outsource this activity to third parties. Some hotel chains, for example, use hospitality students to conduct a sales blitz that is essentially a telephone-based cold-calling campaign.

Telemarketing is widely used as a more cost-effective way of prospecting than using a salesperson. Telemarketing, sometimes called telesales, is a systematic approach to prospecting using the telephone and, sometimes, other electronic media such as fax and e-mail. Telemarketing is usually performed by the staff of customer contact centres. These are either in-house or outsourced. Outbound telemarketers make outgoing calls to identify and qualify leads. Inbound telemarketers receive calls from prospective customers. In addition to prospecting, telemarketing can be used to manage other parts of the customer lifecycle: cross-selling, handling complaints, winning back at-risk or lost customers, for example.

E-mail

A growing number of companies are using e-mail for new customer acquisition. E-mail offers several clear advantages. A very large proportion of business decision-makers have e-mail, although this does vary by country and industry. It is very cheap, costing about the same to send 1000 e-mails as it does to send one single e-mail. It is quick and simple for recipients to respond. Content can be personalized. Production values can be matched to audience preferences: you can use richly graphical or simple textual content. It is an asynchronous prospecting tool. In other words, it is not tied to a particular time-frame like a sales call. E-mail messages sit in mailboxes until they are read or deleted. It is a very flexible tool that can be linked to telesales follow-up, 'call-me' buttons or click-throughs.

When e-mail is permission based, response rates can be extraordinarily high.[5] However, there is growing resistance to spam e-mail. E-mails are spammed when they are sent to large numbers of recipients who have not been properly screened. What is spam to one recipient is valuable information to another. An important ingredient in e-mail marketing is a process by which prospects are encouraged or incentivized to provide e-mail addresses for future contact.

Sales-force automation (SFA) software, in conjunction with a selling methodology, helps B2B companies to manage the selling and communication activities that are involved in progressing a prospect towards customer status.

Business-to-consumer prospecting

In B2C contexts, the distribution of customer acquisition effort is different. More emphasis is placed on advertising, sales promotion and merchandising. However, all of the techniques described above are also used, but generally in a different way. These will be discussed later. First, we will look at advertising.

Advertising

Advertising is used as a prime method for generating new customers in B2C environments. Advertising is:

> the creation of messages that are communicated to targeted audiences through the purchase of time or space in media owned by others.

Advertising can be successful at achieving two different classes of communication objective: cognitive and affective. Cognition is concerned with what audiences know; affect is concerned with what they feel. Advertising alone is often insufficient to generate behavioural outcomes such as trial purchasing. It can, however, predispose audiences to make an intention-to-buy based on what they learned about and felt towards the advertised product.

Cognitive advertising objectives include: raising awareness, developing understanding and generating knowledge. New customers generally need to be made aware of the product, to understand what benefits it can deliver and to know the product's name and sources. Affective advertising objectives include developing a liking for the product and generating preference.

In high-involvement purchasing contexts, where products or their usage context are personally significant and relevant, prospects will normally progress through a learn–feel–do process when making their first purchase. In other words, before they buy, they acquire information that helps them to learn about and compare alternatives, thus reducing perceived risk. They then develop a preference for, and intention-to-buy, a particular solution. This is an illustration of complex problem-solving by customers. Advertising is one of the sources they can use in the learn–feel part of the process. It is, however, not the only source of information, nor is it necessarily the most powerful.

High-involvement advertising can employ long copy because prospects use advertising to learn about alternatives. Comparison advertising and copy featuring endorsements by opinion formers may be influential. Media that help prospects to acquire and process information are those that have a long dwell-time, such as magazines and newspapers.

Advertising can also evoke powerful emotional responses in audiences. The type of response that advertisers seek in prospects is 'I like the look of that. I really must try it'. This is an affective response linked to a buying intention. Advertisements for fashion items, jewellery and holiday destinations often aim for an emotional response. Television advertisements evoke emotions by their clever mix of voice, music, images and sound effects. Advertisers can pre-test different executions to ensure that the right sort of emotional response is evoked.

In low-involvement contexts, where the product or its usage context is relatively unimportant, prospects are very unlikely to go through a complex and effortful learn–feel–do process. Rather, there will be little or no prepurchase comparison of alternatives. The prospect becomes aware of the product and buys it. There may not even be postpurchase evaluation of the product except in the most elementary of forms. Evaluation may only take place if the product fails to deliver the benefits expected. The purchase model is therefore learn–do. The role of advertising for low-involvement products is to build and maintain brand awareness and recognition. Copy needs to be kept short: prospects will not read long advertising copy. Recognition can be achieved with the use of simple visual cues. Repetition of the advertisement in low-involvement media such as TV and radio will be needed to build awareness and recognition.

Advertisers are concerned with two major issues as they attempt to generate new customers: message and media issues. Which messages will generate most new customers, and which media are most cost-effective at customer acquisition?

Message

It has been suggested that heavy media users are exposed to over 1100 advertisements per week. Yet, how many can the person recall? In an increasingly communicated world, it is a first requirement that an advertisement stand out from the background clutter and claim the audience's attention. Without that, no cognitive, affective or behavioural outcomes can be achieved. Standing out means being different from the mass of advertisements and other stimuli that compete for a prospect's attention. This is a matter both of message creativity and execution, and media selection. What stands out? Black and white advertisements in colour magazines, image-based advertisements in text-dominated media, loud advertisements in a quiet medium, advertisements that leave you wondering 'what was that all about?' and advertisements that challenge your comprehension and emotions.

Message execution is an important issue in gaining an audience's attention. Messages can be executed in many different ways. Execution describes the way in which a basic copy strategy is delivered. Basic copy strategy is the core message or theme of the campaign. Execution styles can be classified in a number of ways: rational or emotional, factual or fanciful, funny or serious. Individual forms of execution include slice-of-life (product being used in a recognizable context), aspirational (associates the product with a desirable outcome or lifestyle), testimonial (the product is endorsed by an opinion-former) and comparative (the advertisement compares one or more alternatives with the advertised product).

Advertisements often close with a 'call to action', such as a suggestion that the audience clip a coupon, call a number or register online. These actions generate useful sources of prospects that can then be followed up.

Pretesting messages on a sample of potential new customers is a way to improve the chances of an advertisement achieving its objectives. Among the criteria you can assess are:

● **recall**: how much of the advertisement can the sample recall?
● **comprehension**: does the sample understand the advertisement?
● **credibility**: is the message believable?
● **feelings evoked**: how does the sample feel about the advertisement?
● **intentions-to-buy**: how likely is it that the sample will buy?

If you buy space or time in media that have local or regional editions, you can conduct post-tests to assess the effectiveness of different executions in achieving the desired outcomes.

Media

Media selection for new customer acquisition is sometimes quite straightforward. For example, there are print media such as *What Digital Camera?* and *Which Mortgage?* that are targeted specifically at new-to-category prospects and are suitable for high-involvement products. An uninvolved prospect will only learn passively about your product; there is no active search for and processing of information. Consequently, for low-involvement prospects frequency is a more important media consideration than reach. These are defined as follows:

Reach: the total number of a targeted audience that is exposed at least once to a particular advertisement or campaign.

Frequency: the average number of times that a targeted audience member is exposed to an advertisement or campaign.

The total number of exposures is therefore computed by multiplying reach by frequency. If your advertisement reaches two million people an average of four times, the total number of impressions or exposures is eight million. For high-involvement products, lower levels of frequency are generally needed. Advertising agencies should be able to offer advice on how many exposures (frequency) it takes to evoke a particular response in an audience member. Krugman claimed that three exposures were enough.[6]

You can compute various media efficiency statistics to obtain better value for money from your customer acquisition budget. These include:

● response rates
● conversion rates.

1	2	3	4	5	6	7	8	9	10	11	12
Vehicle	Date	Readership	Ad space cost ($)	Cost per thousand (CPM) ($)	Coupons returned	Coupon response rate (%)	Orders received from new customers	Coupon conversion rate (%)	Total order value ($)	Average order value ($)	Ratio: Ad cost to total order value
Daily News	15/3	300 000	500	1.67	655	0.0022	200	30.53	10 000	50	1:20
Supermarket tabloid	20/3	500 000	1000	2.00	1205	0.0024	80	6.64	3 200	40	1:3.2
Sunday News	25/3	200 000	600	3.00	350	0.00175	175	50.00	10 500	60	1:17.5
Consumer Colour Magazine	30/3	30 000	1000	33.33	120	0.004	100	83.33	22 000	220	1.22

Figure 8.4 Customer acquisition report

Response rates might include coupons clipped and returned, or calls requesting information [requests for information (RFIs)] made to a contact centre. Conversion rates can include sales made as a percentage of coupons returned, or proposals submitted as a percentage of RFIs.

Figure 8.4 indicates the sorts of statistics that can be used to evaluate and guide customer acquisition strategies.

The figure contains a number of descriptive and analytical statistics for four different print advertising vehicles: cost-per-thousand (column 5: how may dollars does it cost to reach 1000 of the advertising vehicle's audience), coupons returned, coupons returned as a percentage of audience reached, orders received from new customers, coupon conversion rate, total order value received, average order value, and advertising effectiveness ratio (column 12: how many dollars of orders were received per dollar spent on advertising in the vehicle). The Daily News is most cost-efficient at delivering an audience since its cost-per-thousand (CPM) is lowest (column 5). The Supermarket Tabloid returns most coupons (column 6), but runs second to the Consumer Colour Magazine in terms of coupon response rate (the percentage of the delivered audience that returns a coupon, column 7). The coupon conversion rate tells you how many coupon enquiries convert into first-time customers (column 9). The Daily News generates most orders from new customers (column 8), but the Consumer Colour Magazine generates the highest total order value (column 10), the highest average order value (column 11) and the best advertisement cost to total sales ratio (column 12). The Sunday News performs less well than the other vehicles in all categories. It does, however, generate a relatively large number of lower value customers quite cost-effectively. It generated 175 customers spending an average of $60, and for every dollar spent of advertising it yielded revenues of $17.50.

Critics of the use of advertising for customer acquisition claim that advertisements are ineffective at customer acquisition. They argue that advertisements work on current and past customers and therefore impact more on retention.[7,8] Others point to the ineffectiveness of advertising at influencing sales at all. Lodish, for example, concluded that 'there is no simple correspondence between increased TV advertising weight and increased sales'.[9] In another study he found that the sales of only 49 per cent of advertised products responded positively to increases in advertising weight.[10]

Campaign management software can help CRM practitioners to construct, conduct and evaluate advertising campaigns. Such software becomes increasingly important as marketing campaigns become more selective in their audience, and more tailored in their message.

Sales promotion

A sales promotion is:

> any behaviour-triggering temporary incentive aimed at prospects, customers, channel members or salespeople.

Although sales promotions can be directed at salespeople and channel members, our concern here is only with sales promotions aimed at prospects or customers as they climb the early rungs of the value-ladder. As the definition makes clear, sales promotions offer a temporary and immediate inducement to buy a product. They are not part of the normal value proposition. There are many forms of consumer sales promotion.

- **Sampling**: this is the provision of a free sample of the product. This can be delivered in a number of ways: mailed or dropped door-to-door, or bound or packed with a related item. Sampling is expensive not only because of distribution costs but also because it may be necessary to set up a special production run with unique promotional packaging. However, sampling is highly effective at generating trial, especially if the sample is accompanied by a voucher offering a discount of the first regular purchase. Sampling has been used for coffee, breakfast cereal and moisturizer products. It has also been used in the online context service. In 1999, Charles Schwab, an execution-only broker, offered free e-trading to new customers. It signed up 8500 new customers, over 6000 of whom remained active once the 3 month trial period ended.
- **Free trial**: some companies offer products to customers on an approval basis. If they like the product they keep it and pay. Auto dealers offer

test-drives to prospective purchasers. One bedding retailer offered beds on a free trial basis to customers. They delivered the bed to the customer's home and let them try it for a month. If customers did not like it the company collected the bed.

- **Discount**: these are temporary price reductions. This reduces perceived risk and improves value for a first-time purchaser. Discounts can be promoted on-pack or in the media.
- **Coupons**: these act like money. They are redeemable on purchase, at the point of sale.
- **Rebates or cashbacks**: in consumer goods markets, these are often offered on-pack and require collection of proofs of purchase. Their use has extended into automobile and mortgage markets. Take out a loan to buy a car, and receive $500 in cash back from the dealer.
- **Bonus packs**: these are promotions in which the customer obtains more volume at an unchanged price. A customer might get 2.5 litres of juice for the price of a 2 litre pack.
- **Banded packs**: a banded pack promotion offers two, or rarely three, products banded together at a bundled price. A customer might be offered a banded pack of shaving gel and aftershave balm.
- **Free premiums**: these are gifts to the customer. The gift may be offered at the point-of-purchase or in packaging, or require the customer to mail or phone in a request.
- **Lotteries**: a lottery is a game of chance, not involving skill. Consumers are invited to purchase the product and be entered into a draw for a prize. Prizes are highly variable. They range from low-value items to high-value prizes such as personal makeovers, exotic holidays and even fully furnished houses.
- **Competitions**: unlike a lottery, a competition requires skill or knowledge. The prizes are varied, as in the case of lotteries.

Merchandising

Merchandising can be defined as:

> any behaviour-triggering stimulus or pattern of stimuli, other than personal selling, that takes place at retail or other points-of-sale.

Merchandising is designed to influence behaviour in-store or at other points of sale such as restaurants, banks or petrol stations. Merchandisers have available a large number of techniques. These include retail floor plans, shelf-space positioning, special displays, window displays and point-of-sale print. Some forms of merchandising are particularly useful for generating new customers, for example, money-off signs, 'as used by' and 'as advertised' signs. Related item displays place two or more related items together, for example, toppings next to ice-cream or dressings next to salads. Sales of one category assist sales of the other, for example, a new type of topping or dressing. Eye-level positions on shelves are generally more productive than 'reach' or 'stoop' positions. If merchandisers can position new products in these preferred positions sales will be positively influenced.

Other tools for customer acquisition

As mentioned earlier in the section on B2B customer acquisition, B2C companies can also use referral schemes, promotions such as consumer exhibitions, publicity, telemarketing, e-mail and canvassing to generate new customers.

Companies believe that delighted, or even completely satisfied customers will naturally speak well of the company. Eismann, a German frozen food manufacturer, estimates that 30 per cent of its new customers are recruited by **referrals** from satisfied customers.[11] Companies may still choose to develop a customer referral scheme (CRS) (see Case 8.1). CRSs are also known as member-get-member (MGM) and recommend-a-friend (RAF) schemes. These work by inviting existing customers to recommend a friend. Often the recommender is rewarded with a gift. It is important to choose the right customer and the right time to invite a referral. Broadly, schemes are more effective when targeted at a relevant section of the customer base, such as customers who are satisfied or customers who have just experienced excellent service. For example, companies offering roadside assistance to stranded motorists will ask for a referral when the vehicle is repaired and the customer's anxiety levels have been reduced.[12]

The automobile manufacturer Lexus invites up to 300 potential buyers to stylish **events** such as dinner-and-theatre shows or dinner-and-concert performances. The Lexus vehicles are on display. Also invited are current Lexus owners who sit among the prospects and talk to them. Lexus knows from customer satisfaction surveys which customers to invite. It is a very soft sell. Current owners receive no direct reward for participation other than the opportunity to enjoy the event.

Fashion retailers will organize fashion **shows** for current customers who are invited to bring along a friend who might be interested. Party plans have been popular for many years. Distributors of products such as

Case 8.1

Customer referrals at NTL

NTL is a leading Internet, telephone and pay television provider in the UK. The organization has grown through the acquisition of other businesses and now has a large base of over 500 000 customers.

To achieve further growth, NTL started to use its current customers to help them with prospecting. The company developed profiles of customers who had previously referred others. This profile was mapped onto the entire database and current customers matching the profile were contacted. NTL offered one month's free subscription to existing customers who introduced a new customer. This proved to be hugely successful, with 34 per cent of existing customers in the consumer broadband market referring at least one potential customer. After the 2 month promotion was complete, 29 per cent of those referred had signed up for a service with NTL.

Tupperware and Anne Summers sex aids organize parties in their own homes. They invite friends and neighbours organizers along. Refreshments are offered and products are exhibited and demonstrated.

Publicity obtained by Richard Branson, founder of the Virgin Group of companies, enables companies in the group to spend less than major competitors on advertising. Branson excels at gaining publicity. When Virgin Cola was launched in the USA, he hired a tank to roll into Times Square and take a 'shot' at Coca-Cola's illuminated advertising sign. All the TV networks were invited to film the stunt, as were representatives of the press. A huge amount of free publicity was achieved as the brand sought to build its customer base.

Telemarketing and **cold-canvassing** to people's homes is a contentious issue. Many customers feel that these methods are too intrusive. Nonetheless, companies in the telecoms and utility industries still use the method. Selling door-to-door to well-targeted prospects is a different matter. Fuller Brushes, Avon Cosmetics, Collier's Encyclopaedias and Prudential Insurance have a long tradition of door-to-door selling.

Many prospects feel that **telemarketing** for customer acquisition is intrusive. However, outbound telemarketing is a very popular and cost-effective method of qualifying leads.

SMS messaging can also be used for customer acquisition. Because it is text and not voice, it does not have to be answered in the traditional sense. SMS has been used very successfully for local bar and club promotions among adolescents. As the medium is so immediate, offers can be switched on at the last minute for highly perishable cinema and retail offers. As personal communication devices become more popular, so will the distribution of messaging in text and visual as well as video formats, all of which will be increasingly targeted to the prospects' known profiles.

E-mail is also useful for B2C customer acquisition programmes. Over 95 per cent of people with Internet access at home use it for e-mail, often on a daily basis.[13] In the UK, organizations such as Dell Computers, Barclays Bank, Comic Relief and Epson printers have used e-mail to acquire new customers. The same benefits and reservations outlined in the earlier discussion of e-mail also apply in the B2C context.

Recent innovations in new customer acquisition tactics include product placement and the use of pitchers. **Product placement** involves arranging for products to be shown on display or in use in television and movie productions. There is no explicit promotion of the product; it is simply seen in the production. Actors may use the product or it may be used as a background prop. The costs of producing the movie *Minority Report* were fully recovered before it was released. Companies had paid handsomely for their products to appear in the movie.

Pitchers approach prospective customers and ask them to buy a product. Pitching is a well-known practice in street trading, but has now been extended into other forms of retail. For example, pitchers will approach dancers in a club and ask them whether they have tried a new drink, then suggest that they buy some. Pitchers generally are expected to act as if they are unpaid advocates, therefore simulating genuine word-of-mouth.

Key performance indicators of customer acquisition programmes

Practitioners of CRM are concerned with three key performance indicators (KPIs) for these customer acquisition activities:

- How many customers are acquired?
- What is the cost per acquired customer?
- What is the value of the acquired customer?

The ideal combination is a low-cost programme that generates lots of highly valuable customers.

Some customer acquisition programmes may require major capital investment, as well as marketing expense. A supermarket operator may build new stores to increase geographical coverage. A financial services institution may invest in IT infrastructure for a new Internet-based channel. A manufacturer of automotive parts may build a new factory close to prospective customers.

Customer referral schemes are very cost-effective methods of acquiring customers. They cost little to operate but they also generate few new customers. However, the customers generated by these schemes tend to be more loyal (less likely to defect) and higher spenders. Advertising can generate a lot of enquiries, but these may be very poor-quality prospects with low conversion rates into first-time customers and, ultimately, low customer value. This is particularly true if the advertising is poorly targeted. Customers won by a sales promotion may be deal prone. In other words, they are not acquired for the long term, but switch whenever there is a better opportunity.

Companies can compare the relative costs of customer acquisition per channel before deciding how to spend their acquisition dollars. For example, a motoring membership organization knows that its MGM scheme has a direct cost per new customer of £22 compared with £100 for direct response TV and £70 for door-drops. The average is £35. A telecoms company reports that it costs £52 to win a new customer through its RAF programme, compared with an average of £100 and an advertising-generated cost of £200.[12] The costs of acquiring new customers online are variable over time and across categories. In 1999, Amazon.com claimed that it was costing $29 to acquire each new customer;[14] credit-card operators claimed that it cost $50–$75, and mortgage customers cost $100–$250 to acquire.[15]

Costs of customer acquisition are one-off costs that are not encountered again at any stage in a customer's tenure. The costs may include prospecting costs, advertising costs, commissions to salespeople, collateral materials, sales promotion costs, credit referencing, supplying tangibles (e.g. credit cards) and database costs. Many sales managers incentivize their salespeople to find new customers. These incentives, whether cash, merchandise or some other reward, are a cost of acquisition.

Using customer data to guide customer acquisition

In a CRM environment it is often possible to query the current and prospective customer databases for clues to guide customer acquisition. For example, salespeople may have entered data about prospects' satisfaction with competitors' offerings. Those who are less satisfied will be likely to show a higher propensity to switch, and may be worth targeting with an offer.

Data mining can be used to identify which customers show the greatest potential for a company. Queries might include the following.

- What is the profile of customers (or segments) having the greatest lifetime value?
- How were these customer originally acquired?
- What products did these customers originally buy?

With this information it could be possible to identify prospects with the same profile, approach them through the same channels and offer them the same introductory product.

Data mining can also be used to identify which existing customers are most likely to respond to the offer of a product from a category they do not already buy (see Case 8.2). For example, a bank might want to generate new customers for its savings account. A model can be produced that predicts propensity to buy based on current product ownership. Then business rules can be applied that guide the precise composition of the offer.

Case 8.2

Customer acquisition at Telecom New Zealand

In recent years, with deregulation of the telecommunications market and increased competition, Telecom New Zealand has become smarter at using its customer data to guide new customer acquisition and to acquire new business from existing customers.

To achieve this, the organization makes use of its CRM system to undertake data mining. This helps the company to identify a wide range of information such as the segments that might be interested in a new or existing product or service, the growth or declining trends in market segments, the segments that have the highest lifetime value and the channels most successful for acquiring customer segments or selling specific products or services.

Telecom New Zealand estimates that around 50 per cent of all new customers acquired are a result of the use of analysing existing customer data. One illustration is of analysing the customers for existing narrowband Internet services. Telecom New Zealand was able to identify a segment for a new broadband service. Through targeted advertising to this segment, over 18 000 of the existing customers switched to the broadband service within 4 months.

Transactional data can provide insight into the basket of goods that customers buy. If you found that 60 per cent of customers buying frozen apple pies also bought premixed custard, you might think it worthwhile targeting the other 40 per cent with an offer.

Affiliation data can also be used to guide customer acquisition. Customers may be members or otherwise associated with a number of organizations: a university, a sports club or a charity. Affinity marketers recognize membership as an opportunity. Banks such as MBNA have led the way in affinity marketing of credit cards. MBNA, the organization and the member all benefit from the arrangement. MBNA offers a credit card to members of the organization. The organization receives a fee for allowing the bank access to its member data. Members enjoy a specially branded card and excellent customer experience from the bank. Affinity groups include members of the Worldwide Fund for Nature, fans of Manchester United and congregations of the Uniting Church.

Making the right offer

In addition to carefully targeting new customers for acquisition, companies need to consider what offer they will make to the target. Some industries are consistent in their use of entry-level products for customer acquisition.

Insurance companies use car insurance to acquire new customers. Developed countries require drivers to be insured at least at third-party level. Since insurance expires annually, it offers the prospect of repeat purchase. In general, premiums are highly discounted and offer little or no margin to the insurer. However, car insurance does give the company at least 1 year in which to cross-sell additional insurance products: home and contents insurance, travel insurance, health insurance, mortgage protection insurance and so on. Churn rates on car insurance can be as high as 50 per cent, giving an average customer tenure of only 2 years. This is the period in which insurers have to make the cross-sales.

Banks use relatively high interest rates on deposit accounts, or relatively low charges on credit cards. Prudential owns the brand 'Egg', which operates as a disintermediated bank. Case 8.3 shows how the bank used incentive rates to win new credit-card customers. Nearly nine out of 10 customers stayed with the bank when the incentive rates were withdrawn, paying interest at higher rates on balances that were relatively high compared with other banks. Although it was a relatively new bank, Egg was able to cross-sell additional products and services into the customer base, producing a cross-holding ratio of 1.36 average products owned.

Supermarkets price high-demand, frequently purchased items such as bread as loss leaders, in order to build store traffic.

Data mining techniques can be used to explore customer transactional histories to identify whether there are any popular products that customers bought first. Then, it may be possible to identify subsequent purchases made by these customers. These profiles would enable you to target initial and follow-up offers.

Case 8.3

Acquiring customers with the Egg Credit Card

⟨ Quotation from Egg's annual report 2001 ⟩

- 'This has been Egg's most successful six months in terms of customer acquisition with a total of 370 000 net new customers joining Egg, leading to a total customer base of 1.72 million. Growth in customer numbers for the first six months of 2001 has increased by 19% compared to the same period last year. In addition the unit marketing cost on Egg Card, our lead acquisition product, has been reduced to £22 (30 June 2000: £37).

- 'The credit card portfolio continues to perform strongly, with a total customer base of 1.13 million. Our card offerings remain compelling and highly competitive in the market and we are attracting an upmarket customer base whose average monthly balance per account is £1742, approximately double the UK average. We are pleased to report that our card customer base is proving loyal to Egg with 89% of customers who join on incentive rates migrating to paying interest at the full rate.'

Experimentation can be performed on subsets of the customer database. For example, different cells of the recency–frequency–monetary value (RFM) matrix can be treated to different offers to develop an understanding of the propensities-to-buy of different customer groups. If the results were to show that women aged 15–25 were particularly responsive to a health-and-beauty bundled offer, you could search the database for more customers of this type, and perhaps buy in additional lists to target.

Event-based marketing can be used to generate new customers. Many B2C companies can link purchasing to life stages. Events may be private (birthdays, weddings, pregnancy) or public (Christmas, Hanukkah, New Year). For example, finance companies target mortgages at people as they progress through life-stages. Newlyweds and empty nesters whose children have left home are prime targets. Clothing retailers target different offerings at customers as they age: branded fashion clothing for single employed females, baby clothes for new mothers, and so on. If you can associate purchasing with particular life-stage events you will be well placed to target your customer acquisition efforts.

Summary

Customer acquisition is the first issue that CRM practitioners face as they attempt to build a valuable customer base. There are three major decisions to be made: which prospects to target, how to communicate with them and what offer to communicate to them. New customers are of two kinds. They are either new to the product category, or new to the company. In principle, the best prospects are those that have potential to become strategically significant customers. You will certainly want to recruit new customers that generate more profit than they consume in acquisition and retention costs.

Business-to-business prospects are generated in a number of ways, including referrals, interpersonal networks, promotional activities such as exhibitions, trade shows and conferences, advertising, publicity and public relations, canvassing, telemarketing and e-mail.

New customers for consumer companies can be generated from much the same sources as B2B prospects, but much greater effort is put into advertising, sales promotion and merchandising.

As customer databases improve, data mining techniques can be used more productively to recruit new customers. The transactional histories of current customers can be analysed and the cost-effectiveness of different customer acquisition strategies computed. By analysing customer data, companies are better informed about the most promising target prospects, appealing offers or appropriate product bundles. Predictive modelling can determine relationship-starter products, such as car insurance used to acquire customers in the personal insurance market. When sales have been made and the customer's permission to use their information has been obtained, other products can be cross-sold, turning acquisition into repeat purchase and subsequently into customer retention.

References

1. Ford, D. (1982) The development of buyer–seller relationships in industrial markets. In: Håkansson, H. (ed.). *International Marketing and Purchasing of Industrial Goods – An Interaction Approach*, pp. 288–303. New York: Wiley.
2. Peppers, D. and Rogers, M. (1997) *Enterprise One-To-One*. London: Piatkus.
3. Hofmeyr, J. and Rice, B. (2000) *Commitment-led Marketing: The Key to Brand Profits is in the Customer's Mind*. Chichester: John Wiley.
4. Chaffey, D., Mayer, R., Johnston, K. and Ellis-Chadwick, F. (2000) *Internet Marketing*. London: FT Prentice Hall.
5. Godin, S. (1999) *Permission Marketing: Turning Strangers into Friends and Friends into Customers*. New York: Simon and Schuster.
6. Krugman, H. E. (1975) What makes advertising effective? *Harvard Business Review*, March–April, p. 98.
7. Ehrenberg, A. S. C. (1974) Repetitive advertising and the consumer. *Journal of Advertising Research*, Vol. 14, pp. 25–34.
8. Barnard, N. and Ehrenberg, A. S. C. (1997) Advertising: strongly persuasive or just nudging? *Journal of Advertising Research*, Vol. 37(1), pp. 21–31.
9. Lodish, L., Abraham, M., Kalmenson, S., Livelsberger, J., Lubetkin, B., Richardson, B. and Stevens, M. E. (1995) How TV advertising works: a meta-analysis of 389 real-world split cable TV advertising experiments. *Journal of Marketing Research*, Vol. 32, May, pp. 125–39.
10. Abraham, M. M. and Lodish, L. (1990) Getting the most out of advertising and promotion. *Harvard Business Review*, May/June, Vol. 68(3), pp. 50–6.

11. Naumann, E. (1995) *Creating Customer Value: The Path to Sustainable Competitive Advantage*. Cincinnati, OH: International Thomson Press.

12. Buttle, F. and Kay, S. (2000) RAFs, MGMs and CRSs: is £10 enough? *Proceedings of the Academy of Marketing Annual Conference.*

13. LBM Internet, UK. Personal communication.

14. Lee, J. (1999) Net stock frenzy. *Fortune*, Vol. 139(2), 1 February, pp. 148–51.

15. Gurley, J. W. (1998) The soaring cost of e-commerce. *Fortune*, Vol. 138(2), 3 August, pp. 226–8.

Chapter 9

Managing the customer lifecycle: customer retention and development

By the end of the chapter, you will understand:

1 what is meant by the term 'customer retention'
2 the economics of customer retention
3 how to select customers to target for retention
4 the distinction between positive and negative customer retention
5 several strategies for customer retention, including meeting and exceeding customer expectations, finding new ways to add value, creating social and structural bonds, and building emotional commitment
6 the role of customer development
7 why and how customers are 'sacked'.

Introduction

This is the second of the three chapters that look at the critical issues of process and structure for customer relationship management (CRM) implementation. The core CRM processes are customer acquisition, customer retention and customer development. Together, they make up the customer lifecycle. The processes of customer retention and development are the focus of this chapter. Customer acquisition is covered in Chapter 8, and structure is covered in Chapter 10.

In this chapter you will learn about the important issues of customer retention and development.

Managing the customer lifecycle is the last primary stage of the CRM value chain (Fig. 9.1).

We propose that the major strategic role of CRM is to manage a company's relationships with customers though three stages of the customer lifecycle: customer acquisition, customer retention and customer development.

Just as a customer acquisition strategy aims to increase the number of customers in the customer base, a customer retention strategy aims to keep a high proportion of current customers by reducing customer defections, and a customer development strategy aims to increase the value of those retained customers to the company. Just as acquisition is focused, so are retention and development. Not all customers are worth retaining and not all customers have potential for development.

We will deal with the issue of retention first, before turning to development.

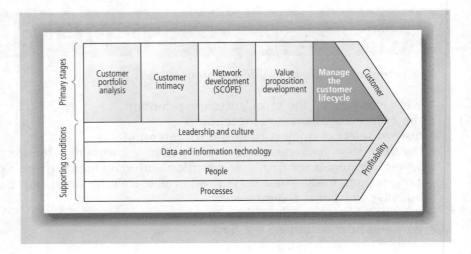

Figure 9.1
CRM value chain

Several important questions have to be answered when a company puts together a customer retention plan.

● Which customers will be targeted for retention?
● What customer retention objectives should be set?
● What customer retention strategies will be used?
● How will the performance of the retention plan be measured?

These issues need to be carefully considered and programmed into a properly resourced customer retention plan. Many companies, perhaps as many as nine out of 10, have no customer retention plan in place. As noted in Chapter 8, most marketing plans fail to distinguish between customer acquisition and customer retention. It is recommended that companies think about these as separate, but related issues, and develop appropriate strategies.

What is customer retention?

Customer retention is the strategic objective of striving to maintain long-term relationships with customers. Customer retention is the mirror image of customer defection. A high retention rate is equivalent to a low defection rate.[1]

Conventionally, customer retention is defined as:[2]

> the number of customers doing business with a firm at the end of a financial year expressed as percentage of those who were active customers at the beginning of the year.

However, the appropriate interval over which retention rate should be measured is not always 1 year. Rather, it depends on the repurchase cycle found in the industry. Consider customer retention in an auto dealership and an insurance broker. Insurance policies are renewed annually, unlike cars. If the normal car replacement cycle is 4 years, then retention rate is more meaningful if it is measured over 4 years instead of 12 months.

Sometimes companies are not clear about whether an individual customer has defected. The problems are created by the following factors.

- **Product-based views of customers**: consider insurance. Insurance companies often have product-based information systems. Effectively, they regard an insurance policy as a customer. If the policy is renewed, the customer remains active. However, take a customer who shops around for a better price and, after the policy has expired, returns to the original insurer. The insurer may take the new policy to mean a new customer has been gained. They would be wrong. Consider industrial chemicals. A customer bought 500 tonnes of hydrogen peroxide last year. This year, owing to a change in manufacturing processes and products, the customer buys a different product and volume, say 50 tonnes of magnesium peroxide. If the database is not smart enough to detect and note the changed order, the supplier's records may show this as a defected customer for hydrogen peroxide and a new customer for the magnesium product.
- **Channel-based views of customers**: telecoms companies acquire customers through many channels. Consider a customer who buys a 12 month mobile telecoms contract from a Vodafone-owned retail outlet. Part way through the year Vodafone launches a new pay-as-you-go product with no contractual obligation. The customer allows her current contract to expire, then buys the new pay-as-you-go product, not from a Vodafone outlet but from a supermarket. Vodafone regards her as a lost customer because the contract was not renewed. In the business-to-business (B2B) market, office equipment dealers have formed into buying groups to leverage better process and service. When a customer stops buying direct from Brother Electronics and joins a buying group, Brother's customer data may report a defection, but all that has happened is that the dealer has begun to buy through a different channel.[3]
- **Multiple product ownership**: a bank customer may have several accounts, such as current, savings and loan. Consider a customer who pays off his debt and closes the loan account. The bank may consider the customer to have defected because its customer data are held in product databases that are not integrated to give an overall view of product ownership by the customer. A customer view would reveal that the customer is still active with current and savings accounts.

Customer defection is the mirror image of customer retention. If retention is high, defection is low. The use of aggregates and averages in calculating customer retention rates can mask a true understanding of retention and defection. This is because customers differ in their sales, costs-to-serve and buying behaviours. It is not unusual for a small number of customers to account for a large proportion of company revenue. If you have 100 customers and lose 10 in the course of a year, your raw defection rate is 10 per cent. But what if these customers account for 25 per cent of your company's sales? Is the true defection rate 25 per cent? Consideration of profit makes the computation more complex. If the 10 per cent of customers that defected produce 50 per cent of your company's profits, is the true defection rate 50 per cent?

What happens if the 10 per cent lost customers are at the other end of the sales and profit spectrum? In other words, what if they buy very little and/or have a high cost-to-serve? It could be that they contribute less than 5 per cent of sales and actually generate a negative profit, i.e. they cost more to serve than they generate in margin. The loss of some customers might enhance the company's profit performance. It is not inconceivable that the company is retaining 90 per cent of its customers, 95 per cent of its sales and 105 per cent of its profit.

A solution to this problem is to consider three measures of customer retention:

- **raw customer retention rate**: the number of customers doing business with a firm at the end of a trading period expressed as percentage of those who were active customers at the beginning of the period
- **sales-adjusted retention rate**: the value of sales achieved from the retained customers expressed as a percentage of the sales achieved from all customers who were active at the beginning of the period.
- **profit-adjusted retention rate**: the profit earned from the retained customers expressed as a percentage of the profit earned from all customers who were active at the beginning of the period.

A high raw customer retention rate does not always signal an excellent customer retention programme. This is because customer defection rates vary across cohorts of customers. Defection rates tend to be much higher for newer customers than for longer tenure customers. Over time, as seller and buyer demonstrate commitment, trust grows and it becomes progressively more difficult to break the relationship.[4] Successful customer acquisition programmes could produce the effect of a high customer defection rate, simply because new customers are more likely to defect.

A high sales-adjusted customer retention rate might also need some qualification. Consider a corporate customer purchasing office equipment. The customer's business is expanding rapidly. It bought 30 personal computers (PCs) last year, 20 of which were sourced from Apex Office Supplies. This year it bought 50 PCs, of which 30 were from Apex. From Apex's point of view it has grown customer value by 50 per cent (from 20 to 30 machines), which it might regard as an excellent achievement. However, in a relative sense, Apex's share of customer has fallen from 67 per cent (20/30) to 60 per cent (30/50). How should Apex regard this customer? The customer is clearly a retained customer in a 'raw' sense, and has grown in absolute value, but fallen in relative value. Consider also a retail bank customer who maintains a savings account, but during the course of a year transfers all but a few dollars of her savings to a different institution in pursuit of a better interest rate. This customer is technically still active, but significantly less valuable to the bank.

Customer retention is an important key performance indicator (KPI) for CRM implementations. Its definition and measurement need to be made with an understanding of the customer profitability issues raised above. It is important to remember that the fundamental purpose of focusing CRM efforts on customer retention is to ensure that the company maintains relationships with strategically significant customers. It may not be beneficial to maintain relationships with all customers. Some may be too costly to serve. Others may be strategic switchers constantly in search of a better deal. Others may perform no useful strategically significant role such as benchmark, door opener, inspiration or technology partner, as defined in Chapter 4.

Economics of customer retention

The economic argument in favour of customer retention goes as follows.[4,5]

- **Increasing purchases as tenure grows**: over time, customers come to know their suppliers. Providing the relationship is satisfactory, trust grows while risk and uncertainty are reduced. Therefore, they commit more of their spending to those suppliers with whom they have a proven and satisfactory relationship. Also, because suppliers develop deeper customer intimacy over time, they can enjoy better yields from their cross-selling efforts.
- **Lower customer management costs over time**: the relationship start-up costs that are incurred when a customer is acquired can be quite high. It may take several years for enough profit to be earned from the relationship to recover those acquisition costs. For example, it can take 6 years to recover the costs of winning a new retail bank customer.[6] In the B2B context in particular, the ongoing relationship maintenance costs such as selling and service costs can be low relative to the costs of winning the account. Therefore, there is a high probability that the account will become more profitable on a period-by-period basis as tenure lengthens. These relationship maintenance costs may eventually be significantly reduced or even eliminated as the parties become closer over time. In the B2B context, once automated processes are in place, transaction costs are effectively eliminated, while Extranets and portals largely transfer account service costs to the customer. In the business-to-consumer (B2C) context, especially in retailing, the claim that acquisition costs generally exceed retention costs is not well proven, in part because it is very difficult to isolate and measure customer acquisition costs.[7]
- **Customer referrals**: customers who willingly commit more of their purchases to a preferred supplier are generally more satisfied than

customers who do not. They are therefore more likely to utter word-of-mouth and influence the beliefs, feelings and behaviours of others. It is likely that newly acquired customers, freshly enthused by their experience, would be powerful word-of-mouth advocates, not longer term customers who are more habituated.[7] Reichheld shows that profit from customer referrals grows as tenure lengthens.[4] Research also shows that customers who are frequent buyers are heavier referrers. For example, online clothing customers who have bought once refer three people; after 10 purchases they will have referred seven. In consumer electronics, the one-time customer refers four; the 10 times customer refers 13. These referred customers spend about 50–75 per cent of the referrer's spending over the first 3 years of their relationship.[8]

- **Premium prices**: customers who are satisfied in their relationship may reward their suppliers by paying higher prices. This is because they get their sense of value from more than price alone. Customers in an established relationship are also likely to be less responsive to price appeals offered by competitors.

These conditions mean that retained customers are generally more profitable than newly acquired customers. Drawing from their consulting experience, Dawkins and Reichheld reported that a 5 per cent increase in customer retention rate led to an increase in the net present value of customers by between 25 and 95 per cent across a wide range of industries, including credit cards, insurance brokerage, auto services and office building management.[9] In short, customer retention drives customer lifetime value (LTV).

Which customers to retain?

Simply, the customers who have greatest strategic value to your company are prime candidates for your retention efforts. These are the customers we defined as having high LTV, or are otherwise significant as high-volume customers, benchmarks, inspirations, door openers or technology partners. You need to bear in mind that there may be a considerable cost of customer retention. Your most valued customers are also likely to be those that are very attractive to your competitors.

If the costs of retaining customers become too great then they might lose their status as strategically significant. For example, top-tier customers may demand customization, just-in-time delivery and price discounts. If this reduces their LTV significantly, and they do not fit into any other strategically significant category, they may be downgraded to tier two.

The level of commitment between a company and a customer will figure in the decision about which customers to retain. If the customer is highly committed, that is, impervious to the appeals of competitors, you do not need to invest so much in retention. However, if you have highly significant customers who are not committed, you may want to invest considerable sums in their retention.

Some companies prefer to focus their retention efforts on their recently acquired customers. They often have greater future LTV potential than longer tenure customers. There is some evidence that retention rates rise over time, so if defections can be prevented in the early stages of a relationship, there will be a pay-off in future revenue streams.[4] Another justification for focusing on recently acquired customers comes from research into service failures. When customers experience service failure, they may be more forgiving if they have a history of good service with the service provider. In other words, customers who have been recently acquired and let down are more likely to defect or reduce their spending than customers who have a satisfactory history with the supplier.[10]

Retention efforts where there is portfolio purchasing can be very difficult. Should effort be directed at retaining the high-share customer with whom you have a profitable relationship, the medium-share customer from whom you might lose additional share to competitors or the low-share customer from whom there is considerable LTV potential? The answer will depend on the current value of the customer, the potential for growing that value, and the cost of maintaining and developing the relationship.

Strategies for customer retention

Positive and negative retention strategies

An important distinction can be made between strategies that lock the customer in by penalizing their exit from a relationship, and strategies that reward a customer for remaining in a relationship. The former are generally considered negative, and the latter positive customer retention strategies. Negative customer retention strategies impose high switching costs on customers, discouraging their defection.

In a B2C context, mortgage companies have commonly recruited new customers with attractive discounted interest rates. When the honeymoon period is over, these customers may want to switch to another provider, only to discover that they will be hit with early redemption and exit penalties. Customers wishing to switch retail banks find that it is less simple than anticipated: direct debits and standing orders have to be reorganized. In a B2B context, a customer may have agreed a deal to purchase a given volume of raw material at a quoted price. Some way through the contract a lower cost supplier makes a better offer. The customer wants to switch but finds that there are penalty clauses in the contract. The new supplier is unwilling to buy the customer out of the contract by paying the penalties.

Some customers find that these switching costs are so high that they remain customers, although unwillingly. The danger for CRM practitioners is that negative customer retention strategies produce customers who feel trapped. They are likely to agitate to be freed from their obligations, taking up much management time. Also, they may utter negative word-of-mouth. They are unlikely to do further business with that supplier. Companies that pursue these strategies argue that customers need to be aware of what they are buying and the contracts they sign. The total cost of ownership (TCO) of a mortgage can include early redemption costs.

When presented with a dissatisfied customer who is complaining about high relationship exit (switching) costs, companies have a choice. They can either enforce the terms and conditions, or not. The latter path is more attractive when the customer is strategically significant, particularly if the company can make an offer that matches that of the prospective new supplier.

In the following sections we look at a number of positive customer retention strategies, including meeting and exceeding customer expectations, finding ways to add value, creating social and structural bonds, and building commitment.

Meet and exceed expectations

It is very difficult to build long-term relationships with customers if their needs and expectations are not understood and well met. It is a fundamental precept of modern customer management that companies should understand customers, then acquire and deploy resources to ensure their satisfaction and retention. This is why CRM is grounded on detailed customer knowledge (Chapter 5). Customers that you are not positioned to serve may be better served by your competitors.

Exceeding customer expectations means going beyond what would normally satisfy the customer. This does not necessarily mean being world-class or best-in-class. It does mean being aware of what it usually takes to satisfy the customer and what it might take to delight or pleasantly surprise the customer. You cannot really strategize to delight the customer if you do not understand the customer's fundamental expectations. You may stumble onto attributes of your performance that do delight the customer, but you cannot consistently expect to do so unless you have deep customer insight. Consistent efforts to delight customers show your commitment to the relationship. Commitment builds trust. Trust begets relationship longevity.

Customer delight occurs when the customer's perception of their experience of doing business with you exceeds their expectation. In formulaic terms:

$$\text{Customer delight} = P > E$$

where P = perception and E = expectation.

This formula implies that customer delight can be influenced in two ways: by managing expectations or by managing performance. In most commercial contexts customer expectations are ahead of perceptions. In other words, customers generally can find cause for dissatisfaction. You might think that this would encourage companies to attempt to manage customer expectations down to levels that can be delivered. However, competitors may well be improving their performance in an attempt to meet customer expectations. If your strategy is to manage expectations down, you may well lose customers to the better performing company. This is particularly so if you fail to meet customer expectations on important attributes.

Customers have expectations of many attributes, for example product quality, service responsiveness, price stability, and the physical appearance of your people and vehicles. These are unlikely to be equally important. It is important to meet customer expectations on attributes that are important to the customer. Online customers, for example, look for rapid and accurate order fulfilment, good price, high levels of customer service and website functionality. Dell Computers believes that customer retention is the outcome of their performance against three variables: order fulfilment [on time, in full, no error (OTIFNE)], product performance (frequency of problems encountered by customers) and aftersales service (percentage of problems fixed first time by technicians). The comments in parentheses are the metrics that Dell uses. Figure 9.2 identifies a number of priorities for improvement (PFIs) for a restaurant company. The PFIs are the attributes where customer satisfaction scores are low, but the attributes are important to customers. In the example, the PFIs are food quality and toilet cleanliness. There would be no advantage in investing in speedier service or more helpful staff.

Kano has developed a product quality model that distinguishes between three forms of quality. Basic qualities are those that the customer routinely expects in the product. These expectations are often unexpressed until the product fails. For example, a car's engine should start first time every time and the sunroof should not leak. The second form is linear quality. These are attributes of which the customer wants more or less; for example, more comfort, better fuel economy and reduced noise levels. Marketing research can usually identify these requirements. Better performance on these attributes generates better customer satisfaction. The third form is attractive quality. These are attributes that surprise, delight and excite customers. They are answers to latent, unarticulated

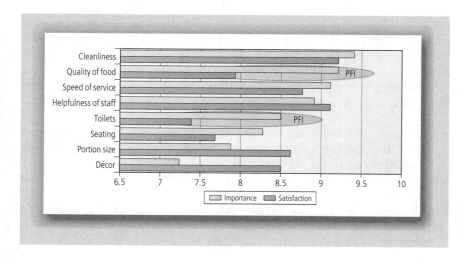

Figure 9.2
Using customer satisfaction and importance data to identify priorities for improvement

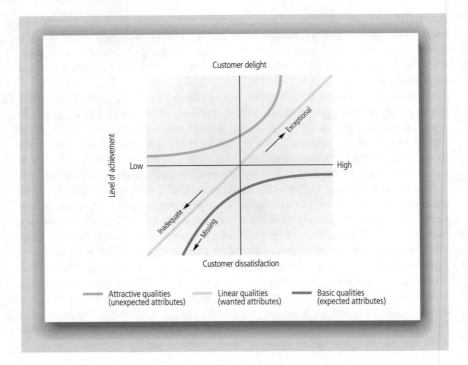

Figure 9.3
Customer delight
through product
quality (Source:
Kano[11])

needs and are often difficult to identify in marketing research. As shown
in Fig. 9.3, Kano's analysis suggests that customers can be delighted in
two ways: by enhancing linear qualities beyond expectations and by
creating innovative attractive qualities.[11]

A number of companies have adopted 'customer delight' as their
mission, including Cisco, American Express and Kwik-Fit, the auto
service chain. Others pay homage to the goal but do not organize to
achieve it. In the service industries, customer delight requires front-line
employees to be trained, empowered and rewarded for doing what it
takes to delight customers. It is in the interaction with customers that
contact employees have the opportunity to understand and exceed their
expectations. The service quality attributes of empathy and responsiveness are on show when employees aim to delight customers.

Exceeding expectations need not be costly. For example, a sales
representative could do a number of simple things such as:

- volunteer to collect and replace a faulty product from a customer
  rather than issuing a credit note and waiting for the normal call cycle
  to schedule a call on the customer
- offer better, lower cost solutions to the customer, even though that
  might reduce margin
- provide information about the customer's served market. A packaging
  company, for example, might alert a fast-moving consumer goods
  manufacturer customer to competitive initiatives in the market.

Some efforts to delight customers can go wrong. For example, sooner is not necessarily better. For example, if a retail store customer has requested delivery between 1 and 3 pm, and the driver arrives an hour early, the truck may clog up goods inwards and interfere with a carefully scheduled unload plan. Many contact centres play music while callers are waiting online. This is to divert the caller's attention and create the illusion of faster passage of time. However, the cycle time of the selected music must not be too fast, otherwise callers will be exposed to the same songs repeatedly. Also, the music needs to be appropriate to the context. Customers may not appreciate '(I Can't Get No) Satisfaction' by the Rolling Stones if they are waiting online to complain.

Companies sometimes complain that investing in customer delight is unproductive. As noted earlier, expectations generally increase as competitors seek to offer better value to customers. Over time, as customers experience delight, their expectations change. What was exceptional becomes the norm. In Kano's terms, what used to be an attractive attribute becomes a linear or basic attribute. It no longer delights. Delight decays into normal expectation, and companies have to look for new ways to pleasantly surprise customers. In a competitive environment, it seems to make little sense to resist the quest for customer delight, because competitors will simply drive up expectations anyway.

Find ways to add value

Companies can explore ways to create additional value for customers. The ideal is to add value for customers without creating additional costs for the company. If costs are incurred then the value-adds may be expected to recover those costs. For example, a customer club may be expected to generate a revenue stream from its membership.

There are three common forms of value-adding programme: loyalty schemes, customer clubs and sales promotions.

Loyalty schemes

Loyalty schemes reward customers for their patronage. The more a customer spends, the higher the reward. Loyalty schemes have a long history. In 1844, in the UK, the Rochdale Pioneers developed a co-operative retailing operation that distributed surpluses back to members in the form of a dividend. The surpluses were proportionate to customer spend. S&H Pink Stamps and Green Shield stamps were collected in the 1950s and 1960s, and redeemed for gifts selected from catalogues. In the 1970s, Southwest Airlines ran a 'Sweetheart Stamps' programme that enabled travellers to collect proofs of purchase and surrender them for a free flight for their partner.[12]

Today's CRM-enabled loyalty schemes owe their structure to the frequent flier programmes (FFPs) that started with American Airlines' AAdvantage programme in 1981. The airline made a strategic decision to use its spare capacity as a resource to generate customer loyalty. Airlines are high fixed cost businesses. Costs do not change much, no matter whether the load factor is 25 or 95 per cent. American knew that filling the empty seats would have little impact on costs, but could impact significantly on future demand. The airline searched its reservation system, SABRE, for details of frequent fliers in order to offer them the reward of free flights.

This basic model has migrated from airlines into many other B2C sectors, such as hotels, restaurants, retail, car hire, petrol stations and bookstores. It has also transferred into B2B contexts, with many suppliers offering loyalty rewards to long-term customers.

The mechanics of these schemes have changed over time. Initially, stamps were collected. The first card-based schemes were anonymous, i.e. they carried no personal data, not even the name of the participant. Then magnetic stripe cards were introduced, followed by chip-embedded cards that carried a lot of personal and transactional data. Innovators developed their own individual schemes (see Cases 9.1 and 9.2). Eventually, these transformed into linked schemes, in which, for example, it was possible to collect air miles from various participating companies such as petrol stations, credit cards and food retailers. Current schemes are massively different from the early programmes. For example, Nectar is a consortium loyalty scheme operating in the UK, and managed not by the participants, but by an independent third party. Its core retail participants are all number one or two in their respective markets: Sainsbury's, Barclaycard, Debenhams and BP. Shoppers register in the scheme, then carry a single magnetic stripe card and collect points that are converted into vouchers redeemable in a wide range of retailers, including supermarkets, off-licences, catalogue retailers, restaurants, hotels, cinemas, travel agencies and tourist attractions. Each of the major retail participants had been a member of another loyalty programme, and customers were able to convert their existing credits to Nectar points.

Case 9.1

The Tesco Clubcard

The cornerstone of Tesco's CRM strategy has been its loyalty programmes. Tesco introduced its first loyalty programme in 1995. Called the 'Clubcard', this loyalty card programme enabled customers to accumulate points with each purchase that could be used to obtain discounts off future purchases.

The Clubcard proved to be very successful: first, in attracting more customers to Tesco stores; second, in capturing valuable information from customers with every swipe of the card, which led to the creation of a powerful database that was made possible through club membership information. For example, the card provided Tesco with vital information such as what products customers were and were not buying, where they were spending their time in the store, and where they were not, as measured by spending. As a result of this initial success, 108 customer segments were identified and specific offers were made to each, such as high-value customers receiving valet parking when they came to shop and other special privileges.

In 1996 Tesco introduced two further loyalty cards, a student card and a card for mothers, with offers specifically targeted to each group's needs.

Case 9.2

Loyalty programme at Boots the Chemist

Boots the Chemist is the UK's leading health and beauty retailer. Ninety per cent of the UK's 60 million population visits a Boots store at least once a year. The company has an annual turnover of around £3 billion from a network of some 1300 stores.

Boots launched their CRM strategy in 1999. It was built around the 'Advantage Card', a loyalty programme enabled by a chip-embedded smart card. The standard reward for purchases is four points for every £1 spent, equivalent to a 4 per cent discount or rebate. This is a very generous rate of reward compared with the other retail sectors, where the major supermarket loyalty schemes represent a 1 per cent saving for customers.

After an initial investment in excess of £30 million, the programme has become the third-largest retail loyalty scheme in the UK. Boots reported that it took 3 years to achieve the programme's revenue objectives and there have been many other benefits such as higher levels of customer retention, increased in-store spending and overall increased profitability.

Boots took its time to introduce the scheme, rather than rapidly following the trend to loyalty schemes in the early 1990s. It conducted extensive market research to determine what customer segments to target, how to differentiate their programme and how to ensure that it fitted the organization's image. The market research discovered that 83 per cent of Boots' customers were female, aged 20–45, who on 55 per cent of their visits to a store purchased a non-essential 'indulgent' item. Considering the results from the market research, the Advantage Card was targeted towards female customers, rewarding them with indulgent items, instead of reducing the cost of their normal shopping.

Since inception the card has become the largest smart card-based retail loyalty card scheme in the world. It currently has 12.3 million cardholders, and more than 40 per cent of transactions in-store are now linked to the card.

It has been suggested that successful schemes deliver five types of value to participants: [13]

- **cash value**: how much is the reward worth in cash compared with what is spent to obtain it?
- **redemption value**: how wide a range of rewards is offered?
- **aspirational value**: how much does the customer want the reward?
- **relevance value**: how achievable are the rewards?
- **convenience value**: how easy is it to collect the credits and redeem them for the reward?

Even if they possess these characteristics, loyalty schemes are not without critics. They can be very expensive to establish and manage. In respect of operating costs, retail schemes typically reward customers with a cash rebate or vouchers equivalent to 1 per cent of purchases. This comes straight out of the bottom line, so a retailer that is making 5 per cent margin loses one-fifth or 20 per cent of its profit to fund the scheme. There may also be a significant investment in technology to support the scheme, and marketing to launch and sustain the scheme. Supermarket operator Safeway dropped its UK loyalty programme, which had been costing about £30 million annually. Shell is reported to have spent up to £40 million to develop its smart card scheme.[14] Unredeemed credits represent liabilities for scheme operators. For example, it has been suggested that if all the unused air miles were redeemed on the same day it would take 600 000 Boeing 747s to meet the demand.[12]

Schemes have become less distinctive and value-adding as many competitors now operate me-too programmes. Fundamentally, these schemes may not be creating loyalty at all. For example, many UK supermarket shoppers carry loyalty cards from more than one super-market.[15] The customer's choice set when grocery shopping includes all suppliers with whom they have a card-based relationship. It is also claimed that customers become loyal to the scheme rather than to the company or brand behind the scheme.[16]

Whether they develop loyalty or not, these schemes certainly reward buying behaviour. Accumulated credits represent investments that the customer has made in the scheme or the brands behind the scheme. When customers get no return from this investment, they can be deeply distressed. Members of at least five airlines, Braniff, Midway, MGM Grand, Legend and Ansett, lost their air miles when their airlines folded. Members of Pan Am's FFP were fortunate to have their credits transferred into Delta Airlines when Pan Am stopped flying. Frequent fliers of Australia-based Ansett forfeited their miles after the airline stopped flying in 2001. Passengers organized themselves into a group to lobby,

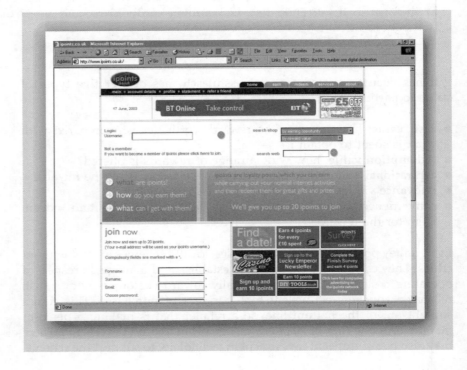

Figure 9.4
ipoints website

ultimately unsuccessfully, for their loyalty to be recognized and rewarded by the company administrators, or prospective purchasers of the airline.

In addition, loyalty schemes are successful enablers of customer insight. Personalized cards are obtained only after registering personal data. Then it becomes possible to monitor transactional behaviour. Chip-embedded smart cards carry the information on the card itself. A huge amount of data is generated that can be warehoused and subjected to data mining for insights into purchasing behaviour. These insights can be used to guide marketing campaigns and offer development. Boots, for example, ran a series of controlled experiments mailing health and beauty offers to select groups of carefully profiled customers. It achieved 40 per cent response rates in comparison to 5 per cent from the control group. For more information on the history and development of loyalty schemes, see Worthington.[17]

The loyalty scheme concept has migrated into the online retail environment. One of the innovators, beenz, which was established in 1998, has not survived. Other scheme brands include ipoints (Fig. 9.4) and mypoints.

Customer clubs

Customer clubs are organizations established by companies to deliver a range of benefits to members. The initial costs of establishing a club can be quite high, but thereafter most clubs are expected to cover their operating expenses and, preferably, return a profit. Research suggests that customer clubs are successful at promoting customer retention.[18]

To become a member and obtain benefits, clubs require customers to register. With these personal details, the company is able to begin interaction with customers, learn more about them, and develop offers and services for them. Clubs can only succeed if members experience benefits that they value. Club managers can assemble and offer a range of value-adding services and products that, given the availability of customer data, can be personalized to segment or individual level. Among the more common benefits of club membership are access to member-only products and services, alerts about upcoming new and improved products, discounts, magazines and special offers.

There is a huge number of customer clubs. One report estimates that there are 'several hundred' in Germany alone.[18] B2C clubs include:

- Swatch the Club (see www.swatch.com)
- The Rolling Stones Fan Club (see Case 9.3)
- The Pampers Parenting Institute (see http://www.pampers.com/en_US/learning/ppi/jhtml)
- Casa Buitoni (see http://www.buitoni.com/index/index.asp)
- The Harley Owners' Group (HOG) (see http://www.hog.com/home.asp)
- Sainsbury's **Little**ones Club (see http://www.sainsburys.co.uk/littleones/default.asp?page = main.asp)
- The Volkswagen Club (see http://www.vw-club.de/).

Case 9.3

The Rolling Stones fan club

- Offers three classes of membership: Premium, Got a Ticket and Basic. Membership at Premium status costs US$95 a year. At the beginning of 2003 benefits included:
  - Access to all the features of the Rolling Stones Official Fan Club website
  - The chance to purchase up to four tickets to one show (two to theatres and clubs) before they go on sale to the general public.
  - A complimentary copy of the new Stones CD, *Forty Licks*
  - A complimentary Official Fan Club hat
  - A code good for 5 per cent off all purchases in the soon-to-be launched Official Fan Club store

There are 650 000 paid-up members of the Harley Owners' Group. They choose from two levels of membership, full and associate, and a variable membership length, from 1 year to lifetime. Among the many benefits are an affinity group Visa card, a membership manual, a touring handbook, a dedicated website, magazines, a mileage programme, membership in over 600 chapters, invitations to events and rallies, and a lot more.

Sales promotions

Whereas loyalty schemes and clubs tend to have a long life, sales promotions offer only temporary enhancements to customer value. Sales promotions can also be used for customer acquisition (see Chapter 8). Retention-oriented sales promotions encourage the customer to repeat purchase, so the form they take differs.

- **In-pack or on-pack voucher**: customers buy the product and receive a voucher entitling them to a discount off one or more additional purchases.
- **Rebate or cashback**: rebates are refunds that the customer receives after purchase. The value of the rebate can be adjusted in line with the quantity purchased, to reward customers who meet high volume requirements.
- **Free premium for continuous purchase**: the customer collects proofs of purchase and mails them in, or surrenders them at retail to obtain a free gift. Sometimes the gift might be part of a collectible series. Customers buying preserves and jams collected proofs of purchase and mailed them in to receive an enamel badge. There were 20 different badges in the series. So popular was this promotion that a secondary market was established so that collectors could trade and swap badges to obtain the full set.
- **Self-liquidating premium**: a self-liquidating promotion is one that recovers its own direct costs. Typically, consumers are invited to collect proofs of purchase, such as store receipts or barcodes from packaging, and mail them in with a personal cheque. This entitles the customer to a discounted premium such as a camera or gardening equipment. The

promoter will have reached a deal with the suppliers of the premiums to buy at a highly discounted rate, perhaps on a sale-or-return basis. Margins earned from the sale of product, plus the value of the cheque, cover the costs of running the promotion.

- **Collection schemes**: these are long-running schemes in which the customer collects items with every purchase. Kellogg's ran a promotion in which they inserted picture cards of carefully chosen sports stars into packets of cereals. Customers did not know what card they had until they bought and opened the pack. These became collectable items.

Bonding

The next customer retention strategy is bonding. B2B researchers have identified many different forms of bond between customers and suppliers. These include interpersonal bonds, technology bonds [as in electronic data interchange (EDI)], legal bonds and process bonds. These different forms can be split into two major categories: social and structural.[19]

Social bonds

Social bonds are found in positive interpersonal relationships between people on both sides of the customer–supplier dyad. Positive interpersonal relationship are characterized by high levels of trust and commitment. Successful interpersonal relationships may take time to evolve as uncertainty and distance are reduced. As the number of episodes linking customer and supplier grow, there is greater opportunity for social bonds to develop. Suppliers should understand that if they act opportunistically or fail to align themselves to customer preferences, trust and confidence will be eroded.

Strong social bonds can emerge between employees in companies having similar sizes, cultures and locations. For example, small and medium-sized businesses generally prefer to do business with similar-sized companies, and Japanese companies prefer to do business with other Japanese companies. Geographical bonds emerge when companies in a trading area co-operate to support each other.

Social relationships between buyer and seller can be single-level or multi-level. A single-level relationship might exist between the supplier's account manager and the customer's procurement officer. The more layers there are between the dyad, the more resistant the relationship is to breakdown. For example, technical, quality and operations people talk to their equivalents on the other side.

Social bonds characterized by trust generally precede the development of structural bonds. Mutual investments in a joint venture are structural bonds. Companies are unlikely to commit resources if there is a low level of trust in the partner's integrity and competence.

Structural bonds

Structural bonds are established when companies and customers commit resources to the relationship. In general, these resources yield mutual benefits for the participants. For example, a joint customer–supplier quality team can work on improving quality compliance, benefiting both companies. Resources committed to a relationship may or may not be recoverable if the relationship breaks down. For example, investments made in training a customer's operatives are non-returnable. In contrast, a chilled products manufacturer that has installed refrigerated space at a distributor's warehouse may be able to dismantle and retrieve it on relationship dissolution.

A key attribute of structural bonding is investment in adaptations to suit the other party. Suppliers can adapt any element of the offer – product, process, price and inventory levels, for example – to suit the customer. Customers also make adaptations. They can adapt their manufacturing processes to accommodate a supplier's product or technology. Power imbalances in relationships can produce asymmetric adaptations. A major multiple retailer might force adaptations from small suppliers while making no concessions itself. For example, it could insist on a reduction in product costs, or co-branding of point-of-sale material, or even attempt to coerce the supplier not to supply competitors.

Different types of structural bond can be identified. All are characterized by an investment of one, or both parties, in the other:

- **financial bonds**: where the seller offers a financial inducement to retain the customer. Insurance companies form financial bonds with customers by offering no-claims discounts, tenure-related discounts and multi-policy discounts
- **legal bonds**: when there is a contract or common ownership linking the relational partners (see Case 9.4)
- **equity bonds**: where both parties invest in order to develop a competitive offer for customers, e.g. the owners of airports invest in the shells of the duty-free retail outlets. The retailer invests in the internal fixtures and fittings
- **knowledge-based bonds**: when each party grows to know and understand the other's processes and structures, strengths and weaknesses
- **technological bonds**: when the technologies of the relational partners are aligned, e.g. with EDI or partner relationship management software
- **process bonds**: when processes of the two organizations are aligned, e.g. the quality assurance programme on the supplier side and the quality inspection programme on the customer side. Some suppliers offer to manage the inventory of their customers and ensure that inventory levels are optimized. This is known as vendor managed inventory (VMI), e.g. chemicals company Solvay Interox enables VMI by using telemetry systems
- **project bonds**: when the partners are engaged in some special activity outside their normal commercial arrangements, e.g. a new product development venture. There may be an exchange of resources to enable the desirable mutual outcome to be achieved, for example an exchange of engineers and technologists between the companies

Case 9.4

Customer retention at Korea Telecom

Korea Telecom places a high level of importance upon creating valuable relationships with customers, both business and consumer, in the telecommunications markets of South Korea and south-east Asia.

The organization places significant emphasis on maintaining high retention rates in markets that are becoming increasingly competitive. To this end, Korea Telecom estimates that it costs around US$185 to gain a consumer for a broadband Internet service. However, for an average customer it takes almost 2 years for the organization to break even with such a service. Consequently, the organization undertakes a number of activities as part of its CRM strategy to retain customers, including offering the bundling of a number of services such as Internet, mobile and home phone at a discount to customers who enter into service contracts for at least 2 years.

- **multi-product bonds**: when a customer buys several products from a supplier, the bond is more difficult to break. There are economies for customers in dealing with fewer suppliers. When a relationship with a supplier of several products is dissolved, the customer may incur significant money, search and psychic costs in searching for one or more replacements. Further, the level of perceived risk attached to a new relationship may become uncomfortable.

Social bonds are generally easier to break than structural bonds. Structural bonds link organizations. Social bonds link people. If the account manager and procurement officer do not grow to trust each other, they may fall out, but this is unlikely to bring down a joint venture.

Build commitment

The final strategy for building customer retention is to create customer commitment. Various studies have indicated that customer satisfaction is not enough to ensure customer longevity. For example, Reichheld reports that 65–85 per cent of recently defected customers claimed to be satisfied with their previous suppliers.[20] Another study reports that 1 in 10 customers who said they were completely satisfied, scoring 10 out of 10 on a customer satisfaction scale, defected to a rival brand the following year.[21]

Several authorities have urged companies to work on developing customer commitment.[22,23] These customers are more than satisfied. They have an emotional attachment to your proposition or company. Committed customers have the following characteristics.

- They are very satisfied customers.
- They believe that your brand, offer or company is superior to other competitors.

- They are involved in your brand, offer or company.
- They have a strong intention to buy that overrides promotional offers from competitors.

Three different form of commitment have been identified: instrumental, relational and values-based.[24]

Instrumental commitment

This occurs when customers are convinced that no other offer or company could do a better job of meeting their needs. They are not just very satisfied, but unbeatably satisfied. All expressed and latent needs have been met. When a customer feels that her bank has the best products, the best access, the best processes, the lowest interest rates on loans and the best reputation, she is committed.

Relational commitment

Customers can become highly attached to a company's people. The emotional tie may be with an individual person, a work group or the generalized company as a whole. Customers who talk about 'my banker' or 'my mechanic' or 'my builder' are expressing this attachment. They feel a sense of personal identification with that individual. Often, these are employees who 'break the rules' or 'go the extra mile' to satisfy customers completely. They are reliable, competent, empathic and responsive. When these employees recover an at-risk customer, they create a friend. Customer-focused organizations make heroes out of these individuals. They are feted and celebrated. For example, American Express tells the story of a customer service agent who responded to a call from a customer who had been robbed, by arranging to have replacement traveller's cheques delivered personally to the customer. He also confirmed the customer's hotel reservation, arranged for a car to collect the customer from the phone booth and notified the police: all above and beyond the call of duty. Customers can also become attached to a work group. In banking, for example, some customers are highly committed to a specific branch and prefer not to transact elsewhere. Finally, customers can become attached to an organization as a whole, believing its people to be better than competitors on dimensions that are important to the customer. They may provide 'the best service' or be 'the friendliest people'.

Values-based commitment

Customers become committed when their values are aligned with those of the company. Values can be defined as:

> core beliefs that transcend context and serve to organize and direct attitudes and behaviours.

Customers have many and varied core beliefs such as environmental awareness, honesty, child protection, independence, family-centredness and so on. Many of these reflect cultural norms. Where these values coincide with those of an organization, the customer may become a committed, highly involved customer. Companies that are accused of using child labour, damaging the environment or otherwise acting unethically place themselves at risk. Nestlé had been accused of marketing infant formula in African countries where the infrastructure made its use dangerous. Many babies died as mothers used unclean water and unsterilized equipment. This is estimated to have cost the company $40 million.[25] Sales of Shell fuel were estimated to have fallen between 20 and 50 per cent during the Brent Spar boycott.[26] The company had planned to decommission the 4000 tonne Brent Spar oil platform by dumping it into the North Sea. Just as customers can take action against companies that they feel are in beach of their values, so can they commit to companies that mirror with their values. Research supports the claim that there is a hierarchical relationship from values to attitudes to purchase intention and ultimately to purchase.[27]

Various companies benefit from values-based commitment, for example Body Shop, John Lewis, Harley Davidson, Co-operative Bank and Virgin.

Body Shop International, the health and beauty retailer, was founded by Anita and Gordon Roddick. The company's values include a refusal to source products tested on animals, and support for community trade, human rights and the environment. A successful and influential business was developed on the back of these values. Body Shop influenced other retailers to become more sensitive to these issues.

The John Lewis Partnership is a UK-based department store with a 140 year history. It is a mutual organization, owned by its staff and incorporated as a trust. Profits are not distributed to external shareholders. Rather, they are shared with employees, who are regarded as partners. The company is reputed to look after these partners very well, including, for example, having a final salary pension scheme.

Harley Davidson, the US motorcycle manufacturer, has a phenomenally committed customer base. When Harley riders replace their bikes, 95 per cent buy another Harley. The bike is a central part of a lifestyle that is grounded on fraternity, independence and rebellion. Image is critical to the Harley rider. In the USA, the average age of a Harley rider is 46 (up from 38 a decade ago), the average salary is $78 000 and the typical cruiser bike costs $17 000. The challenge for Harley is to develop value propositions that appeal to a younger customer.[28]

The Co-operative Bank is positioned in the UK retail banking market as the ethical bank. The mutually owned bank believes that its ethical stance contributed about £20 million to pre-tax profits of £107.5 million reported in 2001. In its annual partnership report, which measures ethical performance, the bank said it had turned down 52 finance opportunities on ethical grounds in 2001. About 41 per cent were rejected because they could damage the environment, including finance for an engineering group to build a pipeline in Sudan. Another 15 per cent were rejected because the companies did not have a satisfactory animal-testing policy or were involved in intensive farming. One-third of the bank's customers moved to the bank because of its ethical and eco-friendly policies.[29]

The Virgin Group is a family of many hundreds of privately owned strategic business units ranging from airline to rail, cosmetics, cola, telecoms, music and financial services. In year 2000 group sales reached US$5.8 billion. The values of the Virgin brand are integrity, value for money, quality and fun. Virgin Group is chaired by its founder, the renegade but highly visible Sir Richard Branson. Customers are attracted to the brand because of its reputation for fairness, simplicity and transparency. Customers trust the brand and rely on it in markets that are new to them. For example, Virgin was a late mover into the index-linked mutual fund marketplace. It still managed to become market leader in 12 months, despite having no history as a financial institution.

Context makes a difference

Context makes a difference to customer retention in two ways. First, there are some circumstances when customer acquisition makes more, indeed the only, sense as a strategic goal. Secondly, customer retention strategies will vary according to the environment in which the company competes.

When launching a new product or opening up a new market, a company's focus has to be on customer acquisition. In contexts where there are one-off purchases such as funerals, infrequent purchases such as heart surgery, or unique conditions such as gave rise to the demand for Y2K compliance software, customer retention is subordinate to acquisition.

The impact of contextual conditions on the choice and timing of customer retention practices has not been thoroughly researched. However, several contextual considerations impact on customer retention practices.

Number of competitors

In some industries, there is a notable lack of competitors, meaning that companies do not suffer badly from customer churn. This typically applies in state-provided services such as education and utilities such as gas, electricity, rail and telecoms, whether deregulated or not. When customers are dissatisfied they have no competitor to turn to. They may also believe that the competitors in the market are not truly differentiated by their service standards. In other words, each supplier is as bad as the others. The result is inertia.

Corporate culture

In corporate banking, the short-term profit requirement of both management and shareholders has resulted in the lack of real commitment to relationship banking. Banks have been very opportunistic in their preference for transactional credit-based relationships with customers.[30]

Channel configuration

Sellers may not have the opportunity to maintain direct relationships with the ultimate buyers and users of their products. Instead, they may rely on their intermediaries. Caterpillar, for example, does not have a relationship with the contractors who use their equipment. Instead, it works in partnership with about 200 independent dealers around the world to provide customer service, training, field support and inventories of spare parts.

Purchasing practices

The purchasing procedures adopted by buyers can also make the practice of customer retention futile. Customers do not always want relationships with their suppliers. For example, government departments in the UK have adopted compulsory competitive tendering (CCT) as their mechanism for making purchasing decisions. The process is designed to prevent corrupt relationships developing and to ensure that tax-payers get good value for money; that is, pay a low price for the services rendered. Every year or so, current suppliers and other vendors are invited to pitch for the business. Price is often the primary consideration for the choice of supplier.

Ownership expectations

The demands of business owners can subordinate customer retention to other goals. For example, Korean office-equipment manufacturers are very focused on sales volumes. They require their wholly owned distributors to buy quotas of product from Korea, and sell them in the served market regardless of whether the products are well-matched to local market conditions and customer requirements. The distributors are put in a position of having to create demand against competitors that do a better job of understanding and meeting customer requirements.[3]

Ethical concerns

Public sector medical service providers cannot simply focus on their most profitable customers or products. This would result in the neglect of some patients and a failure to address other areas of disease management. Private sector providers do not necessarily face this problem. The Shouldice Hospital in Ontario specializes in hernia repairs. Their website, www.shouldice.com, reports that they have repaired 270 000 hernias over a 55 year period with a 99 per cent success rate. They even organize annual reunions. Recently, these events have been attended by 1000 satisfied patients.

Key performance indicators of customer retention programmes

Practitioners of CRM are concerned with a number of KPIs for these customer retention activities, among them the following:

- What is the raw customer retention rate?
- What is the raw customer retention rate in each customer segment?
- What is the sales-adjusted retention rate?
- What is the profit-adjusted retention rate?
- What are the sales and profit-adjusted retention rates in each customer segment?
- What is the cost of customer retention?
- What is the share of wallet of the retained customers?
- What is the customer churn rate per channel?
- What is the cost-effectiveness of customer retention tactics?

The choice of KPI will vary according to context. Some companies do not have enough data to compute raw retention rate per segment. Others may not know their share of wallet (share of customer spending on the category).

The role of research

Companies can reduce levels of customer churn by researching a number of questions:

- Why are customer defecting?
- Are there any lead indicators of impending defection?
- What can be done to address the root causes?

The first question can be answered by contacting and investigating former customers to find out why they took their business elsewhere.

Customers defect for all sort of reasons, not all of which can be foreseen, prevented or managed by a company. For example, Keaveney identified eight causes of switching behaviours in service industries: price, inconvenience, core service failures, failed employee responses to service failure, ethical problems, involuntary factors, competitive issues and service encounter failures. Six of the eight causes of switching behaviours are controllable by the service provider.[31]

Other research has identified six types of defectors:[32]

- **price**: for a lower price
- **product**: for a superior product
- **service**: for a better service
- **market**: for a different market, for example, a transport company that has moved out of road haulage and therefore no longer buys trailers
- **technological**: a customer that has converted from using one technology to another, for example from dedicated word processors to multipurpose PCs
- **organizational**: switches due to political pressure.

The second question attempts to find out whether customers give any early warning signals of impending defection. If these were identified the company could take pre-emptive action. Signals might include the following:

- reduced RFM scores (recency–frequency–monetary value)
- non-response to a carefully targeted offer
- reduced levels of customer satisfaction
- dissatisfaction with complaint handling
- reduced share of customer (e.g. customer only flies one leg of an international flight on your airline)
- inbound calls for technical information
- late payment
- querying an invoice
- customer touch points are changed (e.g. store closes, change of website address)
- preferred customer contact person moves on
- customer change of address.

Customer researchers are also advised to analyse the reasons for customer defection, and to identify the root causes.[33] Sometimes these can be remedied by management. For example, if you lose customers because of the time taken to deal with a complaint, management can audit and overhaul the complaints management process. This might involve identifying the channels and touchpoints through which complaints enter the business, updating complaints database management, or training and empowering frontline staff. Root causes can be analysed by customer segment, channel and product. The 80:20 rule may be applicable. In other words, it may be possible to eliminate 80 per cent of the causes of customer defections with relative ease.

Strategies for customer development

Customer development is the process of growing the value of retained customers. Companies generally attempt to cross-sell and up-sell products into the customer base while still having regard for the satisfaction of the customer. Cross-selling means selling additional products and services. Up-selling means selling higher value (and margin) products and services. Customers generally do not respond positively to persistent and repeated efforts to sell additional products and services that are not related to their requirements. There is an argument that companies should seek to down-sell where appropriate. This means identifying and providing lower cost solutions to the customers' problems, even if it means making a lower margin. Customers may regard up-selling as opportunistic and exploitative, thereby reducing the level of trust they have in the supplier, and putting the relationship at risk. Successful CRM-based customer development activities have a number of characteristics.

- **Data mining**: offers are based on intelligent data mining. Mining tells you what customers have already bought. It can also tell you the probability of a customer buying any other products (propensity to buy), based on their transactional history or demographic/psychographic profile. First Direct, the Internet and telephone bank, uses propensity-to-buy scores to run targeted, event-driven cross-sell campaigns through direct mail and call centres. They aim at high conversion rates through follow-up calls.
- **Customization**: offers are customized at segment or unique customer level. Also personalized is the communication to the customer and the channel of communication – e-mail, surface mail or phone call, for example.
- **Channel integration**: customer development activities are integrated across channels. It is regarded as bad practice to have different channels making different offers to the customer. In retail, this would mean that channels such as stores, web and direct-to-consumer channels act in an integrated, customer-centric manner. Clearly, customer information and customer development plans need to be shared across channels.
- **Integrated customer communication**: the messages communicated to customers are consistent across all channels.
- **Campaign management**: campaign management software is used to develop customer development campaigns and track their effectiveness, particularly in terms of sales and incremental margin.

In mature markets, where customer acquisition is difficult or expensive, the development of retained customers is an important source of additional revenues. For example, in the mature mobile telecoms market, the penetration of handsets is at a very high level. Winning new-to-market customers is regarded as too difficult, since these are the laggards, and expensive to convert. Network operators have begun to focus on selling additional services to their existing customer bases, including data applications, as shown in Case 9.6.

Case 9.5

Tesco's strategy for customer development

The cornerstone of Tesco's customer development programme has been its loyalty card. The retailer uses it to retain, develop and add value to relationships with customers.

Tesco's Clubcard is a loyalty programme that employs magnetic stripe technology. The Clubcard has been extremely popular, with over 12 million members. It continues to grow, with a large number of prominent retailers in the UK becoming affiliated with the programme.

Tesco attributes an average 34 per cent increase in customer spend since 1995 to the programme, which enables the company to target communications and offers much more effectively.

Case 9.6

Customer development at Vodafone

⟨ Extract from the Vodafone Annual Review 2001 ⟩

- 'We expect to see customer growth moderate as most of our markets have now reached a high level of penetration. This means that the rate of future growth will slow, although the potential for more rapid growth still exists in the US, Japan and China, where penetration rates are still at relatively low levels.
- 'Emphasis will move from market growth to the retention of our customers, particularly those of highest value. In addition, we will aim to stimulate more usage of voice traffic and introduce a new range of data applications, to increase the value of our service to our customer base. We must be able to respond to the changing needs of our customers and the new and different services they require, as we move from the relatively straightforward world of nationally operated voice services to the complex world of globally provided voice and data.'

Strategies for sacking customers

Just as employees can be sacked, so it is possible to sack customers (see Case 9.7). Candidates for dismissal include customers who will never be profitable and who serve no other useful strategic purpose. More specifically, these include fraudsters, persistent late payers, serial complainants, those who are capricious and change their minds with cost consequences for the supplier, and switchers who are in constant search

Case 9.7

Sacking unprofitable customers at the CBA

The Commonwealth Bank of Australia (CBA), like many other banks, has been criticized in the media for adopting a strategy of sacking unprofitable customers.

In recent years the bank has closed branches in many areas that were considered unprofitable, particularly in less populated areas of rural and regional Australia. The bank believes that customers are unprofitable if their balance is less than $500. For these customers the bank has introduced higher bank fees. The bank has also trialled the transaction fees of up to $3 when customers withdraw their money over the counter in a branch.

The media has widely speculated that actions such as these by many banks will continue to occur as banks and other financial institutions attempt to shift customers to electronic banking channels, where the cost to the bank of performing a simple deposit or withdrawal transaction can be just a few cents as opposed to a few dollars for similar over-the-counter service in a branch.

for a better deal. McKinsey reports that 30–40 per cent of a typical company's revenues are generated by customers who, on a fully costed, stand-alone basis would be unprofitable.[34] These customers would be potential candidates for dismissal. Nypro, a large plastic injection moulder, had 800 customers and sales of $50 million in 1987 when it decided to move out of low value-add manufacturing. Many of these customers served no useful strategic purpose and by 1997, the company had only 65 customers, all of whom were large, and required value-added solutions rather than cheap moulded products. However, sales revenues were $450 million.

Sacking customers needs to be conducted with sensitivity. Customers may be well connected and spread negative word-of-mouth about their treatment. In the year 2000, UK banks began a programme of branch closures in geographical areas that were unprofitable. Effectively, they were sacking low-value customers in working-class and rural areas. There was considerable bad publicity, the government intervened and the closure strategy was reviewed.

There are a number of strategies for sacking customers:

- **Raise prices**: customers can choose to pay the higher price. If not, they effectively remove themselves from the customer base. Where price is customized this is a feasible option. Banks introduced transaction fees for unprofitable customers.
- **Unbundle the offer**: you could take the bundled value proposition that is sold to the customer, unbundle it, reprice the components and reoffer it to the customer. This makes transparent the value in the offer, and enables customers to make informed choices about whether they want to pay the unbundled price.
- **Respecify the product**: this involves redesigning the product so that it no longer appeals to the customer(s) you want to sack. For example, BA made a strategic decision to target frequent-flying business travellers who they regarded as high value. They redesigned the cabins in their fleet, reducing the number of seats allocated to economy travellers.
- **Reorganize sales, marketing and service departments** so that they no longer focus on the sackable segments or customers. You would stop running marketing campaigns targeted at these customers, stop salespeople calling on them and stop servicing their queries.
- **Introduce ABC class service**: migrate customers down the service ladder from high-quality face-to-face service from account teams, to sales representatives, or even further to contact centre or web-based self-service. This eliminates cost from the relationship and may convert an unprofitable customer into profit. In a B2C context, this equates to shifting customers from a high-cost service channel into a low-cost service channel. Frontier Bank, for example, introduced a no-frills telephone account for business customers who needed no cash-processing facilities. A minimum balance was needed for the bank to cover its operating costs. Customers who did not maintain the targeted credit balance in their account were invited to switch to other products in other channels. If they refused, the bank asked them to close their account.[35]

Summary

This chapter has looked at the important issues of how companies can retain, develop and, if necessary, sack customers. The economic argument for focusing on customer retention is based on four claims about what happens as customer tenure lengthens: the volume and value of purchasing increases, customer management costs fall, referrals increase and customers become less price sensitive. Measures of customer retention vary across industry because of the length of the customer repurchase cycle. There are three possible measures of customer retention. Raw customer retention is the number of customers doing business with a firm at the end of a trading period, expressed as percentage of those who were active customers at the beginning of the same period. This raw figure can be adjusted for sales and profit. Customer retention efforts are generally directed at customers who are strategically significant. These same customers may be very attractive to competitors and may be costly to retain, thus undermining their value and significance.

A number of alternative strategies can be used to retain customers. A distinction can be made between positive and negative retention strategies. Negative retention strategies impose switching costs on customers if they defect. Positive retention strategies reward customers for staying. There are four main forms of positive retention strategy. These are meeting and exceeding customer expectations, finding ways to add value, building bonds and establishing emotional commitment. Companies have a number of methods for adding value, including loyalty schemes, customer clubs and sales promotions. Customer bonds can be categorized as either social or structural. Three different forms of commitment have been identified: instrumental, relational and values-based. What is an appropriate customer retention strategy will be contextually defined. Not all strategies work in all circumstances. In addition to customer retention, two other CRM activities were discussed in this chapter. These are developing and sacking customers. Customer development aims to increase the value of the customer by selling additional or replacement offers to the customer. Sacking aims to improve the profitability of the customer base by getting rid of customers who show no signs of ever becoming profitable or strategically significant.

References

1. Ahmad, R. and Buttle, F. (2001) Customer retention: a potentially potent marketing management strategy. *Journal of Strategic Marketing*, Vol. 9, pp. 29–45.
2. Dawkins, P. M. and Reichheld, F. F. (1990) Customer retention as a competitive weapon. *Directors & Board*, Summer, pp. 42–7.
3. Ahmad, R. and Buttle, F. (2002) Customer retention management: a reflection on theory and practice. *Marketing Intelligence and Planning*, Vol. 20(3), pp. 149–61.
4. Reichheld, F. F. (1996) *The Loyalty Effect: The Hidden Force Behind Growth, Profits, and Lasting Value*. Boston, MA: Harvard Business School Press.

5. Reichheld, F. F. and Sasser, W. E., Jr (1990) Zero defections: quality comes to services. *Harvard Business Review,* September/October, pp. 105–11.

6. Murphy, J. A. (1996) Retail banking. In: Buttle, F. (ed.). *Relationship Marketing: Theory and Practice.* London: Paul Chapman Publishing, pp. 74–90.

7. East, R. and Hammond, K. (2000) Fact and fallacy in retention marketing. Working paper, Kingston Business School.

8. Bain & Co/Mainline (1999) *Consumer Spending Online.* Bain & Co.

9. Dawkins, P. M. and Reichheld, F. F. (1990) Customer retention as a competitive weapon. *Directors & Board,* Summer, pp. 42–7.

10. Bolton, R. N. (1998) A dynamic model of the duration of the customer's relationship with a continuous service provider: the role of satisfaction. *Marketing Science,* Vol. 17(1), pp. 45–65.

11. Kano, N. (1995) Upsizing the organization by attractive quality creation. In: Kanji, G. H. (ed.). *Total Quality Management: Proceedings of the First World Congress.* Chapman & Hall.

12. Gilbert, D. (1996) Airlines. In: Buttle, F. (ed.). *Relationship Marketing: Theory and Practice.* London: Paul Chapman Publishing, pp. 31–144.

13. O'Brien, L. and Jones, C. (1995) Do rewards really create loyalty? *Harvard Business Review,* Vol. 73(3), May, pp. 75–82.

14. Dignam, C. (1996) Being smart is not the only redeeming feature. *Marketing Direct,* September, pp. 51–6.

15. Reed, D. (1995) Many happy returns. *Marketing Week,* 17 November, pp. 7–11.

16. Dowling, G. and Uncles, M. (1997) Do customer loyalty programs really work? *Sloan Management Review,* Vol. 38(4), Summer, pp. 71–82.

17. Worthington, S. (2000) A classic example of a misnomer: the loyalty card. *Journal of Targeting, Measurement and Analysis for Marketing,* Vol. 8(3), pp. 222–34.

18. Stauss, B., Chojnacki, K., Decker, A. and Hoffmann, F. (2001) Retention effects of a customer club. *International Journal of Service Industry Management,* Vol. 12(1), pp. 7+.

19. Buttle, F., Ahmad, R. and Aldlaigan, A. (2002) The theory and practice of customer bonding. *Journal of Business-to-Business Marketing,* Vol. 9(2), pp. 3–27.

20. Reichheld, F. F. (1993) Loyalty-based management. *Harvard Business Review,* March/April, pp. 63–73.

21. Mitchell, A. (1998) Loyal yes, staying no. *Management Today,* May, pp. 104–5.

22. Hofmeyr, N. and Rice, B. (2000) *Commitment-led Marketing.* New York: John Wiley.

23. Ulrich, D. (1989) Tie the corporate knot: gaining complete customer commitment. *Sloan Management Review,* Summer, pp. 19–27.

24. Aldlaigan, A. (2000) Service quality, organisational attachment and relational intention in retail banking. Unpublished PhD thesis, Manchester Business School.

25. Nelson-Horchler, J. (1984) Fighting a boycott: image rebuilding, Swiss style. *Industry Week,* Vol. 220, pp. 54–6.

26. Klein, N. (2000) *No Logo*. London: Harper Collins.
27. Follows, S. B. and Jobber, D. (2000) Environmentally responsible purchase behaviour: a test of a consumer model. *European Journal of Marketing*, Vol. 34(5/6), pp. 723–46.
28. Helyar, J. (2002) Will Harley-Davidson hit the wall? *Fortune*, Vol. 146(3), 12 August, pp. 120–4.
29. Croft, J. (2002) Ethics proves big draw for Co-op Bank. *Financial Times*, 15 May, p. 20.
30. Schell, C. (1996) Corporate banking. In: Buttle, F. (ed.). *Relationship Marketing: Theory and Practice*. London: Paul Chapman Publishing, pp. 91–103.
31. Keaveney, S. M. (1995) Customer switching behaviour in service industries: an exploratory study. *Journal of Marketing*, Vol. 59, pp. 71–82.
32. DeSouza, G. (1992) Designing a customer retention plan. *Journal of Business Strategy*, March/April, pp. 24–28.
33. Hart, C. W. L., Heskett, J. L. and Sasser, W. E., Jr (1990) The profitable art of service recovery. *Harvard Business Review*, July/August, pp. 148–56.
34. Leszinski, R., Weber, F. A., Paganoni, R. and Baumgartner, T. (1995) Profits in your backyard. *McKinsey Quarterly*, No. 4, p. 118.
35. Ahmad, R. and Buttle, F. (2002) Retaining telephone banking customers at Frontier Bank, *International Journal of Bank Marketing*, Vol. 20(1), pp. 5–16.

Chapter 10

Organizing for customer relationship management

By the end of the chapter, you will understand:

1 several ways of organizing the customer interface to achieve CRM objectives, including functional, geographical, brand or product, market or customer, and matrix organizations
2 how IT acts as a proxy for structure in the networked or virtual organization
3 the role of key account management structures in CRM.

Introduction

This is the last of the three chapters that look at the critical issues of process and structure for customer relationship management (CRM) implementation, the fifth and final primary stage of the CRM value chain (Fig. 10.1). The core CRM processes of customer acquisition, customer retention and customer development were addressed in Chapters 8 and 9. In this chapter you will learn how companies organize their customer interface to achieve their CRM objectives.

Organizational structures serve both to enable and to constrain business outcomes. For example, it is very difficult to promote creativity

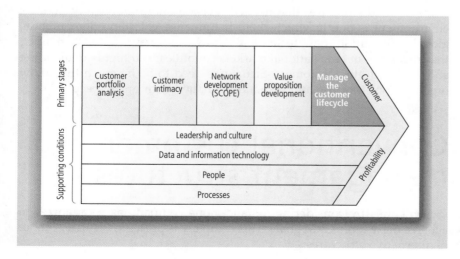

Figure 10.1
CRM value chain

in a rule-bound bureaucracy. Conversely, a bureaucracy is highly conducive to obtaining compliance to standardized business processes. Similarly, it is a struggle to become customer-centric in a functional organization where specialists report upwards within silos, but do not share customer insight horizontally across silos. Consequently, there is no single correct structure that is suitable for all organizations. What is right depends on the strategic goals of the business.

The expression, 'strategy before structure', stems from the work of Alfred Chandler.[1] Chandler was stressing the point that organizations should decide their strategic goals before designing the structure of the organization in order that those goals can be achieved.

Strategic goals of CRM

Companies adopting CRM as their core business strategy need to create an organizational structure that achieves three major outcomes through their marketing, selling and service functions:

- the acquisition of carefully targeted customers or market segments
- the retention and development of strategically significant customers or market segments
- the continuous development and delivery of competitively superior value propositions to the selected customers.

Some organizations achieve these outcomes alone, but often it requires close co-operation with suppliers, partners and other members of the business's network. This adds a degree of complexity to the organizational structure because the structure may have to facilitate the co-operation of several normally autonomous organizations.

These goals have to be achieved in an environment of increasing turbulence. Between the end of World War Two and into the 1970s, the business environment was relatively stable. Businesses could develop strategies and structures that needed revision only infrequently. Today's environment is one in which there is immense volatility: deregulation, global competition, new technologies providing new routes to market, the emergence of new national market economies, and highly demanding and well-educated customers. Structures need to be invented that allow organizations to sense and respond to change with great speed.

Conventional customer management structures

We will start by considering a stand-alone company as it organizes to achieve these three CRM goals. This company is presented with a number of alternative structures:

- functional organization structure
- geographic organization structure
- product, brand or category organization structure
- market or customer-based organization structure
- matrix organization structure.

Functional structure

A functional structure has sales, marketing and service specialists reporting to a functional head such as a director or vice president of sales and marketing. The specialists might include market analyst, market researcher, campaign manager, events manager, account manager, service engineer and sales support specialist. Small to medium-sized businesses with narrow product ranges tend to prefer the functional organization. The three core disciplines that interface with customers – sales, marketing and service – may or may not co-ordinate their efforts, and share their customer knowledge by depositing it in a common customer database. From a CRM perspective it would be better if they did. Elsewhere in a functionally organized business will be other specialists whose decisions can impact on customer acquisition, retention and experience, for example, specialists in operations, human resources and accounts receivable. These experts also would benefit from having access to customer information. Very often, functional specialists feel a sense of loyalty to their discipline rather than their customers.

Geographical structure

A geographical structure organizes some or all of the three core CRM disciplines – marketing, selling and service – on territorial lines. Selling and service are more commonly geographically dispersed than marketing. International companies often organize geographically around the Americas, EMEA (Europe, Middle East and Africa) and Asia-Pacific regions. Smaller companies may organize around national, regional or local areas.

Where customers are geographically dispersed and value face-to-face contact with salespeople, there is a clear benefit in salespeople also being geographically dispersed. Where service needs to be delivered at remote locations, service may also be distributed geographically. Because selling and service costs can be very high, companies try to find ways to perform these activities more cost-effectively. Some companies sell face-to-face to their most important customers and offer a telesales service to others. Others provide service through centralized contact centres that might either be outsourced or company operated. Websites that enable customers to service their own requirements can also reduce cost. Technology companies such as EMC have found ways to reduce service costs by developing a technology-enabled remote problem-sensing and problem-solution capability (see Case 10.1).

One disadvantage of this approach, from a CRM perspective, is that there may be many different customer types in a single geographical area. A salesperson selling industrial chemicals might have to call on

Case 10.1

EMC delivers remote customer service

EMC sells information storage, systems, networks and services worldwide. EMC provides proactive and pre-emptive customer service. EMC systems are configured to identify problems. If an EMC system detects an error or unexpected event, no matter how small, it will automatically call home to the support centre that is available 24/7. Staff immediately research the issue by dialling back into the system. Over 90 per cent of service calls are resolved remotely and most often without the customer even being aware there has been a problem or there being any impact on the information system.

companies from several industries such as textiles, paint or consumer goods manufacture. The applications of the sold product may be diverse; the buying criteria of the customers may be quite different. Some may regard the product as mission critical; others may regard it as insignificant. The problem is multiplied if a salesperson sells many products to many customer groups. The salesperson develops neither customer nor product expertise.

Product, brand or category structure

A product or brand organization structure is common in companies that produce a wide variety of products, especially when they have different marketing, sales or service requirements. This sort of structure is common in large consumer goods companies such as Procter and Gamble and Unilever, and in diversified business-to-business (B2B) companies. Product or brand managers are generally responsible for developing marketing strategy for their products, and then co-ordinating the efforts of specialists in marketing research, advertising, selling, merchandising, sales promotion and service, to ensure that the strategic objectives are achieved. Normally, brand and product managers have to compete for company resources to support their brands, an annual planning cycle inviting the brand managers to submit and defend their marketing plans. Resources are spread thinly across many brands and the company risks becoming focused on products rather than customers. Procter and Gamble found that brand managers became isolated, competing vigorously against each other, focusing on their own goals, rather than those of the corporation. Brands competed against each other, creating cannibalization.[2]

Many multibrand companies have found that brand management is an expensive way to market their offerings. In a worst-case scenario, different product managers might be calling on the same customer on the same day. This certainly gives the impression of a lack of co-ordination and a disregard for the value of the customer's time. The customer may also experience varying levels of service from the different brand or product managers. Some companies have tried to co-ordinate their

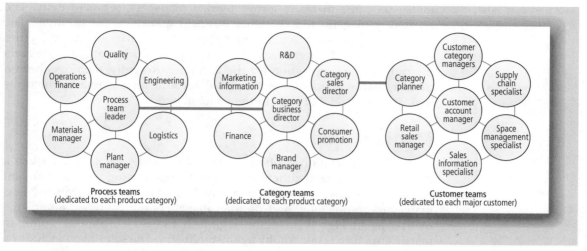

Figure 10.2 Category management at Kraft (Source: adapted from George et al.[3])

product-marketing efforts by appointing product group managers to an oversight role.

More recently, some leading companies have moved to a category management structure. Procter and Gamble did this in the 1980s in response to the problems outlined earlier. Kraft markets a number of different brands, including Louis Rich cold meat cuts and Oscar Mayer hot dogs. The company has now appointed category business directors who co-ordinate a team of functional experts focused on each major category (Fig. 10.2). Brand managers sit on the category team. The category team works with a customer team that is dedicated to each major customer, to ensure that the category offer generates profit for both Kraft and the customer. The customer team works closely with customers to help them to learn how to benefit more from intelligent product assortment, shelf position and promotion decisions. They also help retailers to understand better and exploit their own customer data. Also dedicated to each category is a process team that is responsible for ensuring that business processes are aligned with customer requirements. Typically, the process team addresses issues of quality management and logistics. This sort of structure attempts to integrate product, functional and customer considerations.

Market or customer structure

Market or customer-based organization structures are common when companies serve different customers or customer groups that are felt to have different requirements or buying practices. Dell, for example, sells to SOHO (small office, home office), corporate and government/institutional markets. IBM has refocused its selling efforts on 14 different customer groups. Royal Bank of Canada is rebuilding its organization to focus on customers, not product lines. Market- or customer-based managers come in many forms: market managers, segment managers, account managers, and customer business managers, for example. The roles are responsible for becoming expert on market and customer requirements and for ensuring that the organization creates and delivers the right value proposition for the customer. Recently, there has been a trend towards national, key or global account management, which we look at in more detail later in the chapter.

Matrix structure

A matrix organization is often the preferred structural solution when a company has several different products lines serving several different customer groups. A matrix typically has market- or customer-based managers on one side, and product managers on the other side of the matrix, as in Fig. 10.3. In the high-tech industries, another common matrix structure is geography against industry. The sales team includes a salesperson and a pre-sales consultant. Salespeople are organized into geographical territories, but pre-sales consultants are organized by industry. This allows customers to have not only a geographically convenient point of face-to-face contact but also an industry specialist on whose expertise they can draw.

A variation that is commonly found in multichannel organizations is the replacement of customer managers with channel managers. Multichannel retailers can have several routes to market: stores, catalogues, online retailing, perhaps even a TV shopping channel. Financial services institutions also have many channels: branch networks, telephone

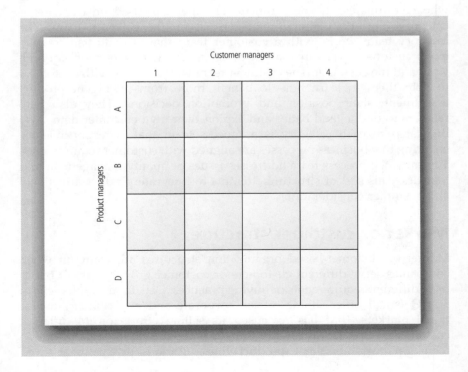

Figure 10.3
A matrix
organization

service, agency operations and Internet offers. Matrix organizations have been popular since the 1970s, when they were felt to facilitate both horizontal and vertical communication, therefore improving co-ordination and reducing inefficiencies.

Market or customer managers in matrices are responsible for developing and maintaining profitable relationships with external customers. In general, they view product managers in the matrix as suppliers. Sometimes the internal product manager will compete against external suppliers to become the market manager's preferred supplier. Then, market managers will form internal customer–supplier relationships, negotiate prices and agree service levels just as they would with outside suppliers. Pricing internal transfers can be a tricky decision. One of two approaches is taken: either the internal supplier sells at external market prices (as if they were marketing to an external customer, and aiming to make a profit), or they sell at an internally agreed transfer price that enables market managers to return a profit on their external transactions and relationships. This price then allows the market manager more flexibility in negotiating price with the external customer.

As an alternative to, or in some cases a prelude to, the development of a matrix organization, many companies have opted for the use of cross-functional teams. A cross-functional team is usually established when a project has implications that span normal functional, product or market lines. A cross-functional team is often used to consider the implications of the adoption of CRM as the core business strategy. It will consist of experts from marketing, sales, service, technology, finance and general management.

Network and virtual organizations

As reported in Chapter 6, we are discovering that networks compete, not just companies. Virgin Atlantic's network competes with the networks of American Airlines and British Airways. Network position both enables and constrains competitive behaviours. A network structure has been described thus: 'de-layered, highly flexible, and controlled by market mechanisms, organizations with this new structure array(ed) themselves on an industry value-chain according to their core competencies, obtaining complementary resources through strategic alliances and outsourcing'.[4]

Clearly, it is no longer a simple matter to know where an organization's boundary lies. This brings us to the role of information technology (IT) in organizational design. The role of IT in a stable corporate environment is to allow senior management to control information and decision-making.[5] As environments become more turbulent, and as companies attempt to understand and forge network relationships, the role of IT has changed. Its role is now to provide information that enables the company and its network members to:

- sense and respond rapidly to changes in the business environment
- collaborate to develop and deliver better customer value propositions
- enhance and share their learning about customers
- improve their individual and joint cost profiles.

The B-2 stealth bomber, for example, was the product of network collaboration. IT was a substitute for a more formalized and centralized organization structure linking the four contributing organizations. It has been suggested that IT functioned as a proxy for organizational structure in two ways: 'First, the information systems aided co-ordination directly by making information-processing less costly. Second, this enhanced information processing made the governance of the project more efficient.'[6]

Therefore, IT has a number of influences on organizational design. It allows information to be shared not only right across an organization – vertically, horizontally and laterally – but also outside an organization with network members. Structure is therefore no longer tied to traditional vertical reporting relationships. In addition, IT enables organizations to adapt the decentralized and networked structures that are necessary if they are to respond successfully to both environmental turbulence and customer expectations.

Customers do not want to learn how the organizations they patronize are structured. They do not want to have queries rerouted from one silo or specialist to another in search of a solution. Customers who hear the words, 'That's not my department. I'll put you through to the right person', or find themselves looping through touch-tone menus in search of a solution, are likely to be dissatisfied customers. Customers want their needs, demands and expectations to be met. Companies therefore need to create an organization structure that enables their products and services to be ubiquitously and immediately available in the channels that customers patronize. Traditional structures, particularly those that are function, geography or product based, struggle to meet these standards.

Structures that are IT enabled are more likely to meet customer requirements. For example, a web-based banking service is open every day and hour of the year. A typical branch-based service is open less than one-third of the time. If the branch network were to replicate the scale of the web-based service, it would require three times the staffing levels, with a concomitant increase in management structure. Even then, this could not match the convenience of a home-accessed banking service, or its price. One report, for example, suggests that a branch-based transaction costs a bank 120 times the cost of an Internet transaction.[7] Some or all of these transaction cost savings can be passed on to customers as improved prices.

At its most advanced, the IT-enabled organization is able to take any sales or service query from any customer in any channel and resolve it immediately. Among the preferred characteristics of such a design are:

- a customer interface that is consistent across channels and easy to use whatever the technology or device

- a first point of contact that takes responsibility for resolving the query
- a back-end architecture that enables the contact point to obtain relevant customer and product information immediately.

These IT-enabled structures eliminate the need for conventional silo-based geography-, function- and product-based arrangements.

Person-to-person contacts

Interpersonal contacts between representatives of the seller and buyer are important, whether they are conducted face-to-face or mediated by technology such as phone, fax and e-mail. On the seller's side these contacts are important for identifying customer needs, requirements and preferences, for understanding and managing customer expectations, for solving problems and showing commitment. Over the life of a relationship, such personal contacts contribute to the reduction of uncertainty and the creation of close social bonds. Interpersonal communication also underpins the development of product and process adaptations that serve as investments in the relationship. These act as structural bonds.

Relationships between individuals on buyer and seller sides tend to be hierarchically matched.[8] Sales representatives meet with buyers; general managers meet with general managers. Researchers have also identified three main patterns of interorganizational contact:[8]

- Controlled contact pattern, where all contacts are physically channelled through a single point of contact, typically a salesperson on the seller's side or a buyer on the customer side. This individual manages all the contacts on the other side of the dyad. There are two forms of this pattern:
  - seller-controlled
  - buyer controlled.
- Co-ordinated contact pattern: many different departments or individuals have direct personal contacts with departments or individuals on the other side, but there is one department or person, usually a buyer or sales representative, who is involved in and co-ordinates all these contacts. There are three forms of this pattern:
  - seller co-ordinated pattern
  - buyer co-ordinated pattern
  - buyer and seller co-ordinated pattern.
- Stratified contact pattern, where individuals and departments on both sides of the dyad manage their own contacts with their equivalents on the other side of the dyad.

These established patterns are breaking down under the influence of new technologies. Now it is possible to have many-to-many communications between contacts on the buyer's and seller's sides, enabled by web technologies. The co-ordination of these contacts is one of the features of CRM application software. Modern communication technologies such as e-mail and the web require the use of multichannel consolidation infrastructures if all types of communication are to be consolidated into a single record of interorganizational contact.

Key account management

A number of B2B companies have adopted a market-based customer management structure variously called key account management, national account management, regional account management or global account management. We use the term key account management (KAM) to cover all four forms. KAM is a structure that facilitates the implementation of CRM at the level of the business unit.

A key account is an account that is strategically significant. This normally means that it presently or potentially contributes significantly to the achievement of company objectives, such as profitability. It may also be a high-volume account, a benchmark customer, an inspiration, a door opener or technology partner, as described in Chapter 4.

Companies choose one of two ways to implement KAM. Either a single dedicated person is responsible for managing the relationship, or a team is assigned, as in the Kraft example earlier. The team membership might be fully dedicated to a single key account, or may work on several accounts. In general, this is under the leadership of a dedicated account director.

The motivation to adopt a KAM structure comes from recognition of a number of business conditions:

- Concentration of buying power lies in fewer hands: big companies are becoming bigger. They control a higher share of corporate purchasing. Smaller companies are co-operating to create purchasing power and leverage purchasing economies. Even major competitors are collaborating to secure better inputs. For example, Procter and Gamble and Unilever, rivals on the supermarket shelf, are co-operating to buy raw materials and input goods such as chemicals and packaging.
- Globalization: as companies become global they want to deal with global suppliers, if only for mission-critical purchases. Global companies expect to procure centrally but require goods and services to be provided locally.
- Vendor reduction programmes: customers are reducing the number of companies they buy from, as they learn to enjoy benefits from improved relationships with fewer vendors.
- More demanding customers: customers are demanding that suppliers become leaner. This means that they eliminate non-value adding features and activities. The corollary is that they want suppliers to supply exactly what they want. This may mean more reliable, more responsive customer services, and just-in-time delivery.

A supplier may decide that it wants to introduce a KAM system, but it is generally the customer who decides whether to permit this sort of relationship to develop. If customers feel that their needs are better met outside a KAM-based relationship, they are unlikely to participate in a KAM programme.

According to one study, suppliers are finding considerable benefits in the adoption of KAM.[9]

- Doing large amounts of business with a few customers offers considerable opportunities to improve efficiency and effectiveness.
- Selling at a relationship level can spawn disproportionately high and beneficial volume, turnover and profit.
- Repeat business can be considerably cheaper to win than new business.
- Long-term relationships enable the use of facilitating technologies such as electronic data interchange (EDI) and shared databases.
- Familiarity and trust reduce the need for checking and make it easier to do business.

Although the research suggests major benefits for sellers, the companies that succeed at KAM are those that perform better at a whole range of management activities, including selecting strategic customers, growing key accounts and locking out the competition. 'Companies that are most effective at developing strategic customer relationships spend more time and effort thinking about their customers' profiles, direction and future needs than the least effective. . . . [T]hey spend relatively less time and effort considering how their strategic customers will benefit themselves as suppliers'.[9]

Concentration of buying power has led to buyers taking charge of relationships. Many companies have supplier accreditation and certification processes in place. To be shortlisted as a potential supplier, vendors often have to invest in satisfying these criteria. Buyers increasingly have documented processes that compel vendors to deal with specific members of a decision-making unit at specific times in the buying process. Under these circumstances, sellers may not have the chance to exhibit their exceptional selling capabilities. What they must do, however, is demonstrate their relationship management capabilities.

Key account management differs from regular B2B account management in a number of important ways. First, the focus is not on margins earned on each individual transaction; rather the emphasis is on building a mutually valuable long-term relationship. The effect of this is that a more trusting, co-operative, non-adversarial relationship develops. Secondly, key account plans are more strategic. They look forward five or more years. Non-key accounts are subjected to more tactical campaigning designed to lift sales in the short term. Thirdly, the KAM (team) is in continuous contact, very often across several functions and at multiple levels of hierarchy. Special access is often provided to customer senior management. Contact with non-key accounts tends to be less frequent and less layered. Fourthly, suppliers make investments in key accounts that serve as structural bonds. Indeed, even the allocation of a dedicated key account manager or team represents an investment in the customer. In addition, suppliers are much more likely to adapt elements of their value proposition such as products, inventory levels, price, service levels and processes for key accounts. Some additional elements might be added to the value proposition for key accounts. This might include vendor-managed inventory, joint production planning, staff training and assistance with the customer's product development and marketing strategies.

Key account management can be thought of as a form of investment management, where the manager makes decisions about which accounts merit most investment, and what forms that investment should take.

A four-step process of KAM is shown in Fig. 10.4. This is essentially the same as the CRM process that we have described in the CRM value chain. First, identify key accounts (same as customer portfolio analysis); secondly, analyse the key accounts (same as customer intimacy); thirdly, develop strategies for key accounts (same as manage the customer lifecycle); fourthly, develop the operational capabilities (same as network development, and value proposition development).

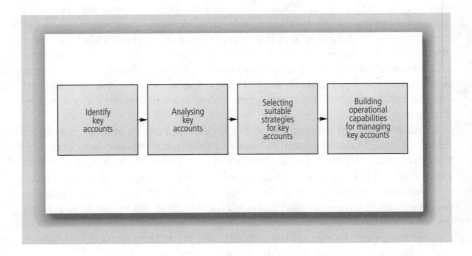

Figure 10.4
Issues in KAM

Researchers have made efforts to understand how KAM develops over time.[10,11] Figure 10.5 shows KAM developing through several stages as suppliers and customers become more closely aligned. As the relationship becomes more collaborative, and as the level of involvement between the two parties grows, the commitment to more advanced forms of KAM grows.

In the pre-KAM stage, a prospective key account – one that shows signs of being strategically significant – has been identified. Because the prospect is supplied by other vendors, the major task is to motivate a modified re-buy, most likely by identifying ways in which the new solution meets customer requirements better. In the early KAM stage, the

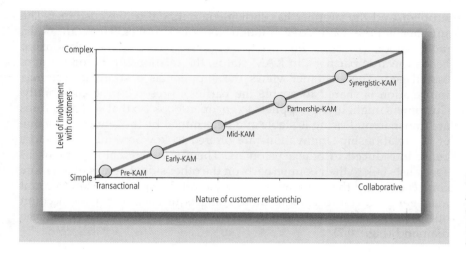

Figure 10.5
A model of KAM
development
(Source: McDonald
and Rogers[11])

new supplier has won a small share of customer spend and is on trial. The early KAM structure often takes the form of a bow-tie (Fig. 10.6), in which the only contact is between single representatives of each company, typically account manager and buyer. These contacts act as gatekeepers, liaising with their own colleagues as needed.

The bow-tie is a very fragile arrangement. If either party does not get on well with the other, the relationship might not evolve. If either moves on or retired, the relationship may be severed. The ability of the supplier company to understand the customer depends on the skills of one person alone. If that person does not enter customer insight into a database, it might be lost forever. Customers will sometimes refuse vendors access to other contacts. This is often designed to demonstrate power.

As it becomes clearer that the relationship is paying off for both parties, it may migrate to mid-KAM status. The customer has come to trust the

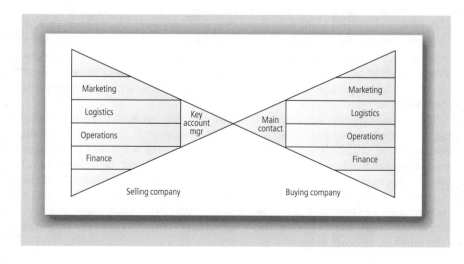

Figure 10.6
Bow-tie structure
for early KAM
(Source: McDonald
and Rogers[11])

supplier, and the supplier has shown commitment to the customer. The supplier is now a preferred, though not sole supplier. There are other, more senior, contacts between the organizations. As the relationship heads towards partnership KAM status, the relationship becomes more established. The customer views the supplier as a strategic resource. Information is shared to enable the parties to resolve problems jointly. Customers might invite suppliers to go 'open-book' so that cost structures are transparent. Pricing is stable and determined by the tenure and value of the relationship. Innovations are offered to key accounts first before being introduced to other customers. There is functional alignment, as specialists talk to their counterparts on the other side. There is much more contact between the companies at every level. The job of the key account manager is to co-ordinate all these contacts to ensure that the account objectives are achieved. This sort of relationship is often represented as a diamond (Fig. 10.7).

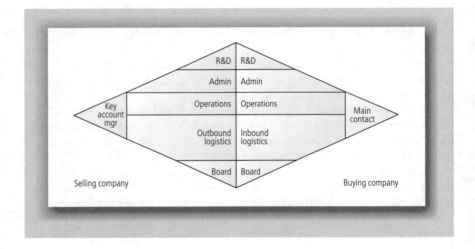

Figure 10.7
Diamond structure
for partnership
KAM
(Source: McDonald
and Rogers[11])

The most advanced form of KAM, identified as synergistic KAM, occurs when a symbiotic relationship has developed. As shown in Fig. 10.8, the boundaries between the two organizations are blurred as both sides share resources and people to work on mutually valuable projects. These might be cost-reduction projects, new product development projects, quality assurance projects or other ventures beyond the scope of their present relationship.

This model should not be taken to suggest that all KAM arrangements migrate along the pathway towards synergistic KAM. Key account management will only advance as far as the parties want. If either party finds they are not benefiting from the arrangement, it can be reversed and become more transactional. Key account status might be withdrawn if the customer ceases being strategically significant, purchases from a major competitor of the supplier, becomes financially unstable, displays unethical behaviour or demands too many concessions, making the relationship unprofitable.

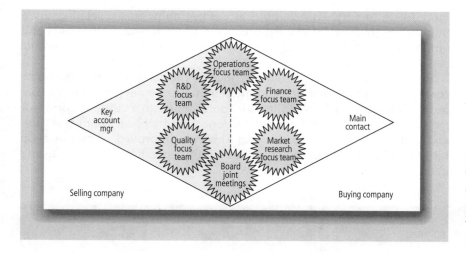

Figure 10.8
Virtual organization
for synergistic KAM
(Source: adapted
from McDonald and
Rogers[11])

There are also situations that can lead to relationship dissolution. This might happen if the customer finds that the supplier has acted opportunistically, thereby breaking trust. Opportunistic behaviours might include ramping up price, betraying confidences to third parties, supplying the customer's major competitors, or artificially restricting supply. Suppliers can also 'sack' customers, for example, when it is clear that there is no prospect of making a profit from the relationship even if it were to be re-engineered to reduce cost.

Progress along the KAM pathway may also be limited by either party's relationships with other companies. This is the network effect that we alluded to in Chapter 6. It may be impossible for a vending machine company to develop a strong relationship with PepsiCo, if it already has a strong relationship with Coca-Cola.

Team selling

Team selling is a form of selling that is often associated with the more advanced forms of KAM. A key account team is assembled that consists of a number of specialists that can sense and respond to customer concerns over a variety of issues. The team might, for example, include people from engineering, logistics, research and development, and sales. Collaborative team selling may even cross organizational boundaries. Representatives from two or more partnering organizations can come together to pitch for new business or service an established customer. Partner relationship management systems facilitate such arrangements by making customer, project and product information available to all partners.

These teams may be thought of as a multiperson selling centre, in much the same way that the customer has a multiperson buying centre, or decision-making unit. The selling centre might have a fixed composition throughout the relationship with the customer, although the make-up is more likely to vary. For example, at the beginning of the relationship a 'hunter' might initially win the account. Later, a 'farmer' takes over and builds the team to maintain and manage the relationship for mutual benefit.

Major decisions for team selling concerns the composition of the team, co-ordination of team efforts and measurement of team performance. Co-ordination can be achieved through conformance to a cultural norm (for example, a focus on customer satisfaction, or mutual benefit), formal rules and plans, deference to hierarchical direction, improved communication facilitated by committee meetings or IT. Intranets can be especially useful in this respect.

Summary

This chapter has examined the issue of organizational structure for the achievement of CRM objectives. Agreeing the CRM strategy is a necessary prelude to deciding on structure. There are several conventional organizational models for the customer-facing parts of a business. They can be organized around functions, geography, products or markets, or they can take a matrix form. As organizational boundaries become blurred, CRM strategies can be seen as being delivered by networks and virtual organizations where IT serves as a proxy for structure. Sharing information across the network acts in the same way as organizational structure to facilitate the achievement of objectives. One important market-based approach to structure is key account management. Key accounts are strategically significant customers in which the selling company is prepared to invest. Key account management can be thought of as comprising a number of forms of structures. Early key account management is often thought of as taking a bow-tie structure; later stages of development can be characterized as taking a diamond shape. The ultimate form of key account management occurs when corporate boundaries dissolve and the buyer and seller work together on projects of mutual interest. Team selling may be an important part of key account management.

References

1. Chandler, A. D., Jr (1962) *Strategy and Structure: Concepts in the History of the Industrial Enterprise*. Casender, MA: MIT Press.
2. Martinsons, A. G. B. and Martinsons, M. G. (1994) In search of structural excellence. *Leadership and Organization Development Journal*, Vol. 15(2), pp. 24–8.
3. George, M., Freeling, A. and Court, D. (1994) Reinventing the marketing organization. *McKinsey Quarterly*, Vol. 4.
4. Miles, R. E. and Snow, C. C. (1995) The network firm: a spherical structure built on a human investment philosophy. *Organizational Dynamics*, Vol. 23, pp. 5–18.

5. Whisler, T. L. (1970) *The Impact of Computers on Organizations.* New York: Praeger.
6. Argyres, N. S. (1999) The impact of information technology on co-ordination: evidence from the B-2 stealth bomber. *Organization Science*, Vol. 10(2), pp. 162–80.
7. Datamonitor (1999) *Banking and E-Commerce: More than Just Another Distribution Channel.* Special report. New York: Datamonitor.
8. Cunningham, M. T. and Homse, E. (1986) Controlling the marketing–purchasing interface: resource development and organisational implications. *Industrial Marketing and Purchasing*, Vol. 1(2), pp. 3–27.
9. Hurcombe, J. (1998) *Developing Strategic Customers and Key Accounts.* Bedford: Policy Publications.
10. Millman, A. F. and Wilson, K. J. (1995) From key account selling to key account management. *Journal of Marketing Science*, Vol. 1(1), pp. 8–21.
11. McDonald, M. and Rogers, B. (1996) *Key Account Management.* Oxford: Butterworth-Heinemann.

Index

Origins of technologies, 59–63
Outsource service providers, 67
Oversight in CRM, 44
Owner/investor relationships, 198–201
Ownership expectations, 319

P3P *see* Platform for Privacy Preferences
PAGs *see* Patient Advocacy Groups
Participants, CRM marketplace, 65–8
Partner relationship management (PRM):
  CRM applications, 88–9
  structures, 345–6
  technologies, 9
Partnerships:
  data and IT, 49
  KAM, 344
  networks, 201–21
Patient Advocacy Groups (PAGs), 209
People:
  CRM value chain, 42, 50–1
  customization, 235
  implementation costs, 29–30
  value for customers, 252–3
People's Lottery, 202
PeopleSoft, 66
Perceived risks, 229–30
Performance indicators:
  business performance, 23–4
  customer acquisition, 288
  customer retention, 319–20
  service–profit chain, 220
Performance issues:
  compliance, 191
  CRM architecture, 70, 72–3
  customer satisfaction, 20–6
  network management and CRM, 183
Perishable services, 233
Person/role modelling, 74
Person-to-person contacts, 339–40
Personalization techniques:
  CRM architecture, 78
  relationships in CRM, 26
  value from communication, 254–5
PESTE analysis, 121–2
PFIs *see* Priorities for improvement
Physical evidence:
  customization, 235
  value for customers, 253–4
Pitching, 287

Platform for Privacy Preferences (P3P), 166–7
Populating databases, 156–7
Portals, 278
Portfolio analysis *see* Customer portfolio analysis
Portfolios:
  definition, 99–100
  purchasing, 273
Positioning issues:
  internal marketing, 216
  networks, 181
Positive retention strategies, 303–18
Power issues, 26
PR *see* Public relations
Predictive modelling, 111
Preferences of customers, 146
Premium prices, 302
Premiums, 285, 312
Primary data, 151
Primary processes, 52
Priorities for improvement (PFIs), 305
Prioritization of CRM, 44
Privacy issues, 164–7
Privatisation, 201
PRIZM customer classification, 150–1
PRM *see* Partner relationship management
Processes:
  alignment, 187–90
  bonds, 314
  costs, 29–30
  CRM value chain, 42, 51–5
  customization, 235
  mapping, 262
  value for customers, 249–52
Processing information, 153–6
Product-based views, 299
Product-oriented businesses, 4
Product–service bundling, 240
Production-oriented businesses, 4–5
Products:
  competitors, 102
  configuration software, 8
  development, 185, 193–4
  management, 85–6
  ownership, 299
  quality models, 305–6
  structures, 334–5
  value, 237–41
Profit-adjusted retention rates, 300
Profits:
  investment in CRM, 30–2
  lifetime value, 127–8